Contemporary Social Work Practice

A handbook for students

Edited by
Barbra Teater

Open University Press

Open University Press
McGraw-Hill Education
McGraw-Hill House
Shoppenhangers Road
Maidenhead
Berkshire
England
SL6 2QL

email: enquiries@openup.co.uk
world wide web: www.openup.co.uk

and Two Penn Plaza, New York, NY 10121-2289, USA

First published 2014

A catalogue record of this book is available from the British Library

ISBN-13: 978-0-33-524603-8 (pb)
ISBN-10: 0-33-524603-6 (pb)
eISBN: 978-0-33-524604-5

Library of Congress Cataloging-in-Publication Data
CIP data applied for

Typesetting and e-book compilations by
RefineCatch Limited, Bungay, Suffolk

Printed and bound in Great Britain by Bell & Bain Ltd, Glasgow

Fictitious names of companies, products, people, characters and/or data that may be used herein (in case studies or in examples) are not intended to represent any real individual, company, product or event.

MIX
Paper from
responsible sources
FSC
www.fsc.org   FSC® C007785

Praise for this book

"This book really is an excellent resource for social work students at an introductory level and for preparation for placements. It provides a comprehensive overview of a range of service user groups as well as specific issues such as domestic violence, homelessness and substance use. Each section is structured around the policy and legislative context and includes comment on theory, challenges and anti-oppressive practice with case examples to aid learning.

The focus on the settings within which social work is practiced is particularly welcome and provides an essential companion to introductory books which look more at values, professional behaviour and skills.

I will certainly be including this book as essential reading for students on introductory and practice preparation modules."

Allan Rose, Social Work Lecturer, Brunel University, UK

"This timely handbook, written by academics, practitioners, service users and managers, is an excellent resource for students and newly qualified social workers. The user friendly format offers a succinct and realistic overview across a range of areas, encourages the reader to engage with diverse case studies and to undertake further exploration."

Mandy Hagan, Senior Lecturer, Manchester Metropolitan University, UK

"It is an excellent student introduction to this diverse profession. Full of information that provides a thought provoking read."

Andrew Ellery, Social Care Professional

To Billie
Thank you for making this book possible.

Contents

Illustrations

Figures

Tables

Box

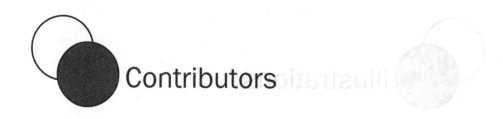

Contributors

Mark Baldwin is Senior Lecturer at the University of Bath. Mark has interests in social work with adults, participatory action research and radical social work. Mark is a member of the National Steering Committee of the Social Work Action Network (SWAN).

Jo Bell BSc, PhD is at the School of Social Sciences at the University of Hull, UK. Jo's current research interests are in self-harming and suicidal behaviour in young people, suicide contagion, suicide bereavement, and the role of the internet and social media in suicide prevention and postvention.

Jill Chonody is an Associate Professor at Indiana University Northwest, USA. Jill teaches Aged Care and Social Work Practice and researches issues related to ageing and ageism.

Jenny Clifford PhD is a Director of a Prisoner Resettlement Charity. Jenny has extensive knowledge and experience of the criminal justice system and retains close links with the University of Bath providing guest lectures and social work placements.

Clare Evans is a disabled person who works as an independent disability and social care consultant with a background in social work and training. Clare has published widely and works also as a practice assessor for social work students and is carrying out research into social work student placements in user-led organisations.

Benedict Fell is a registered social worker and a lecturer in social work at the University of Hull. Ben has a wide range of teaching and research interests which include social work with asylum seeking and refugee populations.

Alinka Gearon is a qualified social worker with over ten years' experience in social care in both statutory and voluntary settings. Alinka has a background in statutory child protection social work and is currently undertaking PhD research into child trafficking, at the University of Bath.

Issy Harvey is a registered social worker with over 25 years' experience, in both the voluntary and statutory sectors, of supporting adolescents to successfully navigate their way to adulthood, including those who find themselves in the youth justice system. Issy currently delivers intensive support services to young people in the London Borough of Hackney.

Caroline Hickman has a background in both social work and psychotherapy, most recently holding teaching and academic posts at the University of East London, University of Plymouth and University of Bath and has worked in private practice as a psychotherapist with children and adults for the past 20 years. Caroline's particular interests are in child observation and the participation of service users and carers, children and young carers in social work education.

Tony Jeffs teaches at Durham University. Tony is a member of the Institute of Social Research, University of Bedfordshire and on the editorial board of the journal *Youth and Policy*.

Debbie Martin is course director to the South West England approved mental health professional programme (Bournemouth University). Debbie provides independent training in mental health and mental capacity law, is a PhD student at the University of Bath, and is also a registered social worker.

Malcolm Payne is a writer and consultant on social work, end-of-life care and social care management, emeritus professor at Manchester Metropolitan University, and an honorary professor at Kingston University/St George's University of London with honorary academic appointments in Finland and Slovakia.

Justin Rogers Dipsw BA, MRes is a registered social worker and a Lecturer in Social Work at the University of Bath. He has practice experience of both fostering and adoption. Justin is currently undertaking a social work PhD at the University of Bath, which explores the experiences of young people in foster care.

Sue Taplin MA/DipSW and DSW is a lecturer at University Campus Suffolk. Sue previously practised as a social worker in palliative care and was awarded a professional doctorate from the University of East Anglia in 2012.

Barbra Teater MSW, PhD is a senior lecturer in adult social work in the School for Policy Studies at the University of Bristol. Barbra teaches and researches on the subjects of social work theories and methods, community practice and adult social work.

John Watson is a lecturer in social work at the University of Hull. John is a registered social worker with experience in the voluntary and statutory sectors, specialising over a number of years in the field of substance misuse.

Michele Winter is currently working as an independent social worker and teacher/trainer. Since qualifying in 1999 she has worked in various adult care fields of practice, most recently as a senior practitioner within a safeguarding adults team. Michele has combined practice with teaching/training including for Bristol City Council and at the University of Bath, Bristol University and the University of the West of England.

1 Introduction

Barbra Teater

Introduction

Social work is a continually evolving profession that has a presence in a variety of sectors in society. This book provides an overview of contemporary social work in order for readers to gauge the wide range of areas in which social work is practised as well as the specific knowledge, skills, and values necessary to practise effectively within each setting. Topics within this book cover settings in which social work takes place, which spans across the statutory, voluntary, private and third sectors but is by no means an exhaustive list. There are, no doubt, other settings or situations where social workers may be present and where students may find themselves on placement.

The book is intended to provide a general introduction and overview and serve as a 'handbook' or initial starting point for gaining information about a particular social work setting. The book should serve as a resource throughout your social work education and first assessed year in social work practice. Each chapter begins with an introduction and overview of the social work setting, which might include the role of the social worker, how service users gain access or entry into the social work service, the prevalence of services users or carers accessing (or not accessing) the service where appropriate, and key issues, definitions or terms that are specific to that social work setting. Each chapter then provides an overview of the necessary legislation in relation to the social work setting as well as the theories, methods and best practice approaches commonly related or used in that setting. A case example will be provided to illustrate the application of the information within the chapter. Each chapter concludes with a further case study for the reader to explore in more depth. The benefits and challenges to working in each social work setting are considered within each chapter as well as anti-oppressive practice considerations. Although each chapter provides a comprehensive coverage of the social work setting, the information provided is by no means exhaustive. The authors intend for the readers to explore the areas in more depth and have provided a list of Further Resources and Suggested Readings and Websites at the end of each chapter. We encourage you to use these resources to further your understanding of the subject and to ensure you have access to the most up-to-date information. The book includes a chapter on service user and carer involvement and I recommend that this chapter be read in conjunction with the other areas of social work practice.

What is social work?

Social work is a profession that works with individuals, families, groups and communities to promote human growth and development and social justice. The definition of social work, as provided by the International Federation of Social Work [IFSW] (2012) is as follows:

> The social work profession promotes social change, problem solving in human relationships and the empowerment and liberation of people to enhance well-being. Utilising theories of human behaviour and social systems, social work intervenes at the points where people interact with their environments. Principles of human rights and social justice are fundamental to social work.

The profession of social work enables social work practitioners to engage and work with individuals, families, groups, and communities in either the statutory or voluntary sectors (as well as private, third sector and independent practices) in order to foster positive human growth and development, initiate and support change, and fight for social justice. Social workers are 'change agents' whereby they focus on problem solving, initiating and fostering change, and enabling all people to reach their full potential (IFSW, 2012). In order to achieve this aim, social workers must have the knowledge, skills and values necessary to work and intervene with individuals, families, groups and communities. This chapter serves as introduction to this book by providing a general overview of the knowledge, skills and values necessary in order to become a competent and effective social worker, which are further expanded upon in each subsequent chapter in relation to specific areas of social work practice.

Knowledge for social work practice

Social workers must have the necessary knowledge in order to practise social work with individuals, families, groups and communities. Knowledge is non-static. Acquiring knowledge is an infinite process; we are continually learning, gaining new knowledge and building upon existing knowledge. Given this, how do social workers gain the 'necessary' knowledge to begin to practise and where does this knowledge come from? According to Trevithick (2012), there are three domains of knowledge that underpin and inform social work: theoretical knowledge, factual knowledge and practice knowledge.

Theoretical knowledge consists of theories that have been adapted from other disciplines, such as social policy, psychology, philosophy and sociology, theories that analyse and describe the role and task of social work, and theories that inform practice perspectives and interventions (Trevithick, 2012). Such theories are used to inform social work practice by describing, explaining and predicting human behaviour, social relations and societal structures, which assist a social worker in assessment and planning for intervention. Social workers must work from a solid theoretical base that serves as a starting point of any piece of work where a social worker refers to the theoretical knowledge to describe and explain what may have contributed to the presenting problem of the service user, predict what may happen if the problem is addressed or not addressed, and inform what course of action the social worker should take in addressing the problem with the service user. Teater (forthcoming) provides a complete overview of the different types of theories that underpin and inform social work practice, which have been collated into one of the following categories: developmental theories; psychodynamic theories; behavioural and social learning theories; humanistic theories; social constructivist theories; systems theories; and critical theories. Utilising, understanding and applying theories in social work practice will then lead a social worker to determine the best course of action, referred to as a method, intervention or approach, with the service user (Teater, 2010).

Factual knowledge consists of the legislation and social and organisational policies and procedures that regulate, dictate and inform social work's roles and responsibilities (Trevithick, 2012). This area of knowledge also requires an understanding of specific problems that require social work intervention and knowledge of specific groups of people, which can be gained through research, gathering of national statistics on specific populations or of people with particular characteristics, and gathering data and information directly from service users and carers.

Legislation and government policies are critical in social work practice as they influence, and often dictate, the ways in which social workers can practise. Each chapter of this book details a specific area of social work practice and specifies the relevant pieces of legislation. As the case examples in each chapter illustrate, the factual knowledge of law is important in determining whether someone is able to access services and the course of action or intervention of the social worker. Legislation specifies the powers (what a social worker *can* do) and duties (what a social worker *must* do) of a social worker (or other helping professional) and often gives guidance on how to respond in certain situations. Although powers and duties are often specified, there are situations where the law does not give a definitive answer in response to what a social worker should do. In such situations, a social worker must take their initiative to research around the issue, explore legislation and policy guidance documents, research case law, and seek advice and guidance from supervisors, colleagues and legal experts. Two pieces of legislation that will cut across virtually all areas of social work practice are the Human Rights Act 1998 and the Equality Act 2010.

The Human Rights Act of 1998 was implemented in 2000 and is based on the European Convention on Human Rights 1950. The primary purpose of the Act is to ensure that public bodies uphold the human rights principles, that Parliament ensures legislation is compatible with human rights principles, and to enable individuals to take cases where their human rights have been breached through the UK courts (Brayne and Carr, 2013). Individuals can only make claims that their human rights have been breached against 'public authorities', which is defined as 'a body carrying out a governmental or public function' (Brayne and Carr, 2013, p. 84). In this sense, local authorities, social service organisations and private companies carrying out statutory functions are public authorities and must uphold the human rights principles. Case law has been critical in determining whether private companies that have mixed public and private functions have to adhere to the Human Rights Act 1998. The articles of the Human Rights Act 1998 that are relevant to social work are as follows:

- Article 2:   Right to life.
- Article 3:   No one shall be subjected to torture or to inhuman or degrading treatment or punishment.
- Article 4:   No slavery or forced labour.
- Article 5:   Right to liberty and security of person.
- Article 6:   Right to a fair hearing.
- Article 7:   No retrospective convictions.
- Article 8:   Right to respect for private and family life, home and correspondence.
- Article 9:   Right to freedom of thought, conscience and religion.
- Article 10:   Right to freedom of expression.
- Article 11:   Right to assembly and association.
- Article 12:   Right to marry and found a family.
- Article 13:   Right to an effective remedy for violation of Convention.
- Article 14:   No discrimination in applying Convention rights.

The Equality Act 2010 consolidates nine main pieces of anti-discriminatory legislation, such as the Race Relations Act 1976 and the Disability Discrimination Act 1995, into one piece of legislation. The Act prohibits various forms of discrimination, including direct discrimination, indirect discrimination, discrimination arising from disability, failure to make reasonable adjustments for a disability, victimisation and harassment, and places a duty on public authorities to promote racial and disability equality (Brayne and Carr, 2013). Section 4 of the Equality Act 2010 lists characteristics of individuals, which are protected under the law (protected characteristics), which include: age; disability; gender reassignment; marriage and civil partnership; pregnancy and maternity; race; religion or belief; sex; and sexual orientation. The law specifies the certain types of discrimination towards someone with a protected characteristic that are deemed unlawful and also specifies when positive action should be upheld to ensure someone with a protected characteristic is able to be included and participate (Brayne and Carr, 2013).

Finally, *practice knowledge* overlaps with theoretical and factual knowledge and is influenced by our life and work experiences and how we use the theoretical and factual knowledge to inform and shape our practice (Trevithick, 2012). Practice knowledge is developed through reflection and critical analysis of our practice, forming hypotheses and problem solving and judicious decision making, as well as intuition, practice wisdom and the use of self (Trevithick, 2012). Social workers particularly develop practice knowledge by using their theoretical and factual knowledge to inform the best course of action, or method with one or more service users and then reflecting and critically analysing their practice. The practice of critical reflection will involve asking oneself the following questions after (and during) a piece of work (Adams, 2009, p. 234):

- What happened?
- How did it compare with previous experience?
- How did I do?
- How well did I do?
- What could I have done better?
- What could I have done differently?

Asking oneself these questions allows the social worker to reflect on the situation and experience and begin to explore what was learnt and how practice will be modified and enhanced in the future. A critical incident analysis is a specific critical reflective tool that promotes reflection of an incident and an evaluation of the piece of work. Parris (2012, pp. 39–40) provides a framework for completing a critical incident analysis, which consists of the following components:

- Describe the incident, what happened, who was involved, what your role was and what you did.
- Reflect on the event and explore the emotions and how you felt.
- How did you deal with the emotions which were evoked for you?
- What issues in terms of values and ethics were involved?
- What theories did you draw on?
- Reflecting back, what worked and what didn't work?
- What might you do differently with the benefit of hindsight?
- What did you learn from this incident?

Participating in critically reflective exercises begins to build social workers' practice knowledge to where they are able to more accurately and effectively plan and implement pieces of work in the future. The three overlapping domains of knowledge – theoretical, factual and practice – are informed by and inform research and the skills and interventions of social work practice.

Skills, standards of proficiency and capabilities for social work practice

Social workers are required to have a specific skill set in order to practise competently and effectively. Trevithick (2012, p. 44) has defined skills as follows:

> A skill is an action with a specific goal that can be learnt, that involves actions performed in sequence, that can be organised in ways that involve economy of effort and evaluated in terms of its relevance and effectiveness. Although these characteristics have been described separately, they interweave and overlap.

Trevithick (2012) proposes that there are approximately 80 generalist skills and interventions in social work practice, which range from interpersonal and communication skills to presenting evidence in court and using humour.

According to The College of Social Work (TCSW) (2012), individuals interested in studying to become a social worker must have an initial skill set where they: (1) communicate clearly, accurately and appropriately to the level of training applied for, in verbal and written forms; and (2) demonstrate an ability to engage with people with empathy. Once qualified, a beginning social worker must have skills in a wide range of verbal, non-verbal and written methods of communication; be able to engage, build, manage and sustain effective relationships; be able to identify and respond to needs; be able to plan, implement and review effective interventions; be able to share information; and be accountable as a professional (TCSW, 2012).

A skill set is only one standard of proficiency or capability needed to practise social work. Social work is a recognised profession that is regulated by the Health & Care Professions Council (HCPC) within England. The HCPC (2012) has identified 15 'standards of proficiency' that registrant social workers must meet. These include the following:

1   Be able to practise safely and effectively within their scope of practice.
2   Be able to practise within the legal and ethical boundaries of their profession.
3   Be able to maintain fitness to practise.
4   Be able to practise as an autonomous professional, exercising their own professional judgement.

5   Be aware of the impact of culture, equality and diversity on practice.
6   Be able to practise in a non-discriminatory manner.
7   Be able to maintain confidentiality.
8   Be able to communicate effectively.
9   Be able to work appropriately with others.
10 Be able to maintain records appropriately.
11 Be able to reflect on and review practice.
12 Be able to assure the quality of their practice.
13 Understand the key concepts of the knowledge base relevant to their profession.
14 Be able to draw on appropriate knowledge and skills to inform practice.
15 Be able to establish and maintain a safe practice environment.

Alongside the HCPC, which is the registering and governing body for social work in England, is TCSW that has set standards, referred to as capabilities, at each level of the social work profession, which ranges from entry into a social work programme to first year of social work practice (referred to as the Assessed Year in Practice [ASYE]) through to the advanced and then strategic levels of social work. TCSW (2012) has developed the Professional Capabilities Framework (PCF), which consists of nine domains in which social workers must demonstrate capability based on the specific level of their practice. The domains are: professionalism; values and ethics; diversity; rights, justice and economic well-being; knowledge; critical reflection and analysis; intervention and skills; contexts and organisations; and professional leadership.

Values and ethics for social work practice

The profession of social work is built upon a solid value base, which primarily consists of respect for the equality, worth and dignity of all people (IFSW, 2012). As discussed above, values and ethics are a necessary aspect of social work and social workers must demonstrate that they are adhering to the value base of social work within their practice. Additionally, students and social workers must continually reflect on their own values and attitudes and explore how their values, attitudes and ethical principles are impacting and influencing their practice. Values can be defined as the 'beliefs that people hold about what is regarded as worthy or valuable' and ethics can be defined as 'matters of right and wrong conduct, good and bad qualities or character and responsibilities attached to relationships' (British Association of Social Workers [BASW], 2012, p. 17).

The values and ethical principles for social work are detailed by the BASW and include the main values of human rights, social justice and professional integrity. Table 1.1 lists the three values and the ethical principles for each.

Table 1.1 Values and ethical principles (BASW, 2012, pp. 8–10)

Value	Ethical principles
1 Human rights	• Upholding and promoting human dignity and well-being. • Respecting the right to self-determination. • Promoting the right to participation. • Treating each person as a whole. • Identifying and developing strengths.
2 Social justice	• Challenging discrimination. • Recognising diversity. • Distributing resources. • Challenging unjust policies and practices. • Working in solidarity.
3 Professional integrity	• Upholding the values and reputation of the profession. • Being trustworthy. • Maintaining professional boundaries. • Making considered professional judgements. • Being professionally accountable.

The social work role

Social workers working within statutory and voluntary sectors as well as private, third sector (e.g. charities and social enterprises) and independent practices will be required to have the knowledge, skills and values as discussed in this (and subsequent) chapters. As you will see throughout this book, social workers predominately work within statutory sectors, particularly in children and families settings or adult social care. Yet, social work is beginning to gain a stronger presence within the voluntary sector, private, third sector and independent practices as well, particularly as local authorities commission services out to the voluntary and private sectors and are taking on more of a commissioning role versus being a provider of services. Social enterprises have recently gained attention when the Department of Education followed by the Department of Health piloted children and families and adult social work practices with statutory functions. Independent social workers are often contracted to complete statutory functions, such as best interest assessors or mental capacity assessors, or provide non-statutory information and advice to fee-paying service users.

Within statutory settings (and in some limited social enterprises and independent practices), social workers primarily provide statutory or 'public' functions as defined by legislation and/or policy guidance. This most often involves completing assessment of need and/or risk, developing a case or support plan, linking the service user or carer to services to meet identified needs, and reviewing the plan. Social workers may collaborate with other professionals, such as teachers, police, nurses, general practitioners (GPs), occupational therapists (OTs), counsellors or therapists in order to complete assessments or to determine the most appropriate services for the service user or carer. Within voluntary, third sector and non-statutory independent practice settings, social workers will still require knowledge of legislation and statutory functions, but may not be administering statutory functions. Social workers will still need knowledge and skills in assessment and services, but may have more flexibility in designing and delivering services and may have more scope for building relationships and implementing social work theories and methods. Social workers within these latter sectors will also collaborate with other professionals. This book covers social work settings across the numerous sectors in which social work takes place.

Summary

This book aims to illustrate how social work is a varied profession that works with individuals, families, groups and communities. As this chapter has discussed, social work has an aim of promoting human growth and development as well as promoting social justice. Such aims can only be met by considering and working with individuals, but equally with communities and within larger social, economic and political structures. In order to work competently and effectively, social workers must have knowledge of theories, methods and legislation, have skills to work with individuals, families, groups and communities, and adhere to the values and ethical principles of the profession. Therefore, the profession requires individuals who are competent, motivated and ready to take on the challenge of gaining the knowledge and skills and promoting the aims of the profession. I hope this book serves as a useful tool as you begin on this journey.

Further resources and suggested readings

Banks, S. (2012) *Ethics and Values in Social Work*, 4th edn. Basingstoke: Palgrave Macmillan.

Brayne, H. and Carr, H. (2013) *Law for Social Workers*, 12th edn. Oxford: Oxford University Press.

Parris, M. (2012) *An Introduction to Social Work Practice: A Practical Handbook*. Maidenhead: Open University Press.

Teater, B. (2010) *An Introduction to Applying Social Work Theories and Methods*. Maidenhead: Open University Press.

Trevithick, P. (2012) *Social Work Skills and Knowledge: A Practice Handbook*, 3rd edn. Maidenhead: Open University Press.

Websites

British Association of Social Workers (BASW) – www.basw.co.uk

Community Care – www.communitycare.co.uk

Health & Care Professions Council (HCPC) – www.hpc-uk.org

International Federation of Social Work (IFSW) – www.ifsw.org

Social Care Institute for Excellence (SCIE) – www.scie.org.uk

The College of Social Work (TCSW) – www.collegeofsocialwork.org

2 Children and families

Alinka Gearon

Introduction

This chapter focuses on children and families social work in the statutory sector, where local authorities are the main provider of social work services termed as 'the bedrock of social work in England' (Social Work Taskforce, 2009b, p. 14). Aimed at social work practitioners considering working with children and families or students starting placements, this chapter introduces the main concepts pertaining to safeguarding and promoting the well-being of children and child protection. Case examples illuminate the social and family problems that occur in children and families practice. The chapter focuses on the centrality of assessment in children and families social work and a model is presented showing the interrelational factors of assessing children's needs: *know-how*, *research*, *abilities*, *child focus*, *reflection* and *process*. Each of these factors of assessment is explored in turn, highlighting key aspects of what is expected of the social work role in working together with children and families.

A central concept of social work practice with children and their families is *safeguarding and promoting the welfare of children*, defined in statutory guidance as 'the process of protecting children from abuse or neglect, preventing impairment of their health and development, and ensuring they are growing up in circumstances consistent with the provision of safe and effective care that enables children to have optimum life chances and enter adulthood successfully' (Department of Children, Schools and Families [DCSF], 2010, p. 27).

Local authorities have a duty to safeguard and promote the welfare of children 'in need' and social workers in children and families practice have a key role in assessing, planning and delivering interventions to families requiring additional support. There are many ways in which children 'in need' may be in danger of not meeting their optimal development (Aldgate et al., 2006) and this is recognised in the definition of children in need under Part III of the Children Act 1989 under s.17(10).

Children are defined as being 'in need' if they are unlikely to reach or maintain a reasonable standard of health or development, or their health or development will be significantly impaired without the provision of services, plus those who are disabled. The Department for Education (DfE, 2011) reported that in England there were 382,400 children in need in March 2011, with local authority children's services dealing with nearly double this amount of cases throughout the year. The most common primary need at initial assessment for these children was 'abuse' or 'neglect', accounting for 44 per cent of cases (DfE, 2011).

Child protection is a part of the duty in safeguarding and promoting the welfare of children. Child protection refers to the activity and process that is undertaken to protect specific children who are suffering, or are likely to suffer, significant harm as a result of abuse or neglect (DCSF, 2010). All social work practitioners engaged in children and families practice need to have a thorough understanding of child protection, the duties and processes, recognise when children are being abused and be familiar with the steps required to protect children from further harm. Abuse takes different forms such as physical, emotional, sexual and neglect, for detailed definitions of each see *Working Together to Safeguard Children* (DCSF, 2010). A person can abuse or neglect a child by inflicting harm or failing to act to prevent harm. A single traumatic event may constitute significant harm; more often significant harm is a compilation of events, acute and long-standing which can affect the child's development. In the year 2010–11, there were 111,700 child protection investigations and 49,000 children were made subject to child protection plans (DfE, 2011). Neglect is the most common initial category of abuse under which children became the subject of a plan (42.5 per cent), emotional abuse is the next most common category (27.3 per cent) followed by physical abuse (13.0 per cent) and sexual abuse (5.4 per cent) (DfE, 2011, p. 4). In the most serious cases, concerns about children fall into more than one of these categories (Chand and Thoburn, 2006) and children can experience multiple forms of abuse.

Children and families social work practice is on the front line of multiple manifestations of social and family problems. Children, including unborn children, can experience harm or potential harm from poor home conditions, parental substance abuse, domestic violence, mental health difficulties, poverty, learning difficulties, lack of parental education or other social difficulties. Any of these factors can singularly or in combination reduce a parent's capacity in providing the care and attention that their child requires to maintain a reasonable standard of health and development. Problems occur when parental capacity is reduced and/or when environmental factors (such as poor housing, deprived neighbourhood areas, lack of community resources) combine to the detriment of children's health, education, emotional wellbeing, social relationships or their developing identity and social presentation. These distinct domains – the child's development needs, parents' capacity to respond to those needs and the wider family and environmental factors – constitute the Assessment Framework (DoH, 2000), the core approach to social work assessments of children's welfare and safety.

Social work practice within children and families services

There are many different social worker roles within children and families practice within local authority statutory services. Qualified social workers are found in various roles, dependent on the structure of teams and the division of casework within children's services departments. Social workers are employed in referral and assessment teams usually responsible for responding to all new referrals, conducting initial assessments and child protection investigations. Some local authorities have teams specifically working with looked after children (children subject to care orders and in foster care), disabled children, leaving care teams (focusing on social work support to teenagers) or asylum teams. Family placement teams typically deal with the provision of foster care and other placements for children and may also specialise in adoption (see Chapter 3). There are also multi-agency or 'co-located' teams where social workers work alongside partner agencies in delivering children and families services. Other settings and roles include out of hours emergency response teams, youth offending teams and local safeguarding children's boards. All of these social work roles are typically within the statutory sector setting. Other important employers of social workers are the (Children and Family Court Advisory and Support Service (CAFCASS, the NHS, voluntary organisations and the private sector.

Assessment

Common to all children and families social work practice are core skills of assessment, planning, child protection and relationship-based social work (Butler and Hickman, 2011). Assessment has been integral to social work practice for many decades although since the 1970s an ideological shift has taken place away from a diagnostic focus, towards understanding the perspectives of service users within a holistic framework (Seden, 2001, as cited in Butler and Roberts, 2004). Assessment practice has developed into a dynamic, interactive and reciprocal process (Butler and Hickman, 2011), one which aims at being child centred, rooted in child development, participative, informed by evidence and a continuing process rather than an one-off event (DCSF, 2010, pp. 133–136). Social workers have a pivotal role in assessments and there are several interconnected factors that shape and influence the practice of assessment. Figure 2.1 depicts the interrelational factors of assessing the needs of children and families: *know-how, research, abilities, child focus, reflection* and *process*.

Process

The process element is a key facet of assessing children's needs. The process of assessment requires social workers to have knowledge of child in need and child

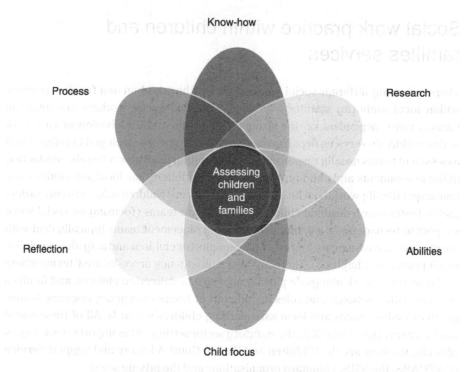

Figure 2.1 Assessing children and families

protection procedures and practice guidance. When there are concerns about a child's safety or welfare a referral is made to children's services. Any person working with children or parents as well as members of the public can make a referral. Referrals are made by the police, health professionals (e.g. GPs, health visitors, midwives, paramedics), education staff (teachers, nursery workers), children centre staff, probation services, drug treatment services and any other agency concerned about a child. On occasion families request support directly or members of the public raise their concerns, often via the NSPCC helpline who then pass on information to children's services.

An initial assessment is commenced if there are concerns about impairment to the child's health and development or the child is suffering harm (DCSF, 2010, p. 144). Examples of the concerns raised in referrals to children's services are given in Box 2.1. In each of the examples, further information is required from the referrer about the nature of concerns, how they have arisen, the needs of the child and family and what involvement the referrer has had. A decision is made within one working day by the social worker together with an experienced line manager on what the next course of action will be, which can be onward referral to another agency, requesting a common assessment framework (CAF), no further action or to commence an initial assessment.

Box 2.1 Concerns raised in referrals to children's services

a   School has raised concerns about a 12-year-old child's increasing challenging behaviour at school, sometimes very aggressive towards other pupils, resulting in the risk of being permanently excluded. Mother has not engaged with school's requests for meetings. It is believed she is experiencing depression due to a recent bereavement.

b   The police have shared concerns about children of a couple experiencing domestic violence. A number of incidents in the last few months have been reported to the police by neighbours but appear to be escalating in severity. The latest incident was witnessed by the children aged five and seven and appears to be exacerbated by father's alcohol use. School reports that the children's behaviour is of concern, the elder child is withdrawn and the younger child is wetting in class. Mother has expressed to school staff that she is ambivalent about ending the relationship.

c   Health visitor shares concerns about a toddler. Health appointments have not been attended, scheduled due to concerns about developmental delay. The health visitor attempted to visit the family at home and found a lot of rubbish has accumulated outside and the curtains were drawn. The parents are known to have a history of substance abuse.

d   The head teacher is concerned about a child at school, aged six, with bruising to his leg. The child has told his teacher that his father has hit him with a belt. Parents do not understand English very well.

e   A 13-year-old girl has been identified by police as at risk of sexual exploitation, going missing from home overnight and on one occasion was found in the 'red light' district area of the town under the influence of alcohol.

f   A midwife is concerned about a couple who appear to have learning difficulties and are expecting their first child. The couple present at antenatal appointments very unkempt, they have financial difficulties and have received an eviction notice from their hostel accommodation due to unpaid rent.

The initial assessment aims to determine whether:

- the child is in need
- there is reasonable cause to suspect the child is suffering, or is likely to suffer significant harm
- any services are required
- if a further core assessment should be undertaken (DCSF, 2010, p. 145).

When there is reasonable cause to suspect the child is suffering significant harm, or is likely to suffer significant harm (evident, alleged or suspected abuse), social workers conduct section 47 enquiries. Where a decision has been made to initiate a section 47 enquiry, an initial assessment would have been carried out and a strategy discussion taken place. The strategy discussion involves children's services, police and relevant agencies and decides upon how the enquiry is undertaken, any immediate action needed to secure the safety of the child and if legal action is required. The core assessment under section 47 of the Children Act 1989 begins following the strategy discussion and is the means by which an enquiry is carried out.

To assist with the process of assessment social workers have at their disposal various assessment tools. Genograms, ecomaps and chronologies are not only useful techniques for sorting through sometimes complex histories and family arrangements, but can also be used as a tool for direct work (Butler and Hickman, 2011). Ecomaps work well with older children as a shared activity and can highlight important friendship networks, strained relationships or other significant figures in the child's life, which can then be used as a prompt to explore particular issues and understand the nature of the child's relationships. Culturagrams are a particularly useful tool for work with culturally diverse families (Congress, 2002, p. 59) as they can illuminate cultural differences in values about family structures, power, rules, traditions and health beliefs. Considering a family only in terms of a generic cultural identity may lead to overgeneralisation and stereotyping (Congress, 1994). By completing a culturagram with a family this is avoided as the family's unique cultural factors are considered aligned with social work as anti-discriminatory practice. The process can help social workers to understand the role of differing cultures in families and assist with assessment of children's needs within a cultural context.

Know-how

The Children Act 1989 is the key piece of legislation for social work practice with children and families. The definitions of significant harm (section 31) and child in need are contained within this act. Under section 47(1) Children Act 1989, there is a duty to make enquiries where the local authority has reasonable cause to suspect that a child is suffering or likely to suffer significant harm. There are no absolute criteria when judging what constitutes significant harm therefore careful assessment of the child's circumstances following an allegation is necessary, with discussion between statutory agencies and the child and family (DCSF, 2010).

The Children Act 2004 was introduced after findings of inadequacies in the child protection framework following the death of Victoria Climbié in 2000. The essence of the Act can be described as promoting inter-agency working but the Act also introduced more in relation to children's rights. A Children's Commissioner was established to promote views of children linked to outcomes from *Every Child Matters* (DfES, 2004). Additionally, the Children Act 2004 requires local authorities to ascertain wishes and feelings of children regarding provision of services, linking to Article 12 of the United Nations Convention on the Rights of the Child (UNCRC).

The key policy document guiding children and families practice is *Working Together to Safeguard Children* (DCSF, 2010). Statutory social work practice with children and families requires practitioners to understand the range of powers and duties under key legislation (for a summary of legislation and the statutory framework see DCSF [2010, p. 336]). The government has revised its statutory guidance on safeguarding children in England, following Eileen Munro's (2011) review of child protection, splitting the existing policy into three separate and much shorter documents: (1) *Working Together to Safeguard Children*: what is expected of organisations responsible for safeguarding children, individually and jointly; (2) *Managing Individual Cases*: a framework for the assessment of children in need. This supersedes nationally prescribed timescales for assessments and focuses instead on the core principles of carrying out good assessments. Local authorities with their partner agencies must develop and publish their own local frameworks for assessment, including guidance on how soon a child should be visited after referral; and (3) *Statutory Guidance on Learning and Improvement*: proposed new arrangements for serious case reviews (SCRs) and child death reviews (DfE, 2012).

Following the tragic death of Baby Peter in 2008, policy and practice have refocused more centrally on 'child protection'. Prior to this the state developed a much broader focus of what constituted risk to children with an emphasis upon 'safeguarding' rather than 'child protection' (Parton, 2011). Since the case of Baby Peter, child protection has become an issue of significant political and policy concern with a renewed interest and priority given to social work within this (Parton, 2011). The government established an independent review of child protection, *The Munro Review of Child Protection* (Munro, 2011), which identified the following principles of an effective child protection system:

1   The system should be child centred.
2   The family is usually the best place for bringing up children and young people.
3   Helping children and families involves working with them (quality of relationship between child and families and professionals impacting on effectiveness of help).
4   Early help is better for children.
5   Children's needs and circumstances are varied so the system needs to offer equal variety in its response.
6   Good professional practice is informed by knowledge of the latest theory and research.
7   Uncertainty and risk are features of child protection work.
8   The measure of the success of child protection systems, both local and national, is whether children are receiving effective help.

The *know-how* of children and families practice and assessment requires practitioners to have good knowledge and understanding of a range of child development theories (Daniel, 2007), child abuse in its varying forms (Corby, 2006) and child exploitation, including new forms of abuse via the internet; social networking sites and chat rooms (CEOP, 2012). Social workers need to recognise the impact of parental problems such as domestic violence, mental health and substance abuse on child development and be able to pick up signs that a child may be experiencing harm through neglect, distress or abuse.

Theoretical aspects of practice include understanding and applying theory-informed methods and approaches such as social systems theory, social constructivism, feminist theory and the ecological perspective. The Assessment Framework (DoH, 2000) is based on the ecological approach (Bronfenbrenner, 1979) focusing on the adaptation between the individual and their environment, the synergistic cycle of influence between the changing individual and the changing environment (Colton et al., 2001). This approach is reflected in the three domains of the assessment, where the welfare of the child depends on interactions between developmental needs, parenting capacity and family and environmental factors (Jack, 2001).

Social workers have at their disposal a range of options when incorporating theories and methods in practice and can select a particular method or theory or choose an eclectic approach (Teater, 2010). Being eclectic can involve choosing different theories and methods, dependent on what is most appropriate for the task and people's situations. For example, assessment requires an ecological approach to ascertain the needs of the child within their family and wider environment. During the assessment process, the social worker may draw on motivational interviewing when working with parents who abuse substances and simultaneously take an empowerment approach in direct work with a child experiencing neglect.

Abilities

Another key element of children and families practice is the *abilities* and skills that a social worker requires for assessment to be a therapeutic and interactive process. Assessment is more than an administrative task and a form-filling exercise; it can be viewed as a social work intervention in itself (Walker and Beckett, 2003) with the capacity to bring about positive change. Even a brief encounter with a child and family can have therapeutic value and pave the way for ongoing relationship-based practice. Service users value being listened to with social workers validating feelings and concerns, which aids the development of trust (Millar and Corby, 2006). A study by Forrester et al. (2008) focused on the skills practitioners used in engaging parents in situations where there are concerns about child welfare found that social workers tended to use a confrontational style with parents, which was unhelpful and created resistance. Whilst the Assessment Framework provides a tool for sharing concerns and creating openness about difficult issues, it needs to be coupled with a skilful approach in being directive yet empathetic. Simultaneously, the role of the social worker is enabling the parent/carer/child to understand why difficult questions have to be asked and requests to see around homes have to be carried out (Ferguson, 2010).

In terms of relationship-based practice, a core skill of social work, Ferguson (2010, p. 1109) observes that 'all homes and the relationships within them have atmospheres and how professionals manage stepping into and negotiating them is at the core of performing social work and child protection and managing risk effectively'. Working in partnership entails negotiating with parents to gain access into homes to see children, sometimes where the social worker's presence may not be welcomed or met with feelings of fear or anxiety, even hostility. Social workers need to be aware of potential avoidance, detraction or an underplaying of the concerns raised and to challenge perceptions honestly and yet remain respectful. Skilful negotiation therefore moves beyond gaining access and raising concerns to building a rapport and setting up an ongoing relationship for the potential intervention required.

A critical approach underpinning practice serves as an effective means of striking a balance between attributing responsibility for harm caused to a child by an adult whilst examining disadvantage and structural factors that adversely affect parenting capacity. Parents and carers with experience of children's services involvement have expressed that good social work should be person centred, where practitioners 'must see service users as whole people' (Cree and Davis, 2007, p. 152) by not immediately focusing on just the problems they have, in order to locate people in their wider contexts. Seeking to understand how income deprivation, poor housing, a lack of education or employment affects parenting capacity helps to see the children and families in a fuller context. Service users value support, which is both practical and emotional including material deprivation and accessing scarce resources (Cree and Davis, 2007, p. 53).

Child focus

Engaging directly with children, listening to their views and ascertaining their needs through direct work requires social workers to have age-appropriate and child-centred communication skills and techniques. Children have identified that effective communication is as much about *being* as well as *doing* and emphasise the need for practitioners to find creative ways to involve and consult them (Luckock et al., 2006). Evidence suggests that children respond better to child-centred communication approaches including the use of techniques such as play, games, activities, creative arts, music and guided reading (Luckock et al., 2006; Lefevre, 2008). These methods 'can be useful in assessment work for gaining information about the child's world, avoiding the kinds of questions that children are often suspicious of' and utilised as 'bridges to open up communication so that the child can become more effectively involved in the therapeutic process' (Luckock et al., 2006, p. 30). For example, as part of the assessment process, books can be used by social workers to involve children in direct work; looking at pictures provides an opportunity to talk about a range of issues, with parents as well as children (Seden, 2008). The method is natural, less stigmatising and more creative than relying on interviews and can help practitioners to understand the impact of life events on children (Seden, 2008).

The absence of touch in relational social work with children is raised by Ferguson (2011) in a current climate of fear; a false conception of a prohibition of touch and risk-averse organisations. Victoria Climbié and Baby Peter were both children in high profile cases that showed a lack of direct contact in the form of touch by practitioners. Engaging in ordinary mobility with children is a way of spotting child abuse, even if it only amounts to taking a few steps with them. As Ferguson (2010, p. 1110) observes: 'effective child protection has to involve not only professional mobility to reach the child, but ensuring that children move.' Walking around rooms in the home, assessing general living conditions, directly engaging with children and asking permission to touch or move with children (when proportionate and appropriate) are all standards of good social work, keeping the child in focus. Interaction with children through listening, playing or observing is vital good practice and provides opportunity to enter the child's world and gain an understanding of their situation.

Reflection

Supervision is a key vehicle by which to reflect on casework, review progress of interventions and clarify issues arising from practice. Effective supervision provides the time and space to examine detailed examples of social work practice as a process of reconstructing practice along more critically empowering lines (Fook, 2002). Fook (2002, pp. 98–102) recommends the technique of *critical incident analysis*, to reflect on any incident of significance in practice, be it traumatic, posing a dilemma or unresolved in nature. The process of deconstructing practice in supervision helps to identify personal assumptions about power and to consider values that each social worker brings to their practice, in order to 'unearth how we ourselves participate in discourses which shape existing power relations' (Fook, 2002, p. 98). Critical incident analysis within supervision therefore allows for oppressive practices to be examined in a supportive, developmental way and helps social workers consider alternative perspectives.

Inevitably the emotions arising from working with families with social, material or health problems and being in close proximity to children who experience abuse and harm is an inherent aspect of relationship-based practice within social work. There is growing evidence that those who work with people who have been traumatised are more likely to develop secondary traumatic stress (Bride and Figley, 2007) or vicarious traumatisation (Palm et al., 2004). Vicarious trauma reactions may include intrusive imagery and thoughts, avoidance and emotional numbing, hyperarousal symptoms, somatisation, and physical and alcohol use problems similar to those experienced by direct trauma survivors (Palm et al., 2004). It is necessary therefore, for social workers to utilise both formal sources of support such as supervision and counselling and informal sources such as support from their colleagues.

Personal coping strategies are an essential self-care skill, to increase resilience and prevent 'burnout'. The types of coping strategies recommended include education related to abuse, supervision, consultation, optimistic perseverance, seeking social support and inner peace and humour (Mederios and Prochaska, 1988). A local authority referral and assessment team consulted for this chapter developed their own social support by practising yoga together on a regular basis. Mensinga (2011, p. 650), a social work educator and yoga teacher, states that yoga practice strengthens the reflexive capacity of practitioners 'leading to a greater health and well-being of social workers and better outcomes for their clients'.

Research

The systematic use of evidence is expected by the requirements of the social work degree and extends into social work practice in children and families. Munro (2011, p. 23) has reiterated the importance of social workers use of research evidence to help them reach the most appropriate decisions, highlighting that 'good professional practice is informed by knowledge of the latest theory and research'. An evidence-informed approach to assessment requires social workers to have wider knowledge in four areas: (1) skills in critical thinking; (2) research skills: (3) knowledge of the particular service user groups being assessed and of social contexts; and (4) knowledge to inform the conduct of the assessment (Crisp et al., 2003, p. 29).

Keeping up to date in developments in social work practice, methods and interventions is therefore another key aspect of assessment that is closely interrelated to the other factors described in Figure 2.1. In assessment practice, evidence from research is used to inform the analysis of why any problems are happening and evidence is used on effectiveness of interventions to guide plans on how to help solve the problems. The sources of available research for social workers include Social Care Online (Social Care Institute for Excellence [SCIE]), social work journals and published research in related disciplines. Other valuable sources of research include the NSPCC Inform website, Barnardo's, Research in Practice, local projects and advocacy services. Research addressing the experiences of children and families in assessments and child protection are particularly valuable in understanding what social work intervention is like for children and parents. Examples of such research are provided in the further resources at the end of the chapter.

Case example

Bringing together some of the key aspects of assessing children and families discussed above, the following case example is used to consider how a social worker may approach the assessment of Marley and his family.

A referral was received from the police stating that the ambulance service was called to the family home to attend to Amanda, mother of eight-year-old Marley. Amanda was unconscious, suspected of having taken an overdose. Marley was present in the house when this happened. Amanda has bipolar disorder and is known to the community mental health team and has a history of self-harm in periods of crises. Marley is supported as a young carer due to his mother's ongoing mental health difficulties. Marley's father passed away a few years ago. Amanda has a partner, John, who usually supports her and Marley when she is unwell, but he is currently serving a custodial sentence for theft. Marley has a grandmother who lives nearby and he stays with her on the weekends. Amanda was kept in hospital overnight under observation and discharged the next day.

As one of the tasks in reviewing the referral, the social worker checks the history of any children's services involvement. The chronology reveals that similar concerns were raised a few months ago. At that time, extended family provided additional support to Marley and children's services recommended a common assessment framework (CAF) to be completed. The social worker discusses her concerns with her manager about a pattern emerging of family difficulties that impact on Marley negatively. An initial assessment is agreed upon as there are concerns about impairment to Marley's health and development and further information is needed to determine if Marley is a child in need under s.17 Children Act 1989. Amanda is contacted by the social worker at the earliest opportunity to discuss the worries about Marley. Amanda is very remorseful and agrees she needs help; a home visit is planned for the assessment. Amanda gives permission to contact her community psychiatric nurse, the young carers project supporting Marley and his head teacher. As part of the information-gathering process, the social worker contacts these key agencies that know the family to contribute to the assessment.

The social worker feels really sad for Marley about the weight of responsibility on his shoulders and is worried about what he has been exposed to at his young age and shares these feelings with colleagues in the duty team. Another social worker expresses sympathy for Amanda, wondering what she would do in her situation. The social worker considers that specific research and knowledge would be of value in assessing this family's needs; the impact on Marley's health and development of poor parental mental health – for example, being exposed to mental distress, an emotionally withdrawn parent, feeling anxiety on behalf of the parent, carrying responsibilities not normally expected at that age and the overall impact on his emotional well-being. Additionally, the social worker obtains information on the presenting symptoms of bipolar disorder, affects of medication and effectiveness of interventions. The social worker is mindful about the initial contact with Amanda, in that she needs to build rapport and trust for any ongoing involvement. In terms of abilities and skills, the social worker prepares for the visit by taking a sensitive, sympathetic and non-blaming approach due to mother's emotional vulnerability, balanced with being clear about the worries about Marley.

In meeting with the family, Marley is spoken to alone with Amanda's consent and the social worker uses the Three Houses Tool (Weld, 2008) to explore Marley's needs and views. The interactive tool allows Marley to put in his own words and drawings what is inside his 'house of worries', 'house of good things' and 'house of dreams'. After the visit, the social worker discusses her analysis of the situation in supervision, why she thinks Marley is a child in need and explores the type of support that may help the family at this time. The manager asks the social worker to reflect on what worked well in the visit and not so well, and what could be done differently next time?

Benefits and challenges to working in children's services

In the present economic climate of increased unemployment and the likelihood of greater social and economic inequalities, the pressures and demands upon social workers are likely to increase considerably (Parton, 2011). Coupled with deep cuts to early intervention services may lead to a further increase in the numbers of children in need and looked after (NSPCC, 2011), increasing social workers caseloads whilst having fewer services for families to help them ameliorate problems. Despite the current backdrop of austerity measures, children and families social work can be hugely rewarding work with satisfaction, degrees of freedom and opportunities to be creative in practice. Social workers in Ferguson's (2010, p. 1112) study expressed a certain thrill that comes from the feeling that you have 'made a difference to people's lives and relieved their suffering by entering the unknown of their homes and lives, such as preventing a child coming into care'. Good social workers can and do make a huge difference in sometimes difficult situations and according to the Social Work Task Force (2009a, p. 5): 'They are needed now as much, if not more, than ever. Their professional skills and knowledge can help people to take back control of their lives, through a genuine partnership between the social worker and the service user.'

Summary

Table 2.1 summarises the key aspects of children and families social work discussed in this chapter, in the dimensions of: *know-how, abilities, child focus, reflection, research* and *process*. These are all interrelated factors that shape and influence the key task of social work – assessing children's and families' needs. One factor interrelates with another: for example, a practitioner's own childhood experience will influence the way the voice of the child is interpreted (*reflection* and *child focus*). The practitioner's relationship-based skills will influence the assessment as an interactive and therapeutic process (*abilities* and *process*). The interconnected factors presented

Table 2.1 Interrelated factors that shape and influence the key task of social work

Know-how	Abilities
Legislation and policy.	Relationship-based practice.
Child development and attachment theories.	Observation, communication, engaging families.
Recognise signs of child abuse and exploitation.	Inclusive approach to participation in assessment and planning: children and carers.
Impact of parental problems on child development: e.g. domestic violence, substance abuse, mental health.	Partnership working with families and other agencies.
	Critical application of theories, frameworks and methods.
Theory-informed approaches: e.g. ecological, systems, structural approach.	Anti-discriminatory approach.
Impact of transitions: resilience and protective mechanisms.	Organisational skills: presentation to diverse audiences (from children to judges); collating information (accuracy/fact distinct from opinion/assumptions).
Family dynamics and family styles.	
Child focus	*Reflection*
Directly engaging children: play, games, activities, creative arts, reading.	Awareness of personal values, biases and experiences of own childhood.
Child-focused practice: observing, listening, interacting – seeing children move.	Supervision as critical reflection.
	Influence of agency values on personal practice.
Participation of children in assessment, planning and processes.	Emotions arising through relationship-based practice.
Ascertaining wishes and feelings of children.	Self-care: formal/informal support and personal coping strategies.
UN Convention on the Rights of the Child, Human Rights.	
Research	*Process*
Evidence-informed approach to assessment.	Child in Need and Child Protection procedures and practice guidance.
	Assessment as interactive/therapeutic process.
Critical use of research sources: SCIE, journals, NSPCC Inform, Research in Practice, Barnardo's, advocacy services, local projects.	Assessment tools: chronologies, ecomaps, genograms, culturagrams.
	Inter-agency collaboration.
Children's and parent's views.	Information sharing.
Develop specialist expertise: Young Minds, Who Cares Trust, Child Poverty Action Group.	
Being up to date: e.g. use of new technologies in child abuse.	

in the model in Figure 2.1 therefore encourage us to practise reflexivity as a 'cyclical process in which we openly study how what we observe affects our thinking and how that then affects what we do' (Payne, 2005, p. 35).

Activity

Read the examples provided in Box 2.1 (p. 15) at the beginning of the chapter of different scenarios where there are concerns about children's welfare. Refer to Figure 2.1 Assessing children and families (p. 14) and the summary in Table 2.1 (p. 24) and consider, for each case (*a* to *f*), who you might approach for an assessment of the child and family.

Questions

Process. Which partner agencies might be especially helpful in this scenario in providing information? What specific tools/techniques do you think might aid assessment?

Know-how. Which parts of the Children Act 1989 apply in this scenario? What theoretical knowledge will you draw on and why?

Abilities. What specific skills do you think are important in approaching the assessment?

Child focus. Which particular child-centred approach could be used given the child's age and situation? How would you try to involve the child in the assessment?

Reflection. What immediate emotional reactions are raised in you by the concerns? Where do these come from? What do you do to manage this?

Research. What research might be of value in this scenario? Where would you find it?

Further resources and suggested readings

Cleaver, H., Nicholson, D., Tarr, S. and Cleaver, D. (2007) *Child Protection, Domestic Violence and Parental Substance Misuse: Family Experiences and Effective Practice.* London: Jessica Kingsley Publishers.

Ghaffar, W., Manby, M. and Race, T. (2012) Exploring the experiences of parents and carers whose children have been subject to child protection plans, *British Journal of Social Work*, 42: 887–905.

Office of the Children's Commissioner (2011) *Don't Make Assumptions – Children and Young People's Views of the Child Protection System and Messages for Change*. www.childrenscommissioner.gov.uk/content/publications (accessed 18 November 2012).

Ofsted (2010) *Before Care – A Report of Children's Views on Entering Care by the Children's Rights Director for England*. www.ofsted.gov.uk/Ofsted-home/Publications-and-research (accessed 18 November 2012).

Websites

Social Care Institute for Excellence – www.scie.org.uk

Social Care TV – *What is social work? Children and families. Introduction to children's social care. Using play and creative arts in communicating with children* – www.scie.org.uk/assets/elearning/communicationskills/cs08/resource/index.html

3 Fostering and adoption

Justin Rogers

Introduction

This chapter provides an overview of social work practice in the field of family place-ment. Family placement services within the context of the UK and more specifically the English public care system are introduced. The different practice areas within family placement are discussed, which include fostering, kinship care, private fostering, respite care and adoption. The key roles and responsibilities of social workers who practise in a family placement service field are examined. For example, completing assessments, attending panels, undertaking duty, as well as providing ongoing support and supervision to placements. The key theories that inform practice in this field are highlighted and discussed with a specific focus on attach-ment theory. The chapter concludes by exploring the benefits and challenges within family placement provision. The ethical, cultural and anti-oppressive dimensions that are inherent within family placement practice will be considered throughout the chapter.

Context

Children and young people enter the public care system for a variety of individual and often complex reasons. These reasons are likely to centre on concerns that they have experienced abuse and/or neglect within their birth families. This may also be coupled with parents who are experiencing mental health and/or substance misuse difficulties. The combination of such experiences with the subsequent separation from their primary caregiver and their placement in public care results in children and young people experiencing 'disrupted pathways' (Schofield, 2003) at an early stage in their life.

In 2011 there were over 89,000 looked after children and young people in the UK (Department for Education [DfE], 2012). After a significant and continued decrease in the number of children in care over the past 30 years, the number has recently started to increase and since 2008 it has risen by 13 per cent to a 15-year high. This recent rise coincides with the inquiry into the death of Peter Connolly and the subsequent increase in care proceedings, particularly in England.

Placement options for looked after children

There are different placement options for children and young people who enter care. A small number remain at home with their parents being supported and supervised by the local authority. However, most children and young people entering care are placed in either a substitute family setting or a residential care setting (e.g. a children's home). The predominant type of placement for children and young people in the UK public care system is foster care, with over 75 per cent of children and young people in care living with foster carers (DfE, 2012). Foster care can be provided by kinship carers who are connected to the child or young person, for example, a family friend or relative. Kinship care accounts for around 15 per cent of foster placements in the UK (DfE, 2012). This differs from family placement practice across the globe: for example, in Spain, the United States and New Zealand where kinship placements are prominent (Nixon, 2007). The vast majority of foster carers in the UK are people recruited and assessed by fostering services specifically to provide care for looked after children and young people with whom they have no pre-existing connection or relationship.

Fostering placements can be made on a short-term basis where carers provide placements in an emergency situation. This may happen, for example, when children are removed from their family and enter care for the first time. Some foster care placements are intended to be long term in order to provide children and young people with permanence and a sense of security and belonging in a family placement. Fostering services may also provide respite carers for parents or long-term carers to have a break from the demands of caring. These different kinds of placement often overlap. For example, a child placed with carers in an emergency may go on to stay on a short-term basis and subsequently they may become part of the foster family and stay on long term until adulthood.

Local authority fostering services are also responsible for overseeing private fostering arrangements. These arrangements are where a person who holds parental responsibility places her or his child in the care of another adult (who is not a close relative) for longer than six weeks. The regulation of private fostering stems from the public inquiry held after the death of Victoria Climbié whose parents placed her in the care of her relatives. Different local authorities undertake differing levels of assessment of private fostering arrangements. However, The Children (Private Arrangements for Fostering) Regulations 2005 place a duty on local authorities to carry out relevant criminal and statutory checks and undertake visits as a minimum standard.

Adoption is another key form of family placement that aims to secure permanence for looked after children. Adopters gain parental responsibility for a child who then is no longer considered looked after by the local authority and instead legally becomes the adoptive parents' child. In 2011, 3700 children and young people left care and became adopted (DfE, 2012). Evidence suggests that in practice adoption is more likely to be the placement choice for infants and younger children (Biehal et al., 2010). For example, in 2012, 74 per cent of the children adopted were under four years old with the average age of an adopted child being three years and eight months (DfE, 2012). Adoption practice is currently under the political gaze and the current process has received criticism from the coalition government with Prime Minister David Cameron criticising the system for delays (Malik, 2012). Cameron also argues that current practice is too focused on matching children with adopters from their own ethnic and cultural background (Malik, 2012). However, the British Association of Social Workers (BASW) argues that the coalition government is not listening to social workers, highlighting how practitioners that are making lifelong decisions for children should be focused on ensuring a child's needs are being met and not about meeting timescales (BASW, 2012). The gravitas of the decision to remove a child permanently from their parent cannot be understated as this is possibly one of the most draconian measures taken by the state against its citizens. BASW also highlights that ultimately speeding up the adoption process will require more resources, such as the need to resource more adoption support services as the adoption breakdown rate is estimated as being as high as one in five placements ending before adulthood (BASW, 2012). As with many areas of social work policy and practice, adoption is undoubtedly an area that the coalition government is seeking to change. Therefore, it would be advisable to read the Community Care website and the British Association for Adoption and Fostering (BAAF) journal *Adoption and Fostering* (references provided in Further Resources), in order to keep up to date with developing family placement issues and contemporary social work practice.

Social work practice within family placement services

In some local authorities fostering and adoption services are undertaken by generic family placement teams where social workers can either specialise in certain aspects of the service or hold a generic caseload undertaking both fostering and adoption work. In other (often larger) local authorities adoption and fostering is undertaken by separate and specialist adoption teams and fostering teams. Neo-liberalism has also undoubtedly had an impact on contemporary family placement practice which is reflected in the 'mixed economy of care' that is evident throughout wider social welfare provision in the UK. This means family placement services are delivered by local authorities and voluntary agencies as well as the independent (private) sector.

Therefore, a social worker may work in a local authority, a voluntary agency or an independent agency and in turn may work within a specialist fostering or adoption team or a generic family placement team. The following section begins to highlight the practice experiences that social workers may gain if working within these settings. A key aspect of family placement practice is working directly with and undertaking home visits to adopters or carers. This highlights a paradox in the work, which is that although family placement is clearly within children's services, the majority of the role of a family placement social worker predominantly involves practice and interactions with adults. In this context it is important to remember that the focus of the work is about meeting the child's needs and acknowledging her or his wishes and feelings as set out in the Children Act 1989. Of course this necessitates regularly making space during a home visit to meet with children in placement in order to hear their voice about their placement arrangements.

Assessment of carers and adopters

At the centre of family placement practice is the need to recruit and assess families to foster and adopt. The assessments of prospective foster carers, kinship carers and adopters have similarities in the formats they follow but they also have some distinct differences. The following section will describe the assessment process for prospective foster carers and then briefly highlight some of the differences when undertaking assessments of kinship carers and adopters.

Assessments of prospective foster carers have two clear aims: (1) to determine an applicant's suitability to foster; and (2) to develop an applicant's skills to foster. It is a process that requires social workers not only to gather information and evidence for their assessment but also to train and prepare prospective carers. This process also provides the applicants with an opportunity to learn about the role of the foster carer and to decide if it is right for them and their family. This involves all prospective foster carers having to attend preparation training days, which can be held over two to three full days where prospective carers learn about issues such as young people's pathways into care, child development and working with birth parents. Over the course of the assessment, which can take around four to six months, the main document to complete is the Prospective Foster Carers Report (PFCR), in practice more commonly known by its old name 'Form F'. The form follows a format devised by the BAAF and starts by bringing together factual information, statutory checks and both personal and employment references. The bulk of the form includes in-depth qualitative information about applicants' family history, their relationship history and their experience of childcare and parenting. The PFCR form concludes with an analysis of all the information gathered, which ultimately leads to an assessment of the applicant's suitability to foster and the recommendation of the assessing social worker as to whether she or he feels the applicants should be approved to foster.

The process for assessing kinship carers is similar and often uses the same PFCR format. However, the report and assessment will also acknowledge and examine the pre-existing relationship a child has with the kinship carer, and in practice the child may well already be living with her or his kinship carers whilst an assessment is being undertaken. A kinship assessment may also have the additional complexity that the carers may be facing the same challenging social and environmental factors as a child's birth parents. Research suggests that some practitioners view kinship assessments negatively with the viewpoint that 'the apple never drops far from the tree' (Hunt et al., 2008); thus, this thought can lead to potentially negative assumptions about kinship care. Such assumptions are not borne out in the research evidence, which finds that children placed with kinship carers achieve outcomes when they leave care (e.g. education, employment) that are generally no worse and in some cases better than their peers who are placed with stranger foster carers (Nixon, 2007; Farmer and Moyers, 2008; Hunt et al., 2008).

The assessments of adopters have similarities to foster carers but are generally more in-depth and often involve more training and home study. The reasoning behind this is that once an adoption order is granted, the families stop receiving supervision from a local authority and go on to parent on their own. The assessment is determining the suitability of the applicants to meet a child's needs over the life course and, therefore, the adoption assessment is of a greater gravitas as it aims to determine the suitability of what is intended to be a lifelong decision. By contrast, with foster carers and kinship carers the supervision and, in effect, the assessment can be seen as more of an ongoing process. Because of this added complexity, the adoption regulations state that adoption assessments must be undertaken by practitioners with at least five years' practice experience or by somebody under the close supervision of an experienced practitioner.

Fostering panels and adoption panels

Once family placement assessments are complete, they are then presented to the agency's fostering or adoption panel. Panels generally meet once a month and assessments usually need to be submitted for panel two weeks prior to the panel date in order to give panel members an opportunity to read the papers. Panels are usually made up of around ten people who either have personal or professional experience of fostering or adoption. For example, panels often include an independent social worker, a legal advisor, a medical advisor and an education professional such as a teacher or education welfare officer. They can also include somebody with experience of fostering/adoption or an adult who has experience of being fostered/adopted. The panel is chaired by an independent social worker who directs the questions that panel members may have for the assessing social worker or the applicants. After a discussion of the assessment and questions to the social worker and applicants, the panel discusses the case alone in order to reach a recommendation. The applicants are usually told of the recommendation at the panel. However, their approval as carers is not official until the agency decision-maker ratifies the decision. The agency decision-maker is usually a senior service manager or director of the agency. The process is very similar for adoption but again it does have added rigour due to the context of adoption decisions as they are meant to be permanent.

Family placement duty

A period on duty in a family placement team generally means a day in the office based on a dedicated duty desk. The duty social worker is usually responsible for answering phone enquiries. These may be from members of the public who may be interested in becoming foster carers, or existing foster carers with queries about their current placements. The duty social worker is also a point of contact for social workers in the children's teams that require placements for children and young people, which may occur over the phone or by social workers dropping by the duty desk to make a referral. Such referrals are often the most important aspect of the duty task where, often at short notice, arrangements are made for emergency place-ments to ensure a child or young person has a place to stay. This process of making placements involves matching the needs, wishes and feelings of the child with the most appropriate carers that have an available placement. In a local authority this can sometimes mean that if there are no available carers the social workers may be required (with agreement from the senior manager) to make referrals via email or phone to independent and voluntary fostering agencies. This highlights that duty work also occurs in an independent or voluntary agency, which involves receiving referrals from a range of local authorities that are seeking placements for the chil-dren and young people in their care.

Adoption placements are generally carried out with matches being approved by a panel. Therefore, as a duty worker in an adoption team the main task centres on responding to telephone enquiries from people interested in adopting and, on occa-sion, enquiries from adults who were adopted who wish to review their case files or contact their birth families.

Supervision visits

In recent years, there has been an increase in professionalisation in fostering, which is evident in the move in terminology from 'foster parent' to 'foster carer' and with family placement social workers titles changing from 'fostering social worker' to 'supervising social worker'. The terminology around home visits or support visits has also changed, with foster carers and social workers now meeting for supervision. This increased formality in the relationship has also brought about increased expec-tations and demands on foster carers. For example, foster carers now undergo annual household reviews with assessment reports written and reviewed by a manager. In the case of newly approved foster carers, a requirement is made for them to return to the fostering panel to provide an update on their progress and experience and foster carers are expected to engage in their own training and development. In local authorities, in particular, this means they often attend the same training days on issues such as child protection or child development as social workers. This highlights how the relationship between carers and supervising social workers is moving towards being seen as a relationship of colleagues, which encourages a team approach to parenting and supporting a placement.

The main role of supervising social workers is to carry out home visits to their caseload of foster carers and provide regular ongoing support and supervision, which is often completed either monthly or every fortnight. Foster carers have the responsibility of dealing with the effects of abuse and neglect and separation and loss on a child or young person, which often impacts on a child's emotional and behavioural development. In supporting a foster carer in this task, a social worker needs to be able to offer practical advice on parenting skills and managing behaviour, as well as offering advice about parenting style, emotional warmth and the importance of building attachments and nurturing a child or young person. Contact with birth parents is another important area of fostering practice with which carers may require support. This may involve advice on how to relate to the birth family when meeting at contact or how to support and care for a child around times of contact. Research evidence suggests that contact is distressing to the parents, children and foster carers (Sinclair, 2005). Of course with some more experienced and qualified foster carers, this advice and support needs to take account of that foster carer's skills. A student on placement or a newly qualified worker would be wise to recognise the potential complexity in this relationship and acknowledge when a foster carer's knowledge and experience surpasses their own.

Legal framework

Children Act 1989

The overriding primary legislation that guides child welfare policy and practice, including family placement work, is the Children Act 1989. This Act introduced the care orders that serve as the legal basis for children and young people entering public care. It also sets out the principle that a child wherever possible should remain with their family, which influences the decisions about whether a child should be brought into public care in the first instance. The Act also highlights and enshrines the principle and need to consider placement with wider family and friends referred to as kinship carers. The Children Act 1989 also makes it clear that the wishes and feelings of children should be taken into account in regard to decisions being made about them. This is an important point to act upon when making any placement for children and young people that is enshrined in legislation.

The Children Act 1989 is also supported by guidance, regulations and national minimum standards for both fostering and adoption and such pieces of secondary legislation have been regularly updated with the most recent revisions being made in 2011 (DfE, 2011). The national minimum standards are used by Ofsted who regulate and inspect family placement services in order to ensure quality. The Education and Inspection Act 2006 and the Care Standards Act 2000 provide the legislative framework for Ofsted inspections. The current inspection framework is undergoing considerable change and a multi-agency inspection framework is currently being developed, which is due for implementation in 2013–2014.

Adoption and Children Act 2002

The Adoption and Children Act 2002 introduced for the first time a duty for local authorities to provide adoption support services. This meant that for the first time adopters were legally entitled to access ongoing support services from a local authority after an adoption order had been granted. Again, how this provision is delivered varies between local authorities; it can be provided within an adoption team or it can be provided by distinct and separate adoption support teams. The Adoption and Children Act 2002 also introduced a new placement option called 'special guardianship', which was intended as a legally secure permanence option for children in placement where adoption has been deemed inappropriate. The order provides carers (either kinship or foster carers) with parental responsibility and legal authority in relation to a child or young person.

Theoretical underpinnings to family placement practice

The key theory that underpins much of family placement practice continues to be attachment theory. The work of Bowlby (1969) and Ainsworth et al. (1979) was applied to family placement in Vera Fahlberg's (1991) classic text *A Child's Journey through Placement*. The contemporary family placement literature continues to focus on attachment (Schofield, 2000; Hughes, 2006; Thomas et al., 2009). This theoretical work highlights the importance of developing bonds of attachment between a caregiver and child through a nurturing relationship, which is vital as it builds resilience and enables children who have experienced abuse and neglect to cope with their past. Attachment is also a key theory that underpins the assessment of prospective carers and adopters. The assessment looks at their experience of being parented and also their experience of parenting in order to understand how this may influence their ability to care for a looked after child and develop attachments with her or him. Some agencies make this focus on attachment theory explicit in their assessments and undertake adult attachment style assessments as part of the assessment process, particularly in adoption. The assessments that are commonly used are known as the Adult Attachment Interview (AAI) (George et al., 1985) or the Attachment Style

Interview (ASI) (Bifulco et al., 2008). Both take the form of structured interviews that have been developed by psychologists. They are undertaken by a practitioner in the team that has been specially trained to analyse and interpret the responses collected.

Systems theory informs a number of approaches to therapeutic work with families and in particular systemic family therapy. It is also an influential and important theory that has influenced social work and family placement. A key aspect of systemic theory and practice is about locating a person within their environment (Kemp et al., 1997; Teater, 2010). This is important in the assessment of prospective carers and adopters and it is usually done in practice by completing an ecomap (Hartman, 1995), which visually represents a person's support network. An ecomap enables the assessing social worker to examine the integration of a person within her or his community and the strength and quality of her or his social networks. In relation to the prospective childcare role, the ecomap highlights the resources that are available to the applicants in order to support them with a child's placement.

Case example

The following case example is intended as an exercise in prioritising needs, a key element of matching. It focuses on the practice dilemmas that are present in attempting to make family placements which meet the ethnic, cultural and religious needs of child. This section includes a short practice vignette with very limited information and then what follows are really 'thoughts out loud', which are intended to demonstrate the complexity and consideration that is required when matching.

Practice vignette

As a family finding social worker you are looking for adopters for a dual heritage child from an African and European background. In a comprehensive and time-consuming search, you have found three potential adopters. The three available families do not reflect the child's heritage. One adoptive family is from a Black Caribbean heritage, one adoptive family is from an Asian heritage and one adoptive family is White British.

Given this information (albeit limited), who do you think would be best placed to meet the child's ethnic, cultural and religious needs and what further information do you need to know in order to reach a decision?

Points to consider

Taking a 'colour-blind approach' to matching would mean determining who is best placed to support the child's wider needs, which could mean prioritising the adopters who will be best at building nurturing attachments and encouraging children with their education. In a society without racism and discrimination this would certainly be the correct approach. However, it does not acknowledge that racism and discrimination exist and that a child or young person of dual heritage may need support in dealing and coping with these at some point in her or his life. It is also important to acknowledge that some adults who were fostered or adopted cross-culturally have also provided clear messages about the negative impact it had on their personal identity, which they attribute to being placed with people who came from a different ethnic, cultural, religious background to their own (Harris, 2006). However, foster carers and adopters may not directly reflect the backgrounds of the children placed in their care, but they may live in a diverse area and have connections with people from diverse ethnicities, cultures and religions. This may mean they have an awareness of diversity and they may be fully able to meet a child's needs and support her or him to have a sound understanding of her or his identity and heritage. It is certainly a complex area of practice that needs to be considered on an individual basis and, as with other aspects of a child's needs, should be matched against what the available prospective adopters can provide and if there are gaps then the required support and training should be identified.

Fundamentally, in an ideal world a dual heritage child with an African and European background would be placed in a perfect culturally matched placement with adopters that are also perfectly matched to meet the child's full range of needs. However, waiting for such a utopian placement could lead to delay, so in practice needs have to be prioritised and decisions do need to be made in order to provide a child with a chance of a permanent family life. Ultimately, for agencies and practitioners to more fully meet the cultural, ethnic and religious needs of children in care the answer is still to proactively work towards recruiting carers and adopters wherever possible from diverse backgrounds. Matching is an exercise in prioritising needs and matching children with the skills and attributes of the carers/adopter available. Recruiting carers from diverse backgrounds widens the pool of skills and attributes and enables better matching not just on ethnic, cultural and religious grounds but across a child's full range of needs.

This case example has attempted to highlight a complex area of practice in a few short paragraphs and is intended to generate some thought about the inherent dilemmas and intricacies in family placement. In reality, linking and matching, for adoption in particular, is carried out in a much more methodical way and generally follows agency policy and procedures. Matching reports and grids that highlight a child's needs with the available adopters' skills and attributes are completed. Decisions are then generally made with the support of supervisors and managers with matches being agreed at panel where assessments and recommendations are presented and given rigorous consideration. For further reading on transracial adoption, Barn and Kirton (2012) offer an overview of the existing research evidence on the topic.

Benefits and challenges to working in family placement

There are numerous benefits and challenges to consider when working in family placement, fostering and adoption. Some of the benefits consist of the following:

- Family placement provides children and young people who may have experienced abuse or neglect with the experience of living in a caring and nurturing family.
- Although there are positive residential units and residential schools that are appropriate for meeting the needs of some children and young people, a family placement lessens the potentially negative impact of institutionalisation in group care settings.
- Being placed in a family setting provides a child or young person with consistent caregivers, an important factor in building secure and nurturing attachments.
- Family placement can provide children in public care with a sense of belonging and permanence through adoption and long-term fostering. Kinship care can also provide this, as well as enable children to grow up connected to their birth families.

Despite these identified benefits, there are also some challenges to acknowledge, which include the following:

- In a UK context, the benefits discussed above are constrained within a context of limited resources. The Fostering Network (2012) estimates a shortage of at least 7000 foster carers. This has an impact on an agency's ability to match children with adopters or carers that are best able to meet their needs.
- Within this context, it is also important to acknowledge that although foster care and adoption have the potential to offer a sense of belonging and permanence, evidence suggests that achieving placement stability is challenging. Young people in foster care experience on average five placement moves before adulthood (Ofsted, 2011), with adoption breakdowns estimated as being as high as one in five. Such adoption estimates are questionable, due to a lack of available data (Pemberton, 2012).

Summary

This chapter has provided an overview of contemporary family placement practice and aimed to introduce student social workers and practitioners to what it is like to work in fostering and adoption. The field of family placement was introduced within the current UK policy context and the legislative and regulatory framework that relates to fostering and adoption has been highlighted. The key day-to-day tasks that social workers undertake in family placement practice have been explored. For example, assessing prospective adopters and carers, presenting assessment reports at panel, undertaking duty responsibilities and providing ongoing support and supervision to carers and adopters. As the chapter highlighted, family placement is an interesting and diverse area of social work practice, and although it presents with pressures and stresses family placement can be a very rewarding area in which to work. Helping to recruit and assess foster carers and adopters and then support them to meet the needs of vulnerable children and young people is both a fulfilling and worthwhile role.

📖 CASE STUDY

As a supervising social worker, you are attending a looked after children's (LAC) review meeting for a child placed with the foster carers that you are supporting.

Kerry is ten years old and has been placed with the carers for the past year; it is hoped she will remain with them on a long-term basis. The LAC review is being held at Kerry's school at the end of her school day. The review is chaired by an independent reviewing officer and is attended by Kerry's social worker and her schoolteacher. Kerry, her foster carers and her parents are all present at the review meeting.

Prior to the review you have had discussions with the foster carers about how problematic contact can be for Kerry, who regularly presents as being anxious and upset before and after contact. The carers express their concern that any increase in contact may have a negative effect on Kerry and the stability of the placement in the long term. However, at the review meeting when the issue of contact is raised by the birth parents asking for it to be increased from monthly to fortnightly, the foster carers respond by saying, 'That sounds lovely, Kerry would really like that.'

Questions

 Why might it be difficult for a foster carer to raise their concerns about increasing levels of direct contact in this LAC review forum?

 What relationships could the foster carers be trying to protect by not voicing their concerns about an increase in contact?

 In this scenario, how could you mediate as a supervising social worker to ensure that the necessary information about Kerry's current experience of contact is shared in an open yet sensitive manner, so that arrangements can be made in the best interests of the child?

Further resources and suggested readings

Fahlberg, V.I. (1991) *A Child's Journey Through Placement.* London: Jessica Kingsley Publishers.

Hunt, J., Waterhouse, S. and Lutman, E. (2008) *Keeping Them in the Family.* London: British Association for Adoption & Fostering.

Schofield, G. (2000) *Growing Up in Foster Care.* London: British Association for Adoption & Fostering.

Websites

Adoption & Fostering Legislation – www.legislation.gov.uk

British Association for Adoption & Fostering – www.baaf.org.uk

Community Care – www.communitycare.co.uk

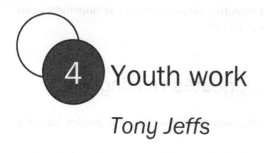

4 Youth work

Tony Jeffs

Introduction

Youth work is not always easy to explain. Even those experienced in the field can encounter difficulty in conveying what they do and why they do it to uninitiated audiences. This is partly because of the enormous range of agencies, big and small, statutory and voluntary, who employ paid and volunteer, full- and part-time youth workers; but also because many of those organisations have different, sometimes incompatible, motives for recruiting a youth worker. The nearest we have to an official definition of youth work is perhaps offered within the National Occupational Standards for Youth Work:

> The key focus of youth work is to enable young people to develop holistically, working with them to facilitate their personal, social and educational development, to enable them to develop their voice, influence and place in society, and to reach their full potential.
>
> (Lifelong Learning UK [LLUK], 2008, p. 3)

Bland, catch-all, ahistorical statements like the above can serve as a starting point but never take critical readers far down the road of discovery. Therefore, this chapter heads in a different direction by commencing with a consideration of the people and agencies involved in youth work, before proceeding to examine the underlying characteristics that make it a discrete sphere of welfare practice.

Structure of youth work

Research undertaken by the Children's Workforce Development Council (2010, p. 9) found the 'youth workforce' to be approximately 6,200,000, of whom 5,300,000 were volunteers. When this is broken down we find around 3,400,000 are involved in sport and recreation, usually helping to run sports clubs and coaching. The next largest is the one million plus who provide various forms of outdoor activities for young people followed by the half million engaged in voluntary youth work. It is this group that provides the backbone of both uniformed youth organisations, such as the Scouts, Guides and Boys' Brigade, and neighbourhood youth clubs, faith clubs and youth groups attached to a plethora of voluntary and charitable bodies.

There are, it should be noted in passing, over 160 operating charities citing youth work as a remit and 34,000 more claiming their mission in part is 'to support children and young people' (Puffett, 2012). Between them, the Scouts and Guides have over 200,000 volunteer helpers servicing approximately 800,000 members. Significantly, after decades of relative decline, both are now growing and have waiting lists that can only be cleared by increasing their roster of helpers by a fifth.

The quantity of volunteers eclipses both the number of full-time youth workers, who comprise around 7000, and the paid part-time workforce of approximately 70,000. Imprecision regarding numbers is because unlike, for example, social work the term 'youth worker' is not a protected title; no requirement exists to register or obtain a licence to practise. Anyone may call herself or himself a youth worker, irrespective of whether or not they have a recognised qualification. Indeed, many voluntary and statutory agencies prefer to recruit individuals with alternative qualifications to undertake youth work. In particular those qualified in counselling, teaching or social work can be favoured to a certificated youth worker. For instance, schools employing youth tutors or school-based youth workers often opt for a schoolteacher with classroom experience. Faith-based organisations, who incidentally now employ nearly double the number of full-time workers found in the local authority sector (Brierley, 2003), regularly recruit as club workers, youth chaplains and youth pastors those individuals fulfilling criteria related to religious belief. Organisations focusing on outdoor pursuits generally prefer those qualified to teach an activity or lead expeditions while the growing number of youth agencies offering information and advice services often favour those with counselling or social work qualifications. Also, many employers select unqualified people who meet other criteria they value. For example, a chosen candidate may have lengthy experience as a volunteer with a project which the agency wisely wishes to exploit, or deep roots in the local community where a club is situated where the person has roots that no 'professional' commuting in could match. Finally, some agencies have very specific traditions that mean they will, if possible, hire 'from the ranks'. As a consequence of this widespread recruitment of 'unqualified' workers, a third of those studying to secure professional recognition do so via part-time and distance-learning courses that allow them to undertake part or all their placements at their place of work (National Youth Agency [NYA], 2012).

Currently, there are around 40 courses in the UK offering professional recognition via undergraduate and postgraduate degrees in youth and community work – almost 1000 complete these annually. At present, the number of such courses is shrinking owing to a shortfall in applications. Reasons for this vary but the prime causal factors are probably: (a) professional drift, with potential candidates opting for social work and other programmes offering bursaries; (b) fears relating to the vibrancy of the job market triggered by reductions in local authority spending on youth services; and (c) poor starting salaries (Jeffs and Spence, 2008). Now, only a fifth of graduates find employment in the statutory sector whereas four decades ago it was closer to eight out of ten (NYA, 2012). The swing in the pattern of graduate employment, which has seen the proportion of full-time workers in 'faith' settings grow as the numbers finding employment in statutory projects fell, has meant it is secular degree programmes that are closing or downsizing whereas those linked to Christian higher education (HE) institutions remain buoyant.

Understandably, other welfare professionals such as social workers and school-teachers are sometimes puzzled as to why youth work is not a state-recognised occupation with controlled entry and registration. As other occupational groups have clawed their way to professional and semi-professional status so those arguing that youth work should follow suit have become more vocal (Wylie, 2010). The core elements of their case are identical to those put forward by every aspirant profession:

> A License to Practice and Registration Scheme which recognises the plurality of the workforce should be introduced to protect the title of 'youth worker' and secure the best people to work with young people.
>
> (Mckee et al., 2010, p. 32)

This justification does not go unopposed. Apart from the usual critiques of professionalisation (Wilding, 1982; Cook, 2008), specific objections are voiced. First, youth work flourishes because it draws from a prolific wellspring of voluntary effort and altruism, relying on what Titmuss (1971) called a 'gift relationship' whereby tens of thousands of citizens freely give of their time and talents to benefit the coming generation. Any extension of the cash nexus, it is argued, as well as heightened state regulation, would seriously damage this delicate plant as it has in relation to social work and education. A service currently costing very little would, if professionalised, either consume incalculable millions of taxpayers' money or more likely, as with adult education, disappear because once regulated the government would recoil from spending what would be required to replace the labour once freely given by volunteers.

Second, youth work as it exists embodies many of the finest values of civil society for in harnessing so much altruism to the common good it teaches young people, by example, a vital lesson regarding the importance of service to others – that citizenship is founded on duties as well as rights. Paid youth workers might preach social responsibility, the importance of altruism and democracy's need for an active citizenry but, like schoolteachers, giving clumsy didactic lessons on the topic their words would rarely impress. By way of contrast, the voluntary youth worker does not need to sermonise on these topics for their willing presence teaches by example.

Third, the history of state-directed and controlled youth work is a truly horrendous one. It was because the example of the Hitler Youth was so pertinent to their members that the committees charged during the 1940s with creating the modern youth service avoided going down that route. Rightly, they saw mass voluntary youth provision, free of state regulation and control, as a bastion against an authoritarian state; a pluralist counterweight to the government regulated and manipulated school system; a walled garden in which young and old together might learn and practise the arts of democracy (Brew, 1946).

Role of central government, local authorities and voluntary sector

It was for all the reasons above that the 1944 Education Act eschewed creating a complex legislative framework regarding what was described at the time as the emerging 'fourth education service'. It was also partly why Scotland never acquired statutory youth services and those drafting the 1944 Education Act made the duty upon local authorities to provide youth services to all intents and purposes optional (Jeffs, 1979); and, incidentally, why central government long refrained from interfering in the voluntary sector, restricting itself to giving small 'headquarter grants' to national youth organisations such as the National Association of Youth Clubs, the National Association of Boy's Clubs, the Young Women's Christian Association (YWCA) and the Young Men's Christian Association (YMCA); 'headquarter grants' to help them support, largely via staff training, their membership. This loose coupling remains in place up to the present time. Indeed, as recently as 2013 the Education Secretary reiterated that 'youth policy' was best left to local government and should not be a 'priority' for central government (Jozwiak, 2013). Although there is a statutory duty on English local authorities under the Education and Inspections Act 2006 to secure young people's access to sufficient educational and recreational leisure-time activities funding for youth services, it is not mandatory; nor significantly is 'sufficient' anywhere defined. Consequently, from 1944 up to the present extraordinary variations occur between what local councils spend on youth services, and more recently it has allowed some to cease all expenditure on such provision.

Before proceeding, some reference regarding how central government has sought to influence the way in which local authorities structure their youth provision will be helpful, even though these only met with partial success as local authorities refused to be corralled. Resulting from this independence has been an incredible tapestry of diversity. Some local authorities chose to open mixed neighbourhood youth centres run by full-time qualified workers while others supported grant-aided voluntary bodies, secular and religious, where the local authority allowed them considerable freedom to as to their modus operandi. A third tranche created community schools with youth and adult education wings often managed by teachers. A fourth grouping amalgamated youth and leisure provision, which invested in all age leisure centres. Other variations were whether or not they invested in outdoor and residential centres for young people, or resourced detached and outreach work.

Similar differences, predominately flowing from historical accident, also occur within the voluntary sector. For example, girls' clubs were concentrated in London, Merseyside, the West Midlands and Lancashire, which meant the National Association of Youth Clubs, which in 1943 grew out of the National Association of Girls' Clubs, was strongest in those regions. Similarly, the YMCA and boys' clubs are unevenly dispersed within metropolitan areas as well as generally absent from rural and suburban localities. Collectively, such disparities mean social workers and others can never predict what provision exists in a locality. Lack of uniformity means no national ethical standards apply as different organisations have their own, nor do common statements of purpose or patterns of 'in-service' training. National co-ordinating bodies exist but rarely speak as one. Given they compete for funding, it is perhaps inevitable that one encounters underlying hostility between them or that they describe each other as 'competitors' (Puffett, 2012).

Difficult times

Until April 2011 central government transferred to local authorities a ring-fenced revenue support grant (RSG) to enable each to provide at least a barebones youth service. In the final year of ring-fenced transfers, local authorities spent on average £77 per head of the 11- to 19-year-old population. Subsequently, this amount has fallen by a third (House of Commons [HofC], 2012). Besides the RSG, central government has offered temporary funding streams in an attempt to restyle local provision. For example, in the 1960s building grants were used to encourage councils to open neighbourhood youth centres, which were initially popular but most soon lost their allure ending up as millstones around the necks of their owners (Ord, 2011). A second flurry occurred between 2007 and 2010 with funding made available to open large, well-equipped Myplace 'hubs' designed to attract youngsters from wide catchment areas to buildings offering a broad array of activities. Few of these 20-plus 'hubs' prospered; one has already closed (Department for Education [DfE], 2011).

The poor success rate of both these attempts to impose a model of practice upon localities reflects a failure to grasp two fundamental youth work tenets. One is that young people prefer facilities that serve their 'natural' communities, be they geographic or cultural. Clubs and projects prosper when they work with the grain of those relationships while few who push against it flourish. Second, external capital funding unaccompanied by long-standing grants to cover wages, repairs and equipment rarely help. Indeed, by saddling projects with heightened running costs these injections usually precede a financial crisis. The history of youth work tells us that if left to manage their own destiny then projects and communities sensibly build what their resources and needs dictate.

During the last two decades, apart from the Myplace initiative, central government has launched almost a dozen, mostly small-scale, targeted funding streams in relation to youth work plus one large-scale catastrophe (the Connexions Service). Amongst the smaller initiatives, the most prominent was the Youth Service Development Fund (YSDF) launched in 2008 with £100 million to spend; it closed in 2011. A pre-condition for the receipt of YSDF funding was that the programme was managed by a partnership involving statutory agencies, third-sector organisations and the private sector. All these funding streams involved bidding procedures, were tied to specific forms of intervention and were time-limited, usually consisting of three years. Collectively, they failed to halt the decline in the size and reach of the statutory sector and probably made matters worse by stimulating pockets of short-term unsustainable growth (Hodgson and Jeffs, 2012). During the last decade, the beneficiaries of state funding have struggled while the Scouts and Guides, who take no government funding, have prospered alongside the faith-based sector, which is overwhelmingly comprised of small independent clubs and projects who receive little or no governmental support.

Connexions Service

The Connexions Service was a large-scale scheme that launched in 1999. The service was initially intended to unify the youth and careers services so that a universal advice and guidance service could be offered to young people via the medium of individual contact, drop-in centres, outreach and detached teams, and centres. Connexions gave each young person a dedicated personal adviser who, alongside other staff, was to help all 14 to 18 year olds make a successful transition to adulthood. Careers officers and youth workers were retrained, alongside new recruits, as personal advisers to deliver the Connexions 'offer'. New offices opened and local authority careers offices plus some youth centres were 're-badged' as Connexions units.

Careers officers often bemoaned their loss of professional status whilst youth workers tended to resent a perceived inferior status within an organisation dominated by the former that focused upon individualised interventions, not informal education and group work. Poor planning meant the geographic boundaries for the Connexions Service were often not coterminus with those of local authorities. Consequently, the Connexions Services 'took over' the existing youth service in some places whilst elsewhere it ran in parallel to a barely unchanged statutory system. Connexions was closed in 2007 after widespread dissatisfaction from head teachers regarding a perceived lack of professional expertise amongst the hurriedly trained personal advisers, a failure on the part of Connexions to halt the growth in the number of young people classified as Not in Education, Employment or Training (NEETs) and resistance from youth workers. Some local authorities kept the 'brand' while others had it erased. Forty per cent of the 'released' funding was relocated to schools for them to 'buy in' services previously provided by Connexions and the remaining 60 per cent was reassigned to the new Children's Trusts (Smith, 2007).

Although a miserable failure, Connexions led to a partial dismantling of the statutory sector without unduly impacting on the voluntary sector. The Connexions service in some areas could not be reassembled; thus some staff were transferred into new children and young people's services to become youth support workers.

Integration

There is a long history of collaboration between youth workers and other welfare professionals and agencies, notably social workers, the police, and probation. Linkages with social workers are historically strong. Many key individuals viewed as the pioneers of social work, such as Mary Carpenter (Manton, 1976), Jane Nassau Senior (Oldfield, 2008) and Octavia Hill (Darley, 2010), are equally honoured as founders of modern youth work.

Social work and youth work are branches of the same tree. Initially, it was common for social and club workers to operate from shared buildings, usually settlement houses and missions. This resulted in many social workers running boys' and girls' clubs in the evenings and club leaders undertaking casework. So close was this relationship that until 1939 they shared, apart from specialist options, a common programme of training and many club leaders described themselves as social workers. In 1940, the appellation youth worker surfaced and discrete youth work training courses commenced following the appearance of mixed youth centres usually managed by local authorities. After that, the focus of social work education increasingly became casework, and group work gradually ceased to have a significant presence, whilst youth work training concentrated on group work and jettisoned casework. Post 1940 until the 1980s, youth work was virtually synonymous with running clubs, centres or youth wings. Graduates from professional training overwhelmingly worked in those settings and most entrants enrolled after being club members, then helpers and part-time leaders. The focus remains on social group work, informal education, and club management consequently has little in common with social work education or worryingly the forms of employment graduates increasingly enter (Jeffs and Spence, 2008).

Historically, collaboration between different youth organisations has been limited or non-existent. Fierce competition to secure members plus abiding religious differences long impeded the development of sustained co-operation at local and national levels. Now competitive tendering is the norm; what little collaboration that once occurred has been supplanted by hostility interspersed with sporadic truces when strategic alliances are negotiated to secure a contract or a march upon rivals. Paradoxically, the intensification of competition occurred when the rhetoric emanating from governmental sources placed unprecedented emphasis upon 'partnership'. Ad hoc and informal linkages between youth projects and statutory youth services existed in the past but usually these were instigated by a 'neutral' and financially stronger statutory sector. Now that the remnants of the statutory sector compete with voluntary agencies for resources, such alliances have become increasingly tenuous.

The arrival of a New Labour government coincided with heightened talk of 'joined up government' and 'partnership working'. This led to the increased involvement of youth workers and youth projects in the activities of youth offending teams (YOTs) and initiatives designed to divert young people from criminal activity, 'high risk' sexual activities and involvement in drug and substance misuse. However, the pace quickened following the publication of *Every Child Matters: Change for Children* (HM Government, 2004) and *Youth Matters* (HM Government, 2005). Soon, local authority youth services were being absorbed into newly created children and young people's services. That change produced no universal structure; rather, as Davies and Merton's (2009, 2010) research shows, it gave rise to diverse managerial configurations. These ranged from the youth service remaining intact and largely unaltered to it being incorporated within a directorate of targeted support and early intervention services, which meant youth workers providing support for identified individuals, and information, advice and guidance for a wider clientele. Overall though, the relocation has 'brought an unprecedented level of complexity into the management of youth work' (Davies and Merton, 2012, p. 156), and within many areas heralded severe reductions in, or the cessation of, funding for the historic core of youth work.

Between 2011 and 2012, local authority spending on youth services fell by a quarter (Puffett, 2012). Integration has also led to redundancies amongst youth workers as well as widespread 're-badging' with them being employed to undertake casework and support roles (Puffett, 2012).

Theoretical and practical underpinnings to youth work

What makes youth work unique? In particular how does it differ from other interventions focusing on or serving young people such as schoolteaching, counselling, lecturing, social work and policing? I argue that the characteristics which distinguish youth work include the following:

- The involvement of young people on a voluntary basis, which recognises their autonomy.
- The rationale for the relationship between the worker and young person has, at its heart, an educational dimension, which requires the worker to operate consciously as an educator, albeit one pre-eminently doing so via the mediums of conversation and dialogue.
- The central focus is upon young people.

These will now be considered in turn.

Voluntarism

Modern youth work, like social work and mass schooling, emerged during the early years of the industrial revolution. Youth work has traditionally operated in the space between formal education on one side and social work on the other (Jeffs and Smith, 2008). All three borrowed from each other and crucially many teachers and social workers were often also club workers just as club workers taught classes or undertook casework. Initially, all three principally worked for bodies linked to religious groups; something that remains the case for a sizeable minority of social workers, teachers and youth workers. This meant they often perceived their foremost task as 'saving young souls' by securing or retaining affiliation to specific creeds or sects. George Williams, founder in 1844 of the Young Men's Christian Association (YMCA), the earliest national and international youth organisation, unambiguously stated its objective was to 'influence religious young men to spread the Redeemer's Kingdom amongst those by whom they are surrounded' (Williams, 1906, p. 112).

In England, legislation in 1862 imposed on schools a national curriculum (then called the Revised Code), and compulsory attendance soon followed (1876). In combination, these created a fundamental divide between schools and youth work: first, because what schools taught became narrowly confined to what the pupils were to be tested on. Consequently, boys' and girls' clubs began offering members access to disciplines, activities, and subjects excluded from school timetables. Second, compulsory attendance meant youth work, like adult education, now belonged to a non-compulsory, autonomous, informal education sector. Unlike schools, clubs possessed the freedom to respond to the expressed and felt needs of members. By focusing on sports, leisure, outdoor pursuits, social education and the arts, club workers could offer a rich and fulfilling educational experience, one which took account of the whole person and might potentially be an attractive alternative to the thin gruel of the school curriculum.

The challenge, therefore, lay in finding ways of engaging with young people whose attendance during their leisure time was voluntary. Workers responded first by undertaking outreach work, which involved going to where the young people were and operating as educators on the streets, in pubs and places of work; that is colonising premises designed for other purpose. Much later, they appended schools and colleges. Thus, youth work has always lacked a sole or discrete location, yet one can now encounter youth workers in hospitals, secure training centres, schools, further education colleges, places of worship, fire stations or homeless projects. The diverse locations have meant that practitioners have acquired a diverse range of titles: for example, youth liaison workers, youth tutors, community workers, youth ministers, youth support workers and youth chaplains.

The second method involved establishing permanent or temporary centres ranging from well-equipped buildings to dilapidated huts or church and village halls. Irrespective of the scale of investment, the worker must entice young people into the building before meaningful youth work can commence. The successful practitioner must be someone whom young people can trust and enjoy spending time with. A miserable, unreliable dullard is doomed to fail. Grumpy, unpleasant social workers and schoolteachers can survive by hiding behind their status and the quasi-legal authority bestowed on them, yet youth workers cannot. The main case for separate provision is that it offers: (1) a venue for activities and educational programmes; (2) an opportunity for young people to manage and control their own space; and (3) a potential refuge where, at least for a short while, young people can find respite from the pressures and unpleasantness of the outside world.

Lilian Robinson, a pioneer of girls' clubs, argued a building for some types of youth work is 'a crying need, a place less dangerous than the street, less noisy and if possible, enclosed' (1937, p. 11). Today workers in 'dangerous localities' similarly advocate the need for centres as places offering 'sanctuary' where young people can relax in safety and enjoy being young (Hirsh, 2005). Others have long held that specialist buildings are unhelpful: (1) they isolate young people from the outside world; (2) they keep them in an atmosphere of artificial immaturity by curtailing contact with adults; and/or (3) they waste disproportionate levels of funding on servicing a building when the income could be better spent on addressing the needs of the most disadvantaged who generally display heightened reluctance to affiliate to centres and clubs.

Debates regarding the relative merits of specialist units versus 'integration' will always rage. These discussions may, however, be something of a distraction for the setting need not determine the focus. The locale is less important than the quality of the relationship between workers and young persons. This does not mean that settings are an irrelevance, for workers must continuously consider the suitability and appropriateness of a given locality. Given the voluntary nature of the engagement, they must make the club attractive and inviting, and street workers must ensure they visit places where young people congregate and then behave in ways appropriate to that setting (Smith, 1988). Irrespective of the locale, practitioners must ensure they present themselves in ways that foster voluntary relationships and opportunities to engage in dialogically based informal education.

Voluntarism always distinguishes youth work from schooling and the bulk of contemporary social work. Voluntarism makes it nigh on impossible for the worker to impose a curriculum, or determine the order and tempo of the learning experience (Jeffs, 2004). Uniquely, it transfers a genuine measure of control over what is taught and what is learnt to the young people. Therefore, the place where the conversation between the young person and the workers occurs is immaterial provided that it does not intrude to shift power into the hands of the worker, or curtail the young person's freedom to question, converse with and challenge the worker.

Educational dimension

How individual youth workers or agencies relate to young people is clearly influenced by their aims and purpose. An evangelical minister seeking to 'bring young people to Christ' may adopt a different modus operandi to a soccer enthusiast keen to encourage youngsters to 'take up the sport', or a detached worker employed to offer support and advice to school truants. They may – but it is dangerous to assume they will – adopt fundamentally dissimilar techniques and methodologies because their motivations vary.

In youth work, assumptions about the role and purpose of the workers based on programme content and methods are risky. Interests and pastimes are something to be exploited for higher educational ends or 'to foster personal and social development' (Department for Education and Science [DES], 1987), not as ends in themselves. Initially a point of contact, activities can be translated into a means of introducing participants to fresh perspectives, alternative ways of understanding their environment, achieving a good life, addressing ethical dilemmas and making the right choices. Therefore, what distinguishes a youth worker from a leisure organiser, coach or dancing master is that the activity is not an end in itself, but a means to an educational end. The educational content and experience becomes not an incidental, but the very raison d'être for the relationship or the justification for engagement between the worker and young person, and, therefore, the underlying purpose for engaging in an activity. Consequently, youth workers like all educators must pay close attention to questions relating to the following:

- *Purpose*. Why am I teaching this?
- *Values*. Am I teaching in a morally acceptable way, which does not demean them or myself?
- *Content*. Is the knowledge and informational material presented in an accessible form? Is it factually correct and relevant?

Youth work unfailingly attracts enthusiasts. Religious zealots, political and social reformers as well as hobbyists exploit it as a means of furthering their own causes, ideals or enthusiasms. Individuals affiliated to particular religious and political positions persistently engage in it to appropriate the hearts and minds of future generations. Suffragettes set up girls' clubs to make links with working-class young women, much as contemporary feminists do. Environmentalists and political radicals, along with religious nonconformists, likewise become involved as they are aware that schools marginalise and censor their viewpoints. Sports and arts organizations wisely run programmers to ensure their survival beyond the present membership. It is right and proper that this should occur, particularly as schools manifestly fail to introduce pupils to many life-enhancing activities and allow few opportunities for meaningful political or theological debate and serious engagement with most social issues.

Generally, the presence of these enthusiasts enriches youth work by bringing vitality and commitment from which many benefit. Yet dangers do exist. Clearly, the voluntary nature of the contact offers a measure of protection against abuse of the youth work process. Indeed, the inherent nature of the relationship makes indoctrination far less of a problem in the informal than formal sectors of education; not least because young people tend to avoid bores at every opportunity. Nevertheless, there are programmes deliberately seeking to curtail debate and restrict dialogue so as to convert, or which are designed to serve the ends of the agency rather than the educational and developmental needs of young people, but what they do does not constitute youth work; not because such workers and projects are misguided or repressive (although they may be both), but because their desire to convert or train supplants the educational needs of the young person as the prime motivation for the relationship. These practitioners have crossed those lines demarcating training from education, and education from indoctrination and replacing doubt with certainty and dialogue with decree.

Young people at the core

Finally, a defining trait of youth work is its focus on young people. This may seem obvious, but it needs appraising. Historically, youth work was directed at those aged 14 to 21, to work with them during the transition from childhood to adulthood. However, the concept of transition has undergone considerable reassessment in recent years becoming broken, extended and fractured (Shildrick and MacDonald, 2007; Roberts, 2009). For most, the length of dependency upon parent(s) has extended with growing unemployment and the advent of mass higher education. Evidence also indicates that the social and personal problems which youth workers are expected to address frequently arise before the age of 14 (Coles, 1995). These and other shifts have helped engender an identity crisis for youth work (Jeffs and Smith, 1994, 2008). Therefore, like social scientists, youth organisations have more flexibly defined the concept of youth. Sometimes this link to the category 'youth' becomes so tenuous that it barely makes sense to describe what the workers do as youth work. Therefore, generic terms such as informal educator or social or community worker might better convey the role. No useful purpose is served by describing as youth work informal education, community work and adult education which is not predominately directed towards addressing the needs of young people.

Many clubs and uniformed groups long ago acquired younger age profiles so that now much of what they do might be more accurately described as 'children's work' or even 'child care'. Detached youth workers are also encountering fewer young people in public spaces so that in many places it might be better designated 'street work', given that they increasingly deal with a broader array of clients. These changes reflect shifting profiles of social need and a reconfiguration of what being a young person means. Rising youth unemployment, the continuation in full-time education of over 80 per cent of school leavers, reformulation of family structures, the escalating popularity of home-based entertainments and sharpening income differentials all serve to reduce the demand for traditional youth services. Therefore we have to be clear regarding whether what is taking place is 'youth work' focusing on young people or a branch of community work.

Case example

During a year, an inner-city youth project catering exclusively for young women and girls receives numerous visits from young women seeking support. They refer themselves, or workers in other youth and community projects have encouraged them to call in. Many come because they are in abusive relationships. In one such instance the young person had been in care and presented with learning difficulties, drug and alcohol issues. She spoke to the youth worker about her violent and abusive partner. When the youth worker contacted social services for information about the young person, the social worker responded in a tone bordering on the hostile and informed the youth worker that they did not believe it was appropriate to share background information with the youth project relating to this young woman. The social worker was adamant they could provide no additional support for this young woman given her age. The young woman maintained contact with the youth worker for a few weeks before opting to disengage from the project.

Summary

The life chances of young people are influenced by many factors. Research indicates that ethnicity, gender, social class, place of residence, health and physical status have a profound impact on the education achieved, employment secured, housing acquired and income enjoyed (Coles, 1995; Ainley and Allen, 2010; Bradford, 2012). The ability of youth workers and projects to reduce the negative impact of those influences is limited. Rhetoric about empowerment or redressing oppression and inequality cannot alter that reality. Compared to the prolonged influence of parents(s), schooling and peers, the youth worker is generally a somewhat transitory and marginal figure in a young person's life. Like individual classroom teachers and social workers, they can only hope for minor victories. But such victories can mean a lot for some and their cumulative potential for achieving, in the words of Horace Mann, 'some small victory for humanity' (Williams, 1937, p. 248), is important. Youth workers, like social workers, do change lives for the better; we know this is the case but must take care never to exaggerate the frequency with which it occurs (Brent, 2004; Williamson, 2004; Forrest, 2013).

So where is youth work heading? With a measure of certainty we can predict that variations regarding what is available in given localities will expand. The pace with which the statutory sector is being trimmed is such that in many areas within a decade it will either have disappeared or be reduced to a residual service. Far fewer neighbourhood centres will be operating and most of those remaining will be managed by voluntary and 'faith' organisations. The drift of statutory workers into youth support and advice and information roles, unless reversed which is unlikely, will mean that the justification for discrete youth work training programmes will be weakened. The vibrancy and vigour of the uniformed and 'faith' sectors is such that both are likely to thrive in the coming years. Voluntary, informal educational work with young people will continue but as in the past the locale where it takes place and the type of personnel involved will have changed – of that we can be sure.

📖 CASE STUDY

X is a school-based youth worker. The head teacher and the management team expect her to focus her attention upon those students who pose behavioural problems and are at risk of disengagement and exclusion. X, despite this expectation, deliberately devotes a portion of her time to building relationships with young people across the ability range. In the youth wing, adjacent to the school, she started a young women's group meeting after school on one evening a week. This attracted a dozen or so older students who were mostly studying for A levels.

Besides meeting for conversation and discussions, the group became involved in 'social action', helping in the youth wing with the junior club and at a nearby community centre. Amongst the members was a young woman in her final year expected shortly to transfer to university. X knew the young woman's older sister had left home suddenly to avoid an 'arranged marriage' and who was rumoured to be living in the United States, but nobody, including the parents, had any real idea where she was.

One day the young woman came to X's office after school and said she had come to say goodbye because she did not wish to leave without saying thank you for all the help and kindness shown by the worker. In particular, she said the young women's group and the social action work had helped her understand a great deal about herself and her place in the world. She proceeded to inform X that her older sister had sent her the air fare and that in order to avoid her now having to marry the man chosen for her older sister she was flying out immediately to join her. Therefore, she would not be returning to school or going to university. She had not told anyone else, including school friends and family, of this decision. She asked the youth worker not to tell anyone, and the youth worker promised she would not do so. After a short discussion they parted. The youth worker never mentioned that conversation to anyone, including colleagues, and the young woman joined her older sister.

Questions

Was X right to flout the expectations of her managers and work with this group?

Should she now disband the group in order to avoid similar events occurring in the future?

Was X wrong to promise the young woman that the conversation would remain confidential?

 Should she have taken steps to prevent the departure of the young woman by contacting parents or the police?

 Should she have passed what information she had to the management team and not simply told them, when asked, that she did not know where the young woman was?

Further resources and suggested readings

Banks, S. (2010) *Ethical Issues in Youth Work*. London: Routledge.

Brew, J. M. (1946) *Informal Education*. London: Faber and Faber.

Spence, J. and Devanney, C. (2006) *Youth Work: Voices of Practice*. Leicester: National Youth Agency.

Websites

Infed (Informal Education Website) – www.infed.org.uk/

Youth and Policy – www.youthandpolicy.org/ (free kindle versions available).

5 Youth offending

Issy Harvey

Introduction

Since the 1990s, social work with children and young people in the youth justice system has become an increasingly politicised area of social policy and law, with frequent legislated changes to guidance and practice. The media feeds public opinion a demonised view of young people whose behaviour is criminal or anti-social and the politicians compete for the popular sound bite to appease them, thus encouraging 'a general climate of intolerance' but 'troublesome' young people are often also very troubled. Those 'involved in persistent offending and very risky behaviours are over-whelmingly the most vulnerable and the most victimised young people in our society' (All Party Parliamentary Group for Children, 2010, p. 12).

Historically, there have been competing tensions between justice, punishment and welfare approaches in the legislation that seeks to control and protect those children and young people committing criminal behaviours. Some have argued that the conflict between social work ethics and legal principles is greater in youth offending team work than in any other area of social work (Pickford and Dugmore, 2012). Providing relationship-based practice (underpinned by the core social work values of respect, empathy, non-judgemental acceptance, advocacy and partnership), which is known from research to produce the best outcomes for the young person, is difficult when young people are reduced to young offenders with the concurrent expectation that intervening agencies should impose 'justice' and sanctions.

Social work with young people (and their parents) who have offended, or are at risk of offending, is therefore complex and challenging, yet it also offers the rewarding possibility of effecting and supporting significant, positive, lifelong changes at the start of their adult lives.

Demographics of young people in the youth justice system

Children can enter the youth justice system as young as ten years old – before this age their behaviour cannot be regarded as criminal – and will not be considered an adult until they are 18. The peak age for recorded offending behaviour is between 15 and 17 years, during the adolescent transition from child to adult. There are 'normal' attributes of adolescence that can increase the occurrence of 'criminal' and 'anti-social' behaviours, such as risk-taking, experimentation, poor decision making, immature management of emotions, and increased influence of peer relationships, which correlate with the peak in offending at this age (Crawford and Walker, 2010). It is not surprising, therefore, that the vast majority of young people who engage in criminal or anti-social behaviours during adolescence will not continue to do so once they mature. In the 1980s this was reflected in the dominant view within juvenile justice teams (as they were then known) that the most effective intervention was 'radical non-intervention' (Pitts, 2003). Since then the youth justice system has become more interventionist in its approach to tackling youth offending behaviours, plus it has widened to include a range of preventative initiatives aimed at those deemed to be 'at risk' of offending behaviour in the future.

In 2010–11 in England and Wales, there were 176,511 proven offences by children and young people. For many of those arrested and charged, this will have been their first offence and they may have been dealt with by a police caution or a youth court diversionary scheme. Youth offending teams (YOTs) supervised a total of 85,300 young people in their communities with 26 per cent of this caseload being children (aged 10–14 years) and 78 per cent being male. Although adolescence is a contributory factor in offending behaviour in teenagers, those young people who get caught up in the youth justice system are not a representative cross-section of the general adolescent population. The Ministry of Justice (2010, p. 4) reports that 'family breakdown, educational underachievement, substance abuse, mental illness and other problems commonly affect young offenders. They are also more likely to have difficulty controlling their behaviour and understanding its impact on others.' Approximately 75 per cent of children in the criminal justice system have speech and communication difficulties (Bryan et al., 2007), and over 65 per cent left school either with no qualifications or not knowing what qualifications they had, compared to just 6 per cent of all school leavers being in this position (Hurry et al., 2005).

Additionally, there is a range of 'criminogenic' factors strongly associated with youth crime, which if present increase the 'risk' that offending behaviour may occur. These factors can be grouped into the following categories: (1) individual characteristics (e.g. hyperactivity and impulsivity, delinquent peer groups); (2) family factors (e.g. harsh or inconsistent parenting, domestic violence); (3) school factors (e.g. low attainment, special educational needs, frequent changes of school); and (4) community factors (e.g. disadvantaged neighbourhood, poor housing). A recent criminology study (Wilkstrom, 2012) followed the lives of 700 English teenagers for five years and examined the impact of environment on teenagers' criminality. It found that certain urban environments, such as 'hotspots' with high levels of social disadvantage and a pro-criminal morality, provide triggers for youth criminality to which some teenagers are much more vulnerable than others. The majority of young people living in these deprived areas 'remain highly resistant to the potential for crime' and do not engage in criminal behaviours. A tiny minority (16 per cent) of children and young people were found to be responsible for over 60 per cent of the youth crimes in these areas.

Levels of disadvantage and vulnerability are highest in the population of children and young people that find themselves forcibly removed from their families and communities. In 2010–11 the average population in 'the secure estate' at any one time was 2070 (under-18s) with 1637 held in young offender institutions (YOIs), 273 in secure training centres and 160 in secure children's homes. Some were remanded (i.e not yet convicted) and some sentenced. Among this population of young people incarcerated, 50 per cent of young women and 25 per cent of young men have been in care and 40 per cent have been assessed as 'vulnerable'. There are high levels of mental health problems with over 33 per cent having a diagnosed mental health disorder (Hagell, 2002) and more than 25 per cent having a learning disability (Harrington and Bailey, 2005). Eighty-nine per cent of young people entering custody had been excluded from school, over 75 per cent have serious difficulties with literacy and numeracy (Parke, 2009) with 15 per cent having special educational needs.

Legal framework

The legislative system reflects shifting social and political attitudes towards the state's role in the control and care of disadvantaged children and young people. Where there are concerns about a young person's welfare, the grounds and process for 'statutory' intervention are laid out in legislation such as the 1989 and 2004 Children and Young Person Acts. This adopts a welfare perspective towards young people in need of support, guidance or care and states that it is in the best interests of children and young people to be raised in families, whenever possible, without state intervention. When a child or young person's behaviour is categorised as 'criminal', additional youth justice legislation applies and sometimes takes precedence over welfare provision. To understand the social worker's welfare role in the context of the youth justice system and the logic underlying contemporary youth justice practice it is useful to be aware of its historical evolution.

A separate legal system for dealing with young offenders was first introduced in Britain with the Children's Act 1908 which created juvenile courts that were distinct from adult courts. The provision of a youth criminal justice system is congruent with international children's rights agendas and reflects the view that children and young people have a different and developing understanding to adults of their own behaviour, are particularly vulnerable, powerless and require special arrangements for their safeguarding and well-being. However, at their inception the same juvenile courts dealt with both criminal and care matters (the 'depraved' and the 'deprived') and, until very recently, juvenile justice policy developments in the UK have oscillated between welfare and justice approaches.

The 1933 Children and Young Persons Act established 'the welfare principle' that is still applicable today, as section 44 of the Act states that 'a court must have regard to the welfare of the child or young person'. It recognised the young offender as a vulnerable, developing character whose behaviour may be caused by psychological or environmental factors that were beyond the young person's control. Attempts to merge the two perspectives of welfare and justice, peaked in the Children and Young Persons Act 1969, which introduced the criminal care order (abolished in 1989 – arguably replaced with anti-social behaviour orders [ASBOs] in 1998) and gave social workers the discretion to draw socially and economically impoverished children and young people into the youth justice system under the guise of preventionism. Pickford (2000) has argued in more detail that the perspectives of justice and welfare, viewing young people who offend as in need of correction or in need of additional care and support, occupy polemical positions that cannot be reconciled.

Following the death of toddler James Bulger in 1993 at the hands of two ten year olds and the ensuing media moral panic with its 'demonisation' of youth (Jenks, 1996), the dominant concept of childhood shifted towards the notion that children can be evil when not controlled and society needs to be wary of them. Many academics have argued that this one case changed the direction of youth justice policy and public opinion in relation to offenders (Jenks, 1996, Pickford and Dugmore, 2012) and the following years have become known as the 'punitive period' (Pitts, 2011). Numbers in custody rose sharply despite an overall reduction in crime levels, until they peaked at nearly 5000 in 2001.

As in other areas of social work and public service delivery, the same period also saw the rise in actuarial risk assessments and managerialism. The 1996 Audit Commission report into the old youth justice teams, *Misspent Youth*, criticised the disparity of practice across the country and lax management as 'inefficient' and 'ineffective'. In 1997, the Green Paper 'No More Excuses', that led to the 1998 Criminal Justice Act, heralded a shift away from the justice and welfare perspectives, both of which highlighted the role of the state in socialising the next generation, to place a greater focus on individual responsibility and parenting. Victims' rights, restorative justice and sanctions on parents, emphasised that although social inequalities might exist, individuals who responded by behaving criminally were responsible and were to blame – and if not them then their parents. This neo-liberal approach accepts that social inequality exists so youth crime cannot be solved and justice and welfare concerns are therefore overridden by the need to manage the problem better and cheaper. This Act gave local authorities the duty to work in partnership with other agencies to prevent and manage youth crime in their areas through establishing youth offender teams that reported back to the centralised Youth Justice Board (YJB).

The Youth Justice Board was set up to produce a national framework to encourage and monitor nationwide consistency in the implementation of the youth justice system, to draw up standards for service delivery and to help disseminate 'effective' practice. The National Standards for Youth Justice were produced in 2000 and updated in 2004 and 2010 (see http://www.justice.gov.uk/youth-justice). The YJB website continues to be an important source of policy and practice information.

The Crime and Disorder Act 1998 also introduced a range of preventative orders (e.g. anti-social behaviour orders [ASBOs] and acceptable behaviour contracts [ABCs]) as sanctions for controlling civil (not criminal) behaviours ('matters'). If 'breached', these civil orders can lead to criminal convictions. The welfare needs of the young person were now matched by the need to assess risk to the public and the likelihood of that young person re-offending. For those who committed serious offences, the Act introduced detention and training orders (DTOs) in which half of the sentence is spent in custody and half under the supervision of youth justice practitioners in the community. The focus of planning and interventions is on risk assessment, reparation, rehabilitation and preventing re-offending. This aimed to improve the effectiveness of custody as a strategy for reducing offending, as figures were showing that more than 78 per cent of young people re-offend within a year of being released from youth detention. The punitive turn announced by the 1998 Criminal Justice Act has been tweaked and added to by a series of further legislation, which are detailed in Table 5.1.

Table 5.1 Legislation for youth offending and youth justice

Legislation	Description
The Youth Justice Criminal Evidence Act 1999	Created the sentence of a referral order for young people convicted in court for the first time.
Powers of the Criminal Courts (Sentencing) Act 2000	S.90 and s.91 introduce special measures for young people convicted of 'grave crimes' and has led to an increase in long-term custodial sentences for young people.
Criminal Justice and Court Services Act 2000	Sentencing of 'grave crimes' is to be determined by judges and not overruled by politicians (e.g. Home Secretary). Gave courts the power to fine or imprison the parents of truanting schoolchildren.
Criminal Justice and Police Act 2001	Introduced electronic tagging as a condition of bail; increased courts' power to deprive young people of their liberty while they are being processed by the courts (i.e. while on remand) and before any criminal act has been proved; extended child curfew orders to geographic areas and not just on specific individuals.
Criminal Justice Act 2003	New provisions made for custody for young people who have committed a sexual or violent offence. YOTs must comply with risk assessments under Multi-Agency Public Protection Arrangements (MAPPA).

(Continued)

Table 5.1 Continued

Legislation	Description
Children Act 2004	Influenced youth justice preventative schemes and informed social work assessments with young people in the youth justice system by encouraging a focus on safeguarding, promoting a child's welfare and educational achievement.
Anti-Social Behaviour Order Act 2008	Extends the power of public bodies in relation to civil orders and allows hearsay evidence to be used.
Criminal Justice and Immigration Act 2008	Introduced the youth rehabilitation order as a generic replacement for nine previously existing, community-based orders; simplified sentencing and improved flexibility of interventions so as to stem the rising numbers of young people placed in the secure estate. Social workers who prepare pre-sentence reports (PSRs) will recommend packages of interventions to the courts (see www.sentencing-guidelines.gov.uk).
Crime and Security Act 2010	Extended the use of anti-social behaviour injunctions to groups or 'gangs' of 14–17 year olds.

The first guide to sentencing defendants under 18 years old was released in November 2009 to coincide with the introduction of youth rehabilitation orders (YROs) and is essential reading for workers in the youth justice system (www.sentencing-guidelines.gov.uk). There was a change in the political administration in 2010 and the coalition government is amending some of the previous policy directions. The key driving factor now is economic – the comparative costs of various interventions and 'value for money'. Ideologically, there is no interest in taking a stance that is 'soft' and shows greater understanding of young offenders or their welfare, but the most expensive and ineffective youth justice strategy is incarceration. Recidivism rates are very high (78 per cent) for young people subjected to this punishment. Across England and Wales, custody rates have been found to vary wildly without any corresponding variations in youth crime rates. Large numbers of children are detained who do not pose a serious threat to the public and the Youth Justice Board currently spends more than two-thirds of its annual budget on placements in the secure estate (NACRO, 2012a). Therefore, for economic reasons, if no other, new legislation has been introduced to address these geographical inconsistencies and decrease the overall numbers of 'bed nights' in the secure estate.

The Legal Aid, Sentencing and Punishment of Offenders Bill 2012 (LAPSO) seeks to do this by making local authorities liable for the overnight costs of every young person remanded whether in a secure care or custody setting. This incentivises them to create cost-effective alternatives, such as remand fostering schemes and intensive bail supervision services, and so reduces the number of young people held in custody awaiting trial. It also aims to decrease the number of young people reaching the custody threshold by proposing a more flexible tariff system. Previously, a young person who re-offended was automatically escalated to a higher tariff sentence regardless of the nature or severity of the offence. This is now replaced with greater professional discretion to determine the most appropriate response based on the severity of the offence and the circumstances of the young person (e.g. a young person can now have more than one referral order).

Social work practice within youth offending teams

Social work with a child or young person is always undertaken with due regard to a child's family. In the UK, the law emphasises a child's 'right to family life' and social workers need to be aware of and understand the legal basis for the provision of services. Legally, the welfare of the child is the paramount consideration but in a contemporary youth offending services context, this basic principle can come into conflict with principles of justice, victim's rights and public safety within the contemporary criminal legal system. In youth justice practice the client, however difficult their background or circumstances, is viewed primarily as a wrongdoer, 'a young offender', who deserves to be punished and controlled.

Different childcare professionals are expected in government guidance to 'work together' to safeguard and protect the welfare of children and young people and in the area of youth justice this has been further legislated for in the 1998 Crime and Disorder Act. This placed a duty on all local authorities to form and fund multi-agency youth offending teams (YOTs) to be led by social services departments (which became children's services in 2000) with professionals seconded from education, health, police and probation. There is a duty to formulate, publish and implement annual youth justice plans with an aim of preventing re-offending. So the risk to the public of a young person re-offending is for youth justice practitioners as paramount as the welfare needs of that young person. The Act stipulated that all YOTs must provide the following services:

- Appropriate adults.
- Assessment of young people for rehabilitation programmes after reprimand/final warning.
- Support for those remanded in custody or bailed.
- Placement in local authority accommodation when remanded.
- Court reports and assessments.
- Allocation of referral orders.
- Supervision of those sentenced to community orders.
- Supervision of those sentenced to custody.

The bifurcate approach to justice and welfare is represented by the different agencies brought together in YOTs (Pickford, 2000). Social work, education and health professionals have a primary duty to focus on the welfare needs of young clients whereas police and probation professionals represent agencies whose primary duty is to prevent and control criminal activity. Guidance initially stipulated how the skills and approaches of these different professionals might be deployed to provide distinct areas of responsibility in delivering these youth justice services. In practice, roles have blurred and a YOT social worker will undertake a multitude of tasks, for example, interviewing and assessing, writing and presenting reports for courts and panels, building relationships with young people and their parents/carers, empowering, supporting and advocating on behalf of young people and challenging discrimination and injustice (Pickford and Dugmore, 2012). It can be difficult to retain a child-focused welfare approach alongside colleagues who adopt a justice position, but it is important to strive to retain a social work identity within any multi-agency environment and to keep an analytical approach to the systems and processes with which you work.

As in other areas of statutory social work, practice is based on skills of assessment, planning, implementation and review in partnership with the young person and their parent/carer. Social workers in the youth justice system will need to know and understand about adolescent development, as this transitional life stage underpins this area of practice. Interventions also highlight the role of parents in controlling and managing their teenager's behaviours. In practice, family relations are often strained by a young person's involvement in the youth justice system with parents feeling powerless to control the behaviour of their child beyond the home so social workers need to offer strategies that support and empower those parents.

Wider children and families social work practice in the last ten years has been reshaped by significant additional procedures and guidance to manage risk, with detailed assessment mechanisms that 'tell the social worker what data about families to collect, how quickly to collect it and what categories to use in recording it' (Munro, 2011, pp. 121–122). Since the 1998 Criminal and Youth Justice Act, the management of risk has also dominated youth justice practice. National standards stipulate the timeframe and format for assessments of children and young people in the youth justice system and the key focus throughout is the assessment of 'risk' in relation to the young person's: (1) risk of serious harm to others; (2) risk of harm to themselves or from others (i.e. vulnerability); (3) likelihood of re-offending (LoR) (Youth Justice Board, 2010, p. 4).

Assessments are structured and standardised through the YJB tool Asset, which requires the identification and analysis of 'criminogenic' factors (see above) while also identifying protective factors, which reduce, prevent or offset the impact of those risk factors. The key tasks of these assessments are as follows:

- Collecting information from a range of sources.
- Recording information clearly and consistently.

- Analysing information to try to understand the young person's behaviour and the circumstances in which it occurred.
- Estimating future behaviour and its potential impact, should it recur.
- Presenting conclusions to others.
- Identifying risk and protective factors to inform intervention plans.
- Sharing information with others.
- Regularly reviewing assessments.

Assessments are also likely to highlight other needs or 'vulnerabilities' that may not be linked to the child or young person's offending behaviour. The *Working Together to Safeguard Children* document (Department of Children, Schools and Families [DCSF], 2010) states: (1) there need to be clear links between youth justice and local authority children's social care both at a strategic level and a child-specific operational level; (2) YOTs have a duty to ensure that their functions are discharged with regard to the need to safeguard and promote the welfare of children.

YOTs are required by law to be part of the local children's safeguarding board and social workers within YOTs need to ensure they are familiar with local safeguarding procedures and processes so that they know what action to take if a young person they are working with is found to be at risk of, or subject to, harm or neglect. Although the law and this assessment tool acknowledge that youth offending services need to pay attention to social inequalities and welfare issues as 'the causes of crime', the focus of interventions is predominantly on individual responsibility and behaviour change.

The Asset assessment should form the basis of any subsequent intervention plan. Intervention plans should be reviewed, with active participation from the young person and their parent/carer, every three months. Effective intervention with young people is likely to combine 'multimodal' methods focusing on the individual, family and social networks, peer associations and schools. Social workers will supervise young people on community referral orders (ROs), youth rehabilitation orders (YROs) and young people on licence following a detention and training order (DTO). As well as challenging difficult behaviour through targeting individual problems such as negative thinking and attitudes, poor problem-solving skills and difficult personal relationships, social workers will support their young clients to secure stable housing, improve family relationships and gain access to education, training and employment. Whyte (2009) argues that 'effective practice' should result in a young person's personal maturation and social development and integration as well as in them ceasing to re-offend.

For all the talk of punishment and coercion, effective programmes rely on the quality of the relationship between the staff working with them and the young person taking part. *The Munro Review of Child Protection* (2011) endorses this view and highlights the importance of social workers moving away from procedural manuals and simply knowing how to collect data, to focusing more on the quality of interactions with service users. Munro provides a detailed list of specific capabilities that are needed in social work with children and young people, such as purposeful relationship building with children, parents, carers and families; skills in adopting authoritative but compassionate styles of working; and knowledge of theoretical frameworks and their effective application for the provision of therapeutic help. Others have argued that these recommendations equally apply to social workers in the area of youth justice practice (Pickford and Dugmore, 2012).

One of the biggest challenges for social work with young people in this context is that these 'service users' are not voluntary and those with the most disturbed and difficult behaviours will probably have had much experience of social care agencies. Those initially most motivated are often less entrenched in criminality and criminal associations (Burnett, 2004). Some young people may be compliant with the technical elements of supervision requirements without engaging in personal change. Compliance is not necessarily an indicator of effective engagement. For others, compliance can be a real sign of change but this may or may not be sustained in the long term. One of the significant factors in effecting positive change that is highlighted by research, but not reflected in the risk-management discourse, is the relentless patience of someone believing in the young person and motivating them to change, rather than just giving up on them.

Theoretical underpinnings

Concepts of childhood, adolescence and human development all influence the criminology theories that underpin different approaches to youth justice. Practitioners have to address the dichotomy underlying the justice/welfare debates, that arise from competing concepts of childhood – children are born innocent and in need of protection from the adult world versus children are in need of discipline and education to become civilised, socially responsible adults (James and James, 2012).

Theories of deviancy, such as labelling and subculture theories, influence debates about the relative merits of preventionism and criminalisation versus diversion strategies in youth crime policy (Junger-Tas et al., 2012). Cultural theories of identity formation during adolescence highlight how teenagers are prone to behaving in ways that 'live up to' the social expectations of their label (Willis, 1977). Diversion strategies (as opposed to prevention) arise from the recognition that the majority of young people do not engage in criminal behaviour and those who do will not be entrenched in such behaviours and, if kept out of the justice system, will not re-offend. Prevention strategies, on the other hand, tend to increase the numbers of young people in contact with the youth justice system (Ross et al., 2011). For example, the introduction of ASBOs and ABCs disregards 'labelling' theories and effectively 'criminalises' youth without positive effect. Recent studies show that in those areas of the country where a commitment to decriminalisation, diversion and decarceration has persisted despite the Crime and Disorder Act 1998, the levels of both reported youth crime and the numbers of young people imprisoned remain significantly lower than in those areas that fully adopted the 'get tough' approach (YJB, 2013).

In 2009, the YJB promoted the evidence-based practice movement, or the 'what works' agenda, through its publication *Key Elements of Effective Practice*. Since then, Ross et al. (2011) conducted a meta-analysis of previously published (predominantly North American) research reports on the efficacy of different interventions, and promotes those that are 'scientifically' measured by the randomised controlled trial (RCT) as having an impact on decreasing the re-offending rates of recipients. Examples of programmes with positive outcomes include social skills training, cognitive behavioural programmes, parent training programmes and multi-modal interventions such as multi-systemic therapy (Ross et al., 2011). However, others have cautioned against the tendency to prescribe such treatments as a universal solution to complex individual characteristics (Prior, 2005).

Modern social work theories relating to relationship-based models of service delivery are based on the psychosocial theory (originating from psychoanalytic and psychodynamic casework) that stresses the importance of understanding individuals, and her or his psychological processes, and the interpersonal relationships of the individual in the context of his or her environment (Newman and Newman, 2012). Theories developed from therapeutic practices inform current relationship-based interventions with importance placed on the practitioner demonstrating warmth/concern, empathy and unconditional positive regard (Rogers, 1976; Egan, 2002). McNeill (2006) found these factors to be centrally important for effecting positive behaviour change in youth justice interventions.

Criminology research has correlated the presence of 'criminogenic risk factors' – four static and 12 dynamic – in a young person's life with an increased likelihood of re-offending. Youth justice practitioners, using the Asset standardised assessment tool (as discussed above), will systematically screen for and rate each of these factors to produce an aggregate score that predicts the degree of risk, or likelihood of that young person re-offending and is applied to determine the level of intervention – standard, enhanced or intensive – that is needed to reduce that risk. This 'scaled approach' is based on actuarial calculation methodology and the belief that an accurate, mathematical enumeration of collective risk factors is possible.

Best practice approaches

As in other areas of child and family social work, the quality of practice, assessments and interventions, is greatly influenced by the quality of professional relationship that the social worker establishes, especially with the young person and their carers. The social worker is likely to first meet the young person and their family at a time when they are anxious, overwhelmed or scared about the justice process. Being aware of power differentials and being able to establish co-operation and communication requires a willingness to listen and to show warmth and empathy; to clearly explain processes and expectations; to involve young people in the planning of interventions; and to view the child or young person as a whole person and not overly identifying a child with a particular problem (Hill, 1999; Morgan, 2006).

Assessment needs to be free of prejudice and this can be proactively addressed by involving young people and their parent/carer in their assessment and the development of their intervention plan. The aim of interventions in the youth justice system is to change an aspect of the young person's behaviour and for this to happen the young person must be motivated also to want it. Someone will only change their behaviour if they see the change as having some beneficial value to them (Miller and Rollnick, 2002). This theory can be combined with the stages of change model (Prochaska et al., 1992) that describes the five-stage process that individuals go through when making changes to their behaviour: pre-contemplation; contemplation; preparation; action; maintenance. There are, however, limitations to how this approach can be applied in situations where young people have been mandated to change their behaviour. Motivational interviewing is a technique that aims to prevent the young person from taking a passive stance towards authority and/or her or his assessment and intervention plans. It is defined as 'a client-centred, directive method for enhancing intrinsic motivation to change, by exploring and resolving ambivalence' (Miller and Rollnick, 2002, p. 25). It is an empowerment-based, anti-oppressive approach as it values the client's views as the expert in their own life.

Social learning theories provide a framework for empowering individuals within their social context. Young people are far less likely to re-offend if they have secure relationships with family, friends and their wider community and are supported to develop relationships that do not centre around crime. Young people who feel they have a stake in their community are less likely to commit an offence in it than those who don't. This makes work with family, friends and the wider community (e.g. employers, community groups and the voluntary sector) as well as with the young person also very important (NACRO, 2012b)

Case example

Peter, a 14-year old boy of dual heritage (White/Black UK), is found guilty of criminal damage and assault (of a police officer). It is his first conviction and he is given a six-month referral order. The YOT worker meets Peter and his grandmother at the office the next day to explain the sentence, what will be required of him and the expectations and importance of his compliance with the plan that will be presented to the referral panel. At this meeting, the YOT worker discusses the offence with Peter and explores his view of these events and his behaviour. Peter is quiet and hostile. The YOT worker reflects back to Peter that he appears to be resentful of the outcome and invites him to explain why. His grandmother responds by saying she thinks it is all her fault as she was the one who called the police. Peter had argued with his younger brother and when she intervened Peter had started smashing up his room. When the police arrived she felt they had made things worse as Peter had reacted by throwing things at them until they managed to restrain him. The assault charge related to Peter spitting in the face of an arresting officer. The YOT worker observed that Peter showed signs of getting agitated when his grandmother described these events and again invited him to share his own perspective. Peter replied that it was unfair because his younger brother had taken his phone and the police had hurt him when they restrained him so he had fought back. Peter had difficulty acknowledging that his own behaviour had started the sequence of events.

The next meeting was at Peter's educational placement, this time without his grandmother. The YOT worker asked Peter what he thought his strengths and difficulties were and in the process discovered that he enjoyed outdoor sports but was no longer doing them. The YOT worker explored this further and found he had recently stopped due to increasing caring responsibilities for his grandmother. He did not see himself as a young carer but he did the family shopping, took his younger brothers to and from school daily, collected his grandmother's prescriptions and organised the occasional meal. The YOT worker also met with the grandmother on her own who explained that although Peter had been in her care since he was three years old his mother, who struggled with alcohol and drug addictions, had intermittently been around but had died six months earlier. She said that Peter never talked about his mother to her. His school had referred him for bereavement counselling but he had refused to go.

The initial referral panel agreed that Peter would be required to do 18 hours of community reparation, attend his educational placement and attend weekly supervision sessions with the YOT worker. Reparation was arranged at the local community centre where Peter was required to attend for two hours every Saturday morning. At first he was kept busy clearing up after the centre's activities but the other volunteers there discovered he had a talent for computer graphics and soon he was designing and printing all their notices, leaflets and posters. The YOT worker enabled Peter to join the local army cadets twice a week by supporting his grandmother to get help from a neighbour if she needed it while he was out. The YOT worker explored the grandmother's care needs with her and encouraged her to find additional sources of support so that Peter could attend school regularly without worrying about her. In the weekly sessions, the YOT worker encouraged Peter to develop his understanding of his behaviours and their consequences. In response to Peter's sense of injury in his altercation with the police, the YOT worker spent a session going through his rights on arrest and considering other ways to manage a situation when he experiences himself as powerless. Peter then shared more about the moments of overwhelming frustration that preceded his outbursts. As the relationship continued, Peter was able to share with his YOT worker that he had previously rejected the counselling because he did not want anyone to think he was 'mad like my mum'. This gave the YOT worker the opportunity to explain how the child and adolescent mental health services

(CAMHS) could help him find new ways to cope with his sense of loss and to give Peter the support he needed to access it.

At the final review of his six-month referral order, Peter had not re-offended and tensions at home had significantly decreased. Both Peter and his grandmother reported that his angry outbursts were far less frequent or serious. He was attending his education unit regularly and was becoming a valued group member. He was found to have learning difficulties that were supported by very structured events. Peter loved cadets and went every week. While doing his reparation at the local community centre he had heard about the Duke of Edinburgh scheme and he had joined with a friend from cadets. This gave him opportunities for fun and adventure in contrast to his responsibilities at home.

Challenges and debates

Many academics have highlighted how the emergence of the risk society has caused assessments to become focused on 'deeds' and increasingly concerned with minimising risk to the public rather than in assessing the young person's needs. The Ministry of Justice (2010, p. 6) views 'the scaled approach' as one which allows the most resources to be allocated to the riskiest offenders as it explicitly matches resources to the level of risk as assessed by practitioners. However, it also attracts much criticism as it negates the possibility that choice, chance and opportunity can influence youthful offending behaviour in unpredictable ways and has been criticised for penalising young people whose circumstances are poor but beyond their control. A refocus on the need for relationship-based practice and greater professional discretion in exercising professional judgement has been called for and the signs are that the YJB will adopt such changes.

Increasingly, government is suggesting that only interventions that demonstrate efficacy or effectiveness should be supported financially, and although this sounds reasonable, in practice it is problematic both in its measure of 'effectiveness' and in its sources of 'evidence'. For example, a programme that showed a significant improvement in participants' self-esteem but not in re-offending rates would, in this context, be seen as ineffective. Also, there are great individual variations in response to the same intervention techniques (Whyte, 2009).

Despite this current policy emphasis on what works, England and Wales continue to lock up more children and young people in the 'secure estate' than almost any other western industrialised society. Custody is an ineffective and expensive way of tackling youth crime and therefore does not adhere to the policy of 'effective interventions'. It does not address the root causes and there is considerable evidence that incarceration actually increases the risk of children continuing with offending behaviours. For example, over 75 per cent of those who are subjected to custody will be reconvicted within one year of their release, compared to 33 per cent of those sentenced to a community order. The UN Convention on the Rights of the Child requires custody to be used as a last resort for those whose offending is so serious that they pose a serious threat to public safety. Practice in the UK has been criticised for contravening these rights as a large proportion of these incarcerated children do not meet that custody threshold.

Institutions are becoming more child centred, despite being a poor environment, particularly for the most vulnerable (All Party Parliamentary Group for Children, 2010). Children in young offender institutions are 16 times more likely to kill themselves than children in the community (NACRO, 2010).

The risk of vulnerability, as well as the risk of re-offending, is addressed within the core profile of Asset. That assessment and its associated vulnerability management plan accompanies a young person if they are remanded or sentenced to the secure estate. There has been criticism of the current narrow definition of vulnerability in these assessments, where vulnerability is primarily focused on the risk of a young person not coping in a young offender institution. The recent government strategy, *Healthy Children, Safer Communities* (DoH, 2009), to promote the health and well-being of children and young people in contact with the youth justice system, recognises for the first time the concentration of special needs in this group. In doing so, it highlights how these factors can make a young person vulnerable to not having the capacity to fully understand the systems and processes they are caught up in and, therefore, they are not in a position to participate fully in planning or even fully understand the YOT programmes of work. The strategy proposes widening the definition of vulnerability to one which addresses all children and young people in trouble with the youth justice system and placing a key corporate duty on children's services to promote their health and well-being through increased access to specialist services. Mental health issues are complex and can be difficult to identify in adolescence. Some YOTs have developed close working relationships with CAMHS services to improve access for these young people, but provision models across the country vary and there is evidence that YOT practitioners have sometimes been reluctant to label a young person with a mental health issue.

Concerns about the numbers of young people in custody, its ineffectiveness and its associated costs have led to renewed government interest in youth justice strategies that could reduce the number of 'bed nights' in the secure estate. Rates for young people remanded into custody (i.e. refused bail) vary widely and do not correlate with the seriousness of the offence. The LAPSO Act 2012 makes local authorities responsible for the full cost of court-ordered secure remands, to 'incentivise' them to develop and invest in alternative forms of remand such as fostering placements and intensively supported and monitored bail schemes. It is hoped that this will result in lower numbers of secure remands. It also gives all children and young people remanded in youth detention accommodation (YDA) looked after child status. This acknowledges that those children and young people viewed as causing the most serious 'trouble' are children in need of additional welfare support.

In times of diminishing budgets, mainstream services tend to adjust their thresholds, which limits services only to those most in need. In many cases children and young people are experiencing multiple problems but any one of them taken on its own may not be sufficient to meet a service threshold. Assessments need to highlight how different factors compound each other to enable these children to access children in need services.

Anti-oppressive practice considerations

The social worker in a youth justice setting is in a clear position of authority when working with young people who are often disadvantaged, progressing through a troubled adolescence, resistant to authority and who may have emotional and/or behavioural problems with experiences of abuse or trauma. It is important therefore to be aware of this power differential and the importance of adopting anti-oppressive practices.

The standardised assessment tool in youth justice settings, Asset, requires practitioners to be aware of social inequalities that are grouped into two types of diversity: (1) those children and young people who can face discrimination due to race/ethnicity, culture, religion, disability, sexuality, age, gender, care status; (2) a range of factors which could pose a barrier to engagement, e.g. children and young people who are themselves carers, young parents, rurality issues, those with literacy/language difficulties (Youth Offending Team, Inspection, 2011).

The criminalisation of young black men (i.e. the disproportionate use of social control methods with this group) has been statistically clear and strongly critiqued for many years. Current figures confirm that black and minority ethnic (BME) groups continue to be disproportionately represented at every stage of the youth justice system: BME youth are six times more likely to be stopped and searched than their white counterparts (despite being no more likely to be caught with anything illegal). There is research evidence which suggests that prejudice, discrimination and stereotyping (Bowling and Phillips 2007) continue to be key factors (Earle, 2011). BME groups are also overrepresented in youth custody figures, both due to being refused bail and to being given custodial rather than community-based sentences, and in YOT caseloads (YJB, 2012). Youth justice practitioners need to be aware that discrimination is also a concern within YOT practice. For example, young people remanded or sentenced to the secure estate should be provided with an initial assessment of their needs and vulnerability but this frequently fails to happen (YJB, 2010). When it does, many young people, particularly those from BME backgrounds, felt that the person completing the assessment did not take the time to understand how they could help.

Girls have always been under-represented in the criminal justice system and there are different theories as to why this might be. Currently, as a consequence of 'early intervention' policies, there is renewed concern that girls are being increasingly drawn into the criminal justice system and at a younger age, with the consequential effects of a criminal record, in spite of there being limited evidence of any increases in their criminality in recent years (YJB, 2012). Asset analysis (YJB, 2012) indicates that young female offenders in England and Wales can be placed into three overall groups of those who commit: (1) offences of theft and handling stolen goods; (2) offences of violence; (3) 'other' offences.

The girls in each group present with a different range of needs and criminogenic factors. Offences of violence by girls appear to have a common pattern in that there is usually a relationship with the victim and it is most often perceived that the victim did something to 'deserve' the violence. In addition, the recent use of alcohol is often linked to the offence/offending pattern. Qualitative data indicate that girls and boys prefer interventions which are stylistically different with girls preferring the building of one-to-one relationships and a female-only environment, whereas boys prefer more structure and rules.

Many of those young people who are 'serious', 'persistent' or 'lifelong' offenders have learning disabilities, vulnerable mental health, conduct disorders and communication difficulties, but youth justice practitioners may not have any specialised knowledge or expertise for how to work effectively with someone who presents with these conditions. An effective social worker will need to be proactive in finding sources of specialist information and resources to inform their response to a range of difficulties with which a young person may be trying to deal.

Summary

Conflict is inherent in the social work role with young people in the youth justice system whose own welfare needs are sometimes compromised by the concurrent need to reduce the risk to the public of the young person re-offending. As in other areas of social work, best practice requires attention to be paid to the quality of professional relationships established with these involuntary service users. However, there are debates about whether current measures of effectiveness take account of the quality rather than just the quantity of professional contacts with young people. In the multidisciplinary settings of YOTs and the secure estate, social workers need to maintain their professional identity and be prepared to advocate effectively for the welfare interests of the child or young person.

📖 CASE STUDY

Danny is a 16 year old White European of Lithuanian origin whose family moved to the UK when he was eight. He was arrested in the city centre at 2pm on a Saturday with three other boys of similar age and charged with possession of a bladed article and conspiracy to rob. Eighteen months earlier, Danny received a six-month referral order, for possession of a knife that he fully complied with and completed. Danny has a diagnosis of attention deficit hyperactivity disorder (ADHD) with mild learning difficulties. He has a good level of attendance at his alternative education provision and is in his last year (year 11) of compulsory school. He lives at home in a three-bed room flat with his parents, younger brother and sister. His mother works part-time as a cleaner and his father supplements his main construction job with late shifts as a minicab driver. Danny has been interviewed and held overnight in the police station. Both parents have attended court. The Crown Prosecution Service (CPS) asks the court to refuse any applications for bail and to remand Danny into custody. Danny's solicitor asks the court to consider an intensive supervision and surveillance (ISSP) bail package and a three-hour adjournment is granted, for the YOT service to prepare this.

Questions

 How would you approach this assessment of the risk Danny poses to the public?

 What welfare concerns might increase the risk of harm to Danny resulting from his behaviour?

 What would you want to establish in your interview of Danny and his parents?

 What other sources of information might you need?

 What might be the key components of any ISSP bail package in this case?

Further resources and suggested readings

Barry, M. and McNeill, F. (2009) *Youth Offending and Youth Justice*. London: Jessica Kingsley Publishers.

Goldson, B. and Muncie, J. (eds) (2006) *Youth Crime and Justice*. London: Sage.

Muncie, J., Hughes, G. and McLaughlin, E. (eds) *Youth Justice: Critical Readings*. London: Sage.

Pickford, J. and Dugmore, P. (2012) *Youth Justice in Social Work*, 2nd edn. London: Sage.

Whyte, B. (2009) *Youth Justice in Practice: Making a Difference*. Bristol: The Policy Press.

Websites

Department of Education – www.education.gov.uk/publications/

Justice for Young People – www.justice4youth.co.uk/resources.html

Race and Criminal Justice Statistics – www.justice.gov.uk/statistics/criminal-justice/race

Youth Crime Prevention Programmes – www.gov.uk/youth-crime-prevention-programmes

Youth Justice – www.justice.gov.uk/youth-justice

Young People and the Law – www.gov.uk/browse/justice/young-people

6 Service user and carer involvement

Caroline Hickman

Introduction

> I was hunched against the back wall of the railway station watching the snow get thicker, the afternoon get darker and my mood get worse. Rumours had started to run through the few remaining people huddled on the plat-form that there were no more trains running that afternoon. Some people had given up and gone. I had no idea how we were supposed to get back to London from Kent if they stopped the trains. I didn't have the money for a taxi, didn't know anyone in Kent (and few enough in London). I was six months into my first social work job after qualifying, and I was sometimes still working hard to make it look like I knew what I was doing, which I did, some of the time, but not in that moment. After an hour of getting more and more frustrated and scared, aimlessly hoping that the man in the (closing) ticket office would magically produce a train, I was on the edge of crying.

There are a number of ways to think about service user and carer involvement and participation across social work practice, research and education, and in service design and delivery. As a qualified social worker, or social work student on place-ment, you will be working with service users and carers in a variety of settings and contexts, sometimes more clearly in partnership, sometimes not. You could be employed in a social work team, maybe in a more authoritative role where you have the power to decide where a service user has to reside or stay for treatment, or be employed in the voluntary and independent sector, or working in a service user or carer led and controlled organisation.

This chapter will provide you with an introduction to some of the key points and discussions that social workers need to think about in training and practice regarding service user and carer involvement and participation. It will examine key theoretical frameworks and models, and look at case studies to create context and help with reflection on questions. A role play and practice example is provided at the end. The chapter will explore what the literature says is important, what service users, carers and young carers say is important, and then explore how to hold together all the different views in order to provide the best possible service to others.

> The snow fell; it grew darker, and colder. I felt completely useless, and lost, and cold, and didn't know what to do. Then I learnt one of those lessons that you just don't see coming. My companion, a long-term user of mental health services that I had taken to visit a rehabilitation community in Kent that he had agreed he may feel able to move to, sat down in front of me, looked me straight in the eye and said, 'It will all be OK, you know Caroline, we will find a way to deal with this. We will get back to London tonight somehow.' He even made me laugh about the state we were in. In an instant the dynamics of our relationship completely changed. I was the one who was being looked after.

Knowledge

Service users and carers: Who are we talking about?

This story opens the discussion with some questions about how we define service users and carers. The reality is that all of us have experience of using services even if it is just visiting a doctor or school counsellor/advisor. We also have experience of caring for others and being cared for in different ways. What defines someone as a user of services or carer of an individual can be a subtle line. It can also become a wall that segregates one group of people from another and leads to a process of 'othering', described by Dalal (as cited in White, 2006, p. 32) as treating one group as though they were somehow less than 'human' or dehumanised. As a social worker, it is important to think about the terms 'service user' and 'carer', to think about the impact of being defined by these terms, and the advantages and disadvantages of the implications of the labels. For example, access to services will usually be restricted to people with these labels. Sometimes, both adult carers and young carers can struggle to define themselves as carers, saying that they are just doing what needs to be done to support their families. While sometimes the label could be comforting and give explanation and meaning to their experience, at other times it could be dehumanising and reduce the person to a list of 'problems' or 'symptoms'. There is no single answer to this question. In practice, the first thing is to be aware of the mixture of feelings that may be attached to the label. Ask yourself if the label is for the benefit of the organisation or the person, and ask the person you are working with what they would prefer to be called.

Critically, Beresford (2000) points to the problematic nature of the term 'service user' because it defines people through their use of services, which is not necessarily the way they might want to identify themselves. Shaping Our Lives national user network argues that 'it is important that "service user" should always be based on self-identification' (Levin, 2004, p. 18) and links the term to being in an unequal relationship with society, entitlement to receive services, the risk of service use over a prolonged period of time which makes the assumption that there is something wrong with the person concerned, and the importance of recognising shared experience of service users with a wide range of other people.

Carers are defined as people who provide care for friends, partners, family or neighbours on an unpaid basis. They will be involved in a range of activities including personal care, financial, physical and psychological or emotional care to people who need support due to age, physical or mental health problems, addiction or disability. Carers UK (2012) estimates that there are approximately 6.5 million people in the UK providing care for ill or disabled family members and friends, which is an increase of 629,000 since 2001. The greatest rise has been among those people providing over 20 hours of care each week, which is the point at which caring starts to significantly impact on the health and well-being of carers and their ability to hold down paid employment alongside their caring responsibilities (Carers UK, 2012).

There are an estimated 175,000 children who could be defined as young carers in the UK between the ages of six and 18 who provide care to others. The care is usually in the home to family members (Barnardo's, 2006), mostly to parents, but is sometimes provided to siblings or grandparents. Being a young carer can impact on a child's development and attachments, lead to loss of contact with extended family and friends, cause difficulties with school such as bullying, underperformance educationally, lead to worries about own mental and physical health, add to anxiety about parent's physical and mental health, cause delayed or compromised transitions to adulthood, and frequently lead to social isolation.

Parents and children can both fear that asking for help from services may lead to removal of the child from the family, which could leave the family even more stressed and fractured. Children can feel that they are responsible for keeping a parent alive, well or out of hospital, and may feel that they have failed if their parent is admitted. It is not simply that being a young carer is a negative experience for a child as some research findings support the argument, sometimes made by the young people concerned, that being a young carer can also bring some positives such as feeling closer as a family (Aldridge and Becker, 2003). Children and young people report that they can feel proud that they are supporting their family and loved ones and their role gives them some satisfaction and sense of responsibility.

Butler and Hickman (2011) describe how some young carers are 'socialised' into the role while others may feel coerced or that they just have no choice. Some will have assumed the role from a young age, while some may take on the role following a crisis in the family or breakdown of other adult relationships. Most important to remember is that 'because of the wide variety of family histories and circumstances as well as the range of caring responsibilities and tasks undertaken by young people, it is clear that this is far from an homogenous group' (Butler and Hickman, 2011, p. 8).

Think about the issues affecting young carers in relation to Molly and her mother Anita in the case example below. What issues would be important for social workers to keep in mind when meeting with both of them, separately and together?

Case example

Molly: Young carer
Molly is a ten-year-old girl who lives with her mother, Anita, in a flat on an estate on the outskirts of the city. No other family live nearby. Anita has suffered from depression for four years since her husband left her and she fell ill. She has been prescribed antidepressants by her general practitioner (GP) but she may not always take them and increasingly refuses to go out of the house; some days she cannot get out of bed. Many days she depends on Molly to monitor her medication, cook, clean and sometimes help her dress. Molly used to do well at school but is now failing tests and seems to have few friends. Molly has recently been involved in a couple of fights with other children at school resulting in detentions. Her teacher thinks that Molly is starting to be bullied by other children because she can look badly dressed, often unwashed, underweight and sometimes falls asleep in class.

Key issues and themes

Participation and power

There are a number of key issues affecting involvement and participation that you could think about in practice. Key questions for both service users and carers are those involving power, authority and control. Beresford and Carr (2012) argue that even if not explicit 'participation is an issue inseparable from power' (p. 29). Engaging with critical questions like the following would help to ground your social work practice in anti-oppressive principles:

- How can I support both individuals and groups of service users and carers to identify and voice their own needs?
- How can I acknowledge and address issues of power, oppression and authority in the relationship between us?
- What level of participation would be meaningful for this person?
- What are the barriers to participation at both an individual and organisational level for us to acknowledge and face?

Consider the question of levels of participation in relation to Peter and Deanna below and think about what levels might be appropriate or helpful, or even welcomed, by both Peter and Deanna.

Case example

Peter and Deanna: Adult carer

Deanna, aged 60, has been a full-time carer for her husband Peter, aged 65, for the last 12 years. Peter was diagnosed with depression after his mother and father died within six months of each other when he was aged 50. He lost his job as a teacher after three years off work and has not worked since. He refused to leave the house at first and was agoraphobic and anxious about meeting people visiting the house. He became very dependent on Deanna and was anxious when she left the house, sometimes talking to her on her mobile whilst she was shopping to keep himself calmer. If she was delayed returning home, he could become very stressed. After counselling and medication, he gained in confidence and now attends a support group for people with mental health difficulties that meets at a local café. He spends a lot of time looking after his garden, reading and walking their dog. His mental health is stable as long as nothing changes around him. He is dependent on his routines remaining stable. Deanna has just been diagnosed with cancer and needs immediate treatment. She is really worried about how Peter is going to cope with her health problems. She's worried that her ill health will cause him to have setbacks in his own mental health and wants to protect him from the full extent of her illness, but also realises she will need his help to cope with her own health and nursing needs.

Organisational context

Participation and involvement should be considered in relation to the organisational context. Warren (2007, p. 57) talks about facilitating participatory practice in organisations where social workers need to distinguish between 'partnership', 'consultation' and 'information sharing' and warns that service user involvement can often be 'managed' by professionals (Braye, 2000) leading to further tokenism. Teater and Baldwin (2012) discuss service user participation in the context of community profiling and the level of involvement of community members in being consulted, to participate or control the activities of a community profile, and the collaborative approach to defining need achieved through community profiling as a social work task. Advocacy and user and carer led services offer different models and opportunities for social workers to engage with people and work in partnership, and often social work placements are provided in service user or carer led organisations.

The principles of partnership are also embedded in policy such as Department of Health (DoH) (2002) guidance, *Keys to Partnership: Working Together to Make a Difference in People's Lives*. The guidance advises that partnership working and information sharing across professional disciplines and agencies is key. This is not simply partnership working between professionals but also between social workers and service users and carers. Areas for involvement include the following: individual care planning and review; the planning and delivery of services; the organisation and management of social work and social care; the development of service user and carer led initiatives; staff and student training; recruitment; and research.

Models and the value base supporting service user and carer participation

The contribution made by service user and carers to the development of the social work value base has been widely documented by writers such as Warren (2007), Weinstein (2010), Beresford (2000) and Beresford and Carr (2012). Grounded in empowerment models of theory and practice that in turn are rooted in groups such as the mental health survivors' movement, civil rights movement and radical social work, the value base is firmly rooted in a political and social and cultural base that aims to give a voice to marginalised groups.

There are a number of models of participation documented in the literature that you can use to help you think about your practice and how the organisations you work in can support and enable service users and carers to get involved. Most well known are the linear and hierarchical models like Arnstein's Ladder (1969), Hart (1997) and Hoyes et al. (1993) that list stages in order of participation and power sharing in the relationship from levels of:

- manipulation
- therapy
- informing
- consultation
- placation
- partnership
- delegated power
- service user control.

Alternately, there are more holistic and circular models of participation discussed by Warren (2007) that because of their intention to place service users and carers at the centre of the model allow for different forms of participation depending on the capacity and circumstances of the people involved. It is important to remember that linear models need to be critically and carefully used as at best they offer a framework and at worst they restrict and categorise people unhelpfully. Real life and people's participation is never as simple but is much more dynamic and dependent on time, context and the circumstances, and the relationship in which it is being considered. These are dynamic and changeable, not static and fixed, as we saw in the case example of Deanna and Peter above.

Diversity, difference and ethical issues

Other key issues to consider are the diversity of the voices of service users and carers and also how different value systems will influence your social work practice, which might include tensions between different value systems and conflict between the social work roles of 'care' and 'control' (Wistow, 2005).

There are always ethical issues to consider, particularly when involving service users and carers in research and teaching and assessment of social work students. Hugman (2005) points to the importance of development of a critical approach to ethics that he argues should be learned through practice experience and through critical examination of the relationship. Participation needs to be considered alongside awareness and sensitivity to other factors such as race and culture, age, gender, sexuality and sexual orientation, faith, beliefs, class and capacity. Financial considerations, access to resources and the impact this has on capacity to participate and get involved are issues that will affect all groups.

We also need to reflect on service user and carer involvement critically and questioningly and think about the ethical issues involved. Sometimes organisations might try to involve service users in a tokenistic way to be able to say they have 'consulted', but what they have consulted on may not mean much at all. Beresford and Carr (2012) identify a number of critical concerns including how organisations could use service user involvement as a 'rubber stamping' exercise to legitimise their services and consultation without offering actual power sharing or genuine participation.

Barriers and opportunities to participation

Barriers and opportunities will be specific to your own local practice and organisation, but generalisations can be made to give you some examples to think about. In many cases, the barriers are likely to mirror the relationship that service users and carers have when trying to access services more generally. Barriers can include changeable personal circumstances that organisations struggle to accommodate, resistance seen through professional attitudes and assumptions, physical, emotional and structural access difficulties, and generally poor communication with service users and carers including failure to provide feedback leading to feelings of participation being a meaningless and tokenistic exercise. Lack of time and organisational resources are often cited as barriers, but you would need to consider if this could also be seen as another form of restriction through attitudes and assumptions and priorities within the groups and organisation concerned.

Warren (2007) helpfully outlines numerous barriers and opportunities to participation and stresses that effective participation depends on a genuine commitment on the part of service providers and policymakers. Braifield and Eckersley (2008) discuss barriers and enablers such as service user motivation to contribute and 'put something back or directly benefit their personal development' (p. 51). This identifies that skills and personal learning can grow from participation, but also raises the concern that service users can fear 'looking stupid' and not being taken seriously, which can influence their decision to participate. Frequently in practice when I start to talk with service users or carers about working with social work students, their first response to me is, 'But what have I got to offer?' It is important to make this clear from the start to help avoid the tokenism that can otherwise dominate. Respectful feedback and training play an important role in generating, supporting and then sustaining service user and carer participation, and in my experience can transcend other barriers such as structural and organisational restrictions by providing a shared and common purpose of 'learning together'.

Case example

Robert and Jane: Children service users
Sally and Mike: Adult service users

Six-month-old Robert was admitted to hospital for evaluation of his failure to gain weight when at 15 pounds he fell below the fifteenth percentile for weight for his age. He is the second of two children (his sister, Jane, is now aged 12) born to working-class parents following an unplanned but normal pregnancy. He weighed almost nine pounds at birth. Robert's mother Sally has had almost constant difficulties with him. He was bottle-fed and had severe colic. The formula used was changed a number of times and his colic was treated but he has continued to fail to gain weight. Sally's husband Mike works away during the week and only spends weekends with the family.

In the hospital, the nurses watched his mother Sally trying to feed him and noticed there was poor synchronicity between them; they were unsure about the amount of bonding they could see. Sally did not seem to know when he was hungry, when he needed to be burped and when he had finished eating. She seemed fed up with trying to feed him and was close to tears a lot of the time. Because of the relationship difficulties between Robert and his mother Sally, feeding was seen to be a distressing experience for both of them, but the nurses found that they were able to feed Robert without difficulty. Medical investigations failed to identify any specific medical condition that might account for his difficulties.

Points to consider

- What issues would you need to think about to help you communicate with the adults (Sally and Mike) and the children (Robert and Jane) in the case study?
- What do you think could be the barriers to participation for both the adults and children in this case?
- What do you think could be the professional attitudes that you may need to face in yourself or in others involved in the case?

Professional attitudes

Sometimes service user and carer participation may prove to be challenging to more than organisations. Even when social workers have the best possible intentions and commitment to person centred/service user centred practice, they can still find themselves practising defensively if they feel under pressure, unsupported and criticised. In your own social work practice, you would want to honestly and openly examine any of your own resistance to service user participation that you can recognise, and how this may mirror or reflect any organisational resistance. You should ask the service users and carers you are working with about the most pressing issues affecting them, their friends and families. Equally, you should find support for yourself in your own practice through supervision, training and peer support to examine your own feelings and attitudes that may lead to defensive practice.

Case example

Mike: Service user

Mike is a 33-year-old man who has been in and out of different psychiatric hospitals and hostels for the last 17 years. His parents had substance misuse problems and he was taken into care at the age of six and remained there until he left at age 16. He has had a number of different diagnoses and has recently been diagnosed with borderline personality disorder. In previous discharges he has refused to engage with support services and he often returns to live in temporary accommodation with friends who themselves have mental health and substance misuse problems, or squats where he has no secure accommodation. He has been referred to various community mental health teams in the past but found it difficult to maintain relationships and misses important appointments. Mike is currently being supported by the assertive outreach team who offer appointments when he thinks he needs them. He likes his new support worker and has started to keep appointments more regularly. Mike has suggested that he would like to get some more help through counselling, and would like to have a different life in the future with a job and family and children of his own.

Points to consider

- What would be the barriers and opportunities for participation and involvement that Mike might face?
- What might be the professional attitudes and the empathetic response needed by Mike to support his participation?

Service users and carer involvement in social work education and research

Social work training programmes are required by the Health & Care Professions Council (HCPC) and The College of Social Work (TCSW) to involve service users and carers as stakeholders in all parts of the design and delivery of programmes. The intention is that students will benefit from their involvement and also develop a better understanding of service users' and carers' experiences and views. Service users and carers will also benefit as newly qualified social workers will enter practice with a comprehensive understanding of the service user and carer perspective and the requirements of social workers for partnership working.

Research with service users and carers is often centred on principles of participation and working 'with' rather than 'on' and service users and carers being less the subjects of study and more co-researchers. Participatory and community-based research methods (Kellet, 2006; Teater and Baldwin, 2012) encourage the involvement of service users and carers in the various stages of the research, such as identifying and prioritising research topics as well as conducting interviews and analysing findings. Weinstein (2010) draws links between service user participation and research accuracy and usefulness of results, arguing that 'if the needs and views of users are reflected in research, results are more likely to be obtained which can be used to improve health, and social care practice' (p. 155).

Tidsall et al. (2009) are interested in the debates surrounding involvement of children and young people in research and how to engage with children in ways that are respectful, mutually beneficial and liberating, rather than exploitative and dominating. Children can benefit from involvement in the research process as they can provide an authentic voice rather than adults interpreting children's experiences and translating findings into adult language and issues, and their involvement can lead to outcomes that are more likely to be meaningful to children.

Theories and best practice approaches when working with service users and carers

Relationship-based social work practice

The relationship between social worker and service user is 'a crucial factor in the effectiveness of social work interventions' (Teater, 2010, p. 7). If the relationship between the social worker and service user is seen as positive by the service user/carer, then the argument follows that all interventions from counsellors, therapists and social workers provide some positive and therapeutic benefit. Factors said to be 'therapeutic' or positive also closely resemble feedback from service users about what they want from their social workers, which includes being supportive, encouraging and warm, trustworthy, reliable and non-judgemental (Warren, 2007). These factors are similar to the 'necessary and sufficient conditions' for the therapeutic process identified by Rogers (1957), which is discussed in more detail below.

Relationship-based practice identifies the professional relationship as the way in which social workers can engage with service users' and carers' lives. Wilson et al. (2011) propose that relationship-based practice core characteristics means recognising that both the professional relationship and the social worker and service user relationship are central parts of any social work intervention, which is linked in turn to the social worker's 'use of self' and reflective practice.

McLeod (2008) makes links between thoughtful reflective practice and the place of 'self' in relationship-based practice through self-awareness and self-knowledge needing to be valued. 'If becoming sensitive to the power-plays in an interaction is a step towards better communication skills, the first requisite for developing that sensitivity is to become more self aware' (McLeod, 2008, p. 117). As a social worker, one of the most important skills you will use is being able to simultaneously think about what is happening to the service user alongside your own thoughts and emotional responses. The aim is that by developing your ability to understand holistically both the service user's and your own responses, you are more likely to feel confident that you are acting in the best interest of the service user or carer.

Narrative approaches

Parton and O'Byrne (2000) see all social work as a potential dialogue or narrative encounter with service users that should focus on their strengths and resources. Narrative social work is described by Roscoe et al. (2011) as a conversation between theory and practice that leads to development in both the service users and social workers. They suggest a three-stage model starting with forming a relationship and engaging with the service user, to story sharing, to exploration and deconstruction of the story. Taking a narrative approach also means developing more awareness of how service users and carers perceive themselves and the world around them (their world view). This understanding helps the development of a narrative empathy in which social workers can increase their empathetic relationship with the service user and carer.

Narrative theories are an extension of social constructivism theory with a focus on the content, context, meaning and importance of the service user's and carer's story and how they see it for themselves. A shared understanding between social worker and service user/carer is developed through listening to the story and then looking for alternative ways to hear or to view the story. Development of this collaborative relationship is vital and then supports you in other practice techniques such as identifying alternative narratives (re-authoring or retelling stories), externalising the 'problems', use of letter writing, looking for unique outcomes and reflective 'curious' questioning.

In practice, personal story telling is part of life story work, sharing stories in support groups, internet support groups and discussion forums, and social and political movements. There are different elements to look for in any story, which can include the following: the emotional narrative; internal and external dialogue; congruence and incongruence in both the story and the telling of it; authenticity and inauthenticity (is the story believable or is there some element that just do not feel true to you); your own empathetic response (or absence of it); and collaboration or the relationship between social worker and service user and/or carer.

Client-centred approaches

Having strong theoretical, legal and policy frameworks in place to support service user and carer involvement and participation is important, but the success of this depends on the relationship between the people concerned, and in turn that relationship is dependent on the social worker's attitude to the people with whom she or he is working.

Professional attitudes can be 'real' and acted on, or imagined; they may be held consciously or unconsciously, 'up for discussion' or held in denial. Social workers need to feel able to work alongside service users and carers rather than assume responsibility for them or 'do things for them'. Contradictory attitudes and values may be exposed when examining service users' rights to take the same risks as other people. Social workers can feel anxious and defensive that they are being criticised for not practising in 'the right way', they may worry about service users making 'bad' choices and themselves being held responsible, and they can worry about no longer being important or needed.

Ballatt and Campling (2011) take a different approach to looking at the relationship in our professional practice and also reintroduce the crucial and missing 'human' element. They focus on the compassionate relationship between social worker and service user/carer and the consequences for both if we fail to sustain this. If we fail to give attention to promotion of kinship, connectedness and kindness, then we will have failed to understand a key component of 'what makes people do well for others' (p. 3). They appeal to organisations to balance attention to systemic and organisational efficiency with valuing the experience of the patient or service user, and make direct links between kindness and well-being, kindness and effectiveness, and positive outcomes for staff and service users as well as organisations. It follows that the opposite would also be true in that a lack of kindness can be 'anti-therapeutic' (p. 33), which is supported with evidence from attachment theory and the biological effects of kindness in aiding the process of healing and recovery.

📖 **CASE STUDY**

'Learning From Each Other' project

Twice a year for the last four years, the social work programme at the University of Bath has invited groups of 40 children and young people (young carers) to join our first year social work students on campus for a series of planned days called 'Learning From Each Other'. We organise activities such as story telling, lectures on group dynamics and family roles delivered to mixed groups of children and students, a young carers' presentation on what they want from social workers, discussions about what makes a good or bad social worker, campus tours, visits to halls of residence, arts and crafts and lots of games. We collated photographs taken during the day (by young carers and students) into slide shows, posters and books to tell the story of the work visually. We provided workshops for the older young carers on writing CV's and how to make an application for further and higher education. Our hope and belief is that these days support widening participation and access to education for groups of young people as well as teaching social work students about young carers.

Discussion on what makes a 'good' and 'bad' social worker

Figure 6.1 and the list compiled in Table 6.1 illustrate the findings from the discussion between the young carers and the social work students about what makes a good and bad social worker.

Role play

The following role-play exercise was designed by a young carers organisation (Off The Record – Bath) to help the social work students to think about how it might feel to be a young carer with high levels of responsibility for your family but also being a child. Below lists the instructions for the students and for the young carers.

Instructions to social work students

You are going to play a young carer who is any age between five and 18 years old. You care for your mum who suffers from schizophrenia. You don't see your dad very often and do most of the caring yourself. This can be very worrying, tiring and emotionally draining. You have been bullied at school and people call your mum names, which really upsets you. Your mum has had to be 'sectioned' before and went to hospital for two months. You were put into care during this time and no one explained what was happening. You want your social worker to tell you why mum gets ill and what you can do to make sure she gets better and never has to go back to hospital.

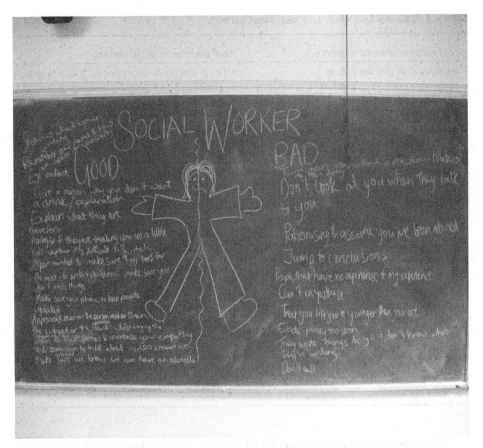

Figure 6.1 What makes a 'good' and 'bad' social worker?

When you have finished the role play, stop playing your role and talk about how it made you feel. You can ask if the young carer has ever had an experience with a social worker and ask them about how it felt and why.

Instructions to young carer
You are going to play a social worker visiting a family who is working in a bad way. You are going to say things that are not true about young carers and their families. The children are going to be played by the social work students and they care for their mum who has a mental health problem called schizophrenia. The children were put into care when mum was ill last time. This is your first visit.

When you have finished the role play, stop playing your role and talk about how it made the students feel. If you have ever had an experience with a social worker you can talk about how it felt and why.

Table 6.1 What makes a 'good' and 'bad' social worker?

'Good' practice for social workers	'Bad' practice for social workers
• Show us what you are writing.	• Don't turn down tea/coffee without a reason – makes us feel dirty.
• Remember our names and how to spell them properly.	• Don't look at you when they talk to you.
• Make eye contact.	• Patronising and assume you've been abused.
• Give a reason why you don't want a drink (tea/coffee) explanation to us.	• Don't jump to conclusions.
• Explain what you are there for.	• People that have no experience of my experience may not understand.
• Apologise if you are treating them like a little child – acknowledge it is difficult to switch roles between carer and child.	• Can't empathise.
	• Treat you like you are younger than you are.
	• Invade privacy too soon.
• Be open minded to make sure they look for the worst – to protect children – make sure you don't miss things.	• They write things down but you don't know what they're writing.
• Make sure you phone us to keep people updated.	• Don't call or visit when they say they will.
• Be approachable and focus on the person rather than the subject or the issue – whilst bringing the person to the issue.	
• Listen to our stories and make sure you show us that you care.	
• Make sure we know we can have an advocate.	
• Ask permission to talk about issues and respect our answer.	

Then, switch to playing a good social worker and talk about how that feels. You can initiate the discussion by asking the young person (played by the social work student) her or his name, ask how she or he is feeling and what she or he would like to happen. When you have finished, stop playing your role and talk about how it made the students feel.

Finally

The service user and I both agreed later that this was a turning point in our work together. Being stuck in the snow changed the relationship between us. He said that seeing me in such a vulnerable state (mess) made him realise that he had something he could contribute (meaningfully) to our work together and so he could also see himself moving out of hospital and changing his life. I realised that not knowing what to do was sometimes exactly the right thing to do. And paradoxically seems to be exactly what was needed. What seemed like hours later (but probably wasn't) a train did arrive, we managed to fight our way on to it and we made it back to London that night, both rather changed, I think, by our visit and not as either of us had anticipated.

Further resources and suggested readings

Beresford, P. and Carr, S. (2012) *Social Care, Service Users and User Involvement.* London: Jessica Kingsley Publishers.

Gosling, J. and Martin, J. (2012) *Making Partnerships with Service Users and Advocacy Groups Work: How to Grow Genuine and Respectful Relationships in Health and Social Care.* London: Jessica Kingsley Publishers.

Warren, J. (2007) *Service User and Carer Participation in Social Work.* Exeter: Learning Matters.

Websites

Carers UK – www.carersuk.org

Involve, National Institute for Health Research – www.invo.org.uk

Shaping Our Lives – www.shapingourlives.org.uk

Working Together – www.serviceuserandcarertoolkit.co.uk/index.html

7 Learning difficulties

Mark Baldwin

Introduction

Although people with learning difficulties can live full and rewarding lives, and this is increasingly the case, history tells us that people with learning difficulties are a group who have experienced severe marginalisation and oppression over the years and for many this continues. From the eugenics movement that included extermination in Nazi Germany and compulsory sterilisation across Europe and in Sweden as recently as the 1970s through to cases of violence against people with learning difficulties (Williams, 2009) and in residential settings, for example, Winterbourne View (Flynn, 2012), people with learning difficulties have been subject to bullying and violence at a higher rate than most other citizens of the UK.

In addition, there is evidence that people with learning difficulties experience poor outcomes in other areas of life. This is notably in relation to health outcomes (Small, 2009; Williams, 2009), employment, education and personal relationships. I want to make the case that people with learning difficulties are a marginalised group of people who experience discrimination and oppression. The majority of people with learning difficulties are not treated as full citizens and do not experience life in the same way as most others, as a result of disabling attitudes and because of poor access to public goods and services that most of us take for granted. In addition, people with learning difficulties have needs that even in a non-disabling society require reasonable adjustment from general services or individualised support from specialist services in order to meet their specific needs.

Social work is a profession that is driven by a unique commitment to social justice and human rights (International Federation of Social Work [IFSW], 2012). As professionals, we are committed to righting the wrongs of social injustice by acting as advocates for oppressed users of services. We are also educated to understand the nature of oppression and to model a participatory, inclusive and empowering practice, which will provide opportunities for people to control their lives.

Social workers also have skills in assessment and knowledge of resources which are there to meet the general needs of people with learning difficulties and the unique needs of each individual. We have skills in recognising abuse and knowledge of the policy, law and practice there to protect individuals from violent or degrading treatment. We act as advocates on behalf of people with learning difficulties who experience problems in receiving services from our own or other organisations. Through our knowledge of formal and informal services and resources in local communities, local authority areas and nationally, we can put people with learning difficulties in touch with services that are there to meet their needs, particularly their need for autonomy (Doyal and Gough, 1991), self-determination (Duffy, 2003) or control over their own lives (Department of Health [DoH], 2009; Williams, 2009).

It is for these reasons that people with learning difficulties are likely to need social workers at some point in their lives. For some people with learning difficulties who are experiencing great trauma and marginalisation, it may be their social worker who is the only person there to stick up for them, listen to what they have to say and ensure that their voice is heard. This places a heavy duty on social workers to adopt a practice which enables people with learning difficulties to control their lives.

To be effective in the lives of people with learning difficulties, social workers need to understand the law that is there to facilitate service users to take control of their lives and to protect them. We need to understand the policy guidance that provides the framework for effective practice within organisations. We need to have knowledge of theory that informs understanding of learning difficulties, of human development, of communication, of power relationships and their potential for both positive and negative outcomes, and we need to understand the concept of discrimination and how this relates to citizenship or the lack of it in the lives of many people with learning difficulties. Most of all, social workers need a commitment to the values of social justice and a willingness to put that commitment into a professional practice which is not just person centred, but which enables individuals to have their voices heard and their wishes respected and addressed.

This chapter will begin with a look at the language used to define people with learning difficulties, the prevalence of people with learning difficulties as users of social work services, and the problems of language, labelling and discrimination. We will then turn to an exploration of what social work for people with learning difficulties looks like in organisational settings. The chapter will then look at the legislation and policy that relates to people with learning difficulties. There is a great deal of useful theory that helps us understand social work for people with learning difficulties, telling us how we ought to practise and providing us with benchmarks to evaluate the effectiveness of that practice. I will explore some of this theory by looking at best practice for people who have learning difficulties, and how it fits with knowledge skills and values for professional social work. Certain aspects of this best practice might be problematic to put into action in contemporary social work agencies but will be argued as essential if the policy rhetoric of *Valuing People* (DoH, 2001), the White Paper that defines public policy in this area, is to be realised. The chapter will conclude, by way of summary, with the views of people with learning difficulties to whom I have spoken when I have asked them what kind of social worker they would find most helpful and effective.

Definitions and prevalence

The problem of language and labelling

According to labelling theory (Becker, 1963), labelling and stereotyping is the process by which people that are seen as different are identified and marginalised. Many people who use social work services, including those with learning difficulties, are subjected to this process of identification, stereotyping, labelling and discrimination. It is an invidious process which seriously affects people's life chances. Social workers need to understand this process so that they can eradicate it from their own practice.

Despite this understanding, what happens in practice is that nobody gets a sniff of a service until they have been thoroughly identified and labelled by the process of assessment. This is the case for people with learning difficulties, the latter phrase being just one of the labels attached to a significant minority of people. What is interesting about labels is that they are, in their negative connotation, generally imposed on people. What is interesting about the label 'learning difficulties' is that it is the one people with learning difficulties have chosen, and that is why it is the term I will be using in this chapter.

The label commonly utilised in government policy and documentation and picked up by local authorities is learning disability. Whilst the terms used to describe people with learning difficulties in the past are pejorative or abusive, the phrase learning disability, which is used in policy literature, is unhelpful. It is the social model that defines disability as discrimination imposed upon people with physical or learning impairments or difficulties. Disability is not something owned by the individual. Therefore, for government to utilise the phrase 'people with learning disabilities' reveals that they do not accept the social model of disability but rather the medical model which sees the impairment as the disability. This process individualises people with learning difficulties and turns them into problems requiring solutions rather than seeing them as people who may require help to deal with difficulties but who otherwise are citizens like anyone else.

For the reasons above, definitions of learning difficulty, and the prevalence of people so defined, need to be approached carefully. Some care services will start their categorisation by looking at intelligence quotient (IQ) scores, although this method is unhelpful because, as Small (2009) points out, there are 3 per cent of the population with an IQ below the key score of 70 but there are people with a higher score who are still in need of services. The government document on safeguarding vulnerable adults, *No Secrets* (DoH, 2000), has a definition of a vulnerable person which would include people with learning difficulties, but this seems a negative approach to defining a section of the population by assuming they are 'automatically vulnerable'. What about the 'structural factors that influence vulnerability' (Small, 2009, p. 51)?

Williams's (2009, p. 7) definition is useful as he defines a person with a learning difficulty as 'someone who has been labelled as having difficulties in cognitive understanding, but is someone with rights [. . .] and who may need help and support to claim and exercise those rights'. He adds that such a person is someone 'whose needs and interests are not well catered for by societal structures or by the interactions of other people; he or she is a survivor of struggles to overcome disadvantage, and may need help to continue to do so' (p. 7).

As far as prevalence is concerned, Williams (2009) cites an NHS survey (2005) which suggests that 2.2 per cent of the population have a learning disability but, of that proportion, 22 per cent are not known to statutory services. Local authorities will use these percentages to estimate need in their area so they are useful in that sense.

Fundamentally, when we are thinking about people with learning difficulties it is essential to remind ourselves of the vision for this marginalised section of our communities that the government White Paper *Valuing People* (DoH, 2001) presents. The updated version of this (DoH, 2009) states that people with learning difficulties are 'people first', that they have the 'right to lead their lives like any others', that they have the right to be 'treated with the same dignity and respect', and to be enabled to have the 'same aspirations and life chances as other citizens' (DoH, 2009, p. 10). This policy, based on the theories of normalisation (Wolfensberger, 1972) and accomplishment (O'Brien and Lyle, 1987) is the bedrock of effective practice for people with learning difficulties.

In writing a chapter on people with learning difficulties, it is important to note not only what I will cover but also what I cannot within the space. I will not be looking at children with learning difficulties. The period of transition from childhood to adulthood is of great importance to young people with learning difficulties as there is evidence (DoH, 2001; Carnaby and Lewis, 2005) of services failing to ease the transition from children to adult services. I will explore some of the themes in this regard, but I will mostly be focusing on adults (18-plus). Social work services for this group of potential service users are predominantly located in local authority adult care services or in integrated health and social care organisations, some of which are social enterprises divorced from the NHS and local authorities. Typically, social workers will be located in integrated community learning difficulties teams (CDLTs).

Social work practice in learning difficulties services

Individuals with a learning difficulty may access social work services in numerous ways. Many people will, as children, already be known to the education and health authorities and ought to be referred on to adult social care (and social work) services through the process known as transition (Carnaby and Lewis, 2005). This process has not worked well in many areas (DoH, 2001), with individuals being left with little support to enable them to live full and rewarding lives as adults. Many authorities have now, under pressure from an alliance of national organisations such as the Valuing People team, carers and people with learning difficulties themselves, set up specialist services to ensure that young adults receive support as they move from childhood and the education system to adult life.

Most local authorities or adult services organisations will have specialist learning difficulties teams to receive referrals, make assessments and link service users to resources. These are generally integrated teams of professionals from nursing, psychology, psychiatry and occupational therapy as well as social work who will work together, in an ideal setting, as an integrated community learning difficulties team (CDLT) to ensure the best possible outcomes for individuals referred to them.

A referral coming into the team, from a relative, general practitioner (GP), friend or member of the community, from another organisation such as a school, voluntary organisation or the police (if there is a need for safeguarding) or a referral from the person with learning difficulties themselves, will be allocated for assessment to the individual professional with appropriate knowledge. Where these issues are to do with social matters such as relationships, position in the community, need for occupation, housing or where an individual is believed to be in need of safeguarding from abusive behaviour, more than likely a social worker will be the allocated person.

Assessment of need is a duty under section 47 of the NHS and Community Care Act 1990 and there has been a considerable amount of guidance on how to carry out such an assessment so that it focuses on the individual and his or her expressed or apparent needs (needs-led assessment), rather than his or her fit with existing services (resource-led assessment), or indeed his or her eligibility for access to services under the fair access to care services (FACS) criteria (eligibility-led assessment).

When assessing need, it is worth noting that Doyal and Gough (1991) argue that it is critical autonomy which is (in addition to basic needs such as food, shelter, safety and warmth) the universal need that all human beings require to be met. This concept urges us to consider the ways in which service users' voices can be heard so that they have autonomy in how their needs are assessed. Critical autonomy is important because individuals and communities require understanding of their needs in order to make realistic and effective choices. People with learning difficulties are often assumed not to have critical autonomy. It would be part of the social work role to enable people to learn how to make judgements, with support. This concept of need as autonomy is helpful because it reminds us that it is service users who must be at the centre of the assessment of need, to avoid professionals, politicians, managers or family carers with other agendas making decisions for people with learning difficulties.

This theory of need fits with the 'exchange' model of assessment that is argued by Smale, et al. (1993) as the best fit with the empowering, user-centred, needs-led practice that the policy rhetoric suggests. This model starts from an assumption that service users are experts in their situations. It assumes the worker has expertise in the process of problem-solving with others and takes responsibility for arriving at the optimum resolution of problems within resource constraints (Smale et al., 1993). The *exchange model* is contrasted with the *questioning model*, which reflects a traditional professional approach in which practitioners assume they have the expertise to understand service users, their needs and the appropriate resources to meet them, as well as the *procedural model* in which managers construct tools of assessment which measure deficits in functionality so that appropriate services can be provided to fill the gaps.

Despite this, the tools that are required for assessment in integrated adult services organisations tend to reflect the procedural model. These models, based on the medical model of disability and focused on deficits in function, may be helpful for managers establishing the eligibility of people to access services and to manage scarce resources, but it is not congruent with the principles of person-centred practice or personalisation, which are the government policies in meeting the need of adult service users (DoH, 2007, 2012). The procedural approach 'undermines autonomy and independence' (Small, 2009, p. 62), and is therefore at odds with the rhetoric of government policy.

Another difficulty that usually precedes the assessment process is the making of judgements as to whether an individual fits the eligibility criteria laid out in the FACS (DoH, 2003). This process is used to establish an individual's priority in relation to four levels: critical, substantial, moderate or low. Most authorities in England and Wales only provide services at the critical and substantial levels, with many only meeting needs when they have reached the critical level (e.g. an emergency requiring immediate action). This policy undermines government rhetoric of choice and control. How can anyone have choice or control when they are in the kind of emergency envisaged by these priority criteria?

The current policy being implemented within statutory adult care services is personalisation and person-centred practice. As far as social work practice in contemporary organisations is concerned, personalisation will mean assessing people with critical or substantial needs and then providing them with a personalised budget that will establish an amount of money that they, their carers and supporters or the local authority can utilise to purchase services to meet their needs. The tool currently being developed in some statutory organisations is the resource allocation system (RAS). The tool can be used by service users and their carers or by professional practitioners to establish the amount of money they are entitled to, assuming they meet the eligibility threshold.

Risk assessment is an area for social work practice that has become huge in the wake of personalisation. Personalisation is intended to enable individuals to take control of the services that they require and to give them more choice in how their needs are met. It was recognised that this policy puts some individuals into vulnerable positions. Having amounts of money that are theirs to spend on services has proved tempting for some carers and others who have abused the trust of those in receipt of personalised budgets. In addition, where people have been left with no access to collective services, such as day services, they are then at the mercy of support systems such as personal assistants that they are responsible for organising, managing and maintaining and this can leave them vulnerable as well (Ferguson and Woodward, 2009). In order to address this vulnerability the practice of safeguarding has been developed (see Chapter 11).

Legal framework

The key policy for safeguarding is *No Secrets* (DoH, 2000) which requires local authorities to make arrangements to safeguard vulnerable adults. The Association of Directors of Adult Social Services (ADASS) published a framework of good practice (2005), which included the following main principles:

- *Empowerment*. Presumption of person-led decisions and informed consent.
- *Protection*. Support and representation for those in greatest need.
- *Prevention*. Better to take action before harm occurs.
- *Proportionality*. Proportionate and least intrusive response appropriate to the risk presented.
- *Partnership*. Local solutions through services working with communities who have a part in reporting neglect and abuse.
- *Accountability*. Transparency in delivering safeguarding.

No Secrets (DoH, 2000) defines abuse as consisting of single or repeated acts. It may be physical, verbal or psychological, it may be an act of neglect or an omission to act, or it may occur when a vulnerable person is persuaded to enter into a financial or sexual transaction to which he or she has not consented, or cannot consent. *No Secrets* lists the types of abuse as physical, emotional, sexual, financial, neglect, or discriminatory (including hate crime). Since then, two further categories have been added, including institutional, in the wake of institutional abuse, for example, Winterbourne View (Flynn, 2012).

The threshold for an investigation requires the following three areas to be satisfied: (1) Is the person a vulnerable adult? (2) Have they been abused by a third party? (3) Did this result in significant harm? Usual practice is to seek consent from the person with learning difficulties, but where there are immediate concerns it may be necessary to act to protect a 'vulnerable' adult without consent. This would be particularly the case if the individual was assessed as lacking 'capacity' under the Mental Capacity Act (MCA) 2005.

No Secrets (DoH, 2000) states safeguarding requires a multi-agency approach. After information has been gathered a strategy meeting involving all parties, including the service user and supporters, would be organised. At this meeting, protection planning would be discussed, agreed and put into place. Given the eligibility thresholds, this work has become a major priority within statutory services with it being a large proportion of what a social worker working with people with learning difficulties would be doing on a day-to-day basis. Whilst this work is clearly very important, it has, in some organisations, been at the cost of more creative and preventative work.

Organisational policy and procedure ought to provide a good framework for dealing with risk and the Mental Capacity Act provides the legal framework. The five principles of the Act outline effective practice:

1   A 'person must be assumed to have capacity unless it is established that he lacks capacity' (section 1(2)).
2   A person cannot be treated as unable to make decisions 'unless all practical steps to help him to do so have been taken without success' (section 1(3)).
3   A 'person is not to be treated as unable to make a decision merely because he makes an unwise decision' (section 1(4)).
4   Action taken to be in the 'best interests' of the individual (section 1(5)).
5   Any action should be as least 'restrictive of the person's right and freedom of action' as possible (section 1 (6)).

The Act states that a person lacks capacity if she or he is unable to make a decision for herself or himself in relation to a matter due to 'an impairment of, or a disturbance in the functioning of the mind or brain' (section 2(1)), which clearly affects some people with learning difficulties. The Act provides a test that needs to be carried out to determine capacity, insisting that

A person is unable to make a decision for himself if (s)he is unable:

a   To understand the information relevant to the decision
b   To retain the information
c   To use or weigh that information as part of a process of making the decision or
d   To communicate the decision (either by talking, using sign language or any other means).

(MCA 2005, section 3 (1))

The Act also points out that capacity can fluctuate and that a decision to take action to protect someone, or, especially depriving them of their liberty (Deprivation of Liberty Safeguards [DOLS]) only relate to the period within which they lack capacity. Such decisions, therefore, need to be regularly reviewed.

Where decisions are complicated or contested, the Court of Protection can, under section 15, use its power to make 'declarations' as to whether a person lacks capacity. Where the court has decided that an individual lacks capacity, it can make decisions on a person's behalf, and/or appoint a deputy to make those decisions. The following covers relevant policies and legislation in relation to working with people with learning difficulties.

Valuing People (DoH, 2001) and *Valuing People Now* (DoH, 2009): *Valuing People* was developed by the DoH professionals and politicians with the active assistance of people with learning difficulties and their supporters. The four principles of *Valuing People* are: rights, independence, choice and inclusion. In practice, the document suggests advocacy, self-advocacy, person-centred planning and direct payments as the key approaches to achieve these principles.

Our Health, Our Care, Our Say (DoH, 2006) and *Putting People First* (DoH, 2007): *Our Health, Our Care, Our Say* was produced following consultation with the public including users of learning difficulties services (see In Control website for their significant role in self-directed support and personal budgets). The document has four main goals: (1) Better prevention and early intervention; (2) More choice and a stronger voice; (3) Tackling inequalities and improving access to services; (4) More support for people with long-term needs. This White Paper is the basis for most mainstream policy today as the principles were taken on by the current coalition government. It also laid the way for the document *Putting People First* which 'sets the direction for adult social care over the next 10 years and more' (DoH, 2007). This document describes a society where people can have choice and control in their lives and has a focus on early intervention and prevention (DoH, 2007).

Equity and Excellence: Liberating the NHS (DoH, 2010a); *Caring for our Future: Reforming Care and Support* (DoH, 2012): coalition policy has reiterated previous government policy (DoH, 2010a, 2012), although the push towards a market of care with increased privatisation of health and social care services has been a priority for the coalition. People with learning difficulties have noted these moves in some areas of the country, notably resisting the closure of day services in a campaign in Edinburgh in which people with learning difficulties wore tee-shirts proclaiming 'We are not for sale' as they noted that service users are becoming commodities within a lucrative market for private companies in the UK (Ferguson and Woodward, 2009).

A Vision for Adult Social Care: Capable Communities and Active Citizens (DoH, 2010b): this document lists areas of focus with none of them very different to Labour policy. These are prevention; personalisation; personal budgets, preferably as direct payments; partnership; plurality, with the variety of people's needs provided within a market; protection, ensuring safeguards against the risk of abuse or neglect; productivity; people, focusing on the whole workforce, including social workers, alongside carers and the people who use services, to lead the changes proposed (DoH, 2010b).

Equality Act 2000: this is another central piece of legislation for social workers working with people defined as 'disabled' because disability is one of the nine 'protected characteristics' listed in the Act. Anyone with a protected characteristic, such as someone with learning difficulties, is protected by the Act against direct and indirect discrimination and victimisation. Local authorities have a duty to promote disability equality and carry out impact assessments to ensure their policies or procedures do not unwittingly discriminate against people. In addition, the Equality Act requires organisations to change the way services are delivered by providing extra equipment if necessary (i.e. duty to make reasonable adjustments). See also the Human Rights Act 1998 as discussed in Chapter 1.

Case example

Ellie lives at home with her parents Frank and Martha. She is a 37-year-old black woman with learning difficulties who has not received services since leaving special schooling when she was 17. She is described by her parents as aggressive and demanding. She has virtually no speech.

Ellie's parents are in their seventies and not in good health. They want Ellie to remain living with them but find it hard to cope. Ellie was referred following a visit by their GP to see Frank who had presented with severe chest pains. Their GP was concerned that the stress of caring for Ellie was getting too much.

Ellie has a younger sister, May, who lives nearby and is married with three children. May feels her parents are overprotective and that Ellie would benefit from living independently. This view has caused problems in her relationship with her parents, who feel that Ellie does not have the capacity to live away from home and that she would be vulnerable to abuse or exploitation if she attended services.

Ellie's final school report described her as a happy young person with an interest in other people and a love of art – both viewing it and painting. She was also interested in music at school and particularly enjoyed singing and dancing. Her speech was described as poor but she was able to express her wishes using speech, Makaton and other communication, including writing and drawing. She had friends at school but no longer sees them, although several live close, living independently with support. You discover that there were two particular teachers at her school whom Ellie was close to. These teachers express an interest in reconnecting with Ellie as part of their project to keep in touch with former pupils. A People First group meets in Ellie's town and they run different groups for people with learning difficulties, including a 'speaking up' group and a support group for people living independently. People First has been commissioned by the local authority to provide advice and guidance for people with learning difficulties interested in getting a personal budget. There used to be a day centre for people with learning difficulties in the town but this has been closed in the wake of the policy shift to personalisation and the desire of the local authority to get eligible people on to personal budgets. There are a couple of informal day and evening clubs run by voluntary organisations, aimed at people with learning difficulties.

The organisation you work for has a policy of only meeting needs at the critical and substantial levels but has a stated policy to provide early intervention and preventative services where possible. Some colleagues have managed to advocate on behalf of service users through decision-making processes and the panel has agreed to fund one or two people with learning difficulties who do not strictly meet the eligibility thresholds.

Best practice in professional social work for people with learning difficulties

Person-centred planning (PCP) is one of the principle approaches that policy and normative literature on social work for people with learning difficulties tells us is the best way to proceed (Carr, 2008; Small, 2009; Williams, 2009). In Ellie's case it is right to start with Ellie herself, although the 20 years which have elapsed since she left school will have entrenched Frank and Martha's views about Ellie's capacity. For this reason, it will be important to maintain good contact with Ellie's parents and offer them the opportunity for an assessment of their needs as carers under the Carers (Equal Opportunities) Act 2004.

PCP requires the social worker to focus on Ellie herself, concentrating on her strengths, preferences and aspirations (Carr, 2008). She should be the person at the centre of the process of assessment so that her voice can be heard and she can express her choices (Small, 2009; Williams, 2009, Duffy and Fulton, 2010). Providing information, advice and advocacy so that Ellie can make an informed decision is essential. The concept of 'normalisation', enabling people with learning difficulties to have similar lifestyles to others, and 'socially valued roles' (Small, 2009, p. 53) is helpful here.

The required outcome, from government policy, is that someone like Ellie should be offered a personal budget or direct payment, which she can use to purchase, with assistance, the services that will meet her needs. People with learning difficulties were originally denied access to direct payments (DPs) by law as they were assumed to lack capacity, and even following a change in the law, people with learning difficulties are still one of the groups missing out on DPs. This denial is often the result of paternalistic attitudes from social workers (Baldwin, 2006).

There are two problems in adopting a person-centred approach with Ellie. First, there is Frank and Martha's overprotectiveness and, second, Ellie herself appears to have little in the way of communication skills and is also 'aggressive and demanding'. Brewster and Ramcharan (2005) argue that PCP requires good communication skills to gain knowledge from service users and their circle of support. It is often the case that parental obstruction to self-directed support comes in the wake of experiences that services are not appropriate to their children's needs. It may be that Frank and Martha were concerned at the lack of attention paid to Ellie's cultural needs. An anti-racist and culturally sensitive approach might persuade them that you are serious in understanding their concerns. In addition, Ellie is potentially vulnerable and her parents would need to see that, whatever path is taken, Ellie is not placed in danger. Williams (2009) argues that if a parent thinks their child is getting the best help, they may be less likely to be overprotective.

In working with Ellie and her family it is important to work with people's 'capacities and not their deficits' (Small, 2009, p. 59). This fits with the social model of disability, and would roll back the ways in which Ellie has been marginalised from ordinary living over the previous 20 years. Capacity is a word frequently used in social work for people with learning difficulties, as it fits with the safeguarding agenda. There will be many occasions in which social workers will need to make a judgement, using the mental capacity checklist, to assess whether an individual is able to be a part of decision making in their lives. For Ellie, the relationship that enables her to speak her mind, which gives her a degree of autonomy and self-determination in the process of assessment, will be the best way of reaching that goal.

There has been a tendency within social work to focus on individuals, adopting a problem-focused approach. The practice of PCP in social work for people with learning difficulties concentrates on the individual in their community. Research has shown (MacConkey, 2005) that people with learning difficulties are unlikely to have many friends in their networks so building community support or circles of friends is a key to effective social work for people with learning difficulties. Circles of support enable the person to learn social skills that are likely to stop them being seen as 'difficult' and enable them to build their self-confidence (MacConkey, 2005; Williams, 2009).

In order to build circles of support, and to work towards community inclusion for Ellie, it is necessary to adopt a community approach. As her social worker you would have the resource of her parents, her sister and her friends and teachers from school. Extending her network of friends and support into the service user led organisation People First may enable Ellie to feel listened to and respected. People with learning difficulties are often marginalised within communities, so her parents' concerns may be built on reality. Reaching out to that community, through a range of community social work methods (Teater and Baldwin, 2012) will have the effect of reducing ignorance, prejudice and oppression.

An advocacy may also be appropriate. Advocacy can be internal for the social worker (standing up for the needs of the service user within your organisation) or it can be external (providing support and advice for an individual such as Ellie). Advocacy involves 'standing up for the rights of the person' (Williams, 2009, p. 121). It means protecting people with learning difficulties from harm, 'helping them to have a voice' and 'arguing for more resources to meet their needs' (p. 121). Advocacy is informed by principles of autonomy and choice (Williams, 2009) and enabling rather than doing things for people (Duffy, 2003).

Brandon and Brandon (2001, p. 20) link advocacy to empowerment, which enables the person with learning difficulties to 'take decisions and make choices in all areas of life'. They argue advocacy is a tool for ensuring autonomy – enabling people to express their own needs and personhood. Advocacy is about a transfer of power, reducing social control and bringing the social back into social work. Chomsky (2003), the anarchist writer, argues that we should all, in our daily lives, seek to avoid the illegitimate use of power. He speaks of using legitimate power to ensure his grandson is safe on a busy street, but notes that examples of power being wielded to prevent someone doing something they wish to do are almost invariably illegitimate. Using the Chomsky maxim requires a critically reflective approach to our practice (Fook, 2002). In working with someone like Ellie we would need to constantly reflect on the way in which we were using our power. Was it person centred? Would Ellie approve of what we are doing? Does it result in her needs being met? If all of these questions can be answered with assurance that our actions are in her best interests, then such advocacy will be a powerful tool in identifying and meeting her needs.

When putting together the series of actions that will meet Ellie's identified needs, it will be crucial to work in alliance with key people. Ellie has to be at the centre of this process, but it will also require the involvement of others. Finding collaborative ways of working with Ellie and her circle of support in the design, delivery and evaluation of services fits well with what is increasingly known as co-production (Carr, 2008). Brandon and Brandon (2001) refer to a model for working towards autonomy in co-production 'being told; being consulted; being a partner; being in control'. Ellie being in control, with backing from her circle of support, is a feasible goal to be aiming at and a very different one to the life that she has been living for 20 years. This is an area where social work really can and does make a difference in people's lives.

Benefits and challenges to working with people with learning difficulties

There may be people who will say that the proposed approach to social work for people with learning difficulties is too optimistic and does not take into account the reality of reduced budgets and managerialist targets. Williams (2009), for instance, argues that social work practices such as advocacy can put social workers at risk from managerially inclined managers. Williams (2009) and the radical literature (Baldwin, 2011) reminds us of the importance of using social work values, the law, policy and practice guidance to argue our position. Most statutory organisations sign up to the rhetoric of government policy, which reflects the PCP approach, choice and control for service users. We need to hold politicians and managers to account for the policies that they make. They reflect the demands of the service user movement and fit perfectly with social work values. We will have to work collectively as a profession to defend this set of values and this way of working. In general, social work for people with learning difficulties has often shown the way in good practice, but we can do even better. We will do better when we stick together as a profession, using collective action in alliance with people with learning difficulties to build a better approach to practice. This would be a person-centred, community-based practice built on the autonomy of individuals and communities so that we can all be in charge of our own lives (Duffy and Fulton, 2010).

Social workers: What do people with learning difficulties say they would like?

I spent time talking to people with learning difficulties, most of them from Wiltshire People First. I asked them, 'What would make a good social worker?' I am grateful to them all individually and to Wiltshire People First, for taking my questions seriously and for answering candidly. Their responses are summarised below.

Relationships

Listening was described as a key skill. 'A good social worker will listen and put himself out. Some couldn't be bothered, didn't want to do it, listen to me that is. They took note of other people's views, parents and staff instead of me.' One person who had social workers who did not listen said, 'Tell them that they should always take time and listen to the person. Don't talk quickly. Don't assume that just because they have a disability they can't do things'. Another person said that she felt scared of the power her social worker had. It was 'Interesting in the end. I felt I could speak out. I found it hard to explain. They made me feel more comfortable. They spoke to me bit by bit and took my hearing difficulty into account. I asked if I could say what I want to say and when they said "yes", the social worker listened to me.'

   Taking time to get to know the individual is hard with resource constraints in social work organisations, but this was important to the people I spoke with. 'It is important that she knows me, knows when I am saying I am OK but I'm not.'

   One person I spoke with told me, 'It won't work unless you have that working relationship before you go into those personal details.' She had a direct payment, which she used to employ a number of personal assistants (PAs) and she said of her social worker, 'She knows the ins and outs of me and when I am not well. She knows how to advise the staff what to do to help me – a mellow chat with the staff about what they can and can't do. Sometimes I want to know [what they are talking about], sometimes I don't. Mostly I feel in control.' This same person said that there are some special skills that students need to learn at university but mostly they need 'good communication skills, respect for individuals and they should treat other people as they want to be treated themselves'.

Offering choices

The importance of listening needs to be demonstrated in consequent action as well. One person stated that a social worker should be 'listening to what I want and doing what I ask. He wouldn't move me where I wanted to be only to where he knew.' Knowledge of a range of community services that would meet needs is also a quality for social workers.

Making things happen

'The social worker helped me to get a direct payment. The social worker did an assessment and listened to me and helped. I know how to ask and who to ask, but there are some people, even in Speaking Up Groups, who don't know who to ask. If anything goes wrong or I want to move on, she knows the people who will help me, refer me on.'

Problems of resource shortfalls

Some people I spoke with had a social worker when they needed one but then that person disappeared. Unless there is a regular review system, which does not operate in many areas, problems will not be identified or dealt with. One person said to me, 'Service users need a named person to contact, but, because of resource problems, all you get is a call centre to contact which is not helpful.' Another concluded, 'There should be more funding and more social workers' if what service users want and need is to be met.

Questions

 How do the views of the service users expressed in this example match with your views of social work?

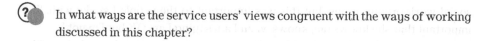 In what ways are the service users' views congruent with the ways of working discussed in this chapter?

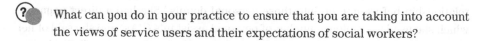 What can you do in your practice to ensure that you are taking into account the views of service users and their expectations of social workers?

Further resources and suggested readings

Cambridge, P. and Carnaby, S. (2005) *Person Centred Planning and Care Management with People with Learning Disabilities*. London: Jessica Kingsley Publishers.

Grant, G., Goward, P., Richardson, M. and Ramcharam, P. (eds) (2005) *Learning Disability: A Life Cycle Approach to Valuing People*. Maidenhead: Open University Press.

Williams, P. (2009) *Social Work with People with Learning Difficulties*, 2nd edn. Exeter: Learning Matters.

Websites

Circles Network – www.circlesnetwork.org.uk

Imagine: Finding New Stories For People Who Experience Disabilities – www.dimagine.com

In Control – www.in-control.org.uk

Mencap – www.mencap.org.uk

8 Physical disabilities

Clare Evans

Introduction

The legal definition of disabled people is defined by the Equalities Act 2010: 'A person has a disability for the purposes of the Act if he or she has a physical or mental impairment and the impairment has a substantial and long-term adverse effect on his or her ability to carry out normal day-to-day activities (S6(1)).' This includes people with long-term mental health issues, people with learning difficulties and those with frailty of old age in addition to disabled people with physical impairments, long-term conditions and sensory impairments. According to the Department for Work and Pensions (DWP) (2012), 6.1 million (20 per cent) of women and 5.4 million (18 per cent) of men were disabled in the UK during 2010 to 2011 and Contact a Family (2012) reports there are 770,000 disabled children under the age of 16 in the UK, which equates to one child in 20.

Historically, social work has grown up within separate local authority departments defined by long-term budgetary headings and a medical model of 'disability'. Therefore, those using social care services have been grouped separately into those with mental health problems and those with learning difficulties, whilst disabled people with physical and sensory impairments have been generally grouped in the same department as older people. This means local authority departments have gathered statistics about disabled people with physical and sensory impairments under the age of 65 and, separately, those of older people. The Office for National Statistics identified that 566,000 service users received social care services from 2008 to 2009, and 65 per cent of the service users who received community-based services had a physical disability. In local authority social services from 2010 to 2011, 32 per cent of male service users and 42 per cent of female service users under the age of 65 had physical disabilities whilst 82 per cent of male and 84 per cent of female service users had physical disabilities in the over-65 care group.

Statistics about disabled children from the age of 0 to 18 are gathered separately from adults. According to Contact a Family (2012), only 8 per cent of families with disabled children get services from their local social services.

All local authority social work departments operate using nationally defined eligibility criteria that define which disabled people and children are entitled to services. Most social work is provided to those entitled to the service after assessment, yet some voluntary organisations, sometimes with a particular emphasis or stress on community development techniques, do offer social work services to those deemed less in need.

Many of the adults and children described above may be in households with other family members who play a significant caring role in relation to them (e.g. partners and children sometimes referred to as 'young carers'). According to the Office for National Statistics, around six million people (11 per cent of the population aged five years and over) provide unpaid care in the UK and it is anticipated that by 2037 the number of carers will increase to nine million (Carers UK, 2012). Approximately, 1.2 million men and 1.6 million women aged 50 and over in England and Wales were providing unpaid care representing 16 per cent and 17 per cent of older men and women respectively. Such family carers are now recognised in legislation as having their own entitlement to a formal assessment of need and allocation of service resources if they reach the necessary needs threshold.

Social work practice within physical disability services

There are two broad access routes into social work services within the local authority for disabled people with physical and sensory impairments depending on the nature of their impairment and how it was referred. Those who obtain their physical impairment through trauma or a sudden development or deterioration of a condition are often referred through a hospital social work department at the time of preparing to leave hospital. This in itself can define the immediate social work tasks as the pressure for hospital beds influences the initial primary goal. The other route to access services, through the community, could include referrals by general practitioners (GPs), district nurses, family carers or self. This is often due to deteriorating conditions and for individuals who now feel they need external assistance beyond the family. Families of disabled children are able to use the same routes of referral including self-referral.

As a result of either entry route, or another into local authorities, disabled people with physical impairments will have contact with social workers in a similar way. Within local authorities, social workers work alongside occupational therapists (OTs) and community care co-ordinators in meeting disabled and older people's needs. Such a referral may not necessarily bring immediate contact with a social worker, although everyone is entitled to ask for a full community care assessment of need. In recent years, there has been the development of care co-ordinators who are not professionally trained social workers but assist by responding to perceived need in a referral, for example, a piece of complex equipment or the supply of information. However, the needs of disabled people with physical impairments are often complex, involving emotional as well as practical support, and should be seen as referrals needing a full assessment by a social worker.

The local authority social worker carrying out the community care assessment will have responsibility for assessing need holistically with the service user under the fair access to care services (FACS) national definitions (DoH, 2003, 2010). This leads to identifying how much support the service user is entitled to, and from April 2013 each service user will be told her or his indicative personal budget for social care support from the assessment process. The social worker has the responsibility to explain that support can be provided through arrangements made by the local authority, though usually subcontracted to commercial or voluntary sector providers, such as domiciliary care. Alternatively, the service user can receive her or his support through a direct payment (DP), which service users can spend on social care support in ways they choose and is drawn up in a support plan approved by the social worker based on the indicative budget cost.

Independent organisations led by disabled people and independent brokers, some-times qualified as social workers, are available to support service users in planning their most suitable social care support. Whether the support is arranged in house or as a direct payment, it is subject to financial assessment and means testing, yet those not eligible for free ongoing services are still entitled to a full assessment of need.

In carrying out assessments in response to referrals, social workers in local authorities carry out a variety of roles to enable service users to meet their needs better in the community. They may link with other professionals in the department, such as occupational therapists, link with community nursing teams or voluntary organisations that are able to provide community-based support, such as transport and shopping assistance. An additional role may include one of providing informa-tion and supporting the family to talk together about the disabled person's needs being met in other ways including, perhaps, a changed role for the family carer. Social workers in voluntary organisations will play a similar role related more specifically to the role of the agency, for example, helping people make their support plans or in meeting the needs of carers.

All families with a disabled child with significant needs have a right to self-refer to a social service team. Most local authorities have separate children's disability teams providing social work support until the child is aged 18. Like adults, all disabled children are entitled to a holistic assessment and the parents of the child to a separate carers' assessment if the impact of the disability on the carers is signifi-cant. At times, social workers link with particular sections of the National Health Service (NHS) as is relevant to the individual child's need, such as the speech and language service or the wheelchair service.

Social workers must also consider aspects of safeguarding; for example, supporting service users to examine risk as they plan the assistance they need. The social work safeguarding role has gained recognition in recent years in relation to the safeguarding of adults who use social care services in the same way as the need for the protection of children. This can be a source of tension between social workers and disabled adults with physical impairments since consideration of risk taking is not necessarily seen as legitimate and they themselves do not identify as 'vulnerable'. However, the shared recognition that disabled people with physical impairments can be put in vulnerable circumstances in a number of ways can be the starting point for discussing risk taking and avoiding unnecessary risks.

Legal framework

Before 1970 assistance with disabled people and their families came through the health service or charities. Often the charities grew out of local need linked to specific impairments and were established by those wishing to do good rather than disabled people themselves. Many of these grew into large national charities which still exist today albeit renamed to better describe their current role (e.g. the Spastics Society became SCOPE, Cheshire Homes became Leonard Cheshire Disability and the Royal National Institute for the Deaf has become Action on Hearing Loss). The assistance growing out of the health service was inevitably linked to people's medical condition.

The Chronically Sick & Disabled Person's Act 1970 led to services for disabled people becoming a social services' responsibility for the first time. Mostly the responsibility for disabled people with physical impairments was attached to welfare departments already established to assist older people. This Act established disabled people for the first time as a group in society requiring services and led to much improved physical access in society as well as in social care. The National Health Service and Community Care Act 1990 led to the reorganisation of adult social services following the Griffiths Report (DoH, 1989) stressing the importance of community care facilities and establishing the importance of assessment of needs rather than expecting individuals to fit into traditionally provided services. The Children Act 1989 also brought in separate provision for disabled children.

Social workers operate within this legal framework, which has also been modified to reflect the still increasing emphasis on encouraging the take-up of direct payments and personal budgets within the wider political agenda of personalisation (DoH, 2007), marketisation and consumer choice and control. Thus, the Community Care (Direct Payments) Act in 1997 was followed by the Direct Payments Act, which extended direct payments take-up to all adults who were able to manage them with support. More specifically for disabled people with physical impairments, the *Improving the Life Chances of Disabled People Report* (Prime Minister's Strategy

Unit [PMSU], 2005) provided an agenda for disabled people and children across all government departments, which placed the expectations of social work firmly within this policy framework nationally.

Theoretical underpinnings

The 1970 Chronically Sick and Disabled Act was significant because it was the first time that disabled people with long-term conditions were recognised in legislation as being entitled to have their needs met in various aspects of their lives including social care. This was at a time also when disabled people were developing their own identity through the growth of the disability movement defined by Campbell and Oliver (1996) as one of the new 'social movements'. This legislation led for the first time, for example, to local authorities being required to provide equipment and adaptions within homes to assist disabled people to remain living there.

A strong theoretical understanding of meeting the needs of disabled people through independent living according to their wishes also came at that time from disabled people themselves in America through the independent living movement. This was quickly adopted by disabled people in the UK, and documents listing the rights of disabled people to independent living, as defined by them, were produced both by the Derbyshire Centre for Integrated Living and the Southampton Centre for Independent Living and followed by other centres for independent living. The 12 rights of disabled people to achieve independent living are defined by the Southampton Centre for Independent Living (2012) as follows:

1   Full access to our environment.
2   A fully accessible transport system.
3   Technical aids – equipment.
4   Accessible/adapted housing.
5   Personal assistance.
6   Inclusive education and training.
7   An adequate income.
8   Equal opportunities for employment.
9   Appropriate and accessible information.
10 Advocacy (towards self-advocacy).
11 Counselling.
12 Appropriate and accessible health care provision.

These rights to provide the same quality of independent living as other citizens have included requiring local authority social workers to use resources for social care, such as to employ personal assistance, provide equipment and obtain accessible housing. This philosophy of independent living, led by disabled people themselves, gradually became adopted by professionals, including social workers, and was incorporated in legislation such as the Direct Payments Act 1997. It was also congruent with the wider philosophy of a mixed market of social care and the emphasis on meeting service users' needs and customer care. This idea has been strengthened in more recent legislation, which now requires social workers to offer all adult social care service users the opportunity to have their support in the form of direct payments if they wish and are able, either independently or with support, to manage them.

However, Oliver et al. (2012) point to the reluctance of some in the social work profession to accept the role of working alongside disabled people to assist them in achieving needs they have identified. Early models of social work were based on the medical model of disability, which tried to support disabled people to fit into existing society by making adaptions to adjust. The social model of disability (Goodley, 2004), in contrast, recognises the need for society to change in order to remove the barriers which a disabled person faces. Thus, any institutional power that social workers have through their role should be used to assist service users to navigate the system, and wider society, to reduce and eliminate barriers to achieving independent living. Priorities for a disabled person may include a provision of resources to enable the employment of sufficient personal assistance and/or the purchase of equipment to overcome any physical barriers and to meet identified need more fully. Today's emphasis on rationing in the social work role may create difficulties in being able to meet the service user's needs.

Certainly the government policy document *Putting People First* (Department of Health, 2007) puts personalisation and a changed role for social work at the heart of the current social care agenda for all adult care groups, which emphasises independent living and service user choice and control for all. Whilst essentially individualistic and entirely focused on individuals' needs, there is also recognition of the importance of peer support in assisting people to gain confidence to take control over their services and, therefore, their lives. This has raised the profile of organisations of disabled people being commissioned to deliver social care services and provide peer support, and there is a growing interest in their role in using social workers as staff within their organisations. Certainly social work students on placement in disabled people's organisations recognise the value of the learning in working alongside disabled people as equals (Evans, 2012).

Safeguarding vulnerable people, which includes disabled people with physical impairments, has been a newly emphasised role within social work in adult social care although familiar for longer in all work with children.

Best practice approaches

Personalisation, which has underpinned recent legislation, is congruent with social work theories and methods of practice, such as a person-centred approach (Teater,

2010) and a community development approach (Teater and Baldwin, 2012). The person-centred approach has enabled social workers to focus on the needs of service users within their community and to encourage service users to build their support plan with themselves at the centre. Unfortunately, the financial restrictions on the amount of care packages and the rationing social workers have been required to put into practice within local authorities has put severe limits on the amount of support available to service users. However, using a community development approach, social workers can ensure they use all resources available in the community and support service users to be part of that community to maximise the effectiveness of support available.

The more recent emphasis on community participation by all, including marginalised groups, together with concepts of carer and user involvement, first enshrined in legislation in the 1992 Community Care and NHS Act, has encouraged disabled people to get involved in giving their views collectively as well as individually about social care. This in turn can lead to increased feelings of empowerment and well-being by service users, which can itself be therapeutic and increase service users' self-esteem. Therefore, social workers can encourage such participation for therapeutic as well as political purposes. However, such involvement needs to inform policy and bring about change or service users will view it as tokenism and retreat from participation.

Social workers working alongside disabled people with physical and sensory impairments and their carers must take into account all aspects of service users' lives and needs in working with them. Whilst it is sometimes said that this group of service users know how to meet their own needs and do not need social work support beyond signposting, there is evidence that disabled service users really value the intervention of social workers and their assistance in navigating the system to obtain the support they need to live lives in the community built on the social model of disability. This can mean helping them and their families break down the barriers within society – physical, institutional, attitudinal and linguistic. Professional advocating on behalf of service users for scarce resources, such as appropriate housing, can lead to effective breakthroughs in accessing services.

The need for discussion with service users about risk taking in the context of recognising their right to take risks but not to put others at unnecessary risk is best developed within a relationship of trust. The importance of making explicit these risks at the time of support planning, for example, and a strategy being developed to deal with them is a far more satisfactory experience for service users than restrictions put on the kind of assistance they can receive. These issues are often highlighted by direct payments if service users choose to employ their own personal assistants within the home. Safeguarding, however, is relevant beyond social care in relation to hate crime and, as Oliver et al. (2012) point out, to the 'assisted dying' debate and the threat of being forced to live in an institution. Scragg and Mantell (2011) show practical examples and case studies of the relevance of safeguarding adults in social work.

The guiding principle for social workers working with this group of service users is to respect the mantra of the disability movement to decide 'nothing about us without us'. Service users' views about their own needs and how they should be met should be the starting place of all planning and delivery of services and is conducive to establishing a long-term working relationship. Unfortunately, current patterns of working and measuring performance often require workers to close a case unless there is intensive current work and so the opportunity for a long-term relationship is lost.

Case example

Colin and his wife, Cynthia, and their two teenage children live in a market town in Wiltshire. Five years ago Colin, 51, was diagnosed with multiple sclerosis (MS) and had to give up work two years ago because his condition deteriorated and he is now at home every day. Cynthia has gradually taken on a caring role as Colin's condition has worsened and has now reduced her working hours to be at home more to care for Colin. The children, John aged 15 and Rachel aged 13, live busy lives joining in school activities, but miss the family outings they all used to have and now spend most of their time at friends' houses. Recently, Cynthia has been diagnosed with depression and Colin has asked social services to be considered for the local residential care home for young adults to relieve his wife of her caring role as he feels the family would function better without him being there. What approach do you take in responding to Colin's request?

It is important that Colin's situation is seen in the context of his family and their place in the community using a community development, person-centred approach, which takes into account the social model of disability.

Colin is likely to have low self-esteem and feel disempowered by his medical diagnosis and subsequent contact with the medical services and the poor prognosis they have given him. He could potentially benefit from meeting others who have been through a similar experience and come to terms with giving up work, yet still feel valued as citizens and family members. He may at first be ambivalent or reluctant to such suggestions of peer support and may need opportunities for discussions with a social worker to look more widely at his situation rather than just consider residential care. A social worker may suggest that Colin be introduced to a local organisation of disabled people who run peer support groups or workshops for people in his situation.

Colin's request may be led by a misunderstanding of the financial situation and the services to which he is entitled. To provide him with up-to-date information relevant to himself and his family, Colin will need to be given specialist advice about benefits for himself and his family and also his entitlement to services. Because his condition has deteriorated slowly, he may not have been advised of his entitlement to a full social care assessment from the council or advice about financial management for the future now that he is not working. Therefore, the social worker can provide an assessment and outline the support in the community to which Colin is entitled, which could include using direct payments to give him maximum control to arrange support which suits his lifestyle. Colin and Cynthia may need specialist independent advice about how to protect their assets and maximise their income for the future. Cynthia will need to be involved in these discussions with Colin to decide how much of a caring role she is prepared to play if Colin stays at home.

Turning to Cynthia more specifically, her GP may have missed a possible relationship between her recent depression and increased carer's role. The social worker should work with Cynthia to help her recognise herself as a carer entitled to help in her own right and provide knowledge of financial assistance, a carer's assessment and the opportunities of membership of the local carer support group.

Finally, more general open discussion about their situation between Colin and Cynthia may help them look at John and Rachel's position and role in the family. It may be they would wish to be more included but not overburdened with Colin's weekly routine to feel they can contribute to the family and feel part of the current situation. Colin's moves to come to terms with his situation and become empowered may also lead him to have a role to play in their school or leisure life. The social worker might want to consider returning to the subject of the purpose of Colin's original referral in a discussion with the whole family, which was to be considered for residential care. This could enable the family to consider and reject this alternative while addressing Colin's feelings of worthlessness and marginalisation within the family.

Benefits and challenges to working with people with physical disabilities

The professional social worker working with disabled people with physical and sensory impairments and their carers have the opportunity of building on the strengths of the service users and carers to enable them to rediscover full lives they may have previously lived, or discover the opportunity of positive lives for the first time. Jointly identifying goals and the support needed to achieve them together with the opportunity of reviewing progress each year is satisfying and can demonstrate the effectiveness of professional social work intervention.

This benefit has been reinforced by the trends in social policy and social work theory, which have encouraged professionals to be service user led and move away from the traditional pattern of fitting service users into existing services. Research about the effects of institutionalisation (Miller and Gwynne, 1972) and the loss of residents' individual identity, together with the action of disabled people themselves in breaking out from such institutions, has led to the discrediting of this model of service which together with its high costs makes it only a solution of 'last resort'.

Instead, patterns of social care assistance such as direct payments have become seen as the ultimate in providing service users with choice and control over their lives and services. Whilst this remains so, such provision is affected by rationing and a lack of access to resources. A lack of resources makes it more difficult in the current economic climate for social workers to release sufficient funding for individual service users to live by independent living principles with access to resources to enable them to have 24-hour support and participate fully. The closure of the Independent Living Fund to new applicants has highlighted this difficulty. The importance of social workers using voluntary resources within the community to compensate as far as possible is one of the current challenges.

The overall policy of the marketisation of social care with multiple providers including a large growth in the commercial sector is held up as offering more choice of service to consumers. However, this statement assumes service users have the skills and confidence to make those choices – often at a time when their lives are in disarray after trauma or family crises. Social workers in local authorities, unable to make recommendations about choices of service, need to be aware of community resources that can assist service users, such as assertiveness training run by disabled people's organisations.

Social workers working with disabled people with physical and sensory impairments from voluntary sector settings will face the same challenges but have more flexibility in how they can assist people and often more time in which to do so. Depending on whether the setting is related to housing, volunteering, support planning or broadly community based will depend on the exact nature of the benefits and challenges of working with this group.

'Transitions' is the name given to disabled children's move from the children's section of the local authority to adult social care. While a smooth transition of services as the service user moves from childhood to adult life has been the subject of central policy guidance, it has been difficult to deliver at local level because of the competing demands of department budgets. This remains the challenge for social workers in relation to maintaining professional standards.

Anti-oppressive considerations

Disabled people have been identified as a marginalised and discriminated against group for over 30 years and recent legislation has identified them as having 'protected characteristics' like other groups such as race, age and gender. Therefore, all social workers will be working within the broad legal framework of the Equalities Act 2010. In addition, statutory social workers operate within the local authority disability equality duty. The legislation will affect the service users in all aspects of their lives; for example, employment and access to services in addition to adult social care.

There are also considerations relating to gender, race and culture, which social workers should be aware of in order to avoid anti-oppressive practice, particularly in relation to expectations of independent living. For example, in some cultures and groups the right of disabled people and children with physical and sensory impairments and long-term conditions to have access to the same quality of life as other citizens is not upheld and so working with family members in the interests of the service user may produce conflict difficult to resolve (Peters, 2011). The social worker in some cases can play a key role in facilitating discussion and assisting different family members to move towards each other in attitudes. Likewise, different expectations of men's and women's roles in the home by different members of the family may affect their assumptions about what support should be provided.

The usefulness of such flexible support as direct payments is its ability to adjust to individuals' situations, and the accompanying guidance shows how they can be used in relation to different cultural considerations. For example, whilst the use of direct payments to pay family members for providing social care is usually not permitted, in some circumstances where service users cannot find care support from their own culture, apart from within their own family, there is flexibility about how they can be used.

Overarching all these considerations is that social workers need to consider the needs of the service user as paramount and acknowledge that the needs of the personal informal carer should be considered as separate and entitled to support as well.

Summary

Disabled people with physical impairments are not a large proportion of those seeking assistance from local authorities and so it is not always recognised as a social work specialism in its own right. However, it has been shown that this group of people in need often require the use of the social worker over time to build fulfilling lives in addition to the short-term presenting problem to the local authority. Social workers with a strong commitment to disability equality and a good understanding of the rights of independent living can give service users the confidence to make plans for a fulfilled life as equal citizens. The need for the provision of practical support such as equipment and domiciliary care is accompanied by the need for the social worker to establish a relationship of ally and support to the service user to self-advocate within the wider society. Since people's needs must be met holistically and disabled people are often part of family units, it may mean that the social worker will be working with family carers as well to achieve the results identified by the user.

📖 CASE STUDY

Susan is a 45-year-old single parent with the progressive long-term impairment of rheumatoid arthritis for 12 years, who lives with her daughter, Flora aged 12 and a half in a small town. She has been working as a clerical officer in a local office and received disability living allowance in addition to her wage, but has no means tested benefits. Susan's condition has gradually deteriorated and at a recent visit to her GP she accepted his suggestion that she have a referral to the local social service department to see what help they could provide to make life easier for herself and Flora. You have now been asked to follow up this referral to the local authority and need to prepare to visit Susan.

Questions

(?) *Financial.* Is Susan's wage sufficient for Flora and herself? How is she affected by recent benefits changes? Is Susan aware of further help she can get through the Department of Work and Pensions Access to Work Scheme? Does she need information about public transport concessions for disabled people and their carers?

(?) *Family dynamics.* Flora has grown up as the child of a disabled mother. How much practical assistance does she give her mother? Does she identify as a young carer? Are there any recent changes in Susan's physical impairment making things difficult for Flora and Susan? Does Flora need any external support as a carer, if necessary, and have the support of school?

(?) *Aids and adaptions for independent living in the home.* Susan's condition has deteriorated so you need to ask her about any assistance required in the home, such as stairlifts, bath seats and hoists, grab rails, raised toilet seats, walking aids, or grabbers for picking up dropped items. Is she in need of a wheelchair from the NHS? Susan may not be aware such things exist or how she can access them.

(?) *Personal care and support.* Susan may not be aware of her possible entitlement to assistance with getting up in the morning and the opportunity of a full community care assessment.

(?) *Opportunities to use community resources.* Is Susan aware of community organisations and the support they provide to disabled people, such as transport schemes for hospital appointments, assistance with shopping and gardening help? What is available in Susan's geographical area?

Peer support resources. Does Susan identify as a disabled person? Would she gain confidence and energy from being a member of a local organisation of disabled people where she will meet people with more experience of using services and campaigning for a better society? Is it relevant for Flora to identify as a young carer? If so, does she want to link in with others?

Further resources and suggested readings

Campbell, J. and Oliver, M. (1996) *Disability Politics: Understanding our Past, Changing our Future.* London: Routledge.

Department of Health (DoH) (2010) *Putting People First: Planning Together—Peer Support and Self-directed Support.* www.thinklocalactpersonal.org.uk/_library/Resources/Personalisation/Personalisation_advice/PT_Final (accessed 19 November 2012).

Morris, J. (1993) *Community Care or Independent Living.* York: Joseph Rowntree Foundation.

Morris, J. (1993) *Independent Lives: Community Care and Disabled People.* Basingstoke: Palgrave Macmillan.

National Centre for Independent Living (NCIL) (2008) *Peer Support and the Personalisation: A Review Prepared for the Department of Health.* http://tinyurl.com/3zzunsu (accessed 24 May 2011).

Oliver, M., Sapey, B. and Thomas, P. (2012) *Social Work with Disabled People,* 4th edn. Basingstoke: Palgrave Macmillan.

Think Local, Act Personal Partnership (2011) *Think Local Act Personal: A Sector-wide Commitment to Moving Forward with Personalisation and Community-based Support.* www.thinklocalactpersonal.org.uk/_library/Resources/Personalisation/ (accessed 19 November 2012).

Websites

Equality and Human Rights Commission – www.equalityhumanrights.com

Think Local, Act Personal – www.thinklocalactpersonal.org.uk/

9 Older adults

Barbra Teater and Jill Chonody

Introduction

Within the UK and many other western countries, 'older' adults are those individuals who are aged 65 years and older. Older adults constitute the majority of health and social care service users, which is expected to rise as the population continues to age (Department of Health [DoH], 2010a). In 2010, 17 per cent of the UK population was 65 years or older and is expected to increase to 23 per cent in the year 2035. The largest population increase will be experienced in the 85 years and older age cohort (Office for National Statistics [ONS], 2012a).

Classifying individuals by age leads to an assumption that these cohorts have shared needs, experiences and aspirations. Older adults are not a homogeneous group and not everyone over the age of 65 will have the same types of needs nor require similar types of services. Despite this, the likelihood of receiving social care services does increase with age and typically occurs at a time when coping skills may not be adequate to address a physical, emotional or social need (Jones, 2012). Older adults may be referred or seek social care services due to physical frailty or impairment, mental health difficulties, financial difficulties, caring responsibilities and needs, housing needs, substance misuse, or abuse or neglect.

Social work practice with older adults

Older adults tend to access social work services when they experience a change in their physical, mental or emotional health and at times when their coping skills may be overwhelmed given the presenting problem(s). This could lead to older adults accessing services that are designed to focus on specific needs, such as older adult mental health teams or multidisciplinary older adults teams. Other available services might encompass all adults (18 plus) with a specific need, such as physical disabilities or learning disabilities, which is in contrast to those services that include generic adult teams, such as short-term (reablement), long-term, safe-guarding or hospital-based teams. Because older adults are not a homogeneous group, they do not require a specific 'older' adult service as they are most likely experiencing difficulties that can be faced by an adult of any age. Separating out services by age could be seen as a form of ageism. Yet for some older adults, their ability to cope with stressors may be exasperated by poverty, poor housing, social isolation and exclusion, changes in social and personal support networks and ageism (Jones, 2012), which social work teams specific to older adults could more fully address. Late life depression and dementia, although not a normal part of the ageing process, are two conditions commonly experienced by individuals over 65 years, which serves as a strong rationale for mental health teams specific to older adults.

When considering statutory services, many local authorities will require older adults to go through the same entry and access routes as all adults, except for those local authorities that have specific older adults teams (e.g. 65-plus mental health teams). The primary task of social workers when working with older adults is to assess for and implement social care within the community. Community care was defined by the Department of Health (DoH) in *Caring for People* (1989), which served as the basis for the National Health Service and Community Care (NHS & CC) Act 1990 that underpins the majority of social work activities with adults. Community care means providing services and support: those people who are affected 'by the problems of ageing, mental illness, mental handicap or physical or sensory disability need to be able to live as independently as possible in their own homes, or in "homely" settings in the community' (DoH, 1989, p. 3).

In working under community care legislation, social workers will be tasked with completing an assessment of need, suggesting a package of care to meet the needs, or referring to outside services if needs cannot be met, and completing a review of the package of care. The majority of clients who receive community care assessments and community-based services are older adults. Of the clients who received services in 2010–11 in England, 1,064,000 were age 65 and over, and 510,000 were age 64 and under. The majority of older adults (82 per cent) were receiving community-based services, followed by 16 per cent who received residential care and 7 per cent who received nursing care. In 2010–11 in England, over 660,000 new clients had completed community care assessments, 454,000 of these clients were age 65 and over (ONS, 2012b).

The reason for entering services can be dramatically different for adults over 65 compared to those who are aged 18 to 64. In 2010–11 in England, 82 per cent of older adults (18 per cent for 18–64 year olds) were receiving services for physical disabili-ties, 71 per cent (29 per cent for 18–64 year olds) for vulnerability, 46 per cent (54 per cent for 18–64 year olds) for mental health, 9 per cent (91 per cent for 18–64 year olds) for learning disabilities, and 8 per cent (92 per cent for 18–64 year olds) for substance misuse (ONS, 2012b). As the data demonstrate, social workers working in adult services most likely work with older adults at some point.

Assessment

Assessment is the core task in social work with older adults. Several pieces of legislation (see Legislation section below) place a duty on local authorities to provide an assessment of an individual's need and what community care services may be essential to address those needs along with a duty to provide certain services. An assessment of need does not automatically lead to receipt of services as provided or supported by the local authority. An individual's assessment must first highlight a level of need, or reach a particular threshold of 'eligible need', to qualify for funded social care services. The threshold of need is based on the *Fair Access to Care Services* (FACS) guidance (DoH, 2003a), which was modified through the *Prioritising Need in the Context of Putting People First: A Whole System Approach to Eligibility for Social Care* (DoH, 2010b), yet is still referred to as FACS criteria within local authorities. The eligibility criteria consist of four bands of need: (1) low; (2) moderate; (3) substantial; (4) critical. Low need usually involves being unable to carry out one or two personal care needs, domestic routines, education or work requirements, or social support or relationship breakdowns. Critical need constitutes life threatening situations, significant health problems, significant support and relationships breakdowns, or possible abuse and/or neglect. Many local authorities set the eligibility criteria at critical and substantial leaving those who are assessed as moderate or low ineligible for services. Social workers should ensure that the assessment (in collaboration with the older adult) is thorough and considers physical, social and emotional aspects. It is important for the social worker to consider certain issues that are common amongst older adults, such as social isolation, physical frailty or impairment, depression and poverty. These factors may be exacerbating the presenting problem or creating a barrier to meeting a need. Social workers should also seek to identify potential carers who may benefit from a carers assessment.

If an older adult meets the eligibility criteria for social care services, then she or he will have an assessment of finances to determine whether the services will be paid by the local authority or if she or he will have to contribute to the cost of non-residential care (DoH, 2003b). Many local authorities have a finance team that takes responsibility for client assessment of finances and billing. In regard to care homes, the government has established that individuals with £23,250 in savings will have to pay for the full cost of their care home fees, whereas individuals with less than £23,250 may qualify for council-funded care. The cost of residential and non-residential care is a separate issue to the amount (and cost) of care for which the client is eligible, which is often based on the assessment and determined through the resource allocation system (RAS). The RAS determines the amount of money that should be made available to meet a client's need and is referred to as her or his personal budget.

In conducting assessments, social workers may discover information that will require further attention, such as disclosures or suspicions of abuse or neglect or concerns about an individual's capacity to make decisions. In such situations, the social worker must follow the procedures as outlined within her or his organisation. Safeguarding concerns may require a referral to a specific safeguarding team and/or to the police (see Chapter 11 for an overview of safeguarding adults). Questions of capacity will require the social worker to review the Mental Capacity Act 2005 (see below) and may require a referral for a mental capacity assessment. Alternatively, this assessment may be completed by the social worker.

Package of care

A package of care refers to the activities and services that are provided to meet the needs as specified in the assessment, which may include services within the home or residential care. Social workers should work closely with clients to determine the best way to meet their identified needs. In-home services could include assistance with dressing or hygiene, taking medication, preparing meals or shopping for food, or transport and participation in local social activities. Often, social workers will work closely with occupational therapists (OTs) to assess the home for any adaptations that could maximise independence. Payment for services could be provided directly by the local authority either through services that it provides or commissions. Alternatively, payment may take the form of a personal budget or even direct payment. As previously discussed, a personal budget is the amount of money that is deemed necessary to meet the individual's assessed needs. A direct payment is a cash sum given to an individual to pay for the services to meet her or his assessed needs. Direct payments enable individuals to have choice and control over commissioning services: However, direct payments cannot be used to pay for residential care.

Reviews

The social worker (or other team member) will be responsible for reviewing the package of care during a timeframe specified by the local authority, which may consist of a six-month or yearly review. This is an opportunity for the social worker to reassess needs and the package of care and assist the individual in meeting his or her needs in the most effective way. For example, combining statutory and voluntary sector services, such as attending a social club at a community centre in addition to home care, may be the best way to achieve those needs.

Specialised services

The services discussed above describe general social work in adult services. In many local authorities, specialised services for older adults do exist, usually through an older adults mental health team. Mental health services are often separated along age cohorts, such as child and adolescent mental health services (CAMHS), working age and older adults. Although older adults represent a heterogeneous group, some commonalities, particularly in regard to mental health, do emerge. Mental health is defined by the World Health Organisation (WHO) (2005) as 'a state of well-being in which the individual realises his or her own abilities, can cope with the normal stresses or life, can work productively and fruitfully, and is able to make a contribution to his or her community' (p. 2).

Older adults (expect for the oldest old) are found to experience less mental ill health than younger persons, but are worse off in terms of signs of good mental health (Westerhof and Keyes, 2010). Similarly, depression is less prevalent among older adults than younger adults (Fiske et al., 2009), yet is the most common form of mental ill health in later life and can greatly impact an individual's physical, mental and social functioning (Blazer, 2003). Specific factors are found to contribute to the late onset of depression, including changes in daily activities (e.g. retirement), changes in social interactions (e.g. loss of relatives and friends), and experiencing physical decline (Holvast et al., 2012).

While depression may affect a person at any life stage, dementia is a mental health condition that mainly affects older adults. In the UK, 800,000 people are living with dementia, 170,000 of whom are 64 years of age or younger. The likelihood of developing dementia increases with age, and over one-third of people over the age of 95 have some type of dementia (Alzheimer's Society, 2013a). Dementia is defined as follows:

> A syndrome which may be caused by a number of illnesses in which there is progressive decline in multiple areas of function, including decline in memory, reasoning, communication skills and the ability to carry out daily activities. Alongside this decline, individuals may develop behavioural and psychological symptoms such as depression, psychosis, aggression and wandering, which cause problems in themselves, which complicate care, and which can occur at any stage of the illness.
>
> (DoH, 2009, p. 15)

Although the research is still unclear about the specific causes of dementia, several types of dementia have been identified, and all of them cause chemical changes in the brain that eventually lead to the death of brain tissue (DoH, 2009). These include: Alzheimer's disease; vascular dementia; Lewy body dementia; fronto-temporal dementia; with other types of syndromes or diseases causing forms of dementia (e.g. Korsakoff's syndrome; Creutzfeldt-Jakob disease) (Alzheimer's Society, 2013b; DoH, 2009).

Specific social services for older adults can be justified based on the common factors that can contribute to mental ill health in later life and the prevalence of dementia amongst the older adult population. In particular, specialised services and practice approaches for older adults with dementia are important as the majority of individuals with dementia are over the age of 65.

Community and preventative types of services

The services discussed above highlight current social work practices within statutory social work. It should be noted that there is equally a great amount of work specific to older adults that occurs outside, or alongside statutory services. Age UK is a voluntary organisation that provides advice, support and services for older adults. Many local Age UKs provide social clubs and lunch clubs, which enable older adults within the community to come together and receive social support and interaction. Other voluntary organisations, such as the WRVS, provide support services to older adults in their homes to assist ongoing independence. Many of these voluntary services can be considered preventative in nature as they aim to reduce social isolation and to prevent (or delay) the need for statutory services. Local authorities provide information of voluntary organisations offering older adult specific services.

Legal framework

Specific legislation related to older adults does not exist. Therefore, social workers must utilise various pieces of adult legislation that might be applicable. The main points of each of the pieces of legislation and policy guidance documents are highlighted below, first in respect to community care, and then in relation to protecting vulnerable adults and assessing for mental capacity. The government is currently constructing a new piece of legislation that will consolidate all of the adult social care to improve clarity and equability. The draft of the Care and Support Bill is with Parliament, and enactment is anticipated sometime in 2013. The White Paper, *Caring for Our Future: Reforming Care and Support* (HM Government, 2012) details the contents of the Care and Support Bill.

The main piece of legislation in regard to working with adults in the statutory sector is the National Health Service and Community Care (NHS&CC) Act 1990. The Act was developed based on the White Paper, *Caring for People: Community Care in the Next Decade and Beyond* (DoH, 1989), which sought to reduce the number of people in residential care by focusing on an agenda to provide care within the community. Local authorities were encouraged to take a step back in providing social care, and in turn individuals would have more freedom to seek and obtain care from the private and voluntary sectors. Under this legislation, the role of local authorities is to assess for needs, provide a package of care to meet these needs, and support individuals to remain within the community. Section 47(1) of the NHS&CC Act 1990 places a duty on local authorities to provide an assessment of need to any person who appears to be in need of community care services. As stated previously, individuals must meet the local authority's threshold of need (usually substantial or critical) to receive services. The NHS&CC Act 1990 works alongside previously established legislation relating to health and social care services, which includes the following:

1   **Part III of the National Assistance Act (NAA) 1948**. Section 21(1) places a duty on local authorities to provide accommodation for 'persons who by reason of age, illness, disability or any other circumstances are in need of care and attention which is not otherwise available to them'. Section 29(1 and 4) places a duty on local authorities to provide advice and support on services, facilities for rehabilitation and adjustment to disability, and occupational, social, cultural and recreational activities.

2   **Health Services and Public Health Act 1968**. Section 45 gives local authorities the power to provide services to older people, such as social work support, practical assistance and adaptations in the home, meals and recreation, and travel assistance for older people.

3   **Chronically Sick & Disabled Person's Act 1970**. Section 2 places a duty on local authorities to provide services to adults who fall under the criteria of section 29 of the NAA 1948. Such services as listed until section 2(1) include practical assistance in the home, access to recreational facilities both within and outside the home, travel assistance, work adaptations in the home, holidays, providing meals, and access to a telephone.

4   **Mental Health Act 1983**. Places a duty on local authorities and health services to provide after care services for individuals detained under the Act. If an individual who has been detained for treatment under section 3 is discharged to residential care under section 117, then there shall be no charge for the services.

5   **Health and Social Services and Social Security Adjudication Act 1983 (HASSASSA)**. Allows local authorities to recover a charge for services provided, such as domiciliary services, if they deem it reasonably practical for her or him to pay.

6   **Community Care (Direct Payments) Act 1996**. Requires local authorities to offer cash payments (i.e. direct payments) to individuals who have been assessed as having eligible needs, are disabled, and are aged 16 and over, or those who have parental responsibilities for a disabled child. Direct payments will only be provided to those who are assessed as willing and able to manage the direct payment either alone or with support.

7   **Community Care (Delayed Discharges Act 2003)**. Requires local authorities to provide an assessment for community care services in a timely manner in order to reduce a delayed discharge from health services.

Within England, there is currently no legislation related to the protection of vulnerable adults within social services. However, social workers are required to work within the policy guidance of *No Secrets* (DoH, 2000) when encountering suspected abuse or neglect of an adult. This guidance defines various forms of abuse (physical, sexual, psychological, financial or material, neglect and acts of omission, and discriminatory) and describes procedures for establishing an inter-agency response to abuse or suspected abuse (refer to Chapter 11 for a thorough overview of protecting vulnerable adults). Although the *No Secrets* guidance is not legislation, it can be used alongside criminal and civil laws that aim to protect adults. In England, adults must give their consent to an investigation of abuse or neglect.

Social workers may come across particular individuals who they suspect might not have the capacity to give consent. In such circumstances, the social worker must refer to the Mental Capacity Act (MCA) 2005, which states that a person lacks capacity if 'he is unable to make a decision for himself in relation to the matter because of an impairment of, or a disturbance in the functioning of, the mind or brain' (section 2(1)). A mental capacity assessment will determine capacity in regard to making a specific decision by assessing the individual's ability to: (1) understand the information relevant to the decision; (2) retain the information; (3) use or weigh that information as part of the process of making the decision; or (4) communicate his decision (whether by talking, using sign language or any other means) (section 3, MCA 2005). Capacity of the individual must be assumed until proven otherwise. If a person lacks capacity regarding a specific decision, then section 4 of the MCA outlines how to make decisions in the person's 'best interests'.

There is also no specific legislation that addresses dementia, but in 2009 the Department of Health published the National Dementia Strategy. The strategy consisted of 17 key objectives that focus on awareness, early diagnosis, access to services and intervention, quality information, improved quality of care, and more research on dementia (DoH, 2009). In 2010, the National Dementia Strategy was reviewed and updated to focus specifically on: 'good-quality early diagnosis and intervention for all; improved quality of care in general hospitals; living well with dementia in care homes; and reduced use of antipsychotic medication' (DoH, 2010c, p. 6). Social workers should be aware of how dementia can affect older adults with whom they work and how social care services can be shaped to best meet their needs.

Theoretical underpinnings

The personalisation agenda serves as the prominent theoretical underpinnings of current legislation, which seeks to give clients 'maximum choice, control and power over the support services they receive' (HM Government, 2007, p. 2). This agenda was supported through the White Paper *Our Health, Our Care, Our Say* (DoH, 2006) and the government's paper *Putting People First* (HM Government, 2007). Personalisation purports that the individual, with her or his strengths, resources, aspirations and preferences, should be the centre focus when assessing and implementing social care services. The individual should have the say and control over what her or his needs are and how they should best be met. The personalisation agenda underpins a variety of person-centred approaches, such as person-centred planning, person-centred care, person-centred support, independent living, and self-directed support (Carr, 2010).

Theories of the ageing process also underpin approaches to practice, which attempt to explain the extent to which older adults are engaged and active within society on social, political and economic levels. 'Active' ageing was developed in the late 1990s by the World Health Organisation (2002) and is defined as 'the process of optimizing opportunities for health, participation, and security in order to enhance quality of life as people age' (p. 12). Active ageing involves the empowerment of older adults to make decisions about their life, participate in family and community life and have access to services and resources. The extent to which an older adult is able to engage in 'active' ageing is theorised to be based on: health and social care services, behavioural determinants, personal determinants, physical environment; social determinants; economic determinants, and the impact of culture and gender differences (WHO, 2002; Ostwald and Dyer, 2011).

Active ageing was developed in response to the less inclusive theories of ageing, such as 'healthy' or 'successful' ageing (Ostwald and Dyer, 2011). Successful ageing is proposed to involve low probability of disease and disease-related disability, high cognitive and physical functional capacity, and active engagement with life, which includes high social activity and social relationships (Rowe and Kahn, 1987, 1997). Biomedical models of successful ageing focus on good physical and mental functioning whereas sociopsychological models focus on life satisfaction and social functioning; neither of which allow for older adults to consider themselves ageing successfully despite experiencing disease, disability or disengagement from society (Bowling and Dieppe, 2005). Views and theories of 'successful' ageing should allow for older adults to define 'successful' ageing in their own terms.

Prominent social psychological theories of ageing include disengagement theory, activity theory, continuity theory and Erikson's (1950) Eight Stages of Man. Disengagement theory (Cumming and Henry, 1961) assumes that ageing will lead to a gradual withdrawal or disengagement from society. Individuals may maintain some strong relationships with certain people while withdrawing from others. This process of disengagement is natural and allows older adults to come to terms with retirement, loss of social roles and, ultimately, death (Davidson, 2011). Activity theory (Havighurst, 1963) proposes that as individuals age their activities and roles begin to shift, due to retirement, children ageing and social networks changing, which can have an impact on their identity. Individuals attempt to maintain their involvement in activities and hold on to their identity, defined roles, sense of well-being and value by finding close substitutions (Hall, 2012). Continuity theory (Atchley, 1989) holds that individuals age while maintaining the same values, preferences and patterns of behaviour that they experienced and developed over the life span: 'how we are as younger people will be how we are as older people' (Hall, 2012, p. 15). Finally, Erikson's (1950) developmental theory purports that older adults will experience a life stage (ego integrity versus despair) in which they will reflect back on their lives and determine if their life has been a good one. This process of evaluation allows an older person to find peace with the decisions that she or he has made throughout life as she or he prepares for mortality. Criticisms have been lodged against these theories in part because they do not fully account for differences associated with culture, ethnicity or gender. Furthermore, each assumes that individuals will, should or can age in a particular way (Davidson, 2011; Hall, 2012).

Best practice approaches

Social work with older adults in statutory services is currently influenced by person-centred practice, which is based on the person-centred approach by Carl Rogers (1959). Rogers stressed the significance of expressing empathy, genuineness and unconditional positive regard when developing therapeutic relationships and promoting positive human growth and development. Within adult social care, person-centred practice and person-centred planning are defined as follows:

> A values-based perspective about what each of us would wish to experience with regard to choice, independence and dignified treatment if we were cast in the role of the service user. Person-centred planning is designed specifi-cally to 'empower' people, to directly support their social inclusion, and to directly challenge their devaluation.
>
> (Hall, 2012, p. 11–12)

Current practice within statutory services would suggest the use of personal budgets and direct payments as a way in which to maximise choice and control for the older adult. Personal budgets and direct payments can allow individuals to have flexibility in meeting their needs by specifying the types of services and, in the case of direct payments, hire and manage their own staff. Although the basic assumptions underpinning direct payments fit within social work values, such as choice, control and empowerment, not all older adults feel comfortable or confident in managing their own care, hiring and maintaining care staff and overseeing records and finances (Glendinning, 2008; Lymbery, 2010). Lymbery (2010) argues that older adults may not actually be seeking independence; rather they may want acknowledgement of changes in their lives that have contributed to their need for support while also having the freedom to exercise choice and control where they can. To truly implement person-centred practice (often referred to as the personalisation agenda), a social worker would offer the option of direct payments and provide as much information as possible for the client to make an informed decision about how best to meet her or his needs.

Person-centred practice also extends to working with older adults diagnosed with dementia and is outlined in the NICE/SCIE (2006) clinical guideline (CG42) *Dementia: Supporting People with Dementia and their Carers in Health and Social Care*. This guideline stipulates that individuals with dementia should have their needs and preferences considered and respected when receiving care and when deciding who should (or should not) be involved in their care. Individuals should have the opportunity to make informed decisions in partnership with those providing care, and health and social care staff should consider the view of carers and relatives. Where an individual does not have the capacity to make informed decisions, a mental capacity assessment should be complete under the Mental Capacity Act 2005.

The NICE/SCIE (2006) guideline, and policy on dementia, is heavily influenced by the work of Kitwood (1997) and Brooker (2004) who argue that individuals with dementia should be seen first as a person rather than a person diagnosed with dementia. Kitwood's (1993) 'enriched model' (also known as dialectic model) forms the basis of the person-centred care by acknowledging that a person with dementia is affected not only by cognitive impairment, but physical health, personal biography, individual personality and a social environment, all of which need consideration. This model recognises that no two individuals will have the same experience of dementia, and several types of interventions may be utilised depending on their individual needs. These interventions may include mapping, life story work or reminiscence (Batson et al., 2002; Gibson, 2011), music therapy (McDermott et al., 2012), memory training, and/or cognitive stimulation therapy (Spector et al., 2000). It is important to consider how communication needs may vary by individuals, and social workers should use communication tools to assist in implementing a person-centred approach, such as talking mats or the use of art as a medium for communication (Killick and Craig, 2012).

Case example

Ann has called social services as she is becoming increasingly concerned about her mother, Rosemary. Rosemary is a 76-year-old white British female who has lived on her own since her husband passed away ten years ago. Ann reports that she has visited her mother on several occasions to find the front door completely open, her mother confused about what day and time it is, her mother wandering around in the back garden and losing items of importance such as keys and bank cheques. Ann states that she and Rosemary went to visit her GP, and the GP diagnosed Rosemary with early onset dementia. Ann is a single mother of two teenage children, works a full-time job and states that she does not feel she can cope with the amount of time that her mother requires of her. Ann would like to see if the local authority can provide any help for Rosemary.

The social worker made an appointment with Rosemary and Ann at Rosemary's house to complete a community care assessment. Rosemary asserted that she was perfectly fine to remain living in her own home, but Ann was adamant that she would not be able to provide all the necessary support, such as cooking, cleaning, and ensuring her mother attends to her personal hygiene, takes her medication and pays her bills. Based on the assessment, Rosemary met the eligibility criteria for social services support and was allocated a personal budget. Rosemary and Ann stated they did not want the personal budget in the form of a direct payment as they did not want to be responsible for the funds.

In a subsequent meeting, the social worker, Rosemary and Ann discussed how Rosemary would like to use her personal budget to meet her needs. Rosemary acknowledged that Ann was providing a lot of care and agreed to have a worker from a care agency come to the house four times a week to prepare meals, remind Rosemary to take her medication and attend to Rosemary's personal hygiene. Rosemary talked with the social worker about her interests in gardening and desire to be involved in the community, as she was when her husband was alive. The social worker recommended that Rosemary attend the local community centre run by Age UK on a Wednesday when there was a lunch club and activities in the afternoon, included gardening. The social worker was able to organise transport for Rosemary to go to the centre by liaising with a community charity that seeks to engage older adults who are socially isolated. Finally, the social worker completed a carers assessment for Ann, referred Ann to the carers centre for support and was able to provide a one-off direct payment for Ann to purchase a new washing machine. Rosemary and Ann both felt relieved that extra support would be in place.

The social worker reviewed the package of care in six months to assess for any changes in needs and to review Rosemary's perspective of whether the services were meeting her needs. Rosemary is continuing to reside in her own home, is active in the local community centre, and Ann feels less pressure and more secure in her mother's safety.

Benefits and challenges to working with older adults

Statutory and voluntary organisations are experiencing budget cuts and financial difficulties, which are creating challenges to social work delivery. Many social workers have high caseloads and are under pressure to follow processes and procedures that monitor performance. The impact of 'managerialism' and the focus on performance management have left less time for social workers to spend with individuals while more time is spent focusing on completing forms and ticking boxes.

The use of eligibility criteria in defining need has often left individuals who could benefit from social services without support. The eligibility criteria are counterproductive to prevention if the threshold is set to substantial or critical whereby access to services can only occur once individual needs are quite high and/or a crisis has ensued. Moving the eligibility criteria down and offering preventative services could preclude or delay deterioration in physical, mental and social health. Although personalisation and putting the individual at the centre of services is important, older adults may need more support and information to make decisions and take control of their services (Baxter and Glendinning, 2011) especially if they are becoming more reliant on others to meet their physical, mental and/or social needs. This is often difficult to implement when social workers are pressed for time and funding is restricted.

Despite the challenges above, some benefits and advances are being made in terms of services for older adults. The personalisation agenda has enabled social workers to implement the values of social work practice by promoting choice, independence and empowerment. Social workers are encouraged to use the person-centred planning to the client's advantage and be creative in the types of services that are sought to best meet needs. There is also a strong voluntary sector that can provide services for older adults, such as Age UK, and social workers should be utilising and supporting older adults to benefit from these preventative and supportive services. Lastly, there is an acknowledgement by the government and many statutory and voluntary organisations for the need to more fully understand and address dementia and health and well-being in older adults. Social workers should equally be educating themselves about best practice approaches when working with individuals with dementia and incorporating this growing knowledge into their practice.

Anti-oppressive practice with older adults

When working with older adults – just as one would work with any other age group – special consideration should be given to cultural differences as they relate to preference for care, the experience of ageing, and the manner in which they approach changes associated with ageing and new problems. For example, in some Asian cultures, older adults hold a higher status and are considered wise. Therefore, an older Asian client who is living in the UK may have difficulties when coping with a culture that does not defer to elders and often dismisses the experience and perspective of an older person. In fact, youth-based cultures often exclude older people, which can impact everything from television programming to the way in which health care is delivered. Social workers may need to help advocate on behalf of older clients to ensure that they are receiving the services and care that they need. Furthermore, cultural perspectives also influence the way in which ageing is experienced for men and women. In western cultures, women who are past child-bearing age are often seen as non-sexual beings and therefore less valuable in society; this can result in being ignored completely by younger people and social exclusion. As men age, they may find that employers actually value them less. In some studies, it has been found that employers see older employees as having less ability to learn new technology and more resistance to change (Chiu et al., 2001; Van Dalen et al., 2008). Positive contact between younger people and older people has been shown to influence attitudes toward older adults. In sum, ageism is a product of how a particular culture limits people as they become older through social norms and values, and addressing it will require a complex set of approaches at both the social and individual level. As social workers we can advocate for fair and equitable services for older adults, and as individuals we can confront those stereotypes that seek to limit the opportunities, contributions and outlets for older adults.

Summary

This chapter has addressed social work practice with older adults by exploring the social work role in terms of assessing and implementing community care and the rationale for specialised services, particularly in relation to depression and dementia. Social workers must have a foundational knowledge of adult legislation and how the various pieces can be used when working with older adults. Safeguarding procedures and assessing for mental capacity are also critical when encountering suspected abuse or neglect or determining an older adult's ability to make decisions. The personalisation agenda is leading the future of adult social care and the basic values and principles of empowerment, choice, control and independence are common factors in the current best practice approaches. Despite the principles and values being congruent with social work values, social workers must acknowledge that the degree to which an individual wants to have choice and control may vary, especially when someone is becoming increasingly dependent due to physical or mental impairment. As older adults constitute the majority of users of social services, social workers need to recognise some of the common factors among older adults that may require services, while also acknowledging variations in individual and cultural views and experiences of ageing.

📖 CASE STUDY

Peter is a 90-year-old white British male who was admitted to hospital after falling and breaking his hip. Peter lives alone and his only living relative is his nephew, Steven, who is 45 years old and lives with his partner and two children in a village one hour away. Up until his injury, Peter was active in the community and at home. He would visit his friends at the local pub and was able to maintain his home and meet his personal needs. Peter will be discharged from the hospital after receiving necessary treatment. Although Peter can walk again, he has to use a Zimmer frame and states that he feels very weak. Peter has full expectations of going back home, but is worried about how he will be able to resume his lifestyle. The hospital has contacted adult social services requesting an assessment for community care services after he is discharged.

Questions

 What are the local authority's duties in relation to Peter?

 What tools would you need to use to determine whether Peter is entitled to social care services?

 Who will be responsible for paying for any social care services?

 What services and support would you recommend for Peter?

 How could you assist Peter in maintaining independence and helping him to resume his desired lifestyle?

Further resources and suggested readings

Crawford, K. and Walker, K. (2008) *Social Work with Older People*, 2nd edn. Exeter: Learning Matters.

Hall, B. and Scrag, T. (eds) (2012). *Social Work with Older People: Approaches to Person-Centred Practice*. Maidenhead: Open University Press.

MacDonald, A. (2010) *Social Work with Older People*. Cambridge: Polity Press.

Ray, M. and Phillips, J. (2012) *Social Work with Older People*. Basingstoke: Palgrave Macmillan.

Tanner, D. and Harris, J. (2008) *Working with Older People*. London: Routledge.

Websites

Age UK – www.ageuk.org.uk

Alzheimer's Society – www.alzheimers.org.uk

Department of Health – www.dh.gov.uk

SCIE: Older People Resources – www.scie.org.uk/topic/people/olderpeople

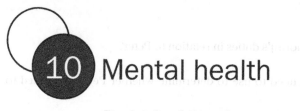

10 Mental health

Debbie Martin

Introduction

The theoretical basis of mental health remains a contested area (Tew, 2012). Medical, psychological and social theories offer differing perspectives on the causes of mental ill heath, yet arguably the most dominant discourse in western society is that of a disease model, much in the same way as physical ill health. Symptoms are used to categorise illness, categories allow prediction of occurrence of symptoms, and the disease may be controlled by treatment (Horwitz, 1982; Moncrieff, 2009). In contrast, the social model looks to social causation as explanation for mental distress. However, in practice, health and social care professionals work together and accept that the most likely cause of mental ill health is a complex interaction between a range of medical, psychological and social factors (Golightley, 2009), which is referred to as the biopsychosocial approach.

The diagnosis of mental disorder by general practitioners (GPs) (in primary care) and psychiatrists (in secondary services) is aided by the use of the *Diagnostic and Statistical Manual of Mental Disorders (DSM-IV-TR)*, published by the American Psychiatric Association, currently in its fifth edition. The manual details everything from anxiety disorders to sexual disorders as forms of mental disorder. The ever-increasing classification system arguably means that more people fall within the scope of mental disorder. This broadening clinical concept of mental disorder was mirrored in legislative change in 2007 when the legal definition of mental disorder, for the purpose of inclusion within the scope of the Mental Health Act 1983 (MHA) (the primary legislation providing for the care and treatment of the mentally disordered), became 'any disorder or disability of the mind' (section 1 MHA), as opposed to the more restrictive classification system of the 1983 Act. The Mental Health Act Code of Practice offers some assistance to those grappling with the concept of mental disorder by stating that the following clinically recognised conditions fall within the Act's definition of mental disorder:

Affective disorders, such as depression and bipolar disorder; schizophrenia and delusional disorders; neurotic, stress-related and somatoform disorders, such as anxiety, phobic disorders, obsessive compulsive disorders, post-traumatic stress disorder and hypochondriacal disorders; organic mental disorders, such as dementia and delirium (however caused); personality and behavioural changes caused by brain injury or damage (however acquired); personality disorders; mental and behavioural disorders caused by psychoactive substance use . . .; eating disorders, non-organic sleep disorders and non-organic sexual disorders; learning disabilities . . .; autistic spectrum disorders (including Asperger's syndrome) . . .; behavioural and emotional disorders of children and adolescents.

(Department of Health [DoH], 2008a, p. 20)

However, the Code of Practice goes on to state that 'this list is not exhaustive' (DoH, 2008a, p. 20), and in practice, regardless of the clinical diagnosis a person will fall within, the scope of the legal definition of mental disorder provided that a medical practitioner considers their presentation to constitute is 'any disorder or disability of the mind'. Whether this broadening concept of mental disorder is the result of greater knowledge, or a more lenient social construct of mental disorder, it remains the role of social workers, along with other health and social care professionals, to offer care and treatment to the growing number of those considered in need.

Mental illness is reported to be the largest single cause of disability in UK society, with one in four adults experiencing mental illness at some point during their lifetime and one in six experiencing symptoms at any one time (DoH, 2012a). However, mental illness is not the preserve of adulthood as children and older adults are equally affected. One in ten children aged five to 16 years is reported to experience a clinically diagnosable mental health problem, and at any one time more than a million children and adolescents will have a diagnosable mental illness (DoH, 2011a). About 750,000 people in the UK are thought to have dementia and this number is expected to double in the next 30 years (DoH, 2012b).

The reader will by now have identified that there are a number of terms used to describe the concept of mental health, for example, mental distress, mental ill health, mental illness and mental disorder. Similarly, there are a number of terms used to describe those affected by mental distress, for example, patient, person and service user. These terms are used interchangeably throughout this chapter, but where possible terms will be used that are compatible with the context, for example, patient when referring to the MHA, and person when referring to the MCA, as these are the terms adopted by the statutes.

Social work practice within mental health services

Whilst many mental health problems can be dealt with within primary care services, some require intervention from secondary services, which specialise in the diagnosis and treatment of mental disorder. The transition from primary to secondary services is usually facilitated by way of GP referral. Secondary services commonly comprise of community-based mental health services and in-patient services.

Social workers usually work within community services (typically working alongside nurses, occupational therapists, psychologists and psychiatrists), which are designed to meet the specific needs of certain groups. For example, the needs of younger people are met by child and adolescent services, adults by community mental health teams, and those aged over 65 years by older people's services. However, mental health service provision is under continual revision, which has resulted in increasing numbers of specialist services, for example, early intervention, recovery, crisis, and assertive outreach teams. Regardless of the nature of the service, almost without exception the policy and legislation governing the delivery of care and treatment is the same.

The primary policy in which mental health professionals operate is the care programme approach (CPA), and although aimed at adults of working age in receipt of secondary services, the principles should be applied to those in secondary services regardless of age (DoH, 2008b). CPA was a government initiative introduced in 1991 in an attempt to bring about seamless services to those experiencing mental disorder. At a time when health and social services operated independently of one another, CPA aimed to establish one key worker whose role was to co-ordinate care planning, risk assessment and review of patient care. CPA has undergone a number of revisions, the latest in 2008, but it remains the framework in which mental health services operate. The person performing the key role is now referred to as the care co-ordinator who may be from a health or social care background. Regardless of professional qualification, their role under CPA is to assess, plan, review and co-ordinate a range of treatment, care and support for those in contact with secondary mental health services. This approach should be undertaken in conjunction with service users (ensuring a person-centred approach), and with other relevant parties.

CPA is also intended to support the care and treatment of those subject to compulsion under the MHA (see Legal framework section below). Whilst CPA offers an approach in working with those with more complex needs, it is not the only policy initiative offering good practice guidance. CPA should be read in conjunction with other recent mental health policy and guidance, for example, *No Health Without Mental Health*, aimed at establishing parity of esteem between services for people with mental and physical health problems (DoH, 2011b), and the Code of Practice Mental Health Act 1983 (DoH, 2008a).

Legal framework

The Mental Capacity Act 2005 (MCA) and the Mental Health Act 1983 (MHA) are the primary legislative frameworks providing for the care and treatment of those with mental disorder. The MCA allows for the provision of care and treatment in circumstances where the person lacks mental capacity to consent, and where the care and treatment is in the best interests of the person. Incapacity and best interests can be determined by anyone who wishes to intervene in the best interests of the person, for example, a social worker. To establish incapacity the test at sections 2 and 3 of the Act must be applied. First, the person wishing to make the decision (referred to as the decision maker) must establish whether the person has an 'impairment of, or a disturbance in the functioning of, the mind or brain' (s2, MCA) that is interfering with the person's ability to make a specific decision. Second, they must establish whether the person is able to make their own decision. The person will be deemed incapable of making their own decision if they are unable 'to understand the information relevant to the decision, to retain that information, to use or weigh that information as part of the process of making the decision, or to communicate his decision' (s3, MCA). Where the decision maker determines that the intervention is in the best interests (s4, MCA) of the person, they are able to act provided the care and/or treatment does not amount to a deprivation of the person's liberty. Where restraint is necessary, it may be used provided that it is a proportionate response to the likelihood and seriousness of the harm to the person (s6, MCA).

In contrast, the MHA enables enforced treatment for the purpose of protecting others in addition to the need to provide for the health and safety of the patient. Whilst the MCA can be operated by anyone concerned with an incapable patient, the MHA only empowers certain professional groups to operate its provisions. It is usual that social workers appointed into mental health teams are expected to train to become approved mental health professionals (AMHP). AMHPs play a vital role in deciding whether or not to operate compulsory provisions under the MHA. Whilst nurses, occupational therapists and psychologists in addition to social workers can train to become AMHPs, the number of AMHPs from professions other than social work remains negligible. Therefore the statutory functions of AMHPs continue, in the main, to be operated by social workers. The following 15 functions under the MHA are performed by AMHPs.

1. Deciding whether to make an application for compulsory admission to hospital, for example, s2 and s4 for assessment, or s3 for treatment
A patient cannot be detained under Part 2 of the Act (civil admissions) unless an AMHP or the patient's nearest relative makes an application for detention. Before making an application the AMHP must interview the patient in a suitable manner and be satisfied that detention in a hospital is the most appropriate way of providing care and treatment (s13(2) MHA). This includes establishing whether the legal criteria for

detention are met, consultation with other interested parties, and consideration of alternatives to detention.

2. *Deciding whether to make an application for guardianship under s7 MHA*
Guardianship enables the imposition of three powers: the power to require the patient to reside at a specified place (for example, residential care); the power to require the patient to attend places for the purpose of medical treatment, occupation, education and training; and the power to require access is given to the patient at her or his place of residence by health and social care professionals. However, there are limitations to these requirements, for example, forced access is not permitted should the patient refuse entry, and medication cannot be imposed. Treatment may only be administered with the consent of the patient, or in the absence of capacity to consent, under the provisions of the MCA.

3. *Informing or consulting the nearest relative under s11 MHA*
The patient's nearest relative provides an important safeguard to those being considered, or made subject to, compulsory provisions under the Act. They are able to object to an application for detention under section 3, or to guardianship under section 7. In addition, they are able to order the discharge of patients subject to detention, guardianship and community treatment orders. They are also in many cases an invaluable source of information, which can assist those offering care and treatment. For these reasons, legislation places a duty on the AMHP to inform or consult the nearest relative prior to making an application where consultation would not be inappropriate, or would not involve an unreasonable delay.

4. *Conveying a patient to hospital under s6 MHA*
Once an AMHP has completed an application for the admission of a patient to hospital, they are authorised to convey the patient to hospital, or to delegate her or his power to another, for example, to the ambulance or police service.

5. *Responding to a nearest relative request for an assessment under s13 MHA*
Under section 13(4) of the Act, the nearest relative has the right to request an assessment with a view to the making of an application for admission to hospital. Should a local social services authority (LSSA) receive such a request, the LSSA must direct an AMHP to consider the patient's case. Where an application for admission to hospital is not made following such a request, the AMHP must put her or his reasons in writing to the patient's nearest relative.

6. *Providing a social circumstances report under s14 MHA following an application by the nearest relative*
Where a nearest relative has made an application for admission to hospital (as opposed to an application by an AMHP) the LSSA in which the patient resides must arrange for an AMHP to interview the patient and provide the managers of the detaining hospital with a report on the patient's social circumstances.

7. Deciding whether they agree with the responsible clinician that a community treatment order (CTO) should be made

Community treatment orders (CTOs) were introduced in 2008, following the 2007 amendments. They are intended to provide a means of compulsion in the community to patients discharged from hospital. The purpose of imposing compulsion by way of a CTO is to prevent patients disengaging from services and treatment, which may lead to deterioration in their health and associated risks. The provision is therefore most commonly used for patients with a history of mental disorder and non-compliance with treatment. A CTO can only be made by the patient's responsible clinician (RC), usually a doctor, if an AMHP is satisfied that the legal criteria are met (s17A, MHA) that any discretionary conditions proposed by the RC are necessary or appropriate, and that it is appropriate to make the order.

8. Deciding whether to extend a CTO under s20A MHA

The initial imposition of a CTO lasts up to six months. After which time, it may be extended for a further six months, and then annually. However, a CTO can only be extended with the agreement of an AMHP. The AMHP must establish whether the grounds for a CTO continue to be met and whether it is appropriate to extend the period of community treatment. Should an AMHP conclude that the criteria are not met, or that it is not appropriate to extend the order the CTO will cease. In these circumstances it would not be appropriate for the RC to seek an alternative view from another AMHP (DoH, 2008a).

9. Deciding whether to revoke a CTO under s17F MHA

As discussed above, the purpose of a CTO is to enforce compliance with a care and treatment regime to avoid deterioration in mental health, and the potential risks that may arise. For this reason, the law enables the RC to recall a CTO patient to hospital if they are of the view that the patient requires medical treatment in a hospital and there would be a risk to the patient's health or safety, or to others if they were not recalled to hospital for medical treatment. Once recalled, the patient can be detained in hospital for up to 72 hours. Should the RC wish to detain the patient beyond this time the agreement of an AMHP must be gained. In order for the AMHP to agree to the revocation of the order (the patient being detained in hospital beyond 72 hours), they must be satisfied that the criteria for section 3 MHA are met and that it is appropriate to revoke the order. The revocation has the effect of detaining the patient in hospital for up to six months, during which time enforced treatment can be given to the patient.

10. Applying to the county court for the appointment of an acting nearest relative under s29 MHA

An AMHP (in addition to the patient, any relative of the patient or anyone with whom the patient is residing) can apply to the county court either to appoint a nearest relative, where a patient does not have one, or to appoint an acting nearest relative, in effect displacing the identified nearest relative because they are either unable to act as such because of mental or other illness; unreasonably objecting to an application being made under sections 3 or 7; because they have exercised their power of discharge (under section 29 MHA) without due regard to the welfare of the patient or the interests of the public; or because they are not a suitable person to act as nearest relative, for example, for reason of abuse (DoH, 2008a).

11. Having the right to enter and inspect premises under s115 MHA

An AMHP is able to enter and inspect any premises (other than a hospital) if she or he believes that a mentally disordered person is not under proper care. The AMHP may only do so at a reasonable time, and if she or he is able to produce documented evidence of her or his AMHP status. However, section 115 MHA does not enable forced entry, and should entry to the premises be denied the AMHP should consider applying to the magistrates court for a warrant under section 135 MHA.

12. Applying to the magistrates court for a warrant under s135 MHA

Section 135 of the Act provides for warrants to be issued by a justice of the peace to allow access to premises. Gaining access to premises without occupier consent or a warrant amounts to a trespass. Therefore, warrants under the Act are most commonly sought where access has been denied to those wishing to provide care and treatment. The Act allows for two differing types of warrants, first section 135(1), which can only be gained by an AMHP. This warrant is typically gained when access has been denied and mental health professionals are sufficiently concerned that an assessment of the patient's needs is necessary to determine whether an application for detention is necessary, or other arrangements for care and treatment need to be made. Provided the legal grounds are met, and the JP is satisfied that a breach of the patient's Article 8 rights are proportionate, a warrant will be issued allowing a police constable to enter the premises (if necessary by force) where the patient is believed to be, if accompanied by and AMHP and a registered medical practitioner. The patient will then be assessed, or removed to a place of safety for up to 72 hours for the purpose of assessment. The second type of warrant (s135(2) MHA) can be gained by any constable or other person authorised under the Act, and allows the taking or retaking of any patient already liable under the Act. Commonly, this will be sought to gain access to patients who have failed to return to hospital after a period of authorised leave of absence from hospital, or for patients recalled from s17 leave of absence, or CTOs who have failed to return to hospital.

13. The power under s18 MHA to take a patient absent without leave into custody

There are a number of circumstances in which a patient who is liable to be detained may be taken into custody or returned to hospital by an AMHP (in addition to others) where she or he is absent without leave; for example, where the patient leaves hospital without the authority of s17 leave of absence, fails to return to hospital following a period of leave, or following recall.

14. Interviewing a patient detained under s136 MHA for the purpose of making necessary arrangement for her or his treatment or care
Section 136 enables a police constable to arrest a person under the MHA if the person is in a public place, it appears that she or he has a mental disorder, and is in need of immediate care or control. The person may be removed to a place of safety (usually a hospital or police station) in the interests of the person or for the protection of others, and be held there for up to 72 hours. During this time the person must be examined by a registered medical practitioner and interviewed by an AMHP for the purpose of making any necessary arrangements for her or his treatment or care.

15. Deciding whether to authorise the movement of a patient between places of safety under s136 MHA
During the 72 hours in which arrangements are being made (under s135 or s136), a constable, an AMHP or anyone authorised by either of them may move the person between places of safety.

The MCA and MHA are both accompanied by codes of practice, which help professionals understand the operation of the Acts, and offer guidance on good practice. However, they are by no means the only statutes governing the actions of those in mental health settings. Those working in mental health settings will also need to familiarise themselves with other statutes, for example, the National Assistance Act 1948, the Health Service and Public Health Act 1968, the Chronically Sick and Disabled Persons Act 1970, Local Authority Social Services Act 1970, Equality Act 2010, the Disabled Persons (Services, Consultation and Representation) Act 1986, the Children Act 1989, the National Health Service and Community Care Act 1990, the Carers (Recognition and Services) Act 1995, the Community Care (Direct Payments) Act 1998, the Human Rights Act 1998, the Care Standards Act 2000, and the Health and Social Care Act 2001.

Theoretical underpinnings

There appears to be a contradiction in approach between the MCA and the MHA (as amended by the 2007 Act). The MCA is intended to assist and support those lacking capacity, and to discourage overly restrictive or controlling behaviour by decision makers. In contrast, the MHA amendments could be argued to have adopted a welfarist approach, as a result of high profile homicides committed by people with mental health problems. Examples of changes arguably concerned with public safety include: the broader definition of mental disorder and the removal of all but one exclusion to use of the Act, both bringing more people within its scope; the lowering of the threshold in relation to the effectiveness of treatment, from that of treatment being *likely* to alleviate or prevent a worsening of the disorder, to a mere intent (*purpose*) on the part of professions to alleviate or prevent a worsening of the disorder, symptoms or even manifestations; and the introduction of the CTO enabling enforced treatment beyond the confines of detention in hospital.

These statutory provisions also have differing approaches to treatment. The MCA allows capable adults to make advance decisions, which are refusals of treatment: the effect being that the specified treatment cannot be imposed on the patient if at a later date they lack capacity and the specified treatment is proposed. However, where an advance decision is a refusal of treatment for mental disorder, detention under the MHA will, in most circumstances, have the effect of overriding the advance decision, thus allowing professionals to impose treatment for mental disorder.

The MCA and the Code of Practice to the MHA 1983 offer a number of principles to support those making decisions. One principle is a less restrictive principle, which promotes the less restrictive intervention necessary, and another principle is participation, which promotes inclusion of patient views. The notion of patient participation and personalisation (the person remaining central to and in control of the process of care and treatment provision) has become a central theme of government policy. *No Health without Mental Health*, a mental health strategy for people of all ages, sets out six objectives aimed at improving mental health and well-being: more people will have good mental health; more people with mental health problems will recover; more people with mental health problems will have good physical health; more people will have a positive experience of care and support; fewer people will suffer avoidable harm; and fewer people will experience stigma and discrimination. This strategy focuses on prevention of mental ill health, well-being and enhancing public mental health. The strategy builds on the *National Service Framework for Mental Health* (DoH, 1999), which established national standards and defined service models aimed at improving quality, and reducing variation in mental health service provision in the UK. *The NHS Plan* (DoH, 2000) implemented the NSF through the creation of new teams, for example, early intervention, assertive outreach and home treatment. The changes were based on 'best available evidence' (DoH, 1999, p. 5). However, research findings equally call into question the effectiveness of such approaches. For example, cognitive behavioural therapy and family therapy, interventions typically offered to those in early intervention in psychosis services, have been found to have no effect on readmission and relapse rates (Garety et al., 2008). More recent studies into the effectiveness of assertive outreach teams (AOTs) in the UK have shown that AOTs are no more effective than community mental health teams at preventing readmission to hospital, or improving health or social functioning (Burns et al., 1999). It is also argued by Nathan and Webber (2010) that the premise of home treatment teams is flawed in that it cannot always be assumed that treatment is best delivered in the least restrictive environment, as hospital treatment will in some circumstances be in the best interests of the patient. This approach can therefore create a dilemma for social workers, especially those with a dual role of care co-ordinator and AMHP.

Best practice approaches

Recent government policy embraces personal recovery (DoH, 2009, 2011), as opposed to clinical recovery. This approach is compatible with social work practice, as it seeks to enable people to live fulfilling lives, rediscovering their personal and social identities. The recovery model may be adopted within existing teams or by specialist teams where individual professionals work alongside patients to establish a recovery plan, typically referred to as a wellness recovery action plan (WRAP), which commonly addresses social, educational, vocational and life skills. Although heralded as a new approach, it arguably mirrors the work of social work of many years, and has been defined prior to inclusion within recent government policy. For example, Anthony (1993, p. 15) gave the following definition:

> a deeply personal, unique process of changing one's attitudes, values, feelings, goals, skills and/or roles. It is a way of living a satisfying, hopeful and contributing life even with the limitations caused by illness. Recovery involves the development of new meaning and purpose in one's life as one grows beyond the catastrophic effects of mental illness.

However, Nathan and Webber (2010) identify a potential problem with this approach, in that some people with severe and enduring mental health problems may not 'recover', which may result in blame and a failure to acknowledge the broader context of poverty, deprivation and unemployment. That said, this approach discourages paternalism and encourages keeping the patient at the centre of decision making.

The personalisation agenda equally encourages patient choice and control by allocating budgets to individuals to purchase their own support, in a way that suits them, and not necessarily health and social care professionals. Direct payments, which have been available for almost a decade, have seen little take-up within mental health services (Care Services Improvement Partnership [CSIP], 2006) and the more recent introduction of personal and individual budgets has seen a slow implementation within mental health services (Bogg, 2010). Whilst this approach is consistent with the theoretical basis of self-determination, concern for risk and the resulting need to control potentially stands in the way of personalisation within the mental health field. Again, social work can play a vital role in advocating patient autonomy to enable service users to make choices whilst ensuring safety.

Case example

Doris is 83 years of age. She lives in her own home with her husband. She has a diagnosis of dementia, and is cared for by her husband and a home care agency. Recently, she has become agitated, and at times she has hit out with her walking stick when her husband has tried to prevent her leaving their home. She has short-term memory problems, and she becomes confused when performing simple tasks, for example, pouring cleaning products into cups, thinking she is making drinks. She has become increasingly frustrated with care staff and no longer wants to receive their support. Her husband is in need of respite, as he has been unable to sleep for some time as he stays awake to prevent his wife leaving the house unaccompanied at night. He is unsure if he can continue providing care for his wife due to the deterioration in her health, her agitation, and his own ill health.

This sort of scenario is not uncommon. In order to intervene, social workers will need to consider a number of options. For example, whether additional support at home could be facilitated, whether Doris and/or her husband would benefit from respite care, whether Doris requires further assessment of her mental health given the reported deterioration, whether specialist residential care is necessary, and what support can be offered to her husband as carer. All of these possible options require knowledge of legislative frameworks, for example: the MCA if Doris lacks capacity to make her own decisions in relation to care and treatment; the MHA should she require in-patient assessment of her mental state; the NHS and CC Act 1990 should she require additional home care; and the Carers (Recognition and Services) Act 1995 to meet the needs of her husband. This is not an exhaustive list of considerations, but it demonstrates the complexities of managing typical situations faced by those with mental health needs, and the necessary range of knowledge needed by those responsible for the provision of care and treatment.

Benefits and challenges to working in mental health services

Social work and the approved social work role (the predecessor to the AMHP role) have been shown to make a positive contribution to mental health service provision (Quirk et al., 2003; Huxley et al., 2008). However, the role arguably faces a number of challenges. The AMHP role, historically the preserve of social work, can now be undertaken by people from other professional disciplines. This change has the potential to lead to a further blurring of roles, and diluted professionals' perspectives caused by multidisciplinary working (Nathan and Webber, 2010). This problem is arguably compounded by the fact that social workers make up a small percentage of the mental health service workforce. Therefore retention of the social perspective within a dominant psychiatric paradigm may prove problematic and, if lost, detrimental to patients. It is therefore important that social workers, whether performing as a care co-ordinator under the CPA framework or as an AMHP undertaking statutory functions, retain their social work values, root their practice in a social perspective, consider patient values and preferences, work within the policy and legislative frameworks, consider available research evidence and exercise independent professional judgement, and in so doing provide a balance to the dominance of psychiatry.

Anti-oppressive practice within mental health services

Mental health social work is perhaps best described as a balancing act between respecting individual autonomy and the exercise of control for the purpose of providing care and treatment. However, the freedoms and restrictions of patients are not the sole focus of mental health social work. Inherent in many decisions is the need to consider the rights of others. As the above case example shows, the needs of others are often intrinsically linked to those of the patient. Consideration of these competing demands is, as with many other aspects of mental health social work, governed by legislation. The European Convention of Human Rights enshrined in English law by way of the Human Rights Act 1998 sets out a number of articles that are of particular relevance to mental health social work, such as article 5, the right to liberty and security, and article 8, the right to respect for private and family life. However, neither are absolute rights. Therefore, professionals are left to determine under what circumstances these rights can be breached, which raises an ethical challenge for mental health professionals. Such an example is the decision of an AMHP to apply for a warrant under s135(1) MHA to gain access to a patient's home. On the face of it, it is a breach of the patient's right to respect for private and family life. However, such an interference may be justified in the interests of the patient's health or for the protection of others.

In addition to the above ethical challenges, particular attention should be paid to those that are overrepresented within the mental health system, for example, Black-Caribbean and Black-African patients (Mental Health Act Commission [MHAC], 2009), and to those with particular needs, for example, children and young people, and those with a learning disability. Wherever possible, professionals should make all reasonable efforts to ensure proper resources are utilised to maximise thorough assessment, and appropriate provision of care and treatment. Codes of practice offer helpful guidance, for example, ensuring assessors have appropriate skills, advocating use of interpreters to aid communication, and mobilisation of specialist services. As a central role of social work is to assess and keep under review appropriate service provision, it is essential that social workers advocate ensuring that the needs of individual groups are understood and met, to avoid oppressive and discriminatory practice and to promote recovery.

Summary

The care and treatment of mental disorder within secondary services is predominated by the biological model. It is therefore imperative that social workers explore the psychological and social factors that impact upon mental health, and in doing so enable individuals to contribute towards their improved mental well-being. As in all areas of social work practice, communication with others is advocated (e.g. CPA) to ensure that the needs of the individual are met, and that risks to the patient and others are minimised. However, the rights of the individual should not be overshadowed without proper justification. Legislation governing human rights and care and treatment is central to mental health social work practice, and assists professionals that are making finely balanced decisions about the rights of the patient and the rights of others. With increasing numbers of people experiencing mental disorder, it is essential that social work continues to work with individuals and their carers, and to have a broader role in challenging the discrimination and stigma attached to those experiencing mental distress.

📖 CASE STUDY

Stephen is 29 years of age. He has a diagnosis of schizophrenia, for which he receives support from a community mental health team. However, he has failed to keep appointments with his care co-ordinator for the last eight weeks. During that time his care co-ordinator has made several home visits and many telephone calls, but nothing has resulted in contact. Concern is growing as Stephen has been without medication treatment for his mental disorder for four weeks. History indicates that Stephen's mental health deteriorates if he stops taking prescribed medication treatment, leading to risks to his health and to others.

Questions

 How might his care co-ordinator gain access to Stephen to assess his mental state?

 If medication treatment is considered necessary, and Stephen is unwilling to co-operate, what are the options available to enforce treatment?

 If detention in hospital is to be considered, who will need to be involved in the assessment process?

If detention in hospital is considered necessary, which section of the MHA would be indicated?

 What after-care provisions may be available to Stephen once he is discharged from hospital?

Further resources and suggested readings

Barber, P., Brown, R. and Martin, D. (2012) *Mental Health Law in England and Wales: A Guide for Mental Health Professionals*, 2nd edn. Exeter: Learning Matters.

Brown, R., Barber, P. and Martin, D. (2009) *The Mental Capacity Act 2005: A Guide for Practice*, 2nd edn. Exeter: Learning Matters.

Peay, J. (2003) *Decisions and Dilemmas: Working with Mental Health Law*. Oxford: Hart Publishing.

Websites

Department of Health – www.dh.gov.uk
Care Quality Commission – www.cqc.org.uk
MIND – www.mind.org.uk

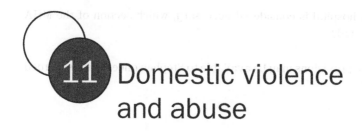

11 Domestic violence and abuse

Michele Winter

Introduction

Domestic violence and abuse (DVA) occurs within all (and more) of the practice areas covered in this book. There is no field of social work that does not have the potential for social workers to work with either 'victims' or perpetrators of DVA.

How DVA converges with statutory social work in terms of safeguarding children is clearly identified in terms of processes and guidance for workers, due to sustained research evidencing the impact of DVA on children psychologically and developmentally (Morley and Mullender, 1994; Kolbo et al., 1996; Hester et al., 2006). Links are routinely made in terms of research, writing and teaching. In practice there are also well-established inter-agency links between DVA services and children's services and partnership working is now more ingrained in practice.

Comparatively, it is my experience that the convergence between DVA and safeguarding adults is not as embedded. The impact of DVA on vulnerable adults (both as 'victims' and as witnesses) is not as routinely recognised and acknowledged, and thus practice is less 'joined up' than it is with regard to children and DVA. Making links more explicit should enable all social workers to competently utilise the theory base and good practice expertise that has been so well established within the DVA field. This is vitally important as there is clear evidence demonstrating that most elder abuse is carried out by a partner or by other family members and that a significant proportion of this is identified as being 'domestic violence' in nature (O'Keeffe et al., 2007). Whilst we know that older people are not the only vulnerable adults, this type of evidence helps us recognise the significant part that DVA can play in adult abuse. Working from this perspective adds a further layer of complexity to our practice with vulnerable adults whilst providing us with a wider theoretical framework on which to draw.

Abuse within institutions such as care homes (e.g. Winterbourne View) and hospitals (e.g. Stafford) has dominated the press recently, which has triggered the government to relook at the need for legislation (including a statutory basis for local arrangements such as safeguarding adults boards), clearer policy/guidance and training, qualifications and registration of care workers. Previously, a review of 'No Secrets' in 2009 involving a national consultation highlighted such needs and promises were made regarding addressing them (Department of Health [DoH], 2010), which were later reneged upon by the new coalition government. It is right that we are now revisiting debates about how legislation might help with regard to safeguarding adults. We do need to learn important lessons and make appropriate changes in our practice with vulnerable adults who live in settings outside of more 'traditional' homes. However, particularly with an ever-increasing ageing population, we also need to recognise that there are comparatively more people being abused within their own homes by people who care for them. We need to address this issue as rigorously as we are trying to address abuse of adults within institutions and as rigorously as we already address abuse of children.

Embedding understanding of DVA within all areas of practice entails sharing knowledge of the underpinning concepts, theories and issues/debates around DVA so as to help social workers practise in the best interest of service users, using processes and experts sufficiently well to help protect, support, offer understanding and enable change in the lives of service users. Where vulnerable adults are involved, DVA must come under the safeguarding adults 'umbrella'. This mirrors how DVA is dealt with for children. Therefore, adhering to this approach ensures anti-discriminatory practice is at the fore, recognising and equally affording the two most at-risk groups in society equivalent gravitas.

Consequently, whilst this chapter will outline the key definitions, theories and concepts of DVA, it will focus on relating and applying these to adult care situations involving vulnerable adults.

Definitions: What is DVA and a vulnerable adult?

The Home Office (2012a) definition, implemented from March 2013, states that domestic violence and abuse is as follows:

> Any incident or pattern of incidents of controlling, coercive or threatening behaviour, violence or abuse between those aged 16 or over who are or have been intimate partners or family members regardless of gender or sexuality. This can encompass, but is not limited to, the following types of abuse: psychological; physical; sexual; financial; emotional.
>
> Controlling behaviour is: a range of acts designed to make a person subordinate and/or dependent by isolating them from sources of support, exploiting their resources and capacities for personal gain, depriving them of the means needed for independence, resistance and escape and regulating their everyday behaviour.

Coercive behaviour is: an act or a pattern of acts of assault, threats, humiliation and intimidation or other abuse that is used to harm, punish, or frighten their victim. This definition, which is not a legal definition, includes so called 'honour' based violence, female genital mutilation (FGM) and forced marriage, and is clear that victims are not confined to one gender or ethnic group.

Within this new definition, the complex nature of DVA is emphasised and the psychological element of power and control made clearer, hence a move from simply DV to DVA. This should help both 'victims', the public and 'helping' agencies recognise that DVA is not just about single acts of violence, and that the psychological impact on victims is just as damaging as any violence they may experience. Furthermore, there is now recognition of the increased vulnerability of 16 to 18 year olds, particularly of girls who are twice as likely as boys to experience abuse from a partner (Home Office, 2012a, 2012c).

In order to link the definition of DVA more explicitly with vulnerable adults, we need to identify 'vulnerable adult' and the related types of abuse. Hence, a vulnerable adult (whilst noting that this term is increasingly used interchangeably with 'adult/person at risk') is as follows:

A person over eighteen who is or may be in need of community care services by reason of mental or other disability, age or illness **and** who is unable to take care of her/himself **or** unable to protect him/herself again significant harm or exploitation.

(DoH, 2000, pp. 8–9)

All elements of the first part must be met along with one element of the second part in order for someone to be classified as a vulnerable adult and for the safeguarding process to be instigated. For example, a person must be over 18, in need (or might be in need) and either be unable to take care of themselves or be unable to protect themselves. Usefully, the Association of Directors of Adult Social Services (ADASS) (2005) expand the concepts within this definition by clarifying that community care services include all care provided in any setting and that when considering if a person is a vulnerable adult consideration must be given to dependency, capacity and duress issues.

No Secrets (DoH, 2000) originally outlined six categories of abuse for adults, which included physical, sexual, psychological/emotional, financial/material, neglect and discriminatory. Institutional abuse is now also recognised as a category. The labelling of someone as a vulnerable adult and the abuse they are experiencing as DVA is not intended to stigmatise, rather it enables access to services and protection with immediate effect as any safeguarding referrals 'jump the queue' in terms of priority status and eligibility.

By examining definitions and concepts together, we are enabled to see the connection between DVA and safeguarding adults. These connections are recognised nationally as demonstrated in the restructuring of specialist police units to incorporate DVA, safeguarding adults, safeguarding children and hate crime. Whilst physically restructuring in this manner may be impossible for social services and health, I would argue that this type of recognition of the interrelatedness can be emulated by social workers just as effectively.

Social workers in whichever field of practice should understand some of the basic theoretical explanations and concepts for DVA. This will help them avoid a 'silo' approach to practice and rather work in a multi-professional way utilising experts from other relevant agencies (including specialist DVA agencies) and sharing their own expertise.

Who experiences DVA?

DVA is gendered with women more likely to be the victims and men the abusers/perpetrators (Home Office 1999, 2011, 2012a; Walby and Allen, 2004; DoH, 2005). DVA is rarely a one-off event and tends to increase in severity over time. The risk factors for disabled women are greater than for non-disabled women (Women's Aid, 2008). Research published by Action on Elder Abuse (2006) estimated that of 2100 older people in the community who had experienced abuse, 35 per cent were carried out by a 'partner' and 33 per cent by 'other family'; 31 per cent of the 'partner' abuse and 20 per cent of the 'other family' abuse categories was identified as being domestic violence.

The gender dynamic around DVA is a result of wider sociological inequalities between the sexes and male privilege. However, there is a caveat here in relation to vulnerable adults where it is important to be aware that DVA can occur within wider familial relationships (e.g. between siblings, from adult children to elderly parents). Whilst we do need to recognise the gender bias in DVA experience generally, we must guard against allowing this knowledge to detract us from recognising DVA dynamics within other familial relationships in relation to vulnerable adults. For example, we know that older people and people with learning difficulties are more at risk of abuse as they are more likely to be dependent on others (Action on Elder Abuse, 2006; O'Keefe et al., 2007; Joint Committee on Human Rights, 2008). Both groups are socially marginalised and have a higher likelihood of having communication difficulties, all elements that make them more easily targeted and less likely to be able to attract help or report abuse. The demographics of DVA become more complex and multi-layered once the convergence with safeguarding adults is recognised, making it vitally important that social workers understand how to recognise DVA, understand how this fits with safeguarding adults work and their role within related processes.

Social work practice around DVA

Social workers will play different roles within social work or social work related settings and will be known by different titles. The following practice examples are therefore not exhaustive.

Workers in voluntary sector services are likely to undertake support work, family support work, specialist DVA work and domestic and family violence prevention work. This often means that social workers, and/or social work students, can initially feel they are not being 'social workers'. However, it is my experience (both within practice and from working with student social workers on placement) that this involves undertaking the front-line therapeutic work that statutory social workers often wish they could do. For example, front-line specialist agencies working with victims (and/or perpetrators) of DVA will be more authentically using group work, advocacy and counselling skills in a way that is rare for statutory social workers to be able to do in this era of increased bureaucracy, where time limitation and contracting out/commissioning mean referral on to specialist support agencies is required. Statutory services now provide the distanced authority figure that assesses, sets up care/protection plans, oversees and monitors in terms of adherence, positive change, and risk abatement and takes 'punitive' action when necessary. Therefore, it is more often the voluntary sector agencies that implement the plans and who undertake the relationship-based 'social work'. In my experience, such agencies are more experienced in working with parents and children than vulnerable adults who could have mental health issues, be drug/alcohol dependent, be elderly and frail or be physically and/or learning disabled.

Classically, a specialist worker might work with the following: a parent and their children to improve the attachment a child has with them; a perpetrator to help him or her understand the impact of his or her behaviour; both parents in order to help them understand child development and best parenting; a child who is beginning to show signs of abusive behaviour towards a parent. Further work may be within a 'refuge' setting or specialist DVA agencies and could involve running the Freedom Programme – group work support set up by experts in the field to predominately help women 'victims' and/or survivors learn about and develop understanding of how the dynamics of an abusive relationship works and strategies for how to keep safer and how to plan to leave safely (see Web Resources list for link to the Freedom Programme)

Ultimately, the aim is to raise consciousness and enable the victim to make empowered decisions. Knowledge is power, according to Lukes (1974), so educating 'victims' is a way towards empowerment and hopefully safety. Workers could also be supporting victims on a one-to-one basis, advocating for them with regard to housing, helping with education and with accessing legal options. Consequently, the work is varied and certainly representative of the skills needed for social work training.

With regard to service user access to these services, this would be voluntary, except where the risk to a victim is so great that referrals can be made without consent. For example, referral to the Multi-Agency Risk Assessment Conference (MARAC) is best done with the consent of a victim, but if this is not forthcoming despite efforts to work with the victim to explain its function, then a referral can be made without consent under the Data Protection Act 1998, s.29(2) and (3)) and the Human Rights Act 1998, articles 2, 3, 8). In the same way, the safeguarding process can be utilised without a vulnerable adult consenting if the risk to them or others is so great that it overrides their right to privacy. This is where one article of the Human Rights Act 1998 can 'trump' another. And this is where the age-old ethical dilemma within social work of choice versus control comes to the forefront. There are no easy answers, but the national principles of safeguarding adults as outlined by the Department of Health (2011, p. 2) can really help guide us in our practice around this issue. The principles consist of the following:

- *Empowerment*. A presumption of person-led decisions and informed consent.
- *Protection*. Support and representation for those in greatest need.
- *Prevention*. It is better to take action before harm occurs.
- *Proportionality*. Proportionate and least intrusive response appropriate to the risk presented.
- *Partnership*. Local solutions through services working with their communities. Communities have a part to play in preventing, detecting and reporting neglect and abuse.
- *Accountability*. Accountability and transparency in delivering safeguarding.

These principles demonstrate that human and civil rights, including self-determination, should be upheld and thus at the forefront of work with vulnerable adults. In summary, the principles offer protection and support whilst promoting individual choice and control. How to empower whilst using our legitimate authority to protect when a duty of care is needed is the complexity inherent in safeguarding adults work but the principles guide us well and work in harmony with social work values and anti-oppressive and anti-discriminatory practice.

Legal framework

Table 11.1 lists the key pieces of legislation in relation to DVA and safeguarding adults.

We can see that in comparison to children's social workers, adult care social workers draw on a plethora of legislation and good practice guidance, much of which is piecemeal, disjointed and obscure. There is no overarching, comprehensive and clear piece of legislation that draws this 'mishmash' together, particularly in relation to vulnerable adults. As a consequence, social workers working within the

Table 11.1 DVA and safeguarding adults legislation and policy

Legislation	Description
National Assistance Act 1948	Section 47 allows for application to a magistrate for compulsory removal from the home in cases where a disabled or ill adult is not receiving proper care and attention from themselves or others.
Theft Act 1968	For financial abuse.
Housing Act 1996	A person can apply to any local authority if they are homeless because of violence or the fear of violence.
Family Law Act 1996	Part 1V, offers protection by way of court orders.
	1. *Non-molestation Order*. Civil court. Aims to stop harassment, pestering or interfering with a person or their children, may include assault or any other violence. Time limited or until a further order is obtained. A breach can invoke imprisonment of up to five years. Applicant must be an 'associated person' (i.e. current or ex-spouse/partner or family member).
	2. *Occupation Order*. Decides who should remain living in the home after violence/harassment. Can exclude the perpetrator from all or part of the home, or from coming within a certain distance of the home, and/or impose a set of rules about living in the home. 'Power of arrest' can be attached. Useful where homes have been adapted as can enable the 'victim' to remain in the home.
	3. *Forced Marriage Protection Order*. Aims to protect someone from being forced (by use of threats or other psychological means) into marriage or attempts to force them, and for those who have been forced into marriage taking into account their health, safety and well-being.
Other Orders	*Restraining Order*. Issued where there have been criminal proceedings for harassment or assault, whether defendant has been found guilty or not. Similar to a non-molestation order but issued via the criminal courts.
	Prohibited Steps Order. Preventative measures to stop something happening (e.g. taking a child).
	Specific Issue Orders. Used to order something to be done (e.g. return a child), documents (e.g. passport).
Protection from Harassment Act 1997	Covers activities which cause alarm or distress, includes awarding damages and restraining orders with the power of arrest.
Human Rights Act 1998	Particularly pertinent:
	Article 2. Right to Life.
	Article 3. Prohibition of Torture.
	Article 5. Right to Liberty and Security.
	Article 6. Right to a Fair Trial.
	Article 8. Right to Private and Family Life.
	Article 14. Prohibition of Discrimination.
Data Protection Act 1998	Gives legal authority to share information to prevent/detect a crime, to protect serious harm or a matter of life or death, for the administration of justice or in the public interest.

No Secrets 2000	Required local authorities to make arrangements to safeguard vulnerable adults (based on Local Authority Act 1970, s7). Includes definitions of a vulnerable adult, abuse, significant harm, categories of abuse, processes.
Sexual Offences Act 2003	Includes concepts of capacity and consent. Consent is described as agreeing by choice by someone who has the freedom and capacity to make that choice. Turned the emphasis away from the 'victim' proving they had been raped/assaulted to the 'burden of proof' lying with the alleged perpetrator with regards to consent. Makes it clear that some people (due to a mental disorder) lack capacity to agree to sexual activity. Prohibits sexual activity between paid workers and their service users who have a mental disorder. Argues that a person lacks the capacity to consent after an act of violence.
Domestic Violence, Crime and Victims Act 2004	Introduced a new offence of 'causing or allowing the death of a child or vulnerable adult' (e.g. via neglect or abuse). Allows same-sex couples and cohabiting couples to apply for non-molestation orders.
Mental Capacity Act 2005	Provides a framework to empower and protect vulnerable people who are not able to make their own decisions. There are five guiding principles. Two criminal offences under section 44 ('ill treatment' and 'wilful neglect') against a person who lacks capacity to make relevant decisions, apply to anyone caring for someone without capacity, including family members, and enables police to apply for a warrant to enter if they suspect a carer of this offence.
Mental Health Act 1983 and 2007	Section 135 – enables a police officer, AMHP and doctor with a warrant to remove to a place of safety for 72 hours where it is suspected that a person with a mental disorder is neglecting himself or herself or being abused.
Children Act 1989 and 2004, United Nations Convention on the Rights of the Child 1989, Working Together to Safeguard Children 2010	Variously make it clear that even if our main remit is working with adults, we need to be mindful of children, take a 'Think Family' approach and refer to statutory children's services when we are concerned a child is at risk including where we are aware of DVA within a household.
Association of Directors of Adult Social Services (ADASS) 2005, 2011	Good practice and threshold guidance for practitioners.
Domestic Violence, Crime and Victims (Amendment) Act 2012	Makes it a crime to cause or allow serious physical harm to a vulnerable adult (or child). Also enables those who fail to report abuse to be prosecuted.
White Paper and draft Care and Support Bill 2012	Proposals to put adult safeguarding on a statutory footing in line with safeguarding children. The idea of powers of entry for social workers is being mooted in cases where a vulnerable adult is suspected to be the victim of abuse, has capacity, they or a third party is refusing entry and coercion or undue influence is suspected.

safeguarding adults arena can be left feeling that there are no 'teeth in the bite' when it comes to protecting vulnerable adults from abuse, or when dealing with perpetrators of abuse, leading to feelings of frustration and impotence.

Theoretical underpinnings and best practice approaches

The immense psychological impact of DVA can affect victim's perception of their situation and thus their decision-making abilities. Further complexities can then be added, such as learning disability, cognitive or sensory impairment, disability, frailty due to age, and/or mental health issues, highlighting just how multifaceted this work can be. How this impact is generated is exposed by examining how manipulation of human behaviour can be achieved. Biderman, a sociologist, investigated how prisoners of war were 'brainwashed', 'conditioned' and 'trained' into being made to do things and how they were controlled. Biderman's (1957) research identified patterns of perpetrator and victim behaviour from which he developed a model of techniques and related effect. The resulting 'chart/cycle of coercion' is now widely used in relation to understanding DVA as there are strong parallels with how victims of DVA are controlled. Thus, this model can help workers and victims identify what is happening, how it is happening and (hopefully) work towards combatting it.

Stages within the cycle include isolation, debility/exhaustion and degradation (Biderman, 1957, p. 619). Isolation is where the perpetrator works to remove outside sources of support, such as social or familial. All support, information and validation begins to come solely from the perpetrator ensuring dependency on him or her. This takes time, is not initially overt and is, therefore, difficult to spot in the early stages. Debility involves incapacitating victims via activities that exhaust them so they are unable to function 'normally'. The victim becomes too weak physically and emotionally to resist which can lead to chronic depression, suicidal thoughts, drug/alcohol dependency and poor health (WHO, 2012). Degradation intensifies the process of gaining control as 'put-downs' and humiliation (sometimes in the presence of others) lead to the victim recognising that submission is ultimately less damaging psychologically and physically. This feeds back into the cycle of isolation with each stage reinforcing the other.

Over time, threats are used to more obviously control and maintain power, leading to escalation for the victim of fear, anxiety and despair. There is also enforcement of trivial/irrational demands to develop a habit of submission and emphasise that resistance is futile. All stages are interspersed with occasional indulgences, where the abuser appears sorry and/or offers a reward for obedience. The whole process creates feelings of confusion, increases anxiety, keeps victims under control, encourages them to be compliant for a 'reward' and creates an environment whereby the victims perception becomes distorted – they lose their own perspective and become monopolised by the perspective of the abuser, feel guilt and that abuse is their fault (Biderman, 1957).

A sense of learnt helplessness (Seligman, 1975), therefore, develops whereby a cognitive shift to the role of 'passive victim' takes place due to repeated exposure to uncontrollable and aversive events. Thus, compliance becomes an unconscious psychological survival trait (Grigsby and Hartman, 1997). Furthermore, the victim develops a trauma bond (Dutton and Painter, 1981) similar to what Hacker (1976) describes as Stockholm syndrome, which is a strong emotional tie due to the dynamic of a power imbalance within the relationship and intermittent violence/abuse alternated with warm, friendly, kind behaviour (i.e. the occasional indulgences described by Biderman). In such a situation, when there are no alternative relationships available, the victim bonds to the positive side of the abuser especially as after abuse the person most readily available to provide support and to ease the emotional distress is the abuser, thus creating an emotional dependence. Knowing this, we can understand that even when it is safe to leave, the victim finds this difficult to do, and how mental ill health (such as PTSD, depression, anxiety disorders) develop and are common amongst DVA victims (World Health Organisation [WHO], 2012).

The concept of 'frozen fright' is also useful to draw upon when working with victims of DVA. This is a state of emotional numbness due to violence, another subconscious survival tactic (Symonds, 1982). Victims of DVA have become so broken down psychologically that what we might deem a 'normal' response to violence (i.e. an uncontrolled panic state such as 'fight or flight') is not invoked. Unfortunately, frozen fright response resembles co-operative behaviour, for example, as seen in rape victims who do not physically fight but remain passive in order to survive. Victims' thought processes appear normal (e.g. they can respond calmly when calling the police) but all of their energy is focused on survival (Symonds, 1982). The elevated state of anxiety that is 'frozen fright' stops the victim from seeing all available options, hence not being able to see a way of escaping/leaving, accessing support services, or envisaging a safer life. Intervention from authorities may also be feared as past experience has taught victims that once helping professions exit the violence and abuse are worse. Lack of understanding of this response can lead to social workers and other professionals making judgements about the victim (e.g. why didn't she or he fight back or leave) as complicit in their abuse.

Biderman's chart of coercion is in effect a 'cycle' model. Cycle of violence theories depict violence either escalating up to severe violence and then back down to a honeymoon phase or as a response to stress (Women's Aid, 2007). Consequently this, and similar cyclical models, have been criticised as not being representative of the constant fear as well as the continual feature of power and control that victims experience in abusive relationships (Women's Aid, 2007). As a way of addressing these concerns, many agencies working with victims (and perpetrators) have adopted the 'wheel' model developed by the Duluth Domestic Abuse Intervention Project (DAIP) in Minnesota (DAIPa, 2011). Using a wheel model helps to visually depict the inter-related and interlinked layers of behaviour as well as keeping a focus on the perpetual feature of power and control. The wheel depicts the most common abuse tactics deliberately used to control or dominate victims within the spokes with the underpinning aim of 'power and control' placed at the centre of the wheel and a surrounding 'tyre' of violence and abuse that holds everything in place.

Since its development, this wheel has been utilised as a tool worldwide. The wheel has also been tailored to other more specific relationships where the 'spokes' offer different headers according to which abusive relationship it is depicting. The wheel that examines abusive relationships between people with disabilities and their unpaid caregivers (i.e. their partner or a family member) enables us to make explicit links from DVA to safeguarding adults as one of the spokes depicts how this 'caregiver privilege' is abused (DAIP, 2011a).

Conversely, the 'equality' wheel (DAIP, 2011b) is used to describe the changes needed to move from an abusive to a non-abusive relationship by helping both victim and perpetrator directly compare a healthy relationship with one that is dominated by power and control. In the equality wheel, 'equality with inter-dependence' is placed at the centre to depict a healthy constant (rather than fluctuating) aim of the caregiver.

The equality wheel is very much in line with person-centred practice as well as anti-discriminatory and anti-oppressive practice. By sharing these wheels we can empower the vulnerable adult by enabling them to recognise the abuse they are being subjected to as well as the treatment they should expect from caregivers. Visual depictions and a more in-depth explanation of the power and control wheel and the equality wheel can be found at the Domestic Abuse Intervention Programs (DAIP) website (http://www.theduluthmodel.org).

In addition to utilising underpinning theories and concepts in a person-centred way, best practice entails partnership working. This includes both the service user and other relevant agencies/specialists and systems that can contribute to safeguarding vulnerable adults who are within a DVA situation. Independent domestic violence advisors, referred to as IDVAs are: 'trained specialists who provide a service to victims who are at high risk of harm from intimate partners, ex-partners or family members, with the aim of securing their safety and the safety of their children' (Home Office, 2012b).

Support can be practical and emotional, can involve advocacy, help in identifying and managing risk and can be around safety planning and options. IDVAs sit on the MARAC and, in relation to safeguarding adults, can be crucial sources of expertise both in terms of knowledge and with regard to working with victims. Consequently, consultation as a minimum is required in order to work in the best interests of vulnerable adults who are experiencing DVA, with involvement at the various stages of safeguarding work including joint working if appropriate.

Another source of information, support, guidance and, crucially, action is the MARAC, which was set up in response to the National Plan for Domestic Abuse 2005. Its aim is to share information about the victim and perpetrator to reduce risk to victims and any children, construct risk management/safety plans, reduce repeat victimisation and improve agency accountability. Sharing of information is key to the process and what agencies could do to support victims, either directly or by intervention with the perpetrator, is explored.

MARAC is a useful multidisciplinary tool in very high-risk situations. It feeds into safeguarding children and safeguarding adults in that key local authority figures are present and cases are cross-referenced on databases to make sure all known relevant information is shared in order to protect. Referral to the MARAC is via a CAADA-Dash Risk Assessment (CAADA, 2012), which is a tool for IDVAs and other professionals to use to assess the level of risk to an individual. Fourteen ticks or more are needed for a referral (CAADA, 2012). However, there is a section where a professional judgement can be stated to justify a referral with less ticks. Here professionals explain other relevant information which may increase risk, such as disability, mental health issues, drug/alcohol dependencies, cultural and/or language barriers and 'honour' based systems (CAADA, 2012). This is where we can make direct links with safeguarding adults as a vulnerable adult is at increased risk due to the additional power imbalance of being dependent on her or his caregiver/abuser. MARAC can refer to safeguarding and safeguarding can refer to MARAC. In addition to being a referral tool, the CAADA-Dash Risk Assessment can be utilised with lower level cases of DVA in order to help a victim begin to recognise their situation.

Case example

Mr and Mrs Peters are both 75 years old, have lived at their home alone since their children moved out decades ago and Mrs Peters provides care for her husband. She is finding this increasingly difficult. Chris, their son, moved back six months ago after his wife took out an injunction due to his violence. Chris is angry and is taking it out on his parents by forbidding them from contacting his wife or children. He has started threatening them to get his own way around the house, regularly ridiculing his father's deteriorating health and taking food and money. Chris is generally taking over the house – the Peters can no longer watch what they want on TV and Chris now has the main bedroom, leaving them to share a single bed or sleep on the floor in the spare room. Mr and Mrs Peters are afraid to challenge Chris due to his temper (he shouts at them and bangs around) and because they know he was violent to his wife. They think he is taking drugs.

The likelihood that this case has come through as a self-referral to statutory services is low. As Jones and Spreadbury (2008) point out, the very fact that someone is a vulnerable adult often impedes them from seeking help. More likely a neighbour, relative or other professional has alerted. Such an alert would lead to a national standardised process starting with an initial gathering of information in order to make a preliminary threshold decision: that is, do Mr and/or Mrs Peters meet the definition of a vulnerable adult. Clearly they do, as there is psychological and financial/material abuse occurring with a very real risk of escalation to physical abuse. Taking into account the power and control apparent and the familial relationship, we can also label this as DVA. Further information from the GP, any other agencies involved (e.g. carers organisations, housing) and the specialist police adult protection unit could add information that would help with our initial risk assessment and planning for proper investigation and protection. All of this would be part of our initial strategy, which might be undertaken over the phone.

During all stages of work, we would need to be mindful of the Safeguarding and MCA Act principles. Mr and Mrs Peters appear to have capacity, although this could be impeded by the coercive dynamics. Any action should be taken with the consent and co-operation of the couple and best practice would be to inform them of the concerns about their well-being and discuss options with them. However, this is a risky situation so careful planning is needed in order not to increase the danger or alienate the Peters. Consequently, it may be that before an inclusive strategy meeting takes place with them present, a professionals meeting is convened to bring together all the information and explore possible ways forward. This could include input from an IDVA worker who is used to dealing with similar situations and who will have expertise around how to make initial contact and work alongside the Peters in order to help mitigate or remove risk to them. Possible outcomes of strategy including what may be in a protect plan are as follows:

- Specialist DVA worker, together with a social worker, engaging the Peters and utilising the CAADA-Dash Risk Assessment and Disability Power and Control Wheel to plan a sensitive conversation around exploring what is happening.
- Explore legal options (e.g. how to remove Chris from their home or manage him within the home) and provide ongoing support.
- Liaison with the specialist police unit regarding intelligence on risk, options regarding theft, protective strategies such as information on how to keep safe, help with getting locks changed, and/or flagging the address as urgent.
- Community care assessment and separate carers assessment to ascertain needs and investigate the situation further. Subsequent provision of any services should alleviate Mrs Peters' carer's role and also offer a monitoring tool as well as giving clear signals to Chris that professionals are aware of the situation and are ready to act if necessary.
- Sharing the protection plan with the GP and other relevant agencies.
- Alerting neighbours, relatives, and/or friends (with the Peters' consent) so others have permission to intervene/seek help on their behalf.

Working with the Peters to devise a protection plan and using the safeguarding process fluidly is crucial in order to work in a person-centred and effective way. Monitoring of the situation is vital. Consequently, regular reviewing to ascertain if the plan is working and ensure choices are revisited – for example, if the Peters do not want police involvement at the moment does not mean they cannot change their minds in the future – would be best practice. Closure around safeguarding would only come once risk is mitigated.

Although possibly not relevant to the Peters, it is worth listing the options if a victim would like to leave the home. Options include accessing a refuge, short-term respite or placement, moving to sheltered accommodation or to a different area (if in social housing) and making a homelessness application for emergency accommodation.

Benefits and challenges in domestic violence and abuse work

Hester (2011, pp. 838-853) argues that there remain 'frustrations and difficulties' and a 'separate planets' mentality within related but differently emphasised services (e.g. child protection, child contact and victim/perpetrator specific services). We can transfer the significance of what she is describing in terms of children directly over into our work with adults around DVA in order to avoid a 'silo' approach to working with vulnerable adults. Rather than merely referring to each other's services, we can work together. This would help address the cultural differences between agencies and lead to a more integrated approach. We can learn much from specialist DVA services in terms of theoretical underpinnings and they can learn much from social work in terms of expanding their repertoire to be more inclusive of less traditional victims of DVA, i.e. the vulnerable adults.

Summary

There is always intent (dynamics of power and control) with DVA – this is what differentiates it from 'ordinary' abuse of a vulnerable adult. Recognition that DVA can be experienced by vulnerable adults adds a layer of complexity to our work as well as additional resources and concepts upon which to draw. Relating theory to practice in a reflective, reflexive way can help us be less judgemental and more empowering in our approach.

The selected concepts and theories shared here are not absolute in terms of DVA and safeguarding work. Many of the models, theories and methods used in other chapters are transferable to this area of practice. It is worth social workers taking time to reflect on how they might need to adapt a particular model and why they might do this, whilst wearing a DVA 'lens' to avoid simply fitting service users into particular models. Finally, sitting with the uncomfortableness of what we might consider 'unwise' decisions, allowing ourselves to 'not know' the answers and not rushing in to problem solve, are all crucial to effective work within the safeguarding and DVA arena.

📖 **CASE STUDY**

Jamila is 34 years old and has bipolar affective disorder. Lately, things are getting worse and she says her partner is finding it difficult to cope with her mood swings. Her partner is her only carer; she has little to do with her family. When you visit, Jamila is very agitated saying she has always been too frightened to tell anyone about her partner's abuse, which is usually verbal and emotional but this time he was physically holding a knife to her throat and saying she would be killed if she called out. Jamila tells you she can't cope and is thinking of 'ending it all'. She is worried because they have a lot of debt in both their names and she is only managing to sleep by drinking. Jamila thinks she may be pregnant as they had sex after the assault.

Questions

 Is Jamila a vulnerable adult under 'No Secrets'?

 Are there any safeguarding children issues?

? What type of abuse may be occurring? How do you know and what are the indicators?

? What might a statutory adult care social worker's role be? Immediately and in the longer term?

? What might a statutory child care social worker's role be? Immediately and in the longer term?

? In what other agencies might a student social worker be placed and what might their role be?

? How might your understanding of DVA help you with your work here in the various roles you might have as a student social worker?

? What might be the ethical, cultural and anti-oppressive considerations here?

Since writing this chapter the Association of Directors of Social Services (ADASS) have published guidance for practitioners and managers on adult safeguarding and domestic abuse. Details of this document are within the suggested readings below.

Further resources and suggested readings

ADASS (2013) *Adult Safeguarding and Domestic Abuse: A Guide to Support Practitioners and Managers*. London: Local Government Association.

Department of Health (DoH) (2000) *No Secrets: Guidance on Developing and Implementing Multi-agency Policies and Procedures to Protect Vulnerable Adults from Abuse*. London: Department of Health.

Hester, M. (2011) The three planet model: towards an understanding of contradictions in approaches to women and children's safety in contexts of domestic violence, *British Journal of Social Work*, 41: 837–853.

Manthorpe, J., Stevens, M., Rapaport, J., Harris, J., Jacobs, S., Challis, D., Netten, A., Knapp, M., Wilberforce, M. and Glendinning, C. (2009) Safeguarding and system change: early perceptions for adult protection services of the english individual budgets pilots – a qualitative study, *British Journal of Social Work*, 39: 1465–1480.

Women's Aid (2008) *Disabled Women and Domestic Violence: Making the Links*. www. womensaid.org.uk/domestic-violence-articles.asp?itemid=1722&itemTitle—aking+the+li nks%3A+disabled+women+and+domestic+violence&section=00010001002200080001&se ctionTitle=Articles%3A+disabled+women (accessed 21 November 2012).

Websites

Freedom Programme – www.freedomprogramme.co.uk

Power and Control Wheel Gallery – www.theduluthmodel.org/training/wheels.html

The CAADA-DASH Risk Identification Checklist – www.caada.org.uk/searchresult. html?sw=DASH

DVA-related contacts

Action on Elder Abuse, national helpline: 0808 808 8141

Broken Rainbow (support for lesbian, gay, bi-sexual, transgender–LGBT-people): 0300 999 5428

English National Domestic Violence: 0808 2000 247

Forced Marriages Unit: 0207 008 0151

Honour Network, national helpline: 0800 5999 247

Male Advice and Enquiry 0808 801 0327

Northern Ireland Women's Aid: 0800 917 1414

Respect (for DVA perpetrators): 0845 122 8609

Scottish Domestic Abuse: 0800 027 1234

Victim Support, national helpline 0845 303 0900

Wales DomesticAbuse: 0808 80 10 800

Women's Aid, 24-hour referral to refuges nationwide: 0808 2000 247

12 Social work in health care settings

Malcolm Payne and Sue Taplin

Introduction

Social workers work in partnership with other professionals in a variety of settings. More specifically, social workers are commonly involved with the health care of clients who are receiving services through the main locations of social work, such as local authority adult social care and children and family services, as well as in many less universal services. Within health care settings, social workers practise in the following five main areas (Payne, 2009): (1) *hospital care*; (2) *other institutions providing health care services*, such as hospices; (3) *primary care*; (4) *community health care services*, such as day centres and specialist community teams; (5) *public health and commissioning*.

This chapter focuses on general, mainly physical, health care settings. Social work in mental health and learning difficulties services, which also involve close relationships with health care colleagues, are dealt with in Chapters 7 and 10 respectively. This chapter will begin with a review of the organisation of social work in each of these five main health care settings and will identify the features of social work that distinguishes its aims and roles from those of health care professionals. The chapter will then move to an examination of the organisational and professional divisions that arise in practising social work in health care. The chapter will then focus more specifically on end-of-life and palliative care, which include services for people who are dying and bereaved. This discussion will provide an example of how the distinctive roles of social work contribute to and create divisions in health care settings. We have elected to focus on end-of-life and palliative care because dealing with emotional, psychological and social issues is accepted in palliative care, the health care specialty, as an integral part of providing an adequate and holistic service. Consequently, social work has an important role to play because the profession aims to focus on these specific aspects of people's needs. In particular, government policy to develop end-of-life care drawing on palliative care experience seeks to incorporate a strong social care contribution. This is typical of the partnership between health and social care envisaged in many other health care specialties dealing with long-term conditions and disabilities. However, such inter-professional and inter-agency partnerships, are hard to establish and maintain and the process by which palliative care developed this policy shift to end-of-life care offers clues about why this is.

Social work settings in health care

Hospital care

Hospital care is the most common location for health-related social workers. Most hospital care is provided through a local district general hospital (DGH), which often has an accident and emergency (A&E) or casualty department providing emergency medical services. Hospitals provide medical and nursing treatment to cure a patient's illness, disability or injury or to reduce the impact of the symptoms, so that patients become self-managing and return home to ordinary life. Most people are treated as outpatients or day patients but there are in-patient facilities, beds, for patients who need operations and nursing that cannot be completed within an outpatient appointment or day treatment. DGHs have a wide range of specialist doctors, nurses and other health care staff, and usually have social workers. All staff are organised around medical specialities, such as surgery, coronary care and renal care. There are some specialised hospitals for very complex conditions, such as specialist hospitals for cancer or heart conditions.

Social workers in hospitals are, therefore, usually attached to specialist teams. Consequently, there is a wide range of social workers with involvement in the major health specialities, particularly those that require long-term care, such as cancer, children, heart disease, geriatric care (the medical care of older people) and renal disease. Because these posts require specialist knowledge, they attract social work staff who have built up an interest, and sometimes training, through experience in a relevant local authority adult or children's social care post. A common alternative model of organisation in hospital social care is for a team of local authority social workers to provide care management and links with children's services from a base within the hospital.

Other institutions providing health care

Other institutions that provide health care usually provide specialist services. Intermediate care units offer rehabilitation for people with long-term medical conditions or disabilities who are building up their capacity to return to ordinary living in their own homes where they manage their own conditions with the support of their family and community. Social workers are often part of specialist teams attached to these facilities. Hospices provide palliative care for people approaching the end of their lives. This medical speciality emerged from care for people diagnosed with cancer and other conditions at the 'end stage', in which curative treatment was no longer possible (Reith and Payne, 2009). Its principle is to concentrate on managing pain and other physical symptoms with expert medical and nursing help, enabling people to maintain a normal life for as long as possible, while also dealing with the emotional consequences of knowing that death is imminent and carrying out practical and social tasks that people often want to complete in the weeks and days before their death. Many hospices are small-scale facilities providing a service in people's homes, which often include care homes and a small number of in-patient beds, and rely on local specialist medical practitioners and general practitioners. A few are larger facilities providing a full range of palliative care expertise and more comprehensive services.

In addition to these hospital-like institutions, nursing homes (the official title is 'care homes with nursing') offer nursing care in a home-like environment mainly for older people who experience frailty and disabilities, which mean that they are no longer able to live independently in their own homes. Care homes offer help with the activities of daily living, where nursing is not required, in a similarly domestic setting. Both care and nursing homes are primarily led by nursing expertise, although most employees are care assistants who often have minimal qualifications. Until the mid-1980s, most care homes were managed by local authority social services, but most are now private or voluntary sector organisations. The better availability of care services in people's own homes, since the 1980s, means that residents are now often very frail, both physically and mentally, and social objectives have been displaced by nursing and physical care priorities. Consequently, care homes rarely employ social workers, although there is considerable engagement with staff from local authority adult social care departments who assess potential residents for local authority care funding and sometimes maintain links between residents and their families where there are difficulties between them.

Primary care

Primary care is so called because it is the local first point of contact between a citizen and the health care services. The aim is to assess the health concerns that a patient presents, provide and supervise treatment, in most cases, and refer the patient to another service if the treatment cannot be provided or completed locally. Primary care services in the UK are organised around a doctor called a general practitioner (GP), who employs a primary health care team (PHCT) of administrators, nurses, health care assistants and sometimes other staff. The other staff might include a counsellor or social worker, and GPs decide the range of people they employ. A long history of projects to place social workers with GPs, so that they are present in this front-line universal agency with high public credibility, has not led to any consistent pattern. Some are seconded from local authorities in a partnership scheme, some employed directly by GPs and in some cases there are liaison workers who promote relationships between (mainly adult) social care departments and GPs (Rummery, 2003). However, most GPs do not have access to social work help, and refer difficulties to the relevant local authority care service in their area.

Community health care services

Community health care services include day centres for older people and for people with particular long-term conditions and disabilities. Specialist services such as drug action teams (DATs), community alcohol services and child and adolescent mental health services (CAMHS) also employ social workers, who often develop a specialist interest while working for local authority adult social care or children's social care posts. CAMHS bridge children's social care and mental health care. These services are often integrated with in-patient health care settings in their specialty.

Public health and commissioning

Public health and commissioning are aspects of health care that involve social workers often in voluntary or third sector organisations concerned with particular health care conditions and practitioners and managers in local authority adult social care. Public health is concerned with preventing ill health through health education, and through measures to improve the environment, remove pollution and improve housing and sanitation. Although from 2013 this is mainly a local authority function, there are close links with local health care services and voluntary organisations advocating for the interests of particular client groups.

Commissioning in health and social care is the process of establishing, planning and financing services appropriate to community needs. It involves assessing the needs of the population served, deciding on an appropriate mix of provision, finding providers that can make the services available in that area and arranging and financing their services. The processes for doing this are in constant change, and after the reforms of the Health and Social Care Act 2012, the pattern of arrangements is still developing. Managers and practitioners work together in various forums to carry out these tasks and employ staff to do this work, either directly or through management consultancy. Social workers, with their background in the social sciences, often bring useful skills to multiprofessional teams engaged in this work, and local authority responsibilities for commissioning social care services overlap and interact with health care commissioning.

Roles of social workers in health care settings

Social workers practising in health care settings are not health care professionals in the same way that social workers practising in children's education departments or working with offenders in criminal justice settings are not education or criminal justice professionals. The distinctive aims of social work, set out in the international definition (IFSW, 2000), are to act as problem solvers, to work to enhance people's personal and social capacity to liberate them from constraints that prevent them from achieving their life goals and to work for social change that removes barriers to broader social improvement in the lives of disadvantaged individuals and social groups. In pursuing these aims, social workers bring a concern for the 'social' into health care interventions. Their work is social in three main ways:

1   They focus on people's social relationships and networks, as well as on their individual needs and resources, and how these contribute to the sources of their health condition and to health care.
2   They are concerned with social institutions that may support or constrain people in meeting their needs. This includes organisations such as social agencies or public and private services and also social institutions in the sense of family, culture or community.
3   By helping individuals, families and communities to resolve present problems, they aim to enhance the resilience and capability of those individuals, families and communities to manage difficulties in the future.

The main roles of social workers in health care settings include the following:

•   Stopping social factors getting in the way of effective health care, by assessing and reporting to multiprofessional colleagues on the social implications of patients' conditions and social barriers to the effectiveness of health care interventions.
•   Contributing social and psychological help to health care provision by identifying social provision that enhances the effectiveness of health care interventions.
•   Interpersonal intervention with patients, their families and informal carers to meet social needs and to deal with emotional and psychological difficulties arising from the impact of the patient's condition on their and their family's and carers' social well-being.
•   Assisting patients and families in applying for social security, social care and other services to meet their social and health care needs.
•   Advocating with other services to ensure that patients' and families' social needs are met.

Where the main role is an extension of local authority care management responsibilities, social workers in health care assess patients who are ready to be discharged back to their homes and for local authority community care services. Many hospitals employ discharge co-ordinators, who are usually nurses or administrators whose job is to liaise with GPs, PHCTs, family members and other community services to co-ordinate support for the patient at home. Social workers might become involved where this is complicated because family relationships present difficulties in making these arrangements or limited informal support is available from friends and family.

Where health care social workers are part of multiprofessional teams caring for patients with long-term conditions, such as heart, lung or renal failure or progressive disabilities such as Parkinson's disease or multiple sclerosis, they often start their work with patients on resolving practical difficulties in managing the disease at home or in other community settings. Another starting point may be ensuring that patients are receiving all the financial and practical support to which they are entitled. Sometimes, this leads on to work with the emotional and social consequences of their illness or the treatment patients are receiving. For example, disability may affect people's sex lives or lead to changes in how they relate to their children or other members of the family. They may become depressed by the limitations that the illness casts over their lifestyle or anxious about the risk of falling or making their condition worse in other ways. Patients with heart conditions may be unable to go out and pursue leisure activities with the freedom they are used to, for example, and patients with renal failure may be subject to very severe dietary restrictions, which take the pleasure out of family meals. Other members of the family may grieve for the loss of the fit and active person that they previously knew, and caring for the patient may mean that they have to give up work, or limit access to educational opportunities or leisure pursuits. Unusual psychological reactions may also be a focus of work. For example, patients may become anxious about their dependence on complex machinery, such as dialysis machines.

Social work–health care divide

Divisions between social work and health care in the UK are sustained by legal, financial and administrative divisions that affect the relationship between central government policymaking and local service delivery (Glasby and Littlechild, 2004). Each UK nation has a slightly different structure and approach to these services. In England, Northern Ireland and Wales, the Department of Health and Education of the relevant government is responsible. In Scotland, social work is part of the education department. Health care organisations in all countries are usually 'branded' NHS (National Health Service) to emphasise to users the range of provision they receive from this politically important care system.

In England, financial support for social care is separated from policy and development, which makes it difficult to co-ordinate the implementation of policy that affects both. In Wales, there is a health and social services minister and policy is more co-ordinated, although local services are still divided between the NHS and local authorities (Stevenson and Boyce, 2005). Most local authorities in England and Wales have adult social care services, but a few have other arrangements, combining social care with other elements of their services. In Scotland, adult social care is provided by local authority social work departments, which merge children's social care, offender and other services together; the NHS is separate. In Northern Ireland, adult social services are provided by health and social service boards, which merge health care and social care services (Review Team, 2011). A similar division exists in the Republic of Ireland. Most European countries replicate such divisions between health and social care, but the arrangements derive from legal and cultural traditions and therefore vary.

In England, the central government Department for Communities and Local Government administers the finance system for local authorities, which determine their provision of social care according to local policies and priorities. The Department of Health is responsible for development of adult social care policy in England; therefore, policy development is separate from financing. The Department of Health in England and the equivalent national departments elsewhere directly manage and fund the NHS. This has come about for two reasons: (1) because of its political importance; (2) because the medical profession has given importance to maintaining independent medical discretion in diagnosis and treatment decisions. The legal basis for social and health care services is a further source of division. Health care legislation enshrines the central political tenet of the NHS: that health care in the UK is free 'at the point of delivery'; that is, no UK citizens pay charges when they receive services, which are funded directly from taxation. Social care legislation has been unconsolidated, and even when legal reform achieves a coherent set of legislation in 2013, a central tenet is that social care provides help for the daily activities of living, which are distinguished from the NHS role of help with illness. Because everyone bears responsibility for their daily lives, while health problems are regarded as exceptional needs, the assumption of social care is that people will make financial contributions to the cost of provision, while health care is wholly financed by the state. Many people find it hard to understand and accept this distinction which means that they must pay for social care help if they are unable to carry out the daily activities of living, yet their inability comes from an illness or disability that is treated free under the NHS.

These administrative, structural and legal divisions interact with other divisions between social work and health care:

1   The generic responsibility of the GP for co-ordinating the health care of individuals and families holistically cuts across the administrative divisions in social care into children's and adults' services and the further division of adult social care into services for older people, disabled people, learning disabilities and mental health.

2   The social work focus on social issues and needs, backed by a social model of explanation based on social science research methods and knowledge, contrasts with the health care focus on identifiable health conditions, backed by a disease model of explanation based on empirical research methods and medical knowledge.

3   The organisational division between social work and health care agencies, which reduces regular interaction between health care staff and social workers.

4   Distinct professional identities derived from separate education and knowledge bases.

5   Different professional organisations, in which health care professionals, and particularly medical practitioners, have a high degree of personal clinical responsibility for their actions, while social work jobs usually involve a higher degree of accountability to a social work agency and political policies.

6   Differing professional ideologies mean that, in health care, problems are seen in health care as first a personal and family responsibility, while social work assumes a greater allegiance to collective social responsibility for people in difficulties.

An important example of these distinctions is debate about the social and medical models of disability. A medical model of practice, which informs most health care organisations and their interventions, seeks to identify conditions of the body and mind, illnesses or disabilities, which through medical interventions may be cured or reduced in their impact. This view is contested by disability and independent living movements of health and social care service users, which argue that disabled people are an oppressed group, excluded from ordinary society because it makes no allowance for the impact of their physical impairments on social participation (Oliver, 1996, p. 22). The development of the social model has led to a movement for social change to transform society and incorporate disability as a natural variation in social living, and has empowered disabled people to value themselves as they are, rather than seeing them as having deficits from a 'normal' ideal of the human body (Shakespeare and Watson, 2002).

Health care focuses on individuals and their bodies, or even on parts of their bodies, in which the physician specialises. Processes such as ageing that are partly social, or social reactions to illness and disability that may affect patients, are of less concern than identifying and overcoming disease or physically disabling conditions. People invest a great deal of their identity in their bodies, their racial, sexual or social identity. For example, women may feel intense psychological reactions to mastectomy operations to cure or prevent breast cancer, since their breasts may represent important aspects of their femininity. Another example is social patterns of consumption, where metabolic illnesses such as diabetes may require restrictions in diet or regular injections of medication, and this affects involvement in ordinary social life. Wider social and family reactions to the processes of becoming ill or disabled, of being diagnosed and living an ordinary life with an illness, its cure or its management, perhaps over a long period of time, also feel less important to health care professionals than physical treatment.

As a result, the culture, education and professional socialisation of health care and social professions leads to markedly different attitudes to health and social care needs. Because the social work role is to assess and work on these aspects of illness that incorporate non-physical and non-medical considerations, social workers represent ideas that are different and to some extent in opposition to the prevailing way of thinking in health care. Because their education is primarily in the social sciences, and their work experience usually starts in local authority social care, they speak a different professional language, are part of a different professional culture, and have not been trained in the medical detail of the conditions or treatments that are well understood by health care colleagues. Therefore, to health care staff, they may seem ill prepared or irrelevant to the main task. To deal with this, many health-related social workers work hard to express and explain the distinctive social objectives of social work, while at the same time providing efficiently a service that meets health care needs as understood by their multiprofessional colleagues. An important part of doing this is to feed back to colleagues what they are doing and why so that they build up a practical under-standing of the social work role and constraints upon it and their contribution to the joint enterprise.

Social work in end-of-life, palliative and supportive care

A significant area of health care in which social workers practise is that of end-of-life and palliative care. This has now broadened to include 'supportive care', which is the care of those who are living with a long-term chronic illness, such as heart, lung or renal failure or even, with advances in its treatment and attendant increased longevity, cancer. Palliative care social workers usually work as part of multiprofes-sional teams based in hospitals or hospices providing care for people with cancer and other life-limiting illnesses, which have reached an advanced or 'terminal' stage where death is likely to occur in the near future.

Working with loss and end-of-life issues are a common feature throughout social work practice across the spectrum of work with children and families to work with adults and older people (Reith and Payne, 2009). Indeed, we all experience loss as part of life. However, it is clear that the experience of loss varies from one individual to another: 'not everyone experiences the same amount of loss [. . .] some may see a situation as a loss whilst others do not. We can [. . .] also observe differences in the ways in which we express loss and in our response to it' (Currer, 2007, p. 6).

Social work intervention within the field of life-threatening illness and end-of-life care in the UK can be traced through the history of the hospice movement and the development of the specialism of end-of-life care (Small, 2001). Dame Cicely Saunders is commonly regarded to be the founder of the modern hospice movement in the UK. She recognised the totality of distress, that can be caused by a diagnosis of cancer (or similar life-threatening illness) in its terminal phase, which has elements of emotional, psychological, financial and spiritual (as well as physical) pain, and therefore the need for a holistic approach to its treatment. This perspective accords well with the tenets of social work (Reith and Payne, 2009).

Significantly, in western society, despite increasing longevity and advances in treatment resulting in constantly improving survival rates, a diagnosis of cancer still seems to confer on the individual a special status. 'Cancer has become the metaphor for the feared death' (McNamara, 2001, p. 30), which can be seen to affect anyone regardless of class, status or financial resources (Beresford et al., 2007, p. 23). Thus, social workers in this field need to be able to work at a psychological level with a high degree of emotional intelligence and recognise the possible effects that a referral to their service may have had on the service user and their family.

Case example

Marilyn was a 65-year-old woman with lung cancer who is currently in a hospice, and who had experienced frightening bouts of breathlessness while at home on her own. Her daughter was concerned about her safety if she returned home. The hospice social worker suggested that they should try to find a weekend when family members would be available if necessary as a test to see how Marilyn would cope at home. An alternative plan was suggested to Marilyn that if this did not work out she could move to residential/nursing care, but visit her home for half days when her family was available. In fact, the weekend at home worked quite well, but when this was extended to weekdays Marilyn could see how anxious her daughter and son were, and so she readily agreed to the option of moving to residential/nursing care.

Benefits and challenges to social work in end-of-life, palliative and supportive care

In 2008, the UK government made a first attempt to co-ordinate policy and practice around palliative care for the forthcoming ten years with its *End-of-Life Care Strategy* (Department of Health [DoH], 2008). The National End of Life Care Programme (NEoLCP) was set up alongside this, to support the implementation of the strategy through engaging key stakeholders and identifying and promoting good practice. Individual frameworks were also established which focused on the different disciplines involved in end-of-life care, and the social care framework, *Supporting People to Live and Die Well – A Framework for Social Care at the End-of-Life* (NEoLCP,

2010), had as one of its objectives to 'strengthen the specialism of palliative care social work' (Objective 4).

Members of the Association of Specialist Palliative Care Social Workers (2006, p. 6) have sought to define the variety of roles that they perform as follows:

> Specialist palliative care social workers offer a wide range of support to patients and families, from practical help and advice around income maintenance, debt counselling, help with housing and accessing other services, through to advocacy, individual counselling and group support. This . . . [may] include bereavement work with adults and children, both as individuals and group setting. Key to specialist palliative care social work is the desire and ability to see people as whole people [. . .] to understand the connections of their lives and seek to act on, rather than ignore, the constraints and discrimination they experience in society.
>
> (Sheldon, 1997; Weinstein, 2008)

What is significant is the variety that exists within the job descriptions of different specialist palliative care social workers, depending on whether they are employed within a hospital, hospice or community team. Even within the hospice movement, the role may vary depending on whether the hospice offers residential/nursing care or daycare/community services.

Beresford et al. (2007) reported on the first major research study that had been conducted into service users' perspectives on specialist palliative care social work in the UK. The findings indicated what service users valued most about their experience of specialist palliative care social work:

1   The importance of the relationship and the preparedness of the worker to be committed to the patient and family's own definition of their needs.
2   Reliability and clarity about what the social worker could do.
3   The significance of a friendly, approachable manner.
4   An emphasis on psychosocial holistic care was valued by patients and carers, including those receiving bereavement support (Beresford et al., 2007; Reith and Payne, 2009, p. 17).

These findings are particularly significant because they provide a challenge to the increasingly 'managerialist' approach to social work in health care, with its growing 'preoccupation with the management of risk and the privileging of outcomes over process' (Lymbery, 2001; Clausen et al., 2005; Holloway and Taplin, 2013). However, it may be that despite its popularity with service users, social work in palliative and end-of-life care is itself under threat. Indeed, the specialist nature of palliative care has long been subject to criticism for being elitist (Douglas, 1992) and for having too narrow a focus on certain types of life-threatening illness, predominately cancer and motor neurone disease (Beresford et al., 2007, p. 23). Likewise the specialist role of social work with people who are dying, people who are caring for people who are dying, or people who have been bereaved seems to be considered by some managers to be a luxury that palliative care services, under pressure to save money, can no longer afford. A number of services have 'replaced' the emotional and psychological support, which was once the province of the social worker, by including it in the job description of other members of the team such as counsellors (some of whom may be working on a voluntary basis) or hospital psychologists, and subsuming the more 'practical' support roles, for example, welfare rights and benefits advice, into those of the nurse or health care assistant (Holloway and Taplin, 2013).

Perhaps there is a need for social workers in this field to diversify, to adapt to the changing situation and to move beyond the narrow parameters of hospice and palliative care and to reach out to where people are actually dying, for example, in nursing homes (see www.stchristophers.org.uk/care-homes#team). Likewise, there is a need to apply the skills and expertise of the palliative care approach within a public health framework of service delivery. For example, Paul (2013) draws on her experience as a hospice social worker in Scotland to describe how she facilitated a bereavement service for children in the local community who had experienced the death of someone significant in their lives regardless of whether that person had received a service from the hospice. Thus, she demonstrated the need to work in partnership with the community to identify and address the need for bereavement support for young people and to build capacity within the community through schools, parent/carer groups and other community services (Holloway and Taplin, 2013).

Anti-oppressive practice considerations

According to Monroe et al. (2011, p. 3), 'responsiveness to individual need and circumstance and attention to issues of cultural sensitivity has been at the heart of palliative care from its inception'. Social workers, through their training and value base, are ideally placed to recognise and address issues of social inequality and to recognise that 'many individuals and communities have experienced histories of injustice and oppression which do not disappear when terminal illness, death and bereavement become part of their lives' (Monroe et al., 2011, p. 3). Monroe et al. (2011, p. 4) have developed a triangle with the three sides depicting the 'complexity of social differences within the holistic model of care' by considering the following: (1) sex and age life cycle issues; (2) bio-social-economic conditions; (3) life circumstance. The three sides are listed in Table 12.1 with the specific variables that need to be considered when understanding individual differences and planning on how to provide the best care to an individual.

Table 12.1 The complexity of social differences (Monroe et al., 2011, p. 4)

Sex and age life cycle issues	Bio-socio-economic conditions	Life circumstances
Gender	Culture and ethnicity	Unemployed people
Old age	Occupation	Travellers
Retirement	Social class	Substance abusers
Mid-life	Sexual orientation	Refugees
Young adulthood	Intellectual ability/disability	Prisoners
Adolescence	Physical ability/disability	Mentally ill
Childhood	Sensory ability/disability	Linguistic minorities
	Urban/rural location	Homeless people
	Rare and chronic medical condition	Gay and lesbian minorities
	Sudden and traumatic death	Ethnic minorities
		Abused and vulnerable children and adults

Summary

This chapter has explored the five main health care settings in which social workers may have a presence as well as the aims and roles of social workers and health care professionals within each of the settings. When working within health care, it is important to acknowledge and understand the organisational and professional divisions that arise in practising social work and how the distinctive roles of social work contribute to and create divisions in health care settings. There was a specific focus on end-of-life and palliative care as social workers can and are beginning to increasingly play a crucial role in this field.

Social workers in the field of end-of-life and bereavement support need to recognise the importance of self-care, supervision and support. Renzenbrink (2008, p. 150) describes the need for 'relentless self-care' and how this might work across organisational, professional and personal support systems. Whether support comes primarily from a staff group (Sheldon, 1997) or from one-to-one supervision (Currer, 2007), the need for reflective practice is paramount. Social workers working in this field need to acknowledge that no amount of skills and expertise 'will be effective if we fail to sustain hope, in our service users and ourselves, that what we do is important and effective, that those who turn to us need not avoid [. . .] genuine feelings in the face of real losses and that we can help them to confront them fully and come to a new understanding' (Weinstein, 2008, p. 166).

📖 CASE STUDY

Joseph was dying of cancer and wanted to visit his family in Africa to see his grand-children, as he had done the year previously. However, his doctor said that his condition had now deteriorated to the extent that he felt it was unwise for Joseph to make this journey. Joseph's social worker asked him to think about journeys that he had made recently and, in particular, to think about how tired he felt after a half day at the hospice day centre. The social worker suggested that Joseph took a three-day rest before coming to the day centre again, and on his return Joseph admitted that he felt exhausted coming to the centre even after the rest.

Questions

 As Joseph's social worker, what might you suggest for Joseph in terms of maintaining contact with his family?

 What other options or services might you suggest when working with Joseph?

Further resources and suggested readings

Beresford, P., Adshead, L. and Croft, S. (2007) *Palliative Care, Social Work and Service Users – Making Life Possible*. London: Jessica Kingsley Publishers.

Currer, C. (2007) *Loss and Social Work*. Exeter: Learning Matters.

Holloway, M. (2007) *Negotiating Death in Contemporary Health and Social Care*. Bristol: The Policy Press.

Payne, M. (2012) *Citizenship Social Work with Older People*. Bristol: The Policy Press.

Reith, M. and Payne, M. (2010) *Social Work in End-of-life and Palliative Care*. Bristol: The Policy Press.

Websites

Age UK – www.ageuk.org.uk

Alzheimer's Society – www.alzheimers.org.uk

Association of Palliative Care Social Workers – www.apcsw.org.uk

Conversations for Life – www.conversationsforlife.co.uk

Department of Health – www.dh.gov.uk

Dying Matters – www.dyingmatters.org

13 Alcohol and other drug treatment

John Watson

Introduction

Working with people with drug problems involves working with some of the most stigmatised and marginalised people in our society. Specialist drugs work is often not traditionally seen as part of the social work domain. In spite of this, social workers have over many years contributed significantly to this field by working in a number of roles in the statutory and voluntary sectors. Social work skills and values can and do make an invaluable contribution, offering a broader perspective in tackling the issues around drug misuse.

What is a drug?

Potential drugs of misuse are psychoactive chemicals, chemicals that have the potential to alter our moods, thought patterns and behaviour to some degree. These chemicals work by interacting with, mimicking or interfering with neurotransmitters, the chemical messengers that carry messages between brain cells, which regulate our moods, our appetites and energy levels. Psychoactive drugs include legal substances in addition to the illegal chemicals we commonly think of as 'drugs'. In fact, the vast majority of us will use some form of drug. There are many complex methods of categorising different types of drugs, but perhaps the easiest is to classify them by their most common effects:

- *Stimulants* – speed up the activity of the central nervous system giving the user a sense of having more energy and alertness. Users may experience increased heart rate and higher blood pressure amongst other physiological effects. Substances include cocaine/crack cocaine, amphetamines, mephedrone, caffeine and nicotine.

- *Sedatives/depressants* – central nervous system activity slows down. The user can experience a slower heart rate, slowed respiratory system and may have a sense of feeling more relaxed. Substances include heroin, methadone, tranquillisers and alcohol.
- *Hallucinogens* – affects the sensory perceptions. The user can experience distortions in what they see or hear. Substances include LSD, magic mushrooms and salvia.
- *Others* – substances that do not easily fit into any single category, which can include cannabis, MDMA (ecstasy), volatile substances (such as glues, gases and solvents) and ketamine.

However, whilst drugs have certain common effects, they do not affect all people in a consistent manner. A drug does not 'make' someone aggressive, happy, anxious or sad by itself. The drug experience is a combination of the chemical, the human being, and the social context in which it is taken. For example, a person drowning her or his sorrows alone following a relationship break-up is unlikely to have the same experience as someone celebrating birthday drinks with friends. Another contributing factor to the effect is the method of taking the drug; for example, effects will come on much quicker when injected. In addition, patterns of use, such as the amount, duration and frequency of usage, will impact on levels of intoxication. Bingeing, taking a large amount within a short time, will commonly mean quicker intoxication. A novice user who has not tried a substance is likely to have a low tolerance and become intoxicated more quickly. However, someone using regularly over a long period can build up a tolerance to that substance and therefore need more to get the same effect. Many users will take more than one drug, a phenomenon known as polydrug use. Inevitably, combining substances can have an impact and certain combinations can increase the risk of overdose. For example, combining sedative/depressants such as alcohol, tranquillisers or methadone will have a cumulative effect, at first increasing intoxication, but potentially further slowing the heart rate and breathing to dangerous levels.

There are three factors that influence how we respond to psychoactive substances, which include the following:

1   *Biological.* Drug/s used; physical health of user; co-current use of medication; tolerance; method of use (injecting, snorting, smoking, orally); patterns of usage (occasional, moderate, bingeing or chronic).
2   *Psychological.* Mental health issues; psychological history/make-up of user; mood at time of usage; issues related to use (loss, abuse, trauma, pain relief, recreational, socially).
3   *Social.* Using alone or with peers; social context of use; stigma and labelling attached to substance/s used.

Prevalence

The vast majority of people who use drugs will not develop problems and many of those that do are able to resolve these without professional support (Best et al., 2006). Nevertheless, there is a population of people whose use causes ongoing issues for themselves and/or others. There is no neat divide between 'normal' users and 'addicts'. Drug issues cover a broad continuum from those whose use is risky, but not causing problems, to people experiencing multiple issues. When studying the prevalence of drug problems, we first need to ask what exactly do we mean by a 'drug problem'? The simple answer is that drug use is a problem when it causes the user and/or others problems. However, in trying to find a standard measure of problematic use most studies rely on the major psychiatric manuals, which define misuse and dependence by categorising different attributes, symptoms and behaviours associated with physical and/or psychological dependence. Physical dependence occurs when certain substances are used regularly over a period of time and when the user ceases using or reduces her or his levels of use very rapidly, she or he may experience certain physical withdrawal symptoms. Drugs noted for producing physical dependence include heroin, alcohol and tranquillisers. Psychological dependence is a need or compulsion to use substances, despite sometimes experiencing adverse effects. Not all drugs produce physical dependence, but all have the capacity to produce psychological dependence to some degree.

However, whilst dependence, physical or psychological, is usually thought of as problematic, much lower levels of use can cause problems for some people, as demonstrated in the following case example.

Case example

Masood is a 16-year-old British Pakistani. He started working for a local supermarket about seven months ago, making new friends, with whom he has started to socialise. He expresses some discomfort about his alcohol usage on these occasions and reports drinking up to three or four pints of beer at times. Relations with his family have been strained as a result of arguments around his drinking. His parents have recently thrown him out and he has since lived a transient lifestyle, sleeping on friends' sofas.

Points to consider

- Would you personally consider Masood's drinking excessive?
- If you drink, how would your own intake compare?

We should never make assumptions around someone's culture and her or his attitudes towards drugs. However, some cultures do have differing views around what substances are acceptable. In Masood's case, his drinking would not be viewed as abnormal by many people from western cultures, but could be viewed as problematic in different cultural settings. Whilst the vast majority of people in contact with services have much higher levels of usage, we must not ignore how different levels can be problematic in certain individual and cultural contexts.

Alcohol misuse

Excessive alcohol usage can cause a variety of physical, psychological and social harms. Bingeing increases the risks of intoxication and consequently the risks of accidents, assault, or anti-social behaviour. Drinking more frequently, over a prolonged period, can lead to issues with physical and psychological dependence. People who are heavily physically dependent can experience dangerous, occasionally life threatening, physical symptoms of withdrawal if they suddenly stop or reduce their usage too rapidly.

Approximately 90 per cent of adults in the UK drink alcohol with the vast majority experiencing no problems. However, around one in four exceed government guidelines as to low risk levels of intake (Cabinet Office, 2004). Within this figure are people drinking at higher levels and showing signs of harm, and further along the continuum are those with symptoms of dependence. Statistics for dependence vary but recent research estimated that around 9 per cent of men and 4 per cent of women (aged 16–74) showed some symptoms of dependence (NHS Information Centre, 2012).

Drug misuse

According to the British Crime Survey, 36.3 per cent of 16 to 59 year olds report trying drugs, whilst 8.8 per cent report use in the last year (Smith and Flatley, 2011). However, this does not necessarily indicate problematic usage. The 2008 drugs strategy estimated there to be 332,000 'problem drug users' (HM Government, 2008). However, a 'problem drug user' here is explicitly defined as a person using heroin and/or crack cocaine. The most recent figure for these users is 320,000 of whom 170,000 are currently in treatment (HM Government, 2010). However, this excludes users of other illegal substances who may also experience difficulties. In addition, the illegality of certain substances and the stigmatisation that their use attracts means that many may be reticent about approaching services.

There are also a number of other legally available substances. A number of over-the-counter and prescription medications are potentially addictive, particularly tranquillisers and certain strong painkillers. A more recent phenomenon is the emergence of 'legal highs': illicit manufacturers have been able to bypass laws by manipulating chemical formulae and producing new substances not covered by legislation. It will take time before these substances feature in official statistics.

Legal framework

All countries have legislation controlling the supply and possession of certain substances. In the UK the main law is the Misuse of Drugs Act 1971, which is one of the strictest in Europe. This Act prohibits the supply or possession of certain substances, introducing a three-level, ABC classification system based on perceived levels of harm. The classification of the drug determines the maximum potential criminal sentence that can be applied. Examples of a few of these drugs and their classifications are given in Table 13.1.

The Act also makes it an offence to allow premises that one manages to be used for drug use, cultivation and supply. This is significant for workers in residential settings, day centres or hostels. In such situations, the worker must take action, which may involve barring the service user from the service, or reporting to the police, depending on the level of the offence and the agency involved. The issue of confidentiality can cause much anxiety for both service users and workers. The Police and Criminal Evidence Act 1984 allows for discretion within a therapeutic relationship, although in a criminal investigation the police may apply for a warrant to access your files (NTA, 2003). You are not expected to automatically report someone to the police for using illegal drugs if they are committing no other offences. However, the rules regarding information sharing for service users on court sanctioned treatment orders are more complex and will be described later in more detail. Government policy has also attempted to promote support and treatment. Until the 1980s, this was predominantly abstinence based. However, the outbreak of the HIV/AIDS virus forced a rethink. The revelation that by sharing injecting equipment people could spread the

Table 13.1 Drug classifications and penalities

Class	Drugs	Penalties for possession	Penalties for supply
A	Heroin, cocaine/crack, methamphetamine, MDMA, methadone (without prescription) any Class B drug prepared for injection.	Up to seven years imprisonment and/or a fine.	Up to life imprisonment and/or a fine.
B	Amphetamines, cannabis, mephedrone.	Up to five years imprisonment and/or a fine.	Up to 14 years imprisonment and/or a fine.
C	BZP, GHB, ketamine.	Up to two years imprisonment and/or a fine.	Up to 14 years imprisonment and/or a fine.

virus amongst themselves and the wider community led to the expansion of a policy of harm reduction, including the prescribing of methadone (as a substitute for street heroin) and the provision of clean needles and injecting equipment. This was a pragmatic response that realised that many users may not be ready to stop and that reducing harm (to the users and community) was the ethical way forward.

The Labour government of 1997–2010 brought increased funding for treatment. The focus, though, was very much on support delivered in conjunction with the criminal justice system (Buchanan, 2010). The Crime and Disorder Act 1998 introduced court sanctioned treatment orders for trigger offences (common drug-related offences). These orders obliged offenders on community sentences to attend support and submit to regular drug testing. Non-compliance, non-attendance, or a positive sample in drug testing could lead to the offender being taken back to court to have her or his order reviewed with the possibility of a custodial sentence. The Criminal Justice Act 2003 replaced the original orders with the more flexible Drugs Rehabilitation Requirements (DRRs). Similar orders have been introduced for offenders with alcohol problems and drug users on bail awaiting a court appearance. The Drugs Act 2005 allowed compulsory drug testing on arrest, rather than charge. Failure to co-operate and attend follow-up assessments is an offence for which the user can be charged, even if they are not charged for the original offence (Buchanan, 2010).

Whilst alcohol is legally available to over-18s from licensed premises, alcohol policy has recently focused on binge drinking and public order offences. Alcohol treatment is often delivered separately from drug treatment in specialist teams or agencies, although many drug users will also have alcohol issues.

The coalition government introduced their strategy in 2010 (HM Government, 2010). Amongst its main points were the adoption of a payment by results system for drugs agencies and an aim to promote more abstinence-based treatment. The move to a payment by results approach has been criticised for the potential for cash-strapped agencies to focus their energies on the most stable service users at the expense of those whose needs are more complex or who are not ready for abstinence (Roberts, 2011; Watson, 2012). Social workers need to be prepared to advocate for their service users' needs and may need to work with service user groups to ensure that the possibilities for such cherrypicking are minimised.

Theoretical frameworks

Historically, substance misuse was seen as a simple choice made out of moral weakness. In the eyes of many politicians and media commentators it continues to be seen as such, contributing greatly to the stigmatisation of drug users (Lloyd, 2010). However, researchers and practitioners have usually cited more complex reasons why people may develop and maintain problems.

The disease model moved away from moralistic explanations and described substance misuse as an illness beyond the user's control. The eighteenth-century doctor Benjamin Rush described it as a disease of the will caused by drinking strong alcohol. However, this model was uncomfortable for western society where the majority of people consumed alcohol. In the twentieth century, attention shifted to separating 'alcoholics' from 'normal' drinkers (Heather and Robertson, 1997). The twentieth-century disease model explained addiction as an inherited mental disorder. This is most famously articulated by the self-help groups, Alcoholics Anonymous (AA) and Narcotics Anonymous (NA), who see addiction as a condition predetermined at birth. This theory proposes that the 'alcoholic' or 'addict' is never able to control their use and that one drink or drug will inevitably lead to disaster.

There is evidence that a significant minority of people with problems may have a genetic vulnerability to developing problems in the presence of other psychological or social triggers (DiClemente, 2006). However, this does not support the idea of a user who is predetermined to become addicted on touching their first drug, regardless of psychological and/or social factors. Furthermore, by splitting users into 'normals' and 'addicts/alcoholics' it fails to acknowledge the wide continuum of problems and has helped to generate stereotypes. Whilst one of the original aims of AA/NA was to promote understanding, their labels 'alcoholic' and 'addict' have become associated with stigmatising stereotypes and myths around the characteristics of the 'typical' substance misuser. Indeed, many people will specifically avoid treatment to prevent themselves becoming associated with these labels and their associated baggage (Hunt and Derricott, 2001).

However, regardless of these debates, drug users often do have medical issues. Undoubtedly heavy use and certain methods of using (particularly injecting) carry greater health risks. As certain substances are physically addictive, using substitute drugs on a gradually reducing dosage, a process known as detoxification, is safer and easier than trying to stop without medical assistance. Certainly, any physically dependent alcohol or tranquilliser user would be ill advised to stop suddenly without medical support. Substitute prescribing (replacing the street drug with a drug prescribed at a steady dose) can help restore stability to chaotic lives and reduce the risk of other harms, such as blood borne viruses, overdoses and drug-related crime. Health professionals were at the forefront of the harm reduction movement in the 1980s, recognising that it is often the ways in which people use that generate the most harm. This model proposes that it is more ethical to focus on the achievable goals of minimising harms, by advising and supporting the user to adopt safer practices, than allowing her or him (and/or others) to suffer until she or he is ready to consider abstinence. It also enables the practitioner to engage with service users who might not normally come forward. This links in with British Association of Social Workers (BASW) code of ethics, which includes the principle to respect service users' rights to make informed decisions and choices (BASW, 2002).

Psychological models

Psychological models see substance use as shaped by choice, but not in simplistic, moralistic terms. Drugs are seen as serving functions in people's lives and even the most seemingly irrational behaviour can carry a purpose. Social learning models see drug misuse as a product of learned behaviours: users come to associate drug use with certain stimuli (classical conditioning); drug use is positively or negatively reinforced as the user perceives benefits, or avoids certain negative experiences (operant conditioning); or a user observes valued role models using and experiencing positive effects (modelling). In addition to these behavioural models we can add cognitive theory, which looks at the roles of automatic thoughts and belief systems in decisions to use or continue using drugs. The case example below highlights some aspects of these theories.

Case example

Mark relapsed after being clean for nine weeks. He had been feeling anxious and depressed and was walking home after a doctor's appointment. He decided to take a short cut. It took him past a pub where his drug-using mates used to gather. He decided to pop in for a quick pint and bumped into an old dealer who offered him some tranquillisers and a £10 bag of heroin. He thought taking some as a one-off might 'help me calm down a bit'. However, after taking some pills and smoking most of the bag he felt guilty that he had 'screwed up'. He felt that he had lost control and began to use heroin more regularly.

Points to consider

- What factors can you see here that may have led to Mark's relapse?
- Think of how social learning and cognitive theories might apply here.

Psychologists have also explored how people change their substance-using behaviour. The transtheoretical model (TTM) of change focused on how people change by identifying the key dimensions in this process (DiClemente, 2006). Central to this model are the stages of change, which describes different levels of motivation:

- **Precontemplation**. The precontemplator has no intention of changing in the near future. They may see no problems, or the negatives of their behaviour may be seen as an acceptable cost of use. As long as no compelling reason to change arises, the individual will remain here (DiClemente, 2006).
- **Contemplation**. The contemplator becomes aware that aspects of her or his behaviour are causing problems. In this stage, the contemplator will feel ambivalent by feeling conflicted between the perceived positives and

negatives of maintaining or changing her or his behaviour. Contemplators can exist on a broad continuum from those with a tiny glimmer of discomfort with their behaviour to a point where they are openly voicing both sides of the change dilemma. A user can be at the contemplation stage for varying lengths of time. To be able to change, the user needs to be willing and ready (it needs to be top of their list of priorities) and the user needs to feel able to change. Here the concept of self-efficacy is vitally important; users won't try to change if they don't believe that they're able (Miller and Rollnick, 2002).

- **Preparation/determination**. A narrow window during which a decision to change has been made. At this point, the user is contemplating targets and action plans for change. They will not remain here long, however, as they will either take action or seek support, or move back to contemplation.
- **Action**. The stage during which the user is working towards defined goals and making changes. Motivation and self-efficacy are higher here than in earlier stages, but they are still vulnerable to triggers to using and relapse.
- **Maintenance**. The targets of the action stage have been reached and as the change is maintained, self-efficacy increases. The danger of relapse is still present until new behaviours become fully integrated into the user's lifestyle with minimum thought or effort.

Motivation can be affected by internal and external factors that result in a re-evaluation of the positives and negatives of usage. Relapse is the norm, motivation can fluctuate on a frequent basis and service users are more likely to fluctuate back and forth through the stages than progress in a linear fashion. The value of the model to workers is to recognise the difficulties of change and enable the tailoring of strategies to the level of motivation. Whilst assessing motivation is not an exact science, it is valuable to be able to recognise that different individuals may require different strategies. For example, precontemplators may not be ready to consider abstinence, but may be open to advice around harm reduction. Alternatively, it may be possible to work with their families and carers around coping strategies, rewarding periods of abstinence and avoiding inadvertently reinforcing substance use (Barber, 2002). A user who may express discomfort about behaviour may well be contemplating change rather than ready to move on. At this stage, rather than pressing ahead with action plans, it is important to address both the pros and the cons of change as the user sees them.

Addressing ambivalence was the central aim of motivational interviewing. This approach recognises that change involves difficulties as well as benefits to the user. Resistance to change is seen as an understandable response to this conflict (Miller and Rollnick, 2002). With the skilful use of active listening skills, it seeks to encourage a discussion around drug use. The drug user is invited to discuss their own feelings around the positives and negatives of maintaining the behaviour or changing. The worker listens carefully for indicators of concern about the behaviour and uses skills such as open questions, paraphrasing and reflection to encourage discussion of these from the service user's perspective. A central element is that the practitioner avoids arguing or debating and recognises that it is the service user's perceptions that are important here. In essence the service user is encouraged to voice her or his own arguments for change; the things that make her or him feel less comfortable and the worker merely reinforces these (Miller and Rollnick, 2002). Self-efficacy is also considered an important component of motivation here and the practitioner looks to boost this by highlighting strengths and successes as the discussion progresses.

Social models

Whilst the transtheoretical model acknowledges the context of change as an influence on how people move through the stages of change, the main focus is on the individual. Advocates of a social model criticise the medical and psychological models' emphases on the individual. Drug use may be seen as a choice but it is recognised that some people have fewer alternatives in life than others. Buchanan (2004) has pointed out that structural inequality and deprivation very often precede substance misuse. Not all substance misusers come from deprived communities, but problems such as poverty, inadequate housing, poor performance in education and unemployment are common precursors to drug use (Reuter and Stevens, 2007). It is argued that insufficient emphasis has been given to these in a system that still emphasises the legal and individual aspects of addiction (Buchanan 2004, 2010). Barber (2002) points out that as social workers we need also to address the social contexts in which drug users live. Hence, social workers within substance misuse agencies are in a strong position to push for a more holistic understanding of drug-related issues.

In addition, substance misusers, particularly users of certain illegal substances like heroin and crack, are subject to a process of 'othering'; being commonly described and presented as different to the majority (Buchanan, 2004). These messages are often transmitted and reinforced by the media and major public figures, who present them as a threat or as the undeserving poor (Watson, 2012). This can result in them facing discrimination in public service provision and encountering unsympathetic, indifferent or hostile attitudes from professionals (Hunt and Derricott, 2001; Lloyd, 2010). The end result is that substance users are further excluded and marginalised. Labels then become self-fulfilling prophesies as the substance user internalises them. Hence, stigma acts as a barrier for engagement and change and reinforces substance use.

Biopsychosocial models

Drug issues often involve aspects of all of the above. The social impacts on the psychological, for example, social deprivation and stigma generate feelings of low self-worth. In the drugs arena, the importance of addressing medical issues remain and whilst social workers will not treat physical health issues directly, a basic knowledge is important in providing support. Service users may ask for advice around different medical options or may need advice around risks, or methods of using. A practitioner in the drugs field who is not able to use basic drugs-related health knowledge will struggle to win credibility with service users or fellow professionals.

The biopsychosocial model is the one to which most modern agencies aspire. This model recognises the medical aspects of drug problems whilst simultaneously addressing psychological and social/environmental factors. This recognises the complexities of addiction, but professionals may pay lip service to the model, whilst still maintaining their own professional bias (DiClemente, 2006). Working within specialist agencies often involves collaboration with practitioners with markedly different perspectives. To make the biopsychosocial model work involves a high degree of skill in inter-professional communication and an ability to understand differing professional perspectives.

Social work roles, best practice approaches and anti-oppressive considerations

Drugs support is delivered in four different tiers with each tier representing a different intensity of intervention (NTA, 2002). Specialist social workers can work at tiers 2 to 4, although it is unusual at present for them to work in residential settings. The tiers and potential roles are outlined below:

Tier 1

This includes any helping professional encountering a drug user, including non-specialist social workers. The main roles here are to identify issues and refer on if necessary.

Tier 2

This includes specialist agencies, usually based in the voluntary sector. Service users do not need a professional referral and can self-refer or often just drop in. Roles here include providing brief interventions, crisis intervention, advice and support around harm reduction and lower risk usage, needle exchanges, motivational work using techniques such as motivational interviewing, giving advice to non-specialist professionals, supporting carers and assessment and referral on to more structured work at Tier 3. Workers need to have basic knowledge of the medical options such as detoxification or substitute prescribing and of the physical health issues related to drug use, such as withdrawal and overdose risks. In addition, a good knowledge of basic counselling skills and the ability to apply the core conditions of congruence, empathy and unconditional positive regard (Rogers, 1961) are vital in engaging and building trust with stigmatised service users, who often lack self-efficacy and self-esteem. Evidence indicates that the attitudes and values of the practitioner are the most important ingredients in supporting change (Miller and Rollnick, 2002). Confrontational approaches and facing down a service user in an attempt to get them to admit to being an 'addict' or 'alcoholic' tend to be counter-productive and only increase resistance.

Assessments will explore the following: drugs/s used; patterns and methods of usage; physical health problems; potential symptoms of drug withdrawal; medication prescribed; mental health issues; risks, including self-harm and harm to others; family networks and childcare responsibilities; housing and social support networks. In addition to this, the worker will need to assess motivation levels and make decisions around what this may mean in terms of immediate support strategies.

The introduction of drug testing for trigger offences has led to drugs agencies placing arrest referral workers in police custody suites. In these challenging environments, the worker's role is to engage with service users around their substance use and assess risks and needs before referring on.

Tier 3

This includes structured community support based in voluntary agencies or parts of the NHS. Roles here include the following: comprehensive assessment; care co-ordination; structured counselling; community based prescribing and group work. These services usually require a referral from another agency. Social workers in these settings will be employed in roles around structured psychosocial support. This can involve cognitive behavioural approaches, skills training and structured day programmes. Comprehensive assessments involve a full assessment of biological, psychological and social factors and an in-depth personal history of changing patterns of usage with associated life events. Ongoing work here can explore the potential high-risk situations and the triggers that can lead to relapse. It is important to think about relapse and potential triggers as soon as change begins rather than once targets are reached. Here cognitive-behavioural approaches remain important in helping the service user become aware of the people, places, emotions, events, times, thoughts and belief systems that can trigger cravings. In addition, psychosocial approaches that focus on aspects of skills training, housing support and living skills are also vital. The emphasis of social work on systemic assessment and approaches can be invaluable here.

Workers may also support service users who are considering in-patient or community detoxification, and/or residential rehabilitation. Whilst medical detoxes are safer and easier for the user than stopping by themselves, they are still an uncomfortable experience in which the user needs to be prepared. Residential rehabilitation is an option for those who have been unable to maintain abstinence with community support but who are still motivated towards abstinence. It involves in-depth residential support in a structured environment. There are different ideological models of rehab, including the 12-steps model (derived from AA/NA), which involves an emphasis on the disease model and elements of spirituality, cognitive-behavioural orientated units and religious-based rehabs. Residential rehabilitation should not be taken on lightly as it often involves moving away from family and friends and usually involves strictly regulated regimes. Some users will prefer different treatment ideologies and this must be discussed in advance before arrangements are made. Users may need support in enabling them to visit potential rehabs. As the most expensive form of treatment, most users will need to seek funding, which is currently held by social service departments. Some departments will have specialist substance misuse teams who prepare service users for residential rehab, assess their readiness and motivation, discuss preferred treatment ideologies, and undertake community care assessments for funding. In other areas, community care assessments are still undertaken by generic adults' teams, whilst the in-depth support may be undertaken by specialist social workers in the statutory and/or voluntary sectors. In planning and preparing for rehab, the worker must also consider aftercare for the service user leaving this structured environment.

These services may be provided to voluntary service users or those whose involvement is a requirement of court sanctioned orders. Services aimed at people on court orders are usually delivered separately. The drugs intervention programme was devised to provide support to substance misusers throughout the criminal justice system from arrest referral onwards. Working with service users on court orders brings with it particular challenges. Social work as a profession has a value base that has traditionally emphasised the importance of autonomy and human rights (Banks, 2012). Balancing this alongside legal requirements is often a complex task.

Collaborative working in these situations also brings new challenges. In addition to working alongside health professionals, probation officers will be closely involved in monitoring compliance with court orders. In these circumstances the rules around confidentiality and disclosure are more complex. There will be information that practitioners are obliged to share with probation officers, such as if someone relapses or gives a positive sample on drug testing. In such cases the order may be reviewed and taken back to court. This does not necessarily mean that the service user will be sent into custody, but it could mean an adaptation in the requirements of the order. In such circumstances, good collaborative working relationships with both service users and probation workers are essential in negotiating the best ways forward.

Tier 4

This involves in-patient detoxification and residential rehabilitation. Detoxification facilities are predominantly staffed by medical professionals whilst residential rehabilitation has traditionally been the preserve of counselling (although some may take on social workers). Social workers in voluntary sector agencies will often provide support to service users leaving residential rehab and/or detoxification. Such support may include further work around relapse prevention and support around resettlement in a new area, or around settling back into their communities.

Benefits and challenges to working with people with drug and alcohol problems

Working in the field of alcohol and other drug treatment can be a rewarding experience, as it often offers social workers the chance to undertake the sort of ongoing therapeutic work that workers in other fields do not get the chance to undertake. However, there are also a number of specific challenges.

As mentioned previously, the issues of confidentiality and information sharing can be more complex with this service user group, particularly, but not exclusively, when working in criminal justice settings. It is often a complex juggling act respecting the rights and autonomy of service users, whilst being open and honest about the potential restrictions to confidentiality. The legal status of certain substances, along with the stigma attached to substance misuse, means that service users are often suspicious and wary when accessing support. They may well also have had negative experiences when dealing with public services in the past (Hunt and Derricott, 2001; Lloyd, 2010). As mentioned previously, good communication and counselling skills are vital here. However, even the most empathic worker will at times struggle with the range of issues and emotions they may encounter. Substance misusers often present with a complex range of physical, psychological and social difficulties, which when brought to the surface can be distressing for worker and service user alike. Workers with high caseloads in time-pressured environments may find it difficult at times to maintain anti-oppressive stances in the face of such pressure. It is vital that workers are able to reflect on the emotions and feelings such pressure may bring to the surface. Utilising supervision in order to identify and discuss such issues is vital in order to avoid burnout.

Finally, it is important to maintain a professional social work identity. Working in a substance use agency involves much work alongside other professionals, in particular from health care and probation. Social workers in this field need to be confident and assertive, whilst respecting the viewpoints and knowledge of other professions. Much like the AMPH role discussed in Chapter 10, roles in substance use agencies are usually open to other professions (in particular counselling and nursing) and may often carry other titles rather than social worker. However, as stated previously, the social work profession with its skills, values and theoretical perspectives has much to offer. Social workers need to remain aware of and take pride in their professional value base, if social perspectives in tackling substance use are to receive the prominence they deserve.

Summary

Substance misuse is the result of a complex range of biological, psychological and social factors. In substance misuse services, good collaborative working is essential to ensure a holistic approach. The legal perspective sometimes adds further challenges here. In working alongside service users, we must remember that stigma has so often shaped their lives and in particular their experiences of public services. Basic communication and counselling skills are vital and labels tend to be counter-productive. Social workers in specialist agencies need a basic understanding of the medical aspects of substance misuse as well as being skilled in understanding psychological and social triggers. In working with users we must try to explore the biological, psychological and social functions of drug use for them in assessing ways forward and be aware of the fluctuating nature of motivation. Working with substance users often means being aware that change is a gradual process and relapse is the norm. Workers must be willing to challenge stereotypes and engage with the most marginalised of service users. Support must address psychological triggers, social support systems, housing and poverty, as well as the physical aspects of drug use. Social workers, with their dual emphasis on the individual and their environment, are ideally placed to ensure that substance users receive the most holistic support possible.

📖 CASE STUDY

This case study involves a service user accessing a direct access (Tier 2) substance use service.

Julie walks into your agency when you are covering drop-in duty. She presents as anxious and upset. You have received a few details from the domestic violence service that encouraged her to approach your service. She is 23 years old and until five months ago was in a long-term violent relationship. At this point she left her partner and took residence in the refuge. The support staff at the refuge state that Julie initially made good progress and moved from the hostel to supported accommodation next door. However, they report that Julie's drinking has recently escalated and that she was hospitalised two weeks ago after deliberately taking an overdose of tranquillisers. They claim that she seems to be neglecting herself and losing weight.

Julie tells you that she has been drinking recreationally since the age of 14. She states that her alcohol use increased not long after meeting her partner six years ago. Her ex was a heavy drinker and she reports that she began to drink on a daily basis. Julie states that her drinking escalated when the violence started and further escalated after losing her job last year. She states that alcohol helps her sleep at night, particularly since the tranquillisers prescribed by her GP no longer seem to work on their own. She tells you that alcohol is her way of coping with stress and anxiety and that she feels ill if she goes too long without a drink. Finally, she breaks down in tears and tells you that she 'hates being this way'.

Questions

 How would you assess her motivation towards change?

 What skills would be vital in engaging with Julie here and ensuring that she returns for further support?

What triggers do you feel may influence Julie's drinking?

What are the main initial risks here and what strengths can you build upon?

Which social work approaches may help you in supporting Julie?

What other professionals and services would you need to work with to support Julie?

What support systems would you wish to explore and strengthen?

Further resources and suggested readings

Barber, J.G. (2002) *Social Work with Addictions*, 2nd edn. Basingstoke: Palgrave Macmillan.
Gossop, M. (2007) *Living with Drugs*, 6th edn. Aldershot: Ashgate.

Websites

Alcohol Concern – www.alcoholconcern.org.uk
Drugscope – www.drugscope.org.uk

14 Housing and homelessness

Barbra Teater

Introduction

Housing is considered a basic human need alongside breathing, food and water (Maslow, 1954). Despite this basic need, social work does not have an established presence within housing and homelessness services, which are often left to housing departments within local authorities or to the private sector. All service users with whom social workers interact will have or will require housing. Therefore, social workers need to have an understanding of housing and homelessness issues in order to provide the best possible service. This chapter will explore the complex area of housing and homelessness by providing definitions and the prevalence of homelessness within England, exploring areas in which social workers will need to consider housing issues, a review of the homelessness legislation and Housing Benefit and a discussion of theories and methods used when working with housing and homelessness. The chapter will provide several case examples to illustrate current practice and calls for social workers to take an anti-oppressive practice approach to tackle the social, political and economic issues that contribute to current housing and homelessness concerns.

Housing and homelessness: definitions and prevalence

Housing and homelessness is a broad phrase that has relevance and meaning to every human being. Classifying 'homelessness' or the extent to which homelessness exists within England is difficult as there are numerous categories of homelessness which are all measured or counted differently, and many times homelessness is hidden or missed within the ways in which it is calculated (Homeless Link, 2013). Under the umbrella of housing and homelessness are several different terms that are used to describe where or how people live or the extent to which people meet criteria that enable them to receive housing under legislation. Such terms include rough sleepers, statutory homeless, hostels and second stage/supported accommodation and hidden homeless. Each of these terms or types of housing is described below.

Rough sleepers

According to the Department for Communities and Local Government (DCLG) (2013a, p. 7), rough sleepers are defined as follows:

> People sleeping, about to bed down (sitting on/in or standing next to their bedding) or actually bedded down in the open air (such as on the streets, in tents, doorways, parks bus shelters or encampments). People in buildings or other places not designed for habitation (such as stairwells, barns, sheds, car parks, cars, derelict boats, stations, or 'bashes').

The definition does not allow for people to be counted as rough sleepers if they are staying in hostels or shelters, campsites or other recreational sites, or organised protest, squatters or travellers (DCLG, 2013a, p. 7). The phrase 'bedded down' is defined as someone either lying down or sleeping and 'about to bed down' is defined as someone who is sitting in/on or near a sleeping bag or other bedding (DCLG, 2013a, p. 7).

The prevalence of rough sleepers is difficult to determine. Local authorities are required to gather data on the number of rough sleeping within their area, which could be calculated by actual counts or through estimates. Whether a local authority conducts rough sleeping counts or provides estimates is based on their assessment of the rough sleeping problem in their area (DCLG, 2013a). The rough sleeping counts and estimates are to include 'single night snapshots' of the number of people who are sleeping rough and should be informed through local intelligence gathered by outreach workers, police and other people who might have contact with rough sleepers (DCLG, 2013a).

The guidance on evaluating the number of rough sleepers was revised in September 2010, which means that the prevalence of rough sleepers prior to 2010 cannot be directly compared to the prevalence of rough sleepers after 2010. Between 1998 and 2010, only those local authorities who suspected they had ten or more rough sleepers were required to conduct a street count. This resulted in 70 local authorities conducting a street count in 2010, which yielded a total of 440 rough sleepers (DCLG, 2010). These figures were drastically increased when the remaining 256 local authorities were required to do a street count, which resulted in an additional 807 rough sleepers for a total of 1247 rough sleepers in England in 2010 (DCLG, 2010). This led to changes in the guidance on calculating the number of rough sleepers with the main differences consisting of the following (DCLG, 2010, p. 2):

- Local authorities have a choice in conducting street counts and are not required to conduct street counts if local intelligence suggests there are less than ten rough sleepers in their area.
- If a local authority decides not to count, then they must provide a 'robust estimate' of the number of rough sleepers in their area. This must be based on local intelligence and should be informed by the basic guidance on how to make estimations.
- The definition of 'rough sleeper' has been expanded to include people who are about to bed down and people in tents (not on campsites or on organised protests).
- Local authorities are encouraged to carry out their counts on the same night as their neighbouring authorities in order to avoid counting twice.
- The time in which night counts take place should be based on local circumstances and can take place from midnight; this will be later in areas where rough sleepers bed down at a later time.
- DCLG will no longer provide officials to oversee the counts, but rather Homeless Link will provide independent verifiers to attend counts.

As of autumn 2012, there were an estimated 2309 rough sleepers in England, which was a 6 per cent increase from the autumn 2011 count of 2181; the majority (557) are based in London (DCLG, 2013a). Of the 326 local authorities that provided figures, 43 conducted night counts of rough sleepers and 283 provided estimates (DCLG, 2013a).

Statutory homeless

The term homeless is often associated merely with people who sleep rough, yet there are other people who are considered homeless because they do not have a their own accommodation (e.g. sofa surfing), are under threat of losing their accommodation or are unable to continue residing in their accommodation. Statutory homeless often include this group of people which is defined as 'those households which meet specific criteria of priority need set out in legislation [Housing Act 1996], and to whom a homelessness duty has been accepted by a local authority' (DCLG, 2013b). Local authorities have a duty to provide housing to homeless households that are eligible for assistance, have a local connection to the local authority, are unintentionally homeless and are considered priority need (see Legal framework section below for further details). Local authorities are required to collect statistics on the number of homelessness applications and those that are deemed homeless according to the Housing Act 1996. It is important to note that many single homeless people do not meet the criteria of being in 'priority need' and are therefore not included in the homeless statistics (Homeless Link, 2013).

Between 1 July and 30 September 2012, local authorities made decisions on 29,130 homelessness applications of which 48 per cent (13,890) were accepted as owed a homelessness duty under the Housing Act 1996 (referred to as homelessness acceptances), which was an 11 per cent increase when compared to the same quarter in 2011 (DCLG, 2012). This was a 6 per cent increase in the total number of homelessness applications compared to the same quarter in 2011 (DCLG, 2012). Twenty-eight per cent of the homelessness applications were found not to be homeless, 17 per cent were found to be homeless, but not in priority need, and 8 per cent were found to be intentionally homeless and in priority need (DCLG, 2012).

As of 30 September 2012, 52,960 households were in temporary accommodation, which was an 8 per cent increase from the same date in 2011 (DCLG, 2012). Of those, 40,090 included dependent children and/or a pregnant woman and 120 households headed by 16 and 17 year olds (DCLG, 2012). Temporary accommodation is often provided while an applicant is waiting to secure suitable accommodation or until a settled home becomes available, is waiting for a decision on the homelessness application, is waiting for the decision of a review or appeal to the county court of the decision on the application, is waiting for a possible referral to another local authority, or the applicant has been found to be intentionally homeless and in priority need and is therefore given accommodation until the applicant can find accommodation for him/herself (DCLG, 2012, p. 10).

Hostels and second stage/supported accommodation

Hostels and second stage/supported accommodation are usually a place of support and accommodation for many single homeless people who have not been accepted as statutory homeless (Homeless Link, 2013). The definition of supported accommodation is 'any scheme which offers services to tenants not normally provided in the mainstream rented sector. Specific client groups could include older people, the homeless, ex-offenders, or women escaping domestic violence' (Cebulla, 1999, p. xiv).

Individuals in supported accommodation may have disabilities or high support needs where the assistance of staff or support workers is needed to support activities of daily living. Although most hostels and supported accommodation serve single individuals without dependent children, some supported accommodation is provided to pregnant women and young parents with children (usually under the age of two years). The type of accommodation is usually provided through either: self-contained units (possibly with an on-site warden, communal facilities and call systems); hostels; shared accommodation with support from either residential or visiting support workers; or self-contained units in the private sector with flexible support workers.

Supported accommodation usually has the focus of providing temporary accommodation to residents in order to build their independent living skills to the point where they can reside in accommodation on their own. There are various types of supportive accommodation that provide specific services for people with physical disabilities, learning disabilities, mental health difficulties, substance misuse, or young parents. The type of support can include counselling and advice, parental support, support in developing independent living skills, such as cooking, cleaning and budgeting money, benefit support, help with education, and/or employment or training.

It is difficult to determine the total number of people who are accessing hostels, supported accommodation and day centres (places for homeless individuals to go during the day for food, shelter and advice and information). A study conducted by Homeless Link (2012) reported 1567 day centres, direct access hostels and second-stage/supported accommodation in England where there are 32,227 bed spaces in second stage/supported accommodation and 9222 bed spaces in direct access hostels. Since 2011, Homeless Link (2012) found 69 fewer second stage/supported accommodation projects, ten fewer hostels, 3.6 per cent reduction in bed spaces in England and 28 per cent more individuals using the average day centres.

Hidden homeless

The prevalence of homelessness as discussed above takes into account those individuals that have been counted as homeless, through a night count or estimation, applied for and have been successful in a 'homeless' application to the local authority, or are those individuals who are accessing hostels or supported housing. What is missing are those individuals who are homeless but do not fall into any of the three categories discussed. This population is referred to as 'hidden homeless'. Hidden homeless is defined as 'nonstatutory homeless people living outside mainstream housing provision' (Reeve, 2011, p. 1). Hidden homeless include people (predominately single people) who have become homeless but have been able to find temporary accommodation by staying with friends or relatives, have become squatters or are sleeping rough but not counted in the night counts by local authorities (Homeless Link, 2013).

Research by Reeve (2011, pp. 1–2) into the prevalence of the hidden homeless had found that 62 per cent of the single homeless people that were surveyed were defined as hidden homeless on the night they were surveyed; 92 per cent had experienced hidden homelessness as some point; 40 per cent had slept rough the night prior to the survey and 76 per cent had slept rough at some point during their episode of homelessness. Further supporting the notion that many homeless people are in fact 'hidden', Reeve (2011, p. 2) found that nearly 50 per cent of rough sleepers surveyed had not had any recent contact with a rough sleeper team. The consequences of being hidden homeless have been found to include the following: lack of security; extremely poor living conditions; criminalisation; exploitation; risk to personal safety; and physical health impacts (Reeve, 2011, p. 3). See the full report by Reeve (2011) for a more detailed account of the prevalence of hidden homeless.

Social work practice within housing and homelessness services

Although housing is seen as a basic human need for individuals, social workers are rarely directly involved in providing housing for individuals. There are no statutory duties placed upon social workers to provide housing. The sole responsibility of providing housing under legislation is placed on the local authorities and is provided under the housing department, which is often separate from social care. Submitting a homeless application does not mean that the person will, ever has or ever will come into contact with a social worker.

Within statutory settings, social workers are most likely to work with individuals or families who have accessed statutory services through reasons other than housing, such as child protection concerns, adult social care, mental health services or youth offending. When working with individuals and families the social worker and service user might identify housing as an issue that needs to be addressed: for example, being homeless or a threat of becoming homeless, problems with paying rent or a mortgage, or the need for extra support with independent living when moving from the home of a carer, being discharged from a drug treatment agency, or being discharged from a section under the Mental Health Act 1983. In such situations, the role of the social worker may be to provide information and advice about service users' rights in terms of social housing applications, homelessness applications, Housing Benefit, rights as a tenant, and services available in the community that provide accommodation or shelter, such as homeless shelters, day centres, hostels and supported accommodation. Social workers may assist individuals in filling out applications, attending meetings or advocating for individuals to receive support or services. In some situations, social workers may find that they need to refer individuals to a Citizens Advice Bureau (CAB) in order to receive advice on entitlements and rights.

Social work students may find that they are placed within a hostel, homeless shelter or supported accommodation setting for their social work placement. Most housing services such as hostels, homeless shelters, day centres and supported accommodation are provided by the voluntary sector. These services are generally supported through funds and grants from the local government, such as the Supporting People fund, through benefits payments, fundraising and other private and charitable funds (Homeless Link, 2012). The agencies rely on volunteers and predominately unqualified staff to provide support and to ensure the running of daily activities. The support staff can provide information and advice and key working sessions, when time permits. Social work students are often tasked with 'key working', groupwork, providing information and advice, and advocating on behalf of service users.

Legal framework

Housing legislation is a vast area that covers private housing, social housing and homelessness. The Housing Acts of 1985 and 1988 cover types of tenancies in regard to the private market and housing associations, The Landlord and Tenant Act 1985 covers tenants' rights against their landlord and the Anti-social Behaviour Act 2003 requires local housing authorities and registered social landlords to have a policy in regard to housing related anti-social behaviour and neighbourhood disruption. This section will focus primarily on homelessness legislation as well as a discussion of Housing Benefit.

The Housing Act 1977, Housing Act 1996 and Homelessness Act 2002 all place a duty on local authorities to provide free advice and assistance to any household that is homeless or threatened with homelessness (DCLG, 2013b). The Housing Act 1996, as amended by the Homelessness Act 2002, is the main piece of legislation in regard to homelessness.

Housing Act 1996

Part 7 of the Housing Act 1996, as amended by the Homelessness Act 2002, provides the statutory framework on homelessness, which is usually delivered through the local authority's housing department. Any household is able to submit a homeless application to the local authority, but they must meet the criteria under Part 7 of the Housing Act 1996 in order for there to be a duty placed on the local authority to provide housing. The criteria include: (1) *eligible for assistance*; (2) *homelessness*; (3) *priority need*; (4) *not intentionally homeless*. In addition, the applicant needs to have a *local connection* (5) to the local authority. Each of these criteria is described below.

Eligible for assistance

Most UK citizens are eligible for assistance. Individuals not eligible for assistance include those that are subject to immigration control (e.g. a person seeking asylum; no recourse to public funds on passport) or if the person has lived abroad (s.185).

Homelessness

A person is considered homeless if he or she has no accommodation available for his or her occupation in the United Kingdom or elsewhere (s.175). A person may also be considered homeless if 'he has accommodation, but he cannot secure entry to it or it consists of a moveable structure, vehicle or vessel designed or adapted for human habitation and there is no place where he is entitled or permitted to place it and to reside in it' (s.175). A person may have accommodation at the time of application, but may still be considered homeless if he or she is threatened with homelessness within 28 days (s.175). Section 177 provides examples of when it would not be reasonable for someone to continue to occupy accommodation. These include: (1) when staying in the accommodation will lead to domestic violence (or other violence) against the person or any person who normally resides in the accommodation, such as a family member; (2) physical conditions in the property; (3) overcrowding; and/or (4) affordability of the accommodation (Homelessness [Suitability of Accommodation] Order 1996).

Priority need

Once a person is deemed eligible and homeless, the local authority must then decide if the applicant is in priority need. A person is considered in priority need if they are one of the following (s.189(1)):

a.   A pregnant woman or a person with whom she resides or might reasonably be expected to reside;

b.   A person with whom dependent children reside or might reasonably be expected to reside;

c.   A person who is vulnerable as a result of old age, mental illness or handicap or physical disability or other special reason, or with whom such a person resides or might reasonably be expected to reside;

d.   A person who is homeless or threatened with homelessness as a result of an emergency such as flood, fire or other disaster.

The Homeless (Priority Need for Accommodation) England Order set out six further categories of applicants with priority need. These include:

e.   A person aged 16–17 who is not a child in need;

f.   A person under 21 who was looked after, accommodated, or fostered between the ages of 16 and 18;

g.   A person aged 21 or more who is vulnerable as a result of having been looked after, accommodated or fostered;

h.   A person who is vulnerable as a result of being a member of the armed forces;

i.   A person who is vulnerable as a result of ceasing to occupy accommodation because of violence or threats of violence likely to be carried out.

Not intentionally homeless

An applicant will not be considered homeless if it has been found that he or she has been made homeless intentionally. Section 191 states that 'a person becomes homeless intentionally if he deliberately does or fail to do anything in consequence of which he ceases to occupy accommodation which is available for his occupation and which it would have been reasonable for him to continue to occupy'.

Local connection

In order for the local authority to provide housing, they must establish that the applicant has a local connection to the area. Section 199 specifies a local connection as an applicant having a connection with the area because: (1) is, or in the past was, a normal resident there, which was of his own choice; (2) because he is employed here; (3) because he has family associations; or (4) because special circumstances result in a local connection to the area.

The local authorities are required to consider the criteria when determining if someone is homeless and, therefore, determining their duties under the legislation. Although the Act does not stipulate a time frame in which decisions need to be made, the Homelessness Code of Guidance (2006) suggest that decisions be made within 33 days (Brammer, 2010). Homelessness decisions can be reviewed, but the request for a review has to be submitted within 21 days of the notification of the decision (Brammer, 2010). Table 14.1 depicts the possible decisions of homelessness applications with the duties of local authorities.

Table 14.1 Homelessness application decisions (Brammer, 2010, pp. 567–568)

Decision	Explanation	Duty/Result
Homeless but no priority need	A person may be eligible and homeless but does not meet the criteria under priority need.	No obligation for the local authority. Provide free advice. Possibly provide housing (based on resources in the local area) if the person is unintentionally homeless.
Priority need but intentionally homeless	A person may be eligible, homeless and priority need, but have made himself/herself intentionally homeless.	Provide free advice. Ensure that temporary accommodation (e.g. hostel) is made available, but only for a time that will enable the person to find his or her own accommodation.
Priority need but threatened with homelessness intentionally	A person may be eligible, priority need and threatened with homelessness, but this threat is deemed to be intentional.	Provide free advice. Once made homeless, the person is entitled to temporary accommodation (e.g. hostel), but only for a time that will enable the person to find his or her own accommodation.
Priority need and unintentionally threatened with homelessness	A person is eligible, priority need and threatened with homelessness that is deemed to be unintentional.	If the accommodation cannot be secured, the local authority has a duty to provide accommodation once the homelessness occurs.
Priority need and unintentionally homeless	A person is eligible, homeless, priority need, and the homelessness is deemed to be unintentional.	The local authority has a duty to provide accommodation to the applicant and any family member who normally resides with him or her.

Under the Homelessness Act 2002, local authorities have a duty to carry out a review of homelessness in their area and develop a five-year homelessness strategy that aims to: prevent homelessness; ensure accommodation for those who are or may become homeless; and provide support for people who are or may become homeless or who have been homeless and need support to prevent them from becoming homeless again (section 2(1)). In 2012 the DCLG put out a call for a joint approach to preventing homelessness through the *Making Every Contact Count* document, which listed the ten local challenges to the sector (DCLG, 2012, p. 4):

1. Adopt a corporate commitment to prevent homelessness which has buy in across all local authority services;
2. Activity work in partnership with voluntary sector and other local partners to address support, education, employment and training needs;
3. Offer a Housing Options prevention service, including written advice, to all clients;
4. Adopt a *No Second Night Out* model or an effective local alternative;
5. Having housing pathways agreed or in development with each key partner and client group that includes appropriate accommodation and support;
6. Develop a suitable private rented sector offer for all client groups, including advice and support to both clients and landlords;
7. Actively engage in preventing mortgage repossessions including through the Mortgage Rescue Scheme;
8. Have a homelessness strategy which sets out a proactive approach to preventing homelessness and is reviewed annually so that it is responsive to emerging needs;
9. Not place any young person aged 16 or 17 in Bed and Breakfast accommodation; and
10. Not place any families in Bed and Breakfast accommodation unless in an emergency and then for no longer than 6 weeks.

Housing Benefit

Housing Benefit is a government benefit, paid by the local council, to assist low-income households to pay rent to either a private landlord, housing association or hostel or guest house (Department for Work & Pensions [DWP], 2012a). In order to be eligible for Housing Benefit, the household has to be low income, have less than £16,000 in savings, and has a rent to pay (i.e. Housing Benefit cannot be used to pay for a mortgage). Households that are illegal immigrants, 'over stayers' or asylum seekers, have 'no resource to public funds' on the passport, reside with a closer member of family, or are full-time students (unless disabled or have children) are not eligible for Housing Benefit (DWP, 2012a, p. 4). The amount of Housing Benefit that a household will receive depends on the household income and savings, household composition, rent costs and housing size. As of April 2011, Housing Benefits have been lowered and are set by the local authority based on the cost of housing within the area. There is a national limit that can be received through the benefit (£400) with the benefit being determined by number of bedrooms as follows (DWP, 2012a, p. 6):

- £250 a week for a one-bedroom property (including shared accommodation).
- £290 a week for a two-bedroom property.
- £340 a week for a three-bedroom property.
- £400 a week for a four-bedroom property.

It is important to remember that these figures are the maximum that can be received through Housing Benefit and many local authorities will have set their Housing Benefit payments much lower based on the housing market within that area. Housing Benefit will most likely be reduced (by the end of September 2013) for many individuals who receive other benefits as well. This is due to the benefit cap to where people receiving benefits will have their total amount of benefits capped at a certain figure: £500 a week for couples (with or without children living with them); £500 a week for single parents whose children live with them; £350 a week for single adults who do not have children, or whose children do not live with them (DWP, 2012b).

Theories and methods in housing and homelessness

One of the fundamental theories in relation to need is Maslow's hierarchy of needs (1954), which presents a pyramid where the base set of needs are to be met before there is an ability to move to meeting the next set of needs. According to Maslow, physiological needs serve as the foundation, which include breathing, food, water, shelter, clothing and sleep – things required for basic survival. These needs are required to be met before moving on to safety and security, love and belonging, self-esteem and self-actualisation. In this sense, when social workers work with service users, they should first consider the extent to which basic needs are being met. If housing is a need for a service user, then the social worker must first address this need before moving on to address other more advanced needs. Social workers, with an understanding that housing is a basic human need, should explore this need when conducting assessments with service users. This could be incorporated into a formal assessment or the social worker could include a discussion of housing informally to gain a full picture of the service users' needs, which will inform the approach and next steps of work together.

Homelessness shelters and hostels tend to work from the frame of reference that basic needs must be met first before moving on to other needs. Assessments often stem from systems theory (Teater, 2010) by gathering information about the person's biological/physiological and psychological health, any dependency issues, family supports and networks and a history of how the person has come to be in the position in which he or she presents. The first step for many assessors in these situations is to assess for physical well-being and once the physical health is stable, then the next step is to apply for or 'sort out' benefits. It is only once the person has his or her basic needs met that the support worker (or social worker) can begin to move to other issues that have presented, such as mental ill health or substance misuse. This approach is supported by research where the factors found to contribute to an exit from homelessness were benefits and government-funded/supported housing (Zlotnick et al., 1999). Those individuals with substance misuse were more likely to have unstable housing while individuals experiencing mental ill health were no less likely than other individuals to obtain stable housing (Zlotnick et al., 1999).

Specific methods to consider when working with housing and homelessness issues might include a person-centred approach, the strengths perspective and empowerment approach, and advocacy, which may be used in conjunction with task-centred social work and crisis intervention (see Teater, 2010 for an overview for each of these methods). Many service users who come into contact with social services may experience some kind of problems with their housing, may benefit or require supported accommodation, may be homeless or may be experiencing a threat of homelessness. The most important approach for social workers to take is one of being person centred, being genuine, having unconditional positive regard and expressing empathy (Rogers, 1957). People may be experiencing stigma and frustration from society because of their housing situation (Belcher and DeForge, 2012) and the government, through restrictive access to housing (Housing Act 1996), cuts in government funding earmarked for homeless initiatives (Homeless Link, 2012) or reductions in Housing Benefit (DWP, 2012b). The first thing is to acknowledge the current position of individuals and listen to their story, what they need and what they would like to happen as a result.

Social workers should also conduct a strengths assessment (Saleebey, 2012) of the individuals and their families and communities in order to acknowledge strengths and resources that can be built upon to overcome the problem(s), address need(s) and promote human growth and development. By taking a person-centred approach and acknowledging and building upon strengths and resources, individuals may begin to feel more empowered and as if they are able to take more control of their lives.

Social workers may also find that they have to take an advocacy role. Service users may not know of their rights under legislation or may have difficulty in presenting their case for accommodation (e.g. social housing, homelessness application) or Housing Benefit. Social workers may be able to assist in gathering, filling out and submitting forms and applications and assist in responding to requests for further information, final decisions or inform service users on their right to an appeal. Referring a service user to CAB may be necessary to ensure that the service user's rights are fully understood and upheld. Support workers (or social workers) working in homeless shelters may need to advocate for the most appropriate type of hostel or second-stage/supportive accommodation for a service user, which is based on his or her needs and knowledge of the housing situation in that particular community.

The government has recently called for a prevention and recovery approach to tackle homelessness in the UK. The *Vision to End Rough Sleeping: No Second Night Out Nationwide* strategy (DCLG, 2011) echoes the practices of many homeless shelters and day centres across the UK where they aim to work with rough sleepers and homeless individuals and families at the earliest possible time with an end goal of having stable accommodation leading to 'recovery'. Once the initial needs of housing are met, then an attempt to address other factors (which are found to contribute to homelessness) should be made. A mixed methods study by Sundin (2012) found eight factors relating to becoming homeless, which consisted of: relationships breakdown; behavioural rebelliousness; childhood abuse; foster care/frequent childhood relocation; substance use; eviction; job loss and jail. The factors that were found to contribute to continued homeless included: adverse life events; substance use; avoidant coping; criminal offence; and ill-health (Sundin, 2012). Such factors need to be acknowledged and addressed in an attempt to reduce the 'revolving door' of homeless shelters and hostels and to encourage and maintain 'recovery'. This strategy and approach should be used in conjunction with methods listed above (person centred; strengths; empowerment) in order to maximise the chances of any changes being maintained by the individual (see Teater, 2010 for an overview of motivational interviewing and the stage of change model).

Case example

This case example is from Reeve (2011, p. 37).

In 2005 Marie, then aged 55 and living alone, formed a relationship and moved into her new partner's home. Marie did not work and was financially dependent on her partner. Three years later they separated and, with no right to remain in the property, she had to leave. Marie approached the local authority and made a homelessness application but was told she was not in priority need. Marie had very little money, no prior experience of homelessness, no family nearby and no knowledge of hostels and other homelessness services so she started sleeping in a local park. She explained that 'I haven't got family down here and I was literally on the streets. I didn't know what to do, I didn't know where to go.'

Marie took a small bag with her containing a sleeping bag and essentials – she has mobility problems and cannot carry much weight – and chose the park over other locations because it afforded a degree of safety, being some distance from other rough sleepers. She spent the days walking around and reading in the library.

Marie had a couple of friends that she could stay with occasionally for a couple of nights but their family commitments prevented them from offering a longer term arrangement. Over the next three months Marie moved between the park and her friends' homes. She was informed by a friend of a local drop-in centre which provided meals, washing facilities and advice. Staff there helped her claim Jobseeker's Allowance (JSA), helped her apply to go on the housing register and made an application to a local housing association with a scheme for the over-55s. In the meantime the willingness and ability of her friends to accommodate Marie dried up and she slept rough in the park continuously for a month. At the end of this month the rough sleeper's team finally found Marie and secured her a place in a hostel.

Benefits and challenges in housing and homelessness services

Housing and homelessness is a very difficult area in which to work. This is mainly due to the lack of affordable housing and the pieces of legislation that restrict access to housing through eligibility criteria. Social workers who are well informed of the legislation, policies and procedures around housing and homelessness will be in a better position to serve service users and provide advice, information and advocacy to meet a basic need of shelter.

Workers within housing and homelessness are faced with several challenges. First, there is not a clear picture of the extent to which people experience housing problems or are homeless. This is due to the way in which homelessness is calculated by the government. The definition of a rough sleeper, provided at the beginning of this chapter, is quite specific and does not include the individuals who walk or move frequently around in the night as they are afraid to 'bed down', due to security issues. It also does not include those individuals who are not present within the specific area in which the 'count' is taking place (e.g. wooded areas, night buses, derelict buildings, staying in squats or with friends).

Second, the restrictions on the homelessness applications' 'eligibility criteria', under the Housing Act 1996, make it very difficult for every homeless person to receive help or assistance. Individuals who submit applications are put under scrutiny to 'prove' that they are eligible, homeless, in priority need and are unintentionally homeless. Many students placed within homeless shelters have reported the difficulty in getting applications through to the local authority and often feel as if the local authorities are taking an approach of 'how can we prove this application is *not* eligible?' over 'how does this application meets the eligibility criteria?'. Social workers who fully understand the housing and homelessness legislation will be better able to assist and advocate on behalf of the service users.

Finally, despite the fact that housing is a basic human need, the funding to many shelters, hostels, day centres and supportive housing is reducing. The greatest loss in housing and homelessness funding occurred when the Supporting People funding was changed from being ring fenced for housing to being a fund given to local authorities to distribute as they wished (Homeless Link, 2012). The funding issue is coupled with the lack of available housing in which to move people after they first enter a shelter or day centre; even the move into a hostel from a shelter could take five or six weeks.

Anti-oppressive considerations in housing and homelessness

There is no doubt that experiencing housing and homelessness problems can lead to stigma and oppression. Society often views housing and homelessness problems as an 'individual' problem where the blame falls on the individual rather than taking a constructive view of the social, political and economic structures and policies that greatly impact on an individual's ability to obtain and maintain accommodation (Belcher and DeForge, 2012). As discussed above, the factors that contribute to homelessness often consist of economic and social variables, such as unemployment, lack of affordable housing, residential mobility in childhood and breakdown in relationships (Belcher and DeForge, 2012; Sundin, 2012). Because of this lack of critical understanding of the factors leading to housing and homelessness problems, society stigmatises individuals by labelling, stereotyping, discriminating and oppressing (Belcher and DeForge, 2012).

The effects of the stigma, indignity and oppression have been found to negatively affect individuals' identities both personally and socially (Williams and Stickley, 2011) and have been found to span across all aspects of their lives, such as their status as parents (Benbow et al., 2011). Social workers must acknowledge the extent to which stigma and oppression affect individuals and should consider how to tackle such oppression on the societal level as well as the individual level. As stated above, social workers must take a person-centred and strengths approach and should be tasked with not only finding shelter for individuals, but also addressing those factors that affect individuals' identities, such as loss of social role and loss of belonging (Williams and Stickley, 2011) and acknowledge that individuals who are homeless do experience strengths, resilience and perseverance (Benbow et al., 2011).

Social workers should also acknowledge that individuals who are homeless do not constitute a homogeneous group. There are differences in sex, age and ethnicity in terms of the triggering factors for becoming homeless. Relationship breakdown was found to be the triggering factor for females regardless of ethnicity (Office of the Deputy Prime Minister [ODPM], 2005)), adverse life events for young homeless and alcohol/drug abuse for mature adults (Sundin, 2012). 'Ethnic minority households are around three times more likely to become statutory homeless than the majority White population' (ODPM, 2005, p. 5). The ODPM (2005) found that social exclusion, poverty and discrimination were the main factors in ethnic minority households becoming homeless as these factors greatly reduced their housing options. Such forms of oppression must be fully acknowledged and understood in order for social workers to best determine the appropriate form of intervention.

Summary

This chapter has provided a brief overview of some of the current issues in housing and homelessness which social workers might encounter. As discussed, there is a wide definition of homelessness within the UK and the prevalence of homelessness is difficult to capture based on the variance in definitions and in how homelessness is 'counted'. Although there are services to address some housing and homelessness problems, these services are usually restricted to meeting eligibility criteria. If the criteria are not met and services are not provided, many individuals remain homeless but become 'hidden' from society and forced to fend for themselves. Funding cuts and staffing issues are challenging the current state of housing and homelessness support. Social workers are best in a position to assist the service users with whom they work by gaining an understanding of housing and homelessness issues, the legislation and eligibility criteria, working closely and in partnership with the many voluntary organisations providing housing and homelessness support, challenging the social, economic and political factors that are contributing to or preventing individuals from suitable accommodation and, most importantly, treating individuals with dignity and respect.

📖 CASE STUDY

Louise is 22 years old and has two children aged three and one. She was referred to children and families services after the police were called to her house for a domestic dispute. Louise's partner and father of her youngest child, Chris, aged 30, was arrested for domestic violence and spent the night in jail. Chris has since been released and Louise refuses to press charges as she is fearful of what Chris might do. Chris is back in the house and children and families services are concerned about the safety of the children. Chris refuses to leave as his name is on the lease. Louise talks to you, as her child and family social worker, and states she would like to leave, but she too has her name on the lease and has nowhere else to go.

Questions

 What are the impacts of this situation for Louise and her children?

 As the social worker for Louise's children, would you suggest that Louise submits a homelessness application?

If yes, what criteria do you think she meets? How soon should she apply? What will you do to ensure the safety of Louise and the children in the meantime? If no, what will you do to ensure the safety of Louise and the children?

 What opportunities are there for multi-agency working?

Further resources and suggested readings

Cowan, D. (2011) *Housing Law & Policy*. Cambridge: Cambridge University Press.

Nooe, R.M. and Patterson, D.A. (2010) The ecology of homelessness, *Journal of Behavior in the Social Environment*, 20: 105–152.

Reeve, K. (2011) *The Hidden Truth about Homelessness: Experiences of Single Homelessness in England*. London: Crisis.

Robinson, P. (2008) *Working with Young Homeless People*. London: Jessica Kingsley Publishers.

Williams, S. and Stickley, T. (2011) Stories from the streets: people's experiences of homelessness, *Journal of Psychiatric and Mental Health Nursing*, 18: 432–439.

Websites

Crisis – www.crisis.org.uk
Homeless Link – www.homeless.org.uk
Shelter – www.shelter.org.uk

15 Asylum seekers and refugees

Benedict Fell

This chapter is dedicated to the memory of John Harston (1944–2012) – a man who made a positive difference to the lives of many.

Introduction

The very fact that this chapter focuses on a specific client population contains an inherent associated risk that the group under focus can become problematised (Parker, 2000). Indeed, as we shall see, this can often extend to assuming all asylum seekers and refugees are in need of social work help when in fact many demonstrate great resilience and determination to help themselves. In addition, a brief look at the titles of other chapters in this book illustrates that people who are referred to as 'asylum seekers' and 'refugees' are not a completely separate group to whom, for example, old age (Chapter 9), disability (Chapter 8), domestic violence (Chapter 11) and substance misuse (Chapter 13) do not apply.

Asylum seekers and refugees are of course human beings and will face the same challenges that life can present to all of us. However, it is my argument that the pre-flight and post-flight experiences of asylum seekers and refugees are sufficiently different from established populations to warrant attention as a separate group. Despite a decline in the numbers of people seeking asylum (House of Commons, 2007), it remains likely that social workers, in both voluntary and statutory contexts, will come into contact with people who are asylum seekers or who have been granted asylum. An understanding of their position, notably a completely separate welfare trajectory for asylum seekers, will be required to enhance the help-giving efforts of practitioners. To this end, this chapter seeks to highlight key areas in understanding the needs of asylum seekers and refugees, whilst recognising that these, as with the established populations, are by no means homogeneous. There is a specific focus on one potentially highly vulnerable group of asylum seekers – unaccompanied asylum seeking children. The chapter begins by clarifying definitions and prevalence of people seeking asylum. It then goes on to briefly discuss the system for claiming asylum in the UK, where the burden of proof rests on the individual asylum seeker and the credibility of their claim. Key legislation and policy is described. Some pointers for best practice are outlined, including a social work process that has emerged in one voluntary agency in the North of England (Fell, 2013; Fell and Fell, 2013).

The asylum 'issue'

Many people living in the UK may be forgiven for thinking that the term 'asylum seeker' is a pejorative one. The asylum 'issue' was one that was high on the political agenda in the late 1990s and early 2000s. This period saw a peak in the number of people seeking asylum in the UK. A perceived 'flood' was stoked by a frequently hostile media (Greenslade, 2005). Noting the language often used in reporting about asylum seekers, the Centre for Social Justice (2008, p. 90) stated:

> The language of asylum is highly charged – and ripe with signification (swamped, tidal wave, draw the line, allow in etc.). It is very physical, geographical, the language of islanders aware of the vulnerability of their separation and interconnectedness.

These media stories have also been accompanied by various myths that have arisen. In no particular order, these have included that asylum seekers are given mobile phones and cars; are predatory around young women; are mainly terrorists seeking to attack the UK; are criminals escaping justice in their home countries. Perhaps the most pervasive media implication is that the majority are in fact posing as asylum seekers when they are here purely for economic benefit (therefore labelled 'bogus'). Large refugee organisations such as the Refugee Council and Refugee Action have done their best through campaigns designed to dispel these myths. Sadly, anecdotal evidence from the author's experience would suggest that they remain.

The gradual decline in numbers of people seeking asylum in the UK has meant a subsequent decline in the issue being at the forefront of the political agenda and newspaper headlines. However, two recent events have served to place the issue back, albeit briefly, into public consciousness. Perhaps the most high profile of these has been the well-publicised case of the Wikileak's founder Julian Assange seeking, and being granted, asylum by the Ecuadorean government in its London embassy. The second follows the refusal of many athletes (notably from Cameroon, Sudan, Ivory Coast and Congo) to return home following the London 2012 Olympic Games (Doyle, 2012; Furness, 2012). This has also occurred following other such high-profile sporting events, offering the citizens of particular countries the opportunity to travel abroad which would not otherwise be offered to them.

Definitions and prevalence

A variety of terms is in the public domain depicting different types of 'migrants' (essentially people who leave their country of origin and travel to another one). Given the plethora of terms, the remarks of one focus group in Centre for Social Justice (CSJ) (2008) research are perhaps quite common: 'I don't understand the terminology – asylum seeker, economic migrant, illegal immigrant. All I know is that they're all bloody foreigners' (p. 30).

Asylum seekers are often referred to as 'forced migrants'. This term denotes that their flight is pre-empted by conditions which are not of their choosing. This is in contrast to those termed 'economic migrants' or people who have made a decision to leave their country for work purposes and to enable a better quality of living. The travel of people across the world is not a new phenomenon and has happened since the existence of the human race (Hayes, 2009). As modern nation states have developed, so have mechanisms by which those states have sought the right to allow who they call citizens ('insiders') to live within their borders. They have also sought the right to decide to refuse those citizens from another country ('outsiders') that may choose to apply to live there.

Undesirable conditions in a home country have always propelled people to seek sanctuary in other countries across the globe. It is human nature to seek stability and safety for oneself and loved ones. For those of us living in the relatively wealthy, stable and democratic west, it can require a difficult (perhaps impossible) mindshift to imagine living in a country where there are constant fears of detainment/imprisonment for disagreeing with a political party/leader; where attacks and rapes are common; where you cannot vote; where membership of a particular religious group can result in murder; where war on the streets is a part of life. These are just some of the many reasons, often referred to as 'push factors', why people flee their countries of origin. Often referred to as 'refugees', the term 'asylum seeker' has arisen because it does not follow that simply arriving in a new country will mean you are granted permission to remain there. Thus the term 'asylum seeker' denotes someone in the process of seeking permanent leave to remain in a new country. If this leave to remain is granted, they become a 'refugee'.

Following the end of the Second World War, nation states gathered together in an attempt to form a consensus about how to deal with the mass displacement of European refugees during that conflict. The result was the 1951 UN Convention Relating to the Status of Refugees. States that are signatories to the convention have a duty to assess claims for international protection from those who have, in the Convention's words, 'a well-founded fear of persecution on the grounds of race, religion, political belief or membership of a particular social group'. The right to claim asylum is also enshrined in article 14 of the Universal Declaration of Human Rights (1948). It can be seen here that a frequently heard term, 'illegal asylum seeker', is a misnomer – it is not illegal to claim asylum. It is important to note, however, that it is not a human right to be granted asylum automatically.

The top ten asylum-seeking-producing countries in 2011 were Iran, Pakistan, Sri Lanka, Afghanistan, Eritrea, China, Libya, Nigeria, Sudan and Bangladesh (Refugee Council, 2012). These countries share two features in common: (1) they are nations where serious human rights abuses are recognised by international authorities as a regular occurrence; (2) they are countries subject to visa regimes by the UK, whose citizens cannot legitimately move to the UK, or other European nations, without visas obtained specifically for the purpose of a visit, to work or to study (Fell and Hayes, 2007). The year 2011 saw a slight increase of 11 per cent (19,865) in the numbers of applications for asylum (Refugee Council, 2012), which, as mentioned, have been in decline since a peak of approximately 84,000 applications in 2002. Research has indicated that, when questioned, the UK public significantly overestimates the numbers of asylum applicants. For example, a 2004 MORI poll showed that UK citizens believed that 23 per cent of the world's asylum seeker population was in the UK when in fact the figure is around 2 per cent (CSJ, 2008). It is by far the poorest countries in the world that bear the burden of the world's largest refugee populations. This again questions the role that the mass media may play in distorting reality.

Flight, arrival and application

Research by Crawley (2010) indicates that asylum seekers have little or no choice as to the destination country they arrive at, challenging the assumption that people choose the UK because it is a 'soft touch', implying that being granted asylum in the UK is easy. The reality is in fact the opposite. There are many means that people will use to travel to a new country and many of them, such as hiding under lorries and/or aircraft, are fraught with risk. People will often pay a smuggler to take them to a destination country clandestinely. The eventual country of arrival will be dependent on that smuggler's own contacts and networks (Crawley, 2010). The UK government expects people to make a claim for asylum as soon as they arrive at a port of entry. Failure to do so may impact upon the credibility of their claim at a later stage. When adult asylum seekers are accompanied by their children, it is the parent(s) that is considered to be the principal asylum applicant. Many asylum applications made in the UK are so-called 'in country' applications, usually after some form of temporary permission to stay, for example, a work/study visa has expired.

The wing of the Home Office that deals with all asylum applications is the UK Border Agency (UKBA). Asylum applicants are allocated a UKBA employee called a case owner who is the named individual that oversees the claim from start to finish. They will also conduct interviews that become crucial in determining the credibility of an applicant's claim because, in the UK system, the burden of proof rests solely upon the asylum seeker to prove that they face a well-founded fear of persecution if they return home. For some applicants from countries that the UK government considers 'safe', the claim may be considered immediately unfounded and the individual may be detained and deported. Applicants are often fingerprinted and issued with an identity card, known as an application and registration card (ARC), which contains electronically stored biometric data about each asylum applicant (Fell and Hayes, 2007).

Legal framework

There is in the UK no legislation setting out a minimum level of care which asylum seekers may expect. The 1999 Asylum and Immigration Act simply allows for financial support and housing whilst an asylum claim is being processed. Support and subsistence arrangements for asylum seekers whose application for asylum is being considered by UKBA are also made under the provisions of the 1999 Asylum and Immigration Act. This legislation set up the National Asylum Support Service (NASS, now referred to as 'asylum support'), which provides weekly cash payments to asylum seekers and provides furnished accommodation mainly subcontracted through the private housing sector. This accommodation is on a 'no choice' basis and can involve asylum seekers and any dependants being dispersed to any part of the UK. The amount of money paid to an asylum seeker depends on their circumstances. For example, in 2012 a single person over 18 who was not a lone parent received £36.62 per week; a couple who were married or in a civil partnership received £72.52; a person under 16 was entitled to £52.96 per week (UKBA, 2012a). These allowances are paid through a local post office upon presentation of the ARC card.

Asylum seekers cannot take paid employment except if they have been waiting more than 12 months for an initial decision from the Home Office about their case, or if they have made further submissions about their case once it has been rejected. In both these cases, permission to work has to be obtained from the UKBA (UKBA, 2012b). Asylum seekers are entitled to free health care whilst their claim is being processed and the children of applicants are entitled to education.

A successful claim will mean that leave to remain in the UK has been granted (person has refugee status), bringing with it access to mainstream benefits, employment and access to the housing market, and also wider access to social care as enjoyed by all UK citizens. If an asylum application is rejected, an appeal may be lodged with the Tribunals Service. The implications of a claim being rejected are discussed later in the chapter.

Needs and responses

It is clear that asylum seekers occupy an uncertain position as they wait 'in limbo' for a decision to be made by an institution about permission for them to stay. Vernon et al. (2008) have coined the term 'Home Office syndrome' – the tendency for the lives of asylum seekers to be exclusively focused on being successful in their claims and their being forced to neglect other basic needs. However, it should not be assumed that problems end once an asylum seeker becomes a refugee. The transition to refugee status presents a host of new challenges, namely settlement in a new cultural landscape, navigating a complex benefits/housing system and finding employment (Fell, 2013).

There has been a large focus on the mental health needs of asylum seekers and refugees. In general, psychological distress is categorised into four broad 'causes':

1   Adverse 'push' experiences in home countries which cause the person to flee, for example, persecution as a member of a certain religious group, war, conflict, threats to life and/or attempts on one's life.
2   The journey to the place where sanctuary is sought. Journeys which may involve travelling thousands of miles in cramped and difficult conditions with strangers and smugglers who may exploit the dependency of their 'passengers'.
3   Distress experienced in an alien and hostile country/culture, which can include a culture of suspicion and racist reactions from local host communities (Parker and Penhale, 2008) coupled with the ongoing uncertainty of their immigration status as their asylum claim is processed.
4   Following rejection of a claim, the likely destitution that arises and fear of being returned to face the persecution that was fled. This stage can also entail a fear of detention and being forcibly returned.

Weaver and Burns (2001) argue that, in general, social workers need a greater understanding of the impact of trauma, including torture, to be effective with their asylum seekers and refugee clients. Post-traumatic stress disorder (PTSD) is the most common psychiatric category employed to describe symptoms arising from traumatic experiences (Kasiram and Khosa, 2008). However, as Friedman (2003, p. 2) observes, many people who are exposed to traumatic events do not necessarily go on to develop PTSD. Watters (2001) notes that this attribution of symptoms to the PTSD category actually does little to determine what interpretations of distress refugees have. These observations again point to the heterogeneity of asylum seekers and refugees and cautions against making assumptions that adverse experiences will always result in psychological distress: 'typically when most refugees are asked what would help their situation they are much more likely to point to social and economic factors rather than psychological help' (Watters, 2001, p. 1709).

Depiction of social work involvement with asylum seekers and refugees has largely been a negative one. As Humphries (2004) has noted:

Social work has only slowly come to accept that an involvement with people subject to immigration controls is its business, because as a profession that deals with some of the most vulnerable people in society, it is now faced with some of the most oppressed people on the planet as its clients. Not only has it become 'involved' with immigrants and asylum seekers, increasingly it has been drawn into a role of constriction and punishment in its work with such groups.

(Humphries, 2004, p. 93)

However, such views can risk obscuring the positive and transforming work that is and can be undertaken. Fell (2013) and Fell and Fell (2013) describe a social work process that has emerged through supportive work with asylum seekers and refugees in one agency in the North West of England. The process that emerged in this work is denoted by the acronym WAMBA and includes features that will be recognisable to social work practitioners in other contexts: *Welcome, Accompaniment, Mediation, Befriending, Advocacy*. As Figure 15.1 depicts, it is a non-linear process and each element will be operating simultaneously to some degree. Each stage will be described in detail below.

- **Welcome.** An asylum seeker or refugee should be made to feel welcome in our agencies and offices. Assessment should be non-invasive and non-intrusive and built on a foundation of trust. For many asylum seekers, the concept of a social work profession may be an alien one and roles and purposes may need careful explanation, usually through an interpreter.
- **Accompaniment.** This is essentially the notion of 'being with' someone as they navigate the uncertainties of the asylum process. This should be offered and not imposed. At its most basic, it is the simple comfort and support we derive from knowing that a named person is there for us.

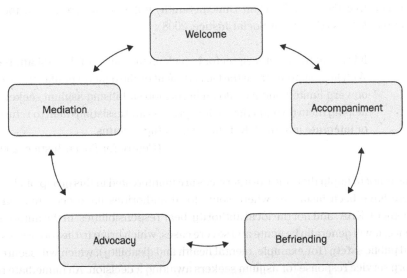

Figure 15.1 WAMBA (Fell 2013, p. 304; Fell and Fell, 2013).

- **Mediation.** The social worker may be called upon to liaise on the client's behalf with UKBA and other agencies. It is important when undertaking this role that the worker does not engender false hopes in their clients. We cannot pretend that immigration laws do not exist. The mediatory role in this process entails standing between the uncertainty of the client and the apparent chaos of the asylum system whilst also trying to facilitate making new supportive links in communities.

- **Befriending.** This is distinct from being a friend. Befriending, carried out as an aspect of the social work role, can provide the 'regular positive experiences and a set of stable, socially rewarded roles in the community' (Cohen and Wills, 1985, p. 311) that might otherwise be a distant aspiration amidst the uncertainty of the asylum seeking process.

- **Advocacy.** Language barriers may increase the need for the social worker's advocacy on behalf of a client. Advocacy with asylum seekers who have not yet been granted refugee status, with its virtual guarantee of access to services and eventual full citizenship, will be different in nature from advocacy with other groups of people who, although they may be excluded in other ways, at least have certain rights as citizens. At the agency in question, various activities that can be described as advocacy took place, such as arranging a bus pass so an asylum seeker could attend UKBA meetings without walking miles to do so, or arranging to accompany an asylum seeker to an appeal hearing when she or he has been unable to obtain legal representation.

This process emerged at a voluntary sector agency. Such agencies undertake the lion's share of supportive work with asylum seekers and refugees. A former Conservative Party leader (Iain Duncan-Smith) notes in the preface to the report *Asylum Matters* (Centre for Social Justice, 2008):

> It is left to the voluntary sector to pick up the pieces of these shattered lives. With little support from the Government or the general public, these groups, on very limited budgets, do an heroic job stabilising asylum seekers' lives, helping them through the asylum process and assisting them to return home or integrate into the UK if they gain refugee status.
>
> (Centre for Social Justice, 2008, p. 5)

This is not to imply that statutory services are uninterested in this group of clients. Yet there have been instances where some local authorities have been unclear about whether UKBA, and not the local authority, bear responsibilities. In the author's experience, it will generally be acute and severe cases, which bring to the fore issues of risk and public safety (for example, mental health and disability), which will secure a statutory service response for asylum seekers awaiting a decision. An immediate responsibility does not follow for single adults in the same way as it does for unaccompanied asylum seeking children (see below). For people awarded refugee status, whether they receive a statutory service will be subject to the same eligibility criteria as applied to citizens of established populations. It must always be borne in mind that often what the asylum seeking client may most desire – leave to remain and refugee status – is not in the individual power of the social worker or agency to give (Fell, 2013).

Refused asylum seekers, destitution and 'no recourse to public funds'

When a single applicant's appeal rights have been exhausted, financial and housing support ceases and asylum seekers may find themselves destitute (Refugee Action, 2006; Fell and Hayes, 2007). Families will continue to receive support and accommodation but may be encouraged to consider voluntary return to their country of origin under the Assisted Voluntary Return for Families and Children programme (International Organization for Migration, 2012). Following the rejection of their claim, all asylum seekers, including unaccompanied minors (see below), face the possibility of forced removal from the UK, if they choose not to return voluntarily to their country of origin. Faced with the prospect of returning to the conditions that caused them to flee, it is not surprising that people choose not to return and many can often go 'underground' to evade detection by the authorities. Local authorities have a duty under Schedule 3 section 14(1) of the 2002 Nationality, Immigration and Asylum Act to inform the UKBA when a person unlawfully in the UK comes to their attention. However, it is unclear to what extent such information, if given, is acted upon by UKBA (NRPF Network, 2011).

People who have their claims for asylum rejected face a particularly difficult challenge and the social work role with this group of people can also become challenging. Rejected single asylum seekers who remain in the UK are considered to be persons with 'no recourse to public funds' (NRPF), as they are now deemed to be unlawfully present in the UK. They effectively become destitute. However, some form of support still remains for rejected asylum seekers with dependants.

Social workers encountering single persons with no recourse to public funds will have restricted powers to assess and assist their clients. There will no doubt be a conflict between the professional duty to assess and attend to the needs of their clients and the restricted range of possibilities caused by their clients' immigration status as persons without leave to remain in the UK.

It may happen that some such people have health and social needs, which would normally be assessed by social services departments under section 21 of the 1948 National Assistance Act. However, the threshold for the receipt of such support is now extremely high in the light of the 2008 House of Lords judgment in M v Slough, where need arising solely from destitution was not deemed sufficient to engage local authority support. Even if the lack of such support might infringe an individual's rights under

Article 3 of the European Convention on Human Rights (prohibiting inhuman or degrading treatment or punishment) and which is incorporated into the 1999 Human Rights Act, an applicant would need to be close to death to be eligible for support (NRPF Network, 2011). Children and their families, for example, in the case of a child born to a destitute mother whose asylum case has been rejected, may still be supported under section 17 of the Children Act, 1989 (NRPF Network, 2011). Thus to qualify for some form of mainstream statutory social work support, a refused asylum seeker must have needs arising over and above their destitution – so called 'destitution plus'.

Section 4 of the 1999 Asylum and Immigration Act provides short-term financial support for destitute asylum seekers in certain circumstances. These include: having a medical condition which prevents a failed asylum seeker from taking steps to leave the UK; being unable to leave the UK because no viable route of return exists; a request for a judicial review of an asylum decision has been granted (UKBA, 2012c). Section 4 support is cashless and takes the form of a smartcard, called the Azure card, which may be used in designated shops to buy food and toiletries to the value (in 2012) of £35.79 per week. The lack of a cash element in section 4 support has obvious implications in restricting what can be actually purchased with it and where, as well as restricting essential travel to legal and medical appointments and to UKBA reporting centres, for example. Crucially, to be awarded section 4 support the rejected asylum seeker must demonstrate that they are taking active steps to leave the country. As mentioned, faced with a choice of returning to conditions that caused them to flee, many will choose not to apply for section 4 and eke out an existence in other ways. Here, church groups and other charities have played an important role in easing the plight of destitution with food and clothes donations.

Case example

Nathan was a 54-year-old asylum seeker from an African country. He was receiving support from a voluntary sector agency called WAYS. Nathan had recently had his appeal for asylum rejected at an asylum and immigration tribunal (AIT) and a further request to the tribunal for a reconsideration of the judge's decision was also rejected. Nathan had his asylum support withdrawn and was effectively considered a person with no recourse to public funds. His accommodation was also withdrawn. WAYS used to give Nathan a food parcel at the drop-in every Tuesday. On one occasion, Nathan asked the social worker Paul to accompany him to a GP appointment as he was getting the results of some tests and wanted Paul to interpret in French. The GP had taken a urine test and explained that Nathan had symptoms which might indicate a possibility of prostate problems and that he would need to go into hospital for a more detailed examination. At this hospital appointment it was confirmed that Nathan had prostate cancer. If he had been British citizen, Nathan could have been discharged for home care and visits by a specialist palliative care nurse, but he clearly had nowhere to live as his asylum support had been withdrawn. A hospital social worker, Michelle, employed within the local authority statutory social work team, phoned Paul (she had been given his number by Nathan). Paul explained Nathan's situation to Michelle, that he was a refused asylum seeker and the implications this had for him in terms of welfare entitlement and accommodation. Michelle arranged a community care assessment under the terms of the National Health Service and Community Care Act 1990. Nathan's cancer had spread rapidly and he met the criteria for services to be provided – he was considered 'destitution plus'. Following his discharge, he was initially accommodated at a residential home where all the residents were much older than him. He was then moved into a terraced house with adaptations as he was beginning to have mobility difficulties at this point. Nathan's condition continued to deteriorate and he died some months later.

Unaccompanied asylum seeking children (UASC)

Where a child is unaccompanied by a parent, that child's claim is subsumed under the parent's claim. However, children often arrive at shores who are unaccompanied by a caregiver. It is perhaps this group of asylum seekers that has received the most attention in the social work literature given their apparent vulnerability (see, for example, Kohli and Mather, 2003; Kohli, 2007). The terms 'unaccompanied' and 'separated' are often used interchangeably. However, there is a subtle distinction, with the latter term denoting that children may arrive in a country with an adult(s) but it might subsequently be established that this adult(s) is either unable or unsuitable to provide care to the child. An unaccompanied asylum seeking child is defined as: (1) an individual who is under 18 and applying for asylum in his or her own right; is (2) separated from both parents and not being cared for by an adult who by law or custom has responsibility to do so (Border and Immigration Agency [now UKBA], 2007, p. 7).

It is a notable observation that many more unaccompanied young men than young women seek asylum in the UK (Kohli and Mather, 2003). Ayotte (2000, as cited in Leggett, 2008, p. 9) suggest some reasons for this gender difference: '. . . boys can be in greater danger in some conflicts; some cultures value boys more than girls and; generally there could be fewer risks involved for a male travelling unaccompanied'.

Wright (2012) notes that there were 1277 UASC applications in 2011 with the majority arriving from Afghanistan. Reliable and accurate figures denoting the prevalence of unaccompanied asylum seeking children can be difficult to come by, however. For example, many children are trafficked into a country and essentially 'disappear'. Some children who are trafficked may avoid bringing themselves to the attention of authorities because they have been instructed by their traffickers not to do so (Department for Children, Schools and Families [DCSF], 2007).

In contrast to adult asylum seekers, UASC do trigger a statutory responsibility under sections 17 and 20 of the Children Act 1989 and 2004. However, first it must be established that the child is indeed under the age of 18. Age assessment is a controversial yet crucial area. It is not an exact science and most unaccompanied asylum seekers tend to be adolescent males with no supporting proof of age (indeed, in many countries births are not registered in the same way as the west). These may at first sight resemble men aged 18 or over.

If a child is mistakenly assessed as over 18, they could be treated as an adult and even detained with other adults. If an adult is assessed as being under 18, this could mean that they become inappropriately accommodated with children with all the risks that this could entail. Accurate age assessment also determines whether responsibility for that person falls to the local authority social services department or UKBA. Once assessed as under 18, a UASC becomes looked after under section 20 of the Children Act 1989 and allocated a social worker. They are given a discretionary period of leave to remain and this is then reviewed when they turn 18. Wright (2012) explores the challenges of working with UASC compared to citizen children in that Pathway Planning has to take account of the reality that the child may be returned to their country of origin.

The Department of Health's 1995 guidance *Unaccompanied Asylum Seeking Children: A Practice Guide* acknowledges that 'these children are by definition living away from their parents: they are children in need' (DoH, 1995, p. 1 as cited in Dennis, 2007, p. 17). The importance of assessment cannot be understated. As Mitchell (2007, p. 48) notes:

> The events precipitating their current circumstances and the way in which individual children and young people have experienced and continue to experience them is likely to differ. Therefore, an ongoing process of assessment is necessary to build an in-depth understanding of the vulnerabilities and competencies of each child or young person, to appreciate the risk and protective factors resulting from their circumstances, and to plan service responses appropriate to their needs and wishes.

We cannot assume that children necessarily want to reflect on family experiences and life in their home country; therefore caution should be exercised. Acknowledging the diversity of pre-flight experiences and the journey, it would be undesirable for us to say with any certainty (as it would with a child who is a British citizen) what the developmental needs of an unaccompanied asylum seeking child are definitely going to be. In her research, Mitchell (2007, p. 51) rated just 32 per cent of 212 assessments with unaccompanied asylum seeking children as 'adequate or better' and outlines the characteristics of these:

- Assessments were timely.
- Evidence was gathered and clear records were kept.
- A range of developmental needs had been considered.

- Due account was taken of possible or evident risks and ways in which these could be mediated.
- There was evidence of practitioners 'weighing up' information and noting shortfalls in information and the potential implications of these.
- Plans were formulated to meet identified needs through a range of clearly defined actions.
- Actions taken were immediate or short term and long term.

Central to assessment with unaccompanied asylum seeking children will be the interpersonal and relationship-building skills of the worker(s) undertaking the work with the unaccompanied child (Kohli and Mitchell, 2007). Many children in exile may not trust authority figures and have limited understanding of who social workers are and what they do (which may account for them initially appearing to withhold certain information). Social workers may be perceived as being linked 'hand in glove' with immigration services which may explain children's reticence about disclosing stories for fear of prejudicing their claim (Kidane, 2001). This is more likely when social workers and immigration officers are co-located (Crawley, 2007).

The importance of access to appropriate interpretation services is also highlighted by *Working Together to Safeguard Children*:

> The need for neutral, high-quality, gender-appropriate translation or interpretation services should be taken into account when working with children and families whose preferred language is not English.
>
> (DCSF, 2006, section 11.44, p. 202)

This approach may take time, not least because of the time required for trust and rapport to be successfully achieved. Raval (2007) provides interesting insights into work between practitioners and interpreters, noting that they must also seek to establish a good working relationship before work with the child can begin:

> Mutual trust is vital for developing a good working relationship and creating a containing working relationship between the practitioner and the language interpreter, and between the two workers and the young person. The young person is unlikely to develop trust and a sense of being contained if they do not experience this between the practitioner and language interpreter.
>
> (Raval, 2007, p. 66)

Kohli and Mather (2003, p. 201) outline three psychological barriers experienced by unaccompanied asylum seeking children after having arrived in the destination country:

> Firstly, as 'strangers in a strange land', they may not know the habits, rules

and customs of their new territories, and have to adapt quickly and fluently in order to settle. Secondly, they may be carrying memories of disintegration following war and be traumatized or haunted by ghosts from the past. They have to depend on the comfort and skill of strangers to make peace with these ghosts. Thirdly, if they are looked after by social services in their country of asylum, they have to find their way through a maze of systems of care and protection, having been through the immigration maze.

Social workers are thus tasked with offering the 'comfort and skills of strangers' (Kohli and Mather, 2003, p. 201) to which many unaccompanied children look to depend upon.

Benefits and challenges to working with asylum seekers and refugees

Working with asylum seekers and refugees does not come without some difficult challenges and rewarding benefits. Some challenges involve the acknowledgement that work has to take place whilst avoiding unwittingly raising false hope in clients. It needs to be made clear that the social worker does not have the power to dictate the outcome of a claim. As in any field, social workers can forge strong bonds with the people they are working with and work can end abruptly. To spend time listening to a person's story and getting to know them, and then realising some hours or days later that they have suddenly been detained and/or deported (possibly to face the persecution they have fled), can present a powerful emotional challenge to workers perhaps coupled with frustration that they could have done more. Asylum seekers and refugees will also often recount stories of horror and suffering which may impact practitioners and, during such times, good supervision and the practitioner's employer/manager may be of vital importance. However, there are also benefits to working with asylum seekers: for example, witnessing the joy that can accompany a positive decision on their claim; helping refugees navigate the UK system to establish a new and safer life for themselves and their families; and seeing an unaccompanied asylum seeking child integrate with foster carers and school and making new friends. Playing a part in many of these journeys can be both a humbling and rewarding experience.

Summary

This chapter has sought to provide some insight into the experiences of asylum seekers in the UK, whilst acknowledging that these are by no means uniform. It has outlined some scope for how social work can make a difference to the lives of people who have risked much to seek safety and security. As a profession that purports to serve vulnerable and marginalised populations, it is clear that social work has much to offer asylum seekers and refugees in working to maximise positive outcomes in their lives, whilst being aware that these lives are also constrained by wider forces outside of their control.

📖 CASE STUDY

Besnik is a young male aged 14 who fled to the UK in 2003 from a country in eastern Europe. He arrived in the UK with some other boys from his home country in a city in the North of England, following a long journey by lorry. He was initially 'age disputed' until his age was confirmed as 14 following a social work age assessment. He was placed in a residential home for children as a 'looked after' child under section 20 of the Children Act 1989. Besnik's allocated social worker was Brian (35). Brian spent a lot of time communicating with him through an interpreter (Besnik had very little knowledge of the English language) to assess his needs and try to get to know him and build trust. Besnik recalls Brian being particularly instrumental in advocating for a place at a local school following some expressions of concern and reluctance by the headmaster. Besnik found school in England 'a shock' and could not understand why some of the children behaved so poorly and disrespectfully towards the teachers. After a year at the children's home, he was eventually considered for a foster placement. This is when he first met his foster carer, Dave, following an introduction facilitated by Brian. Dave had been fostering for some years but had never provided a placement for an unaccompanied asylum seeking child. Dave (55) and his wife Joan (50) were also fostering two other children age (8) and (10) at the time. They got on well at the initial meeting, despite Besnik's difficulty with English, and the placement went ahead. At first, Besnik was reluctant and quiet and did not speak about what he had witnessed at home. Dave, Joan and Bill and the other foster children worked hard at making Besnik feel at home and introducing him to aspects of English culture. Besnik and Dave/Joan recall some cultural 'adjustments' that needed to be made, for example, Besnik was used to a culture where women were generally subservient to males and Besnik assumed that Joan would carry out certain tasks for him, such as cooking food when he asked for it. After some careful explaining and negotiation, Besnik began to understand different cultural understandings and values and was very apologetic. His language gradually began to improve. At 18, Besnik qualified for leaving care services under section 20 of the Children Act 1989 and the Children (Leaving Care) Act 2000. Besnik recalls that Brian, who had been involved with Besnik since his arrival, was an important figure in their lives. According to Dave and Besnik, Brian again stepped in and 'went the extra mile'. Besnik wanted to study at university and Brian liaised with a local university to ensure that Besnik was accepted as a 'home' student and entitled to study. Besnik is now at the end of his first year of a degree and is doing well. With Brian and Dave's assistance, he had to make a new claim for asylum after his discretionary leave expired and he is still awaiting the outcome of this decision. He feels settled and integrated in the UK and calls it 'home'. He is worried that this will be destroyed if the UKBA decide he cannot stay in the UK and he feels that this would breach his human rights. However, he is hopeful because he has a good legal representative and has confidence in him. With Brian's Pathway Planning input, and support from Dave and Joan, Besnik has moved out of Dave and Joan's home but continues to call Dave and Joan 'Mum and Dad'.

Questions

 What do you think were the main factors leading to Besnik's successful settlement in the UK?

 What factors might have been taken into consideration by social services when placing Besnik with a family not of his own ethnic/cultural background?

 What do you think 'going the extra mile' entails? List the skills, roles, tasks and values that Besnik's social worker, Brian, drew on in his work.

 How do you feel that Brian went about successfully establishing trust with Besnik?

Further resources and suggested readings

Fell, P. and Hayes, D. (2007) *What Are They Doing Here? A Critical Guide to Asylum and Immigration*. Birmingham: Venture Press.

Kohli, R.K.S. (2007) *Social Work with Unaccompanied Asylum Seeking Children*. Basingstoke: Palgrave Macmillan.

Websites

Refugee Action – www.refugee-action.org.uk
Refugee Council – www.refugeecouncil.org.uk

16 Rehabilitation and corrections

Jenny Clifford

Introduction

This chapter will provide the reader with a selective overview of the framework for working with offenders in England and Wales and the services provided by statutory and 'third sector organisations' (TSOs). The chapter will consider relevant legislation, policy and practice conditions. The aim of this chapter is to demonstrate the complexity of working with offenders and how social work with offenders can be configured in many ways.

Over the last two decades, work with adult and young offenders has changed beyond recognition, in part due to the raft of legal and policy changes that have emanated within the criminal justice system (CJS), including the independent training of probation officers. Social work services may appear redundant in the ever-changing CJS and work with offenders external to the probation service can appear perplexing. Many mistakenly see the role of TSOs in these circumstances eroded and superfluous. It is here that TSOs can and do play a role in providing a social work service for offenders in many environments. These settings and the experiences they provide can be a challenge to students as a 'definitive' social work role is often less defined.

Alongside the legislative changes, the terms used to define work with offenders can be confusing and misleading. One of the most frequently used terms is 'resettlement'. 'Resettlement' is used conterminously with 'reintegration' and/or 're-entry' all subject to critique (Hedderman, 2007; Raynor, 2007). The interpretation of 'resettlement', as defined by the Ministry of Justice (MOJ, 2011), provides a clear remit in which organisations can operate:

> Assistance and support pre and post release from statutory and non-statutory agencies to enable ex prisoners and their families to prepare for life after prison ... and cope ... without re-offending, to access

accommodation, welfare benefits, education and training, gain employment and address personal problems.

The challenges for workers emerge when faced with offenders who have never experienced stability, support or acceptance, despite the additional difficulties that face young people, women and black and ethnic minority groups. Resettlement may also involve returning to a social network underpinned by criminality and communities experiencing severe social and economic disadvantage, all adding to the pressure to desist from crime. Maruna (2010, p. 2) states 'to desist from crime, ex-offenders need to develop a coherent pro-social identity for themselves'. With limited resources, peer pressure and temptations, the ability to develop and sustain a pro-social identity becomes diminished.

Another frequently used term is 'Rehabilitation'. The impact of rehabilitation was questioned during the 1970s when treatments were producing few results, leading to the classic statement of Martinson (1974) that 'nothing works'. The term 'rehabilitation of offenders' is now mostly considered in terms of factors associated with re-offending. The Home Office (2004) *Reducing Re-Offending National Action Plan* identified specific areas known as 'pathways' that impact on successful rehabilitation/resettlement. These pathways comprise accommodation and support, education, training and employment, health, drugs and alcohol, finance, benefits and debt, children and families, attitudes, thinking and behaviour. These are areas in which effective social work practice can prevail. In 2010, the Justice Secretary Kenneth Clarke confirmed that imprisonment alone failed to reduce re-offending and heralded the new 'Rehabilitation Revolution' with the crucial emphasis being post-release support.

Approximately 90,000 people are released from prison each year. Reconviction rates suggest that around half of those released will have re-offended and possibly been returned to custody within a year (Prison Reform Trust [PRT], 2012). Effective resettlement services are essential in order to reduce re-offending and ultimately reduce the high social and economic cost of crime and disorder. Offender rehabilitation has to be measured, effective and outcome based. Within these parameters, TSOs will play a significant role in the delivery of services, and as such are ideal settings for social workers and social work students.

Social work practice within rehabilitation and correction services

Many TSOs work within custodial and community based settings, which provide a host of services including advice and guidance on employment, housing, education and delivering health and therapeutic experiences. The prison system within England and Wales separates and defines services for men, women and young people. The prison population has been steadily rising over the years, for example, in 2002 it was just under 71,000 and in October 2012 it was just over 86,000. It is now the case that factors related to offending and reducing re-offending are becoming more reliant on the expertise and skills deployed by practitioners.

In 1998, the Diploma in Probation Studies (DipPS) was introduced as a stand-alone qualification formally dissociating the links with social work. Here the role of the probation officer was to be based on established evidence of what was most likely to be effective in order to prevent re-offending and protect the public. The Crime and Disorder Act 1998 created the Youth Justice Board who would oversee the administration of youth justice services within England and Wales and established youth offending teams (YOTS). The Criminal Justice and Court Services Act 2000 created the National Probation Service for England and Wales and subsequently divided probation services into areas. The 2007 Offender Management Act created Probation Trusts and by 2009 35 self-governing trusts were accountable to the Justice Secretary.

In April 2010, the Probation Qualifying Framework (PQF) was introduced replacing the DipPS. The PQF draws in part on the DipPS but is a framework not an award. Trainees are more accountable for their work and can, on completion, apply for probation officer roles that allow them to work with higher risk offenders.

Social work with offenders can take place in a variety of settings where a social work role is not automatically visible. Having placed students in a young offender institution with a TSO worker on specially designed courses, the challenge was manifested during initial supervision sessions. The question always raised was how does this work fulfil social work values and roles? The answer became evident as more experience was gained. Working in a restricted environment, where the balance of care and control competes, is ripe for social work intervention. For many young offenders, the opportunity to develop skills, partake in education and 'have a voice' in discussions is newly encountered. It is well documented in the literature that two-thirds of prisoners have a reading age of 11 or lower. To complete a course of education that enables them to gain a qualification alongside having the opportunity to consider future education/career pathways is an important and empowering social work role. The importance can be considered in the context of resettlement pathways, factors connected with re-offending and, equally, if not more so, the fact that people are prepared to work with and encourage them, thus engendering respect and underlying core social work values and principles, which in turn can be assimilated into their own value system and used in familial relationships.

Community based settings also presents challenges to students. Helping offenders with work-based or education skills in the community is equally as important as the support gained in institutions, particularly as voluntary engagement is often relied on, whereas in custody enforced attendance often prevails.

The importance of building confidence and developing skills in areas such as interpersonal interaction, promoting pro-social attitudes and responses may take place in unexpected locations. For example, helping an offender prepare a CV, fill in a job application form, and provide voluntary work experience placements are ideal settings in which to deploy social work practice whilst engaging with centralised resettlement agendas.

The diversity of practice by professionals and organisations involved in working with offenders should not be underestimated. There are numerous texts available that outline what offender rehabilitation should be (Burnett and Roberts, 2004) and the climate of change and the place of traditional skills therein (Farrow, 2004). Alongside this, practitioners continue to face challenges from the ever-changing legislation, policies and developments that continue to evolve, reinvent and circumvent practice. Practitioners have to develop and work within competing discourses. They need to be creative and identify situations whereby social work roles can be located and/or relocated. Many offenders have complex and multiple needs resulting in chaotic lifestyles. Challenging preconceptions and stereotypes in the community becomes a constant activity for workers. As Moore (2012, p. 131) aptly states: 'If being in prison is enforced exile from society, then returning to the community often constitutes involuntary exile within it'. This is particularly pertinent with regard to finding employment and disclosing criminal offences and is exacerbated when considering offences against the person (Clifford, 2010).

Legal framework

The legislative framework for working with offenders is complex and ever changing, in part due to Criminal Justice Acts (CJAs), which influence policy initiatives and ultimately practice interventions that focus on reducing re-offending. A brief overview of significant chronological events will be discussed. Each TSO will have policies and procedures unique to their area of expertise, and some examples of good practice are considered.

The 1991 Home Office White Paper radically altered the landscape of working with offenders. The dominant discourse of risk management emerged and continues to dominate statutory work with offenders. Conterminously, traditional social work training for probation officers was also experiencing change.

The 2003 CJA introduced some of the most dramatic changes within criminal justice policy – namely the introduction of sentences to detain 'dangerous' offenders. Providing effective risk management and enshrining the principles of 'actuarial justice' (Feeley and Simon, 1992) were implicit within this Act.

The review of correctional services in England and Wales by Patrick Carter (2003), using sources such as the Social Exclusion Unit (2002) report, heralded changes within the CJS that would enable the voluntary sector to become a recognised and supported 'third sector', alongside the need for effective working relationships between prison and probation services. This had been stressed by the 1991 *Joint Thematic Review* by HM Inspectorates of Prisons and Probation Services which, following Carter's report, were merged to become the National Offender

Management Service (NOMS) in 2004 with a stated intention to ensure the effective 'end to end' management of offenders.

Providing 'end to end' offender management for individuals whose offending warranted intensive support and supervision was implemented in the concept of *Integrated Offender Management* (Home Office, 2009). Here, statutory and TSOs co-ordinate and deliver well-managed interventions designed to be individualised to meet the needs of the offender whilst addressing risk factors. This initiative incorporates valuing each partner's skills and knowledge, and considers shared aspects of risk. Ultimately the emphasis is having the offender as the focus of attention, not the offence.

Other initiatives such as payment by results (PBR) have been implemented. Here financial incentives are created for service providers who can demonstrate reduced re-offending. Outcome-based payment models replace bureaucratic targets. Put simply, those who show most long-term success receive extra remuneration. This concept has been introduced in key pathway areas such as employment. In 2012, the Work Programme was introduced which ensured each prison leaver had access to advice and guidance on training and employment; engagement is compulsory. Alongside PBR, social impact bonds are also a favoured method of financing offender interventions incorporating TSOs. There is continuing political emphasis on reducing re-offending and the effective management of offenders. In March 2012, the MOJ issued two consultation papers – 'Punishment and Reform: Effective Community Sentences' and 'Punishment and Reform: Effective Probation Services'. These documents indicate that offender punishment in the community has to be rigorous, well managed and effective.

Social work students who undertake placements with TSOs need to have an understanding of the legislative framework in which statutory supervision is located, and how the Probation Trust has the overall responsibility for managing and supervising community orders and pre- and post-release supervision (see Table 16.1). Familiarisation with CJAs, court orders and custodial sentences is an important part of the learning experience within a placement. It is also essential to ensure that risk management and effective supervision are complemented by the support given to offenders by TSOs.

When undertaking TSO placements, social work students need to be fully aware of policy documents and codes of practice. Such documents may include formal

Table 16.1 Persons supervised by the National Probation Service as at 30 September 2011

Persons Supervised by the Probation Service	232,862
All court orders	125,862
All community sentences	86,410
All pre- and post-release supervision	108,446

(MOJ, 2012)

agreements with statutory partners outlining each other's roles and obligations. Each organisation will have developed different sets of documents. Further to these, students should always consider the Human Rights Act and legislation pertaining to mental health as work with offenders can cross boundaries due to their complex and multiple needs.

Policies that are adhered to on a daily basis should include child protection, confidentiality, complaints, grievance procedures, lone working procedures, equal opportunities, health and safety and data protection. Good practice would indicate that policies on recording and sharing of information are readily available. These are particularly important for social work students, who can be faced with ethical dilemmas relating to information sharing. The list is not exhaustive and organisations will have developed policies that specifically relate to areas of their own practice and expertise. All policies should be regularly updated and amended. Policies should be more than 'compliance' documents; they should be enacted and effective. Students should challenge their effectiveness and can play an important role in design and implementation.

Interventions to practice

The type of intervention will depend on the organisation in which the placement is located. Students need to have an eclectic repertoire of theory and methods in order to meet the diverse needs of offenders. Evidence-based practice and 'what works' philosophies are the fundamental principles that underpin offending behaviour interventions.

The 'What Works' initiatives were launched in the 1990s by the government of the time as an 'aim to ensure all probation practice was based on evidence of success which comprised . . . high quality programmes . . . based on what is known to reduce re-offending' (Home Office 1999, p. 3; Cann et al., 2003). In order to achieve this, programmes had to be accredited and were designed to address specific deficits identified as leading to offending behaviour. Programmes are nationally defined and accredited by the Correctional Services Accreditation Panel (CSAP).

Just as crime and penal policy changes so does the application of programmes/ interventions. However, there are core specific areas, such as addressing anger and violence, drugs and alcohol, domestic violence, sexual offending, and racially motivated offending (McGuire, 2006). The MOJ website provides up-to-date details on all courses and interventions available and how these relate to specific court and custodial orders. As with any area of contemporary social work practice, evidence-based practice remains important in the CJS, particularly in terms of preventing re-offending and promoting community safety.

It is unlikely that in a TSO placement students will be undertaking any official interventions such as accredited offending behaviour programmes. However, they may be working with offenders who have or are undertaking such interventions. It is therefore important for the student to have an understanding of the principles and rationale for the intervention in order to support the work of case managers. Prior to undertaking any observations or case management work, students should be well grounded in the theoretical/criminological debates in particular 'What Works' and how it evolved (McGuire, 1995; Home Office, 1999). The ensuing section will consider some further approaches and practice interventions that are considered of value when working with offenders.

The 'What Works' model for programmes is focused on cognitive behavioural work, which is the most widely used form of intervention with offenders (Losel, 2012). This would be the model that prisoners had engaged with prior to release and would underpin the programmes continued on community orders. Cognitive behavioural approaches aim to remoralise or ethically reconstruct offenders by pro-social thinking (Kendall, 2004). Although this view can be accused of being biased, advocates of the approach would reiterate that distorted thinking is changed in order to help offenders change themselves (Clifford, 2010). Challenging attitudes and increasing the motivation to change lends itself readily to 'motivational interviewing' (Rollnick and Miller, 1995).

Motivational interviewing enables offenders the opportunity to reconsider more systematically the positive and negative consequences of their behaviour and relate these to their value systems (Miller and Rollnick, 2002). The Prochaska and DiClemente (1984) Cycle of Change is a further useful tool in order both to understand behaviour and to work toward sustainable change. Motivational work can take place side by side with cognitive work, task-centred work (Reid and Epstein, 1972) and systems theory (Pincus and Minahan, 1973). Practitioners should also be able to use person-centred approaches (Rogers, 1951) and deploy humanistic frameworks within their practice (Egan, 2010). Given the complexity and multiple needs that accompany many offenders, it is likely that crisis intervention (Roberts, 2005) will be needed, especially in situations that could elicit re-offending such as the loss of welfare benefits or housing. It is particularly important for practitioners in TSOs to work in conjunction with areas that have been identified (where applicable) via statutory assessments such as pre-sentence reports (PSRs) and offender assessment systems (OASys) (Howard et al., 2003), each indicating areas of risk and what support is needed to manage risk. Any work undertaken by TSOs should not be seen or done in isolation but rather any help or support that is offered should have a clearly planned strategy, be co-ordinated and ameliorate problems associated with offending.

Case example

Martin was classed as a prolific offender who had served numerous prison sentences. He was homeless and, despite efforts made by his supervising officer, was unable to secure accommodation before his current period of imprisonment. A few years previously, he had been housed by a charity to which he was re-referred by the prison officer when he was nearing the end of his sentence. After a full risk assessment and interviews, alongside close liaison with his statutory supervisor, Martin was once again housed by the same charity.

Unfortunately, Martin breached the conditions of his accommodation agreement and was evicted. However, he agreed to continue contact with the charity, which offered him mentoring support and help to find future accommodation. He was appointed a social work student as his caseworker in order to achieve this. It should be noted that at the time of his eviction his statutory supervisor had been unable to access an accommodation provider who would be willing to house Martin given his previous responses to housing and his constant returns to prison which resulted in him losing tenancies.

The social work student commenced engagement with Martin on a weekly basis. She attended multi-agency case meetings and brokered support from mental health professionals on Martin's behalf. The relationship between Martin and his caseworker was one based on open and honest exchanges of information. A task-centred approach was initially adopted and this later moved into more a solution focused model, which provided goals for Martin to aim towards, including moving towards independence and lessening support from professionals. After many months of pursuing housing options, and where other professionals openly admitted they could not see where Martin would be accommodated, the social work student secured a tenancy for him based on the additional support package that had been put in place for him via the charity. Martin moved into his accommodation and sustained his tenancy. He continued to receive 'floating support' from a number of sources including his caseworker for a designated period.

Benefits and challenges to working with offenders

One of the greatest benefits when working with offenders is acknowledging that your involvement has contributed to reducing re-offending, which in turn prevents the creation of victims. Addressing the associated underlying causes that led to offending is also rewarding and satisfying work. Witnessing individual's change and progress can incentivise workers. However, relapse presents challenges to workers who can become despondent. For many offenders change will not be an immediate response, if at all. Williams (1992, p. 20) considers: 'workers base their work on the assumption that offenders can change, that recidivism is not inevitable, and that the nature of the professional relationship with clients is influential'. This is of utmost importance when working with people with chaotic lifestyles who may drift in and out of services for a number of years and who may not respond to the interventions applied.

The ultimate goal of any intervention is to elicit change. An emphasis on improving self-esteem and developing insight has shifted to 'protecting the public and rescuing "future victims" by rehabilitative work, rather than the individual' (Garland 2001, p. 176). At times this can be both a challenge and reward for the worker.

Prisoners (and offenders on community based orders) take part in courses/interventions as a means to prevent re-offending and hence reduce any risk to the public. Lewis (1971) suggests prisoners could 'cheat' by participating in programmes in which they had no belief or by disingenuous expressions of remorse. One of the biggest challenges for released prisoners (and those who have completed community based interventions) is maintaining the momentum of what has been learnt and putting this into practice in everyday living situations. Supporting this process provides one of the main benefits of working with offenders – ensuring the core values of protecting the public regardless of one's role within a statutory or TSO setting.

The two extremes of imprisonment, short term and long term, present challenges to workers in a number of areas. When sent to prison more than just liberty is lost. Family and social relationships can become strained and result in deterioration and in some cases complete breakdown. The family, often the 'punished innocents', is left to cope with the aftermath of the offence, societal indignation and managing alone financially and emotionally. There is a wealth of literature relating to prisoners and families (Boswell, 2002; Bretherton, 2010). The maintenance of family relationships presents many challenges, particularly when prisoners are often placed miles away from home. This situation can be compounded when considering offences of a sexual or extremely violent nature, particularly when the term of imprisonment is lengthy and aspects of institutionalisation emerge (Goffman, 1961; Clifford, 2010). In these cases social workers have an important role to play in supporting family reintegration or, conversely, separation, drawing on their wealth of theoretical knowledge. Being estranged from family and established support networks is further complicated by lack of housing and employment opportunities, which are critical factors in the successful resettlement of prisoners.

It is acknowledged that housing is a key factor in reducing re-offending based on the established links between homelessness and offending. Since the introduction of the resettlement pathways, partnerships with TSOs involving housing initiatives have been established. However, research indicates that housing offenders remains problematic, due to factors such as lack of housing stock and difficulties in partnership working alongside prioritising need and policy restrictions. Accessing effective housing advice in custody remains an area of concern, for example, a HMIP (2012) inspection found many prisoners were awaiting specialist housing advice and some were still being released without suitable accommodation (Maguire et al., 2007; Gojkovic et al., 2012). It should be noted that many prisons do have dedicated housing advisors and the links with TSOs and housing providers continue to develop in order to address the issue of homelessness on release.

One of the biggest difficulties facing smaller housing providers is keeping abreast with management changes in prisons and making sure all advisors are aware of and have knowledge of their services in order to ensure effective and maximum utilisation. However, being part of a process that assists offenders into housing and the benefits associated with the end results are numerous and, whilst the challenges are great, each individual success provides the motivation to continue. Once accommodation has been accessed, there are further considerations, which include being able to manage financially and understand the conditions of a tenancy. The stigma (Goffman, 1963) of having a criminal record and how other members of the 'housed' community respond to this knowledge should not be ignored.

Ex-offenders seeking employment can encounter difficulties relating to trust, ability and experience, and stigma. Whilst there is legislation in place (Rehabilitation of Offenders Act 1974) alongside the support of many organisations, having a criminal record remains a barrier for many. One area of disconcertion is the disclosure of an offence to potential employers. Preparing offenders to disclose their offence is an area that requires workers to have knowledge, skills and expertise. Being able to do this whilst not minimising the offending history, or even denying it existed, can be challenging and frustrating at the onset, particularly in times of economic recession, and the dominant discourse of risk management. Spending time addressing areas such as interviewing skills, presentation and effective communication may not appear to have a 'specific' social work role. However, the benefits to those involved are immense. Being part of an organisation that helps prepare people to maximise their potential and gain acceptance within society by playing an active part in the economy of that society is extremely rewarding. There is great satisfaction when individuals take responsibility for their past and have the courage and determination to move forward regardless of the barriers imposed.

Working in the CJS presents both challenges and rewards. Many TSOs have neither the financial capacity nor human resources to tender for contracts in the climate of change within offender services. Some TSOs may decide to work as a subcontractor to larger organisations. Here the risk is in terms of retaining individual identity and autonomy. The landscape is precarious for small organisations that lack the capacity to demonstrate the financial returns necessary to compete in current market conditions with the emphasis on effectiveness, collation of data and demonstrable long-term impact. The loss is even greater to the offenders who miss the opportunity to gain from the benefits of the personalised and experienced services associated with many small TSOs.

Anti-oppressive considerations

Government responses to law and order and ultimately statutory work with offenders historically dovetail Foucault's (1977) 'disciplinary society'. The dilemma for workers in these environments is to build positive working relationships whilst, at the same time, managing their disciplinary powers. Confronting offending behaviour whilst supporting the individual is challenging. The underlying principle of valuing each person as unique, worthwhile and self-determined must be kept separate from confrontation/challenging any offending behaviour (Williams, 1992). Workers may experience ethical/moral concerns and these should not be negated. Supervision provides a forum for these issues and, where applicable, referral to specialist professional support (Brannen, 1988).

Workers within the CJS should oppose oppression and discrimination. The link between racism and the CJS is well documented in the literature (Phillips and Bowling, 2012) coupled with the effect of the terrorist events of 9/11 and the London bombings of 2005, when minority ethnic groups become a visible target. Gender inequalities in sentencing, imprisonment and the treatment of women offenders have been the subject of critique (Corston, 2007a, 2007b). Imprisonment for disabled and/ or elderly offenders creates difficulties within institutions originally built for the able bodied. The challenges facing staff and prisoners are immense (Crawley and Sparks, 2005). Sexual orientation has been subject to discrimination across time. The Howard League Commission on Sex in Prison is an area long overdue for attention. Working in an environment that restricts liberty, whilst imposing sanctions that can be oppressive and discriminatory, is exceptionally challenging.

Once on placement, students will be expected to apply their learning of anti-oppressive and discriminatory practice and demonstrate these in engagement with offenders. Empathy, or the capacity to recognise feelings experienced by another, is an area that can be problematic. Worrall (1992, p. 30) aptly states that 'empathy is the most ubiquitous cliché in social work jargon' – it implies a commonality. This will not be the case for workers dealing with people who have committed very serious violent and/or sexual offences, nor those who are currently street homeless. Similarly, the desire to show service users 'some shared experiences' implies the worker has successfully overcome barriers. It follows that the service user should have the ability to do the same – a disempowering approach. The ability to show respect and recognise individuals as experts in their own current situation whilst helping them make informed choices regarding their situation is a more empowering stance.

The differing organisations working in custodial institutions all bring their own ethical and cultural base and, at times, conflicting values as each follow the political agendas set regarding resettlement and rehabilitation. Managing the divide between care and control is ever present.

Students who have TSO placements which provide services within custodial establishments must consider these issues and refrain from confronting and challenging too vociferously at the onset. Change is more likely to occur when all parties are able to fully understand each other's role and to support and complement each other's work. Adopting a calm rational approach in which to promote good practice and establish a framework for change is more conducive and, whilst this takes time, the end result will be worth the wait. Using an anti-discriminatory action plan linked with legislative developments can assist and provide a tool for constructive arguments, without jeopardising the working relationships established between TSOs and HM Prisons, which can take years to develop.

The restriction of liberty is not confined to imprisonment but applies also when released into the community and as part of community-based court orders as both impose conditions such as where to reside, whom to contact and permissible locations – all of which can impact on relationships, support and progression. Such restrictions can present dilemmas to workers, particularly in TSOs, when considering the possibility of recall to court/custody if breached. The dilemma of disclosing to the appropriate authorities any concerns a worker has must be balanced against the protection of the public. It is vital that workers adhere to following all procedures as dictated under statutory provision, thus maintaining professionalism and credibility by doing so.

Summary

Within this chapter, consideration has been given to working with offenders in custody and the community and some of the challenges that can arise from working in an ever changing, politically driven CJS. Cuts in public spending and the pressure on an overstretched prison system add to the tension experienced by workers and prisoners. The individual circumstances of offenders often mean that practitioners will straddle professional paradigms, at times advocating on behalf of those with mental health issues, brokering specialist services and keeping abreast with new laws and legislation, to name only a few.

Motivating offenders to change is a key role within the CJS. Whilst in custody offenders frequently state their desire to desist from offending, seek work and/or education and training on release. The reality they experience shows that the barriers faced in the community can prevent the continued momentum of desistance gained in custody.

Some released prisoners will pose a continued threat to the public and it is essential that workers in TSOs have the appropriate information, knowledge and skills to work with statutory organisations in managing this risk. It is equally as important to remember that stigmatising all offenders in such a way impedes successful reintegration. Providing support that encourages responsibility and enabling offenders to make choices is empowering for both parties.

This chapter has focused on two critical resettlement areas – accommodation and employment. Housing ex-offenders within community-based settings can present problems when, despite political rhetoric, public opinion still opposes such action. Coupled with the management of risk and the decline of statutory housing funding, demands on housing providers are great. Similarly, when considering employment options, disclosure of a criminal record remains a barrier in times of high unemployment and as demands for skills increase. The Legal Aid, Sentencing and Punishment of Offenders Act 2012 which reforms the Rehabilitation of Offenders Act 1974 will impact significantly on offenders in terms of the number of months and years before a conviction becomes 'spent' and ultimately the time it may take to gain employment, especially in times of economic recession. Overcoming the aforementioned barriers requires support, guidance and opportunities to acquire new skills, attitudes and experiences, all of which can be time consuming. Guaranteeing instant results does little to promote trust and works against successful resettlement.

Students may find themselves placed in organisations without a singular remit. The provision on offer may be varied, specialised, extensive and ever changing. Many smaller organisations have to become 'bricoleurs' in order to remain financially solvent. It is important for students entering placements to be aware of the financial demands and constraints in which they are working in order for them to be creative in service delivery, as it is within some of the smaller organisations that extensive and valuable front line experience is gained.

The challenges may appear to outweigh the benefits, but despite the difficulties considered within this chapter, the rewards of working in the CJS are great. For those committed to social justice and safer communities, each small success is the motivator to continue. However, students need to overcome the desire to have 'social work' clearly defined, but to be as adaptable as the people they seek to assist.

There is a wealth of diversity of provision and the expertise available within small TSOs who are adept at working with 'softer outcomes', such as increasing confidence and self-esteem. The importance of this work should not be underestimated when considering engaging with employment or education options, or fostering pro-social and constructive activities, all of which can result in reducing re-offending. Making a difference to the lives of offenders, enabling them to desist from crime, reintegrate into society and gain a sense of self-worth, reaps rewards for the individuals concerned, their families, the community and society as a whole.

📖 CASE STUDY

Andrew was a first-time offender who received a four-year prison sentence for grievous bodily harm. Due to the nature of Andrew's offence he was seeking to relocate on release from prison. He was housed by a charity that worked with two probation trusts in order to transfer his case between counties. A full information exchange took place in order for the charity to assess the risk Andrew may pose and to ensure that the move was successful. Andrew was very motivated and determined to return to his pre-custody lifestyle, which included being employed. He undertook voluntary work with the charity and engaged fully with his caseworker as part of his support plan. Andrew applied for numerous jobs and was always being turned down. He was becoming despondent with his situation and his caseworker was concerned that this would impact on his thus far successful reintegration. During sessions with his caseworker, they focused on building on Andrew's strengths and abilities and his previous employment history. They also ensured that his offence disclosure was presented in a truthful way and undertook exercises to facilitate this process. Andrew was very animated at having successfully completed an interview and felt sure he would gain employment. However, his euphoria was quashed when he learnt that he was not successful and became convinced that his criminal record was a barrier to employment, as he would always have the offence on record.

His caseworker worked on Andrew's behalf contacting the organisation in question, helping Andrew to have full understanding of the Rehabilitation of Offenders Act, spent and unspent convictions and the possibility of recourse should discrimination occur. Andrew was demoralised, particularly as the job in question was at a much lower level than his previous managerial experiences. Undeterred, his caseworker ensured each session adopted a task-centred approach with an employment focus. With increased confidence, Andrew became more skilled at disclosing his offence at interview, explained his support package and demonstrated his motivation. He was eventually accepted for employment, again a position that was at the starting point of a career ladder. However, he also realised that the experience would lead to him having a work record, references and the opportunity to progress. He continues to receive the support of his caseworker.

Questions

 Discuss the personal and professional implications for individuals with regard to disclosing or not disclosing criminal offences to potential employees.

 Relocating to a new geographical area is an unsettling experience. What specific impacts are there for offenders who relocate?

 When considering your answer make reference to the legal framework and case management issues.

Further resources and suggested readings

Carter, P. (2003) *Managing Offenders, Reducing Crime: A New Approach*. London: Home Office Strategy Unit.

Jewkes, Y. (ed.) (2007) *Handbook on Prisons*. Gloucester: Willan Publishing.

Liebling, A. and Maruna, S. (eds) (2005) *The Effects of Imprisonment*. Gloucester: Willan Publishing.

Maguire, M., Morgan, R. and Reiner, R. (2012) *The Oxford Handbook of Criminology*, 5th edn. Oxford: Oxford University Press.

Maruna, S. and Immarigeon, R. (2004) *After Crime and Punishment: Pathways to Offender Reintegration*. Cullompton: Willan Publishing.

Social Exclusion Unit (2000) *Reducing Re-Offending by Ex Prisoners*. London: Social Exclusion Unit.

Websites

Ministry of Justice – www.justice.gov.uk

17 Self-harming

Jo Bell

Introduction

Self-harm and suicidal behaviour among young people is now a major public health issue in the UK and beyond. Despite wide acceptance that suicide in adolescence is under-reported, it still consistently ranks as one of the leading causes of death for young people between ten and 24 years of age in most westernised countries. Recent research has also drawn attention to the increasing prevalence of self-harm amongst young people, and suggests that social workers and others who work with young people are more likely than ever to encounter this behaviour in their practice. Current estimates show that around 10 per cent of adolescents report having self-harmed, some of which have suicidal intent. It is more common in young females, where presentation at hospital becomes increasingly common from age 12 onwards (between ages 12 and 15 years, the girl-to-boy ratio is five or six to one). This ratio decreases with age in the later teenage years (Hawton et al., 2012).

It is therefore important for practitioners and students of social work to be aware and prepared with relevant skills and knowledge of this important subject as they go into practice. This chapter will critically examine some of the definitions, myths and differences between self-harm and suicidal behaviour; legislative frameworks within which practitioners must work; implications for assessment and intervention, with exercise examples and questions; and benefits and challenges for social workers in this field.

Suicide and self-harm

There is no single, universally agreed definition of self-harm and suicidal behaviour and the terms are often used interchangeably. Very broadly, suicide can be defined as: 'an act of deliberate self-harm which results in death. Deliberate self-harm is an act, which is intended to cause self harm, but which does not result in death. Individuals engaging in deliberate self-harm may, or may not, have in intention to take their own life' (Scottish Executive, 2002).

Self-harm is not a classified mental health disorder, although mental health problems are very often associated with self-harm, in that they co-exist with each other. Nor is there any such thing as a typical person who self-harms. Self-cutting is the most common method of self-harm in adolescents (Hawton et al., 2012) but over-doses (self-poisoning), burning, scalding, hair pulling, biting, and banging heads are also often involved. The onset of self-harm tends to correlate with the end of puberty and this explanation has been used to account for the high girl-to-boy ratio around the age of 13 to 15 years (Hawton et al., 2012). Research by the Mental Health Foundation and Camelot Foundation (2006) reported a range of factors that could trigger self-harm in young people. The most frequent reasons mentioned were: being bullied at school; not getting on with parents; stress and worry around academic performance; parental divorce; bereavement; unwanted pregnancy; experience of abuse in earlier childhood (whether sexual, physical and/or emotional); difficulties associated with sexual orientation; problems to do with race, culture or religion; low self-esteem and self-confidence; and feelings of being rejected. Other reported factors associated with self-harm are alcohol and drug use, mental disorders and mental health problems, and domestic violence (NICE, 2004).

Self-harm is often confused with suicide attempts and suicidal behaviour but they are not the same thing. There are distinct pathways in self-harm and suicide and also points of convergence. The difference is in the intention and motivational basis for the act (Bell, 2011). Sometimes intention and motivation can be inferred from the method used. For example, suicidal intent is more often associated with overdoses, whereas cutting indicates self-punishment and tension relief (Hawton et al., 2012). Most professionals agree that self-harm is a response to profound emotional pain; young people engage in self-harm because they have no other way of coping with problems and emotional distress in their lives. Episodes of self-harm can be triggered as a result of a complex combination of experiences, rather than a single event. So whilst significant changes or events may act as triggers, multiple daily stressors can also accumulate to produce the analogous 'pressure cooker' effect (McDougall et al., 2010; Bell, 2011).

Therefore, although self-harm and suicidal behaviour overlap considerably, it is important that they are understood and responded to differently. Deliberate self-harm needs to be regarded as one of a range of risk factors associated with suicide, rather than as suicidal behaviour. Indeed, the majority of people who self-harm do not go on to take their own lives (this has significant implications for assessment which will be discussed later in the chapter). More often than not then, self-harm is about regulating emotions, survival and coping with stress (Trainor, 2010). For individuals contemplating or attempting suicide, a critical point to understand is that very often they do not want to die as much as they want their suffering to end

(Schneidman, 1996). In other words, suicidal people are often not motivated by a wish to die as much as they are motivated by a desire to escape from what they perceive to be an otherwise unbearable situation (Williams, 2001).

Social work practice within suicide and self-harming services

There is a variety of statutory and voluntary contexts in which social workers may encounter self-harming and suicidal behaviour amongst young people: for example, in child and adolescent mental health services (CAHMS), young offenders, child protection, family support, fostering and adoption, education, probation, hospital and primary health settings. More serious cases are most likely to come to attention of accident and emergency (A&E) services.

Roles occupied by social workers in this area may include assessment and subsequent referral (e.g. CAHMS, GP, alcohol or drug services, other voluntary agencies), advocacy, support, help and advice, and some therapeutic work. The type of referral made will depend on the individual and the assessment of the individual's needs. For example, if the 'risk' is thought to be serious and is the first time brought to the attention of professional and helping services, a referral to CAHMS may be appropriate. If, however, parents and significant others are aware, and the 'risk' is considered to be less serious, a referral to a local voluntary agency or support group may be more appropriate. Advocacy can be equally important in this respect; it may be that the young person needs support in telling their GP, needs help with accessing services or benefits, or even help with finding supportive sites on the internet which they can use in their own time.

Working with suicidal or self-harming young people is a complex area and no single policy or procedure can be expected to cover all eventualities. Risk assessment procedures and policies will differ between different agencies and organisations. Part of the problem with dealing with self-harm and risk of suicide amongst young people for professionals is being able to fit the phenomenon into their existing working context. Professionals from different backgrounds may not share the same perception and understanding of self-harming and suicidal behaviour (Walker, 2012) with the most obvious example being differences between a medical model and social model approach. In addition, a social worker's professional identity in this field may differ from other professionals in terms of value base and assessment skills. For example, they may wish to explore social factors and individual problem-solving approaches. Social workers tend to use more of a reflective practice approach in their work, and this value base is very important. For this reason, it is essential that discussion occurs between professionals as well as the young person themselves regarding the nature of the risk and the function of the behaviour. The benefits and challenges of collaborative multidisciplinary working will be discussed in more detail later in the chapter.

Whatever the access or entry route to services and whether the context is statutory or voluntary, there is a need for clear guidance on information sharing, child protection and confidentiality. The next section deals with relevant legislation, policy documents and codes of practice for social workers working with young people where there is a concern about self-harm or suicide.

Legal framework

Social workers practising with young people where there is a concern about self-harm or suicide need to be clear about the legal frameworks within which they work. They should be familiar with human rights legislation, children's rights (e.g. Children Act 1989) and mental health law (e.g. Mental Health Act 1983; Mental Capacity Act 2005) and how these frameworks interact (McDougall et al., 2010), recognising that children have rights too. They have a right to protection from all forms of violence, including protection from suicide and self-harm. The United Nations Convention on the Rights of the Child (2007) states:

- Children have the right to life and must have the best possible chance to develop fully.
- Children and young people have the right to express a view about things that affect them.
- Children have the right to their own space and privacy.
- Children must be kept safe from harm and given proper care by those looking after them.
- Children have the right to be as healthy as possible.
- Children have the right to be protected from all sorts of exploitation which can damage their welfare.

The human rights framework is set out in the European Convention on Human Rights, the United Nations Convention on the Rights of the Child, and the Human Rights Act 1998. Together these instruments establish important principles in law regarding the rights of children and young people in relation to dignity, respect, decision making and protection. The Children Act 1989 is a key legal framework governing the care and welfare of all children and young people under the age of 18. The United Nations Convention of the Rights of the Child and the Children Act 1989 entitle children to participatory decision-making rights. Of importance here are issues relating to competence, capacity and consent. A young person's competency is determined by their maturity and understanding rather than their fixed chronological age. Within UK law, the 'Gillick principle' refers to the right of a child under the age of 16 to consent to treatment without the need for parental permission or knowledge if they are deemed to be competent to do so (Harbour, 2008). This means the young person must have achieved sufficient understanding and intelligence to enable him or her to understand fully what is proposed (NSPCC, 2008) and is commonly referred to as the 'Fraser ruling'. Their consent must be freely given and the young person must be given appropriate information.

Despite these principles, many young people report that they have not been involved in decisions made about them and frequently have their privacy, dignity and confidentiality compromised (Mental Health Foundation and Camelot Foundation, 2006; McDougall et al., 2010). However, McDougall et al. (2010) point out that although clarity about confidentiality and consent is important to young people, making appropriate decisions about care and treatment is not always straightforward. For example, competence may vary according to the decision being proposed (a young person may be competent to make one decision, but not another); a social worker may be asked by a young person not to share information about self-harming with parents. Difficult decisions may also present themselves when a young person self-harms and then refuses help. Not only are these decisions difficult but they can also provoke disagreements between professionals who may interpret the legal framework differently (Hassan et al., 1999a, 1999b). Therefore, social workers need carefully to consider the legal implications of any decision they take and consent for treatment decisions must always be kept under review (McDougall et al., 2010).

The Mental Capacity Act 2005 covers decisions, particularly decisions on health and social care. The assessment of capacity and ability to make decisions and consent to treatment is different for young people aged 16 and 17. This Act states that all people over the age of 16 have the right to autonomy and independent decision making unless it can be shown that they lack capacity as defined in the Act. People are judged to lack capacity if they are unable to understand information that is given to them; unable to use the information, or retain the information for long enough, to make the decision; or unable to communicate their decision (McDougall et al., 2010).

The first three principles of the Act are always to assume that someone can make a decision (i.e. has capacity) and to help her or him to make a decision (for example, by providing information). Sometimes this can present dilemmas for social workers in practice. There is an important distinction between the capacity to make decisions and autonomy to choose; people can make unwise decisions and that does not mean that they lack capacity. Under the Act someone else can give consent providing it is in the person's best interests. This can also present its own problems.

Finally, the Mental Health Act 1983 deals with the circumstances under which individuals with mental disorders can be detained without their consent. In 2007, the Act was amended to include new guiding principles through a revised Code of Practice, including the expectation that young people admitted to hospital for mental health treatment should have access to appropriate care in an environment suited to their age and development (Department of Health [DoH], 2004). The revised Code of Practice also sets out circumstances where the refusal by a young person of potentially life saving treatment could be overruled and where confidentiality can be breached.

Theoretical underpinnings

The theoretical underpinnings of the Mental Health Act and the Mental Capacity Act are discussed in Chapter 10. Of relevance here are clinical guidelines published by the National Institute for Clinical Excellence (NICE). These guidelines are relevant for all people aged eight years and over. Where guidelines refer to children and young people, this applies to those who are between eight and 16 years. The upper age limit may vary depending on whether the young person is in full-time education or not. They are concerned with how services should respond in the 48 hours after an episode of self-harm and the effectiveness of follow-up treatments, and set standards for the short-term physical and psychological management and secondary prevention of self-harm in primary and secondary care (NICE, 2004). The guidelines are intended for use by self-harming individuals and their families and carers, professionals who are involved in the care or treatment or who may have direct contact with those who have self-harmed, and those with responsibility for planning services. The purpose is to improve standards of care, reduce variations in service quality, and ensure that the needs of children and young people who self-harm, and their families or carers, are met. Relevant health care groups are expected to produce a plan and identify resources for implementation, along with appropriate timetables (NICE, 2004).

According to NICE (2004) guidelines (4.9.1.8), the assessment and treatment of self-harm in children and young people should give special attention to the issues of confidentiality, the young person's consent (including Gillick competence), parental consent, child protection, and the use of the Mental Health Act in young people and the Children Act.

NICE guidelines were developed in part as a response to an objective that covers the need for a 'cultural shift' both within society and amongst professionals. This includes the need for a greater understanding of self-harm as a coping strategy, so that those who self-harm are seen as doing the best they can to survive very difficult circumstances. It also covers the need to move away from seeing self-harm as a 'clinical illness' in itself, rather as a manifestation of emotional distress. Such a shift would imply a move towards a more holistic approach to treatment and a positive step in terms of the frameworks set out above. However, the NICE definition does not differentiate between self-harm and suicide, a point which has been highlighted previously as important. As discussed, although self-harm and suicidal behaviour overlap considerably, for the purposes of intervention and treatment they need to be understood and responded to differently. This will be discussed in the next section in the context of best practice approaches.

Best practice approaches

The starting point for anyone working with self-harming and suicidal behaviour amongst young people is to acknowledge the strength of the social stigma surrounding this behaviour and its associated effects. Joiner (2005) suggested that suicidal behaviour is special in the degree to which it is stigmatised, because the fear and ignorance that surround it are so great. This is because our efforts to understand such behaviour, he argues, take us to the most intellectually and emotionally challenging of mysteries about why and how people overcome the most sacred of life's instincts – self-preservation.

Because of the stigma surrounding it then, many young people engage in self-harming and suicidal behaviour secretly. They are often scared and feel unable to talk about their behaviour or the reasons why they are doing it, harbouring feelings of guilt and shame. This can seriously affect their sense of self-worth and their relationships with families and friends. Therefore the most important factor, at least in the initial stages of assessment, is your attitude as a professional social worker.

Risk assessment

A helpful response would be one in which the social worker does not 'freak out' but is prepared to listen and allow the young person to talk. A young person disclosing self-harm needs to know that the fact they have been able to disclose shows strength and courage and should be allowed to take the discussion at their own pace. Contrary to popular belief, there is no evidence to suggest that asking questions or talking about self-harm or suicide will increase the probability that it will occur. Talking about it, however, will help them to come to some decisions and an increased understanding of their own behaviour (Best, 2006).

It is very important not to focus exclusively on the self-harm itself but on the reasons why the young person has self-harmed. Effective strategies also need to reflect the differences and the overlap between suicidal behaviour and deliberate self-harm. In order to distinguish between the two, one has to explore them in depth with the individual. The functions of the behaviour or the motivational intention behind it need to be established before intervention can begin. This refers to what the individual intends to accomplish by engaging in the behaviour; in other words, what is the goal of the behaviour (Bell, 2013).

Unfortunately, this process may not be as straightforward as it sounds. Walsh (2006) and Miller (2011) point out that eliciting a clear articulation of intent from young people who are engaging in self-destructive behaviour can be difficult. They may be emotionally overwhelmed as well as very confused about their own behaviour and often provide answers that are ambiguous. Assessing intent, therefore, requires a combination of compassion and investigative persistence (Walsh, 2006). Finding the answers depends on asking the right questions; *when* the behaviour started, *how, how often*, and *why*. Direct questions such as 'Do you do this to feel better or to end all your feelings?' can be a helpful starting point for exploring their intentions and how it made them feel. Often when people don't know *why*, being asked to think about what may have triggered the act may help them. Is there a precipitating event? What was going on in his or her life at the time? Other important questions include: Is the young person using drugs or alcohol? What are their social supports (protective factors)? Is the young person able to see any alternatives?

Finally, it is also important not to make assumptions about intent on the basis of previous episodes; a person who self-harms repeatedly might not always do so for the same reason each time (Horrocks et al., 2003). Therefore, each act must be assessed separately and contextually to determine the motivation behind it. For more detailed information on assessment tools and key points in the process of initial assessment, see McDougall et al. (2010).

Intervention and treatment

There is a wide range of intervention models and methods available for suicidal young people and those who self-harm. However, Hawton et al. (2012) caution that there is still a shortage of information and evidence on which to base treatment recommendations, and more research is needed to assess their effectiveness. Nonetheless, two major approaches often used in the short and longer term treatment of self-harm and suicidal behaviour in young people will be the focus of discussion here.

Crisis intervention techniques

The goal of crisis intervention is to take the edge off the pain of the current crisis so as to bring it within a tolerable range. Techniques include harm minimisation and distraction.

Harm minimisation approaches (discussed also in Chapter 13) are predicated on the understanding that the behaviour engaged in functions as a coping mechanism for the individual. As discussed by Watson in Chapter 13, this approach proposes that it is more ethical to concentrate on achievable goals (minimising harms), by advising and supporting the user to adopt safer practices, than try waiting until they are ready to consider abstinence. It also enables the practitioner to engage with young people who might not otherwise seek help. Importantly then, this approach does not try to prevent young people from self-harming, recognising the damage that could be done by removing a key coping strategy – the one thing that keeps them alive (remember this is not about wanting to die it is about wanting to survive).

One popular harm minimisation technique is to use ice cubes instead of cutting. These can be either squeezed in the hands or pressed/rubbed on the skin. The pain from the ice resembles pain from self-injury but the result is not as harmful or dangerous to the body. Many young people who self-harm by cutting will talk about how watching blood run from a wound makes them feel better. One young woman described to her social worker how watching the blood run out was like seeing the bad feelings and tension running away from within her. This act is symbolic but also tangible. She tried the ice-cube technique and described how the sensation was similar but not quite the same, as the melted ice did not look the same as blood. Her social worker suggested she dye the ice cubes with red food colouring (which she did before she froze them). The effect was increased as the melted red ice took on the appearance of blood running from her arm.

Other harm minimisation techniques include snapping wrists with an elastic band; colouring parts of the body to resemble what would happen if they had cut themselves (for example, drawing red lines on parts of the body instead of cutting); or plunging the arm into a bucket of ice water – again the shock of the cold and pain from this will resemble pain of self-harm. Practitioners can also offer advice on reducing risk such as using sterile equipment, how it is done, where it is done, using bandages, etc.

Distraction techniques are methods adopted to help relieve tension and distract a young person's thoughts from the immediate urge to self-harm. Examples include listening to music, relaxation, writing, calling a hotline or support group, or posting on a message board. For some young people relief from tension may come about from physical activity such as running, dancing, smashing ice into a bath (or crying, screaming or shouting); for others it could be writing, drawing or painting.

The use of mood graphs involves charting the intensity of thoughts and feelings over a period of time – say every two or three minutes for 20 to 30 minutes. According to Joiner (2005), this results in some charted improvement in negative mood. This has the dual benefit of distracting the young person engaging in self-harm by having them cognitively involved in another task. It also serves as a way of demonstrating that negative moods are not unmanageable; they are unpleasant states that fade with time. Individuals who chart these feelings over time will see that they lose their edge even over short periods.

Cognitive based techniques

A number of cognitive based techniques have developed over recent years and are often considered to be the leading treatment for suicidal behaviour (Joiner, 2005). These models represent a move away from crisis intervention towards more longer term therapeutic support. Cognitive therapies are underpinned by the notion that our behaviour is contingent upon the ways in which we perceive and think about a situation. The goal, therefore, is to restructure or alter the ways in which young people think and perceive, which should in turn result in alterations and changes in behaviour. These therapeutic techniques are considerably more time consuming than short-term crisis intervention techniques.

Cognitive approaches such as the ICARE technique (Rudd et al., 2000) typically involve identifying particular negative thoughts and connecting those thoughts to general categories of cognitive distortion (such as all or nothing thinking, catastrophising, or overgeneralisation), which are characteristic of constricted suicidal thinking (Schneidman, 1996). The goal in assessing these types of thoughts is to demonstrate their irrationality – how such thoughts are negatively distorted and might involve questions such: How likely is it? Are there any alternative explanations? Will it matter in a year? Exploring alternative interpretations for distorted thinking allows the person to 'degeneralise' their perceptions and restructure them in a less distorted and dichotomous way.

Case example

Jessica is an intelligent and outgoing 16-year-old girl who has recently completed her GCSEs. She plans to study to go to university to train to be a teacher. She has been referred to your agency after a recent incident where she attempted to take an overdose of paracetamol. Her mother discovered her before she was able to ingest the tablets.

Jessica was seen by a social worker at your agency several years ago following an act of self-harm. She has a wide circle of friends and enjoys socialising and regularly 'gets drunk'. Her parents separated when she was ten years old, she has no brothers or sisters and is not particularly close to her parents. Six months ago her auntie died in a car accident. Jessica described her auntie as a second mother. They were extremely close. She has been with her boyfriend for over a year and describes him as her best friend and the only one she can talk to about worries and problems in her life. She discovered via Facebook that her boyfriend had been seeing another girl, and received a message from him ending their relationship. She tells you that she wanted to take the tablets because she 'didn't care' and 'wanted to die'. However, she now regrets her actions and denies current thoughts of suicide although she continues to feel that her life is 'crap' and 'not worth living'. She also admits to urges and thoughts about self-harm.

Points to consider

- What specific skills are important for engaging with Jessica in this assessment?
- What triggers might be influencing this behaviour?
- What therapeutic interventions might be beneficial?
- Which partner agencies and services might be helpful in this scenario (consider both Jessica and her family)?
- Which part of the Children Act 1989/Mental Health Act might apply in this scenario?

Benefits and challenges in suicide and self-harming services

There are a number of challenges involved in working with young people and suicide and self-harming behaviour. This section will highlight consent and confidentiality, risk assessment, legal implications and ethical and anti-oppressive considerations.

One of the most crucial and also challenging aspects of working with self-harming or suicidal young people is in assessing risk. Initial assessments, often made by social workers as the first point of call, need to be as thorough as possible. The outcome decision (intervention, treatment, referral to another agency or specialist service) depends on it. Getting the assessment wrong could mean that you risk referral to an inappropriate agency or implementing an inappropriate intervention or treatment. There is also a risk that you could be making things worse for the young person. When it comes to consent and confidentiality, the question of who needs to know and who has a right to know is critical and needs to be considered in the context of risk. Social workers need to be cautious that informing others against the wishes of the young person would do more harm than good, and informing parents should not be the automatic first step. Thus, deciding whom to inform may well present a number of difficult ethical dilemmas. For example, where it is believed that the response would be harmful or abusive, it may be necessary to avoid informing parents. Similarly, where ongoing or previous abuse by parents lies at the heart of self-harming behaviour, informing parents might not be in the interests of the child at all.

These decisions require professional judgement and discretion and it is not always clear what action should follow: When and to whom should social workers refer cases of self-harm? Do parents have an automatic right to know? If young people have a right to confidentiality, are there any limits to it? They should consider the seriousness of the presenting behaviour and the motivations behind it, any mental health issues, family background, and what led up to it. Social workers also need to carefully consider the legal implications of any decision they take. All decisions need to be fully documented with a clear rationale and kept under constant review. Consent for treatment decisions must always be kept under review.

One of the most important things you can offer a young person in distress is time to talk. This sounds easy, but when pushed for time and resources this can become a major challenge. Most difficult to deal with are young people who are helpless and hopeless; those who have no coping mechanism; or those who fit the revolving door model of being failed repeatedly by systems and services. Such individuals often have enduring histories, may be unable to sustain and maintain relationships, and are hard to reach and engage. Such young people may also be regarded as those who present the highest risk.

As with other areas of front line social work, lack of time and resources, feelings of frustration and lack of efficacy, and concerns about risk and responsibility can take their toll on practitioners in this field. For this reason, it is important that social workers are able to acknowledge and understand their own limits within their professional practice. This requires high levels of self-awareness and regular access to clinical supervision. Social workers need to be able to reflect regularly on their own practice. They need opportunities within a robust support system to go through it – to offload it to formulate a balanced perspective. Ultimately, the most successful work is likely to come about as a result of strong multidisciplinary teams where there is consistency in understanding between and amongst different professionals in terms of the legal framework, risk assessment and understanding of intent, and where professionals feel supported and confident in their practice.

Summary

Where there is a concern about self-harm or suicide, social workers who work with young people should be aware of their professional obligations and the various legal frameworks affecting the care and treatment of young people.

Young people who deliberately harm themselves are giving clear signals that something is wrong. Some episodes are aimed at dying but many are aimed at mobilising help or gaining relief from an overwhelming emotional state and are not directly connected to suicidal intent. Others are ambiguously aimed at both. Some do not wish to die but impulsively act out a wish to change their circumstances. Practitioners should focus on the emotional and psychological distress, and less on the behavioural aspects of self-harm. It is the motivational basis for the act, rather than the act itself, which is relevant.

If young people are at serious risk from self-harm or suicide attempts, then clear referral pathways and a commitment to sharing information across agencies is crucial. Agencies need to work collaboratively with each other in developing and delivering appropriate effective services to individual young people. Issues of confidentiality and consent should be discussed openly, in a manner consistent with the young person's evolving capacities, and jointly understood. If confidentiality needs to be compromised, it should be done respectfully and openly with due consideration of the best interests of the young person. Social workers also need to carefully consider the legal implications of any decision they take and consent for treatment decisions must always be kept under review.

A number of different techniques can be used in crisis intervention for short-term support. Longer term support can use cognitive based models focusing on changing thinking patterns and processes. However, much more research is needed to assess their effectiveness and appropriateness. Social workers, therefore, need to remain vigilant to this issue and open minded in their approach to treatment recommendations.

📖 CASE STUDY

Daniel is 16 years old and has just begun studying for A-levels, having achieved exceptionally good grades in his GCSEs. His school has referred him to your social work agency. Over the last few months, family and professionals at school have become increasingly concerned about his emotional state and behaviour. Daniel has become passionately interested in the Bible and talks constantly about religious issues. He carries a Bible around with him everywhere he goes.

His schoolwork and attendance have deteriorated and teachers have noticed that he is often unable to concentrate during lessons. The school are concerned about his mental health and feel that he might be depressed. He has a good network of friends at school but some have been worried by Daniel's behaviours and unsure about how to react to his unusual behaviour and nonsensical ramblings. Daniel's family are also concerned that he might have been drinking alcohol and smoking cannabis and have begun to associate with a 'bad crowd' outside of school. They feel that this may be influencing his strange behaviour.

Daniel turned up at school last week in an intoxicated state. He smelt strongly of alcohol and began making references to himself as Jesus and needing to be resurrected. He made incisions to both palms on each hand with a knife. He has never harmed himself before and this episode has deeply upset those around him. He has attended today with his parents. He presents as friendly and bright and is able to recognise that the situation at school is a problem. However, his thinking is erratic and he is sometimes unable to stay on topic. He tells you that he is a reincarnation of Jesus Christ and becomes increasingly distracted. Daniel tells you that he is not suicidal but goes on to make references to Jesus Christ dying for the human race and his own wish to be reincarnated. It is difficult to explore these thoughts with Daniel due to his leaving the subject in question and making indecipherable references to philosophy and the Bible.

Questions

 Would you regard this case as high, medium or low risk? Why?

 Which part of the Children Act 1989/Mental Health Act might apply in this scenario?

 Which partner agencies and support services might be helpful in this scenario (consider both Daniel and his parents)?

 What might be some of the major challenges involved in working with this case (think about ethical and legal implications)?

Further resources and suggested readings

Joiner, T. (2005) *Why People Die by Suicide*. London: Harvard University Press.

McDougall, T., Armstrong, M. and Trainor, G. (2010) *Helping Children and Young People*

Who Self-Harm: An Introduction to Self-Harming and Suicidal Behaviours for Health Professionals. Abingdon: Routledge.

Walker, S. (2012) *Responding to Self-Harm in Children and Adolescents: A Professional's Guide to Identification, Intervention and Support*. London: Jessica Kingsley Publishers.

Websites

HOPELineUK, confidential young suicide prevention advice: 0800 068 4141

Life Signs, self-injury guidance & network support – www.lifesigns.org.uk/

Mind – www.mind.org.uk/help/diagnoses_and_conditions/self-harm

National Institute for Health and Clinical Excellence – www.nice.org.uk/cg16

Papyrus, prevention of young suicide – www.papyrus-uk.org/

Selfharm.co.uk – www.selfharm.co.uk/home

Self-injury.net – http://self-injury.net/information-recovery/recovery/distractions

Thesite.org – www.thesite.org/healthandwellbeing/mentalhealth/selfharm

Young Minds – www.youngminds.org.uk/

# References

1 Introduction

Adams, R. (2009) *The Short Guide to Social Work*. Bristol: The Policy Press.

Brayne, H. and Carr, H. (2013) *Law for Social Workers*, 12th edn. Oxford: Oxford University Press.

British Association of Social Workers (BASW) (2012) *The Code of Ethics for Social Work: Statement of Principles*. Birmingham: British Association of Social Workers.

Health & Care Professions Council (HCPC) (2012) *Standards of Proficiency: Social Workers in England*. London: Health and Care Professions Council.

International Federation of Social Work (IFSW) (2012) *Definition of Social Work*. http://ifsw.org/policies/definition-of-social-work/ (accessed 3 March 2013).

Parris, M. (2012) *An Introduction to Social Work Practice: A Practical Handbook*. Maidenhead: Open University Press.

Teater, B. (2010) *An Introduction to Applying Social Work Theories and Methods*. Maidenhead: Open University Press.

Teater, B. (forthcoming) Social work theories, in J. Wright (ed.) *International Encyclopedia of Social & Behavioral Sciences*, 2nd edn. Oxford: Elsevier Science Ltd.

The College of Social Work (TCSW) (2012) *Professional Capabilities Framework (PCF)*. www.collegeofsocialwork.org/pcf.aspx (accessed 13 March 2013).

Trevithick, P. (2012) *Social Work Skills and Knowledge: A Practice Handbook*, 3rd edn. Maidenhead: Open University Press.

2 Children and families

Aldgate, J., Jones, D., Rose, W. and Jeffery, C. (eds) (2006) *The Developing World of the Child*. London: Jessica Kingsley Publishers.

Bride, B.E. and Figley, C.R. (2007) The fatigue of compassionate social workers: an introduction to the special issue on compassion fatigue, *Clinical Social Work Journal*, 35: 151–153.

Bronfenbrenner, U. (1979) *The Ecology of Human Development: Experiments by Nature and Design*. Cambridge, MA: Harvard University Press.

Butler, I. and Roberts, G. (2004) *Social Work with Children and Families: Getting into Practice*, 2nd edn. London: Jessica Kingsley Publishers.

Butler, I. and Hickman, C. (2011) *Social Work with Children and Families*, 3rd edn. London: Jessica Kingsley Publishers.

Chand, A. and Thoburn, J. (2006) Research review: child protection referrals and minority ethnic children and families, *Child and Family Social Work*, 11: 368–377.

Child Exploitation and Online Protection Centre (CEOP) (2012) *Threat Assessment of Child Sexual Exploitation and Abuse*. http://ceop.police.uk/Documents/ceopdocs/CEOPThreatA_2012_190612_web.pdf (accessed 9 October 2012).

Colton, M., Sanders, R. and Williams. M. (eds) (2001) *An Introduction to Working with Children: A Guide for Social Workers*. Basingstoke: Palgrave Macmillan.

Congress, E. (1994) The use of culturagrams to assess and empower culturally diverse families, *Families in Society*, 75: 531–540.

Congress, E. (2002) Using the culturagram with culturally diverse families, in A. Roberts and G.J. Greene (eds) *Social Workers' Desk Reference*. Oxford: Oxford University Press.

Corby, B. (2006) *Child Abuse: Towards a Knowledge Base*. Maidenhead: Open University Press.

Cree, V.E. and Davis, A. (2007) *Social Work: Voices from Inside*. Abingdon: Routledge.

Crisp, B.R., Anderson, M.T., Orme, J. and Lister, P.G. (2003) *Knowledge Review 01: Learning and Teaching in Social Work Education – Assessment*. London: Social Care Institute for Excellence.

Daniel, B. (2007) Assessment and children, in J. Lishman (ed.) *Handbook for Practice Learning in Social Work and Social Care*, 2nd edn. London: Jessica Kingsley Publishers.

Department for Children, Schools and Families (DCSF) (2010) *Working Together to Safeguard Children*. Nottingham: DCSF Publications.

Department for Education (DfE) (2011) *Statistical Release: Characteristics of Children in Need in England, 2010–11*. London: Department for Education.

Department for Education (DfE) (2012) *Working Together to Safeguard Children*. Awaiting publication.

Department for Education and Skills (DfES) (2004) *Every Child Matters: Change for Children*. London: HMSO.

Department of Health (DoH) (2000) *Assessing Children in Need and their Families: Practice Guidance*. London: The Stationery Office.

Ferguson, H. (2010) Walks, home visits and atmospheres: risk and the everyday practices and mobilities of social work and child protection, *British Journal of Social Work*, 40: 1100–1117.

Ferguson, H. (2011) *Child Protection Practice*. Basingstoke: Palgrave Macmillan.

Fook, J. (2002) *Social Work: Critical Theory and Practice*. London: Sage.

Forrester, D., McCambridge, J., Waissein, C. and Rollnick, S. (2008) How do child and family social workers talk to parents about child welfare concerns?, *Child Abuse Review*, 17: 23–35.

Jack, G. (2001) Ecological perspectives in assessing children and families, in J. Horwath (ed.) *The Child's World*. London: Jessica Kingsley Publishers.

Lefevre, M. (2008) Communicating and engaging with children and young people in care through play and the creative arts, in B. Luckock and M. Lefevre (eds) *Direct Work: Social Work with Children and Young People in Care*. London: British Association for Adoption & Fostering.

Luckock, B., Lefevre, M., Orr, D., Jones, M., Marchant, R. and Tanner, K. (2006) *Teaching, Learning and Assessing Communication Skills with Children and Young People in Social Work Education*. London: SCIE.

Mederios, M.E. and Prochaska, J.O. (1988) Coping strategies that psychotherapists use in working with stressful clients, *Professional Psychology: Research and Practice*, 19: 112–114.

Mensinga, J. (2011) The feeling of being a social worker: including yoga as an embodied practice in social work education, *Social Work Education*, 30: 650–662.

Millar, M. and Corby, B. (2006) The framework for the assessment of children in need and their families – a basis for a therapeutic encounter?, *British Journal of Social Work*, 36: 887–899.

Munro, E. (2011) *The Munro Review of Child Protection: Final Report, A Child-Centred System*. London: The Stationery Office.

NSPCC (2011) *Smart Cuts? Public Spending on Children's Social Care*. www.nspcc.org.uk/Inform/research/findings (accessed 17 October 2012).

Palm, K.M., Polusny, M.A. and Follette, V.M. (2004) Vicarious traumatization: potential hazards and interventions for disaster and trauma workers, *Prehospital and Disaster Medicine*. www.impact.arq.org/doc/kennisbank/1000011453-1.pdf (accessed 17 October 2012).

Parton. N. (2011) Child protection and safeguarding in England: changing and competing conceptions of risk and their implications for social work, *British Journal of Social Work*, 41: 854–875.

Payne, M. (2005) *Modern Social Work Theory*, 3rd edn. Basingstoke: Palgrave Macmillan.

Seden, J. (2008) Creative connections: parenting capacity, reading with children and practitioner assessment and intervention, *Child and Family Social Work*, 3: 133–143.

Social Work Task Force (2009a) *Facing Up to the Task: The Interim Report of the Social Work Task Force*. http://publications.dcsf.gov.uk (accessed 9 October 2012).

Social Work Task Force (2009b) *Building a Safe, Confident Future: The Final Report of the Social Work Task Force*. http://publications.dcsf.gov.uk (accessed 9 October 2012).

Teater, B. (2010) *An Introduction to Applying Social Work Theories and Methods*. Maidenhead: Open University Press.

Walker, S. and Beckett, C. (2003) *Social Work Assessment and Intervention*. Lyme Regis: Russell House.

Weld, N. (2008) The three houses tool: building safety and positive change, in M. Calder (ed.) *Contemporary Risk Assessment in Safeguarding Children.* Lyme Regis: Russell House.

3 Fostering and adoption

Ainsworth, M.D.S., Blehar, M.C., Waters, E. and Wall, S. (1979) *Patterns of Attachment: A Psychological Study of the Strange Situation.* Oxford: Routledge.

Barn, R. and Kirton, D. (2012) Transracial adoption in Britain politics, ideology and reality, *Adoption & Fostering Journal,* 36(3–4): 25–37.

Biehal, N., Ellison, S., Baker, C. and Sinclair, I. (2010) *Belonging and Permanence: Outcomes in Long-term Foster Care and Adoption.* London: British Association for Adoption & Fostering.

Bifulco, A., Jacobs, C., Bunn, A., Thomas, G. and Irving, K. (2008) The attachment style interview (ASI): a support-based adult assessment tool for adoption and fostering practice, *Adoption & Fostering Journal,* 32(3): 33–45.

Bowlby, J. (1969) *Attachment.* London: Random House.

British Association of Social Workers (BASW) (2012) *Government's Adoption Plan Risks Exacerbating Problems.* www.basw.co.uk/news/quick-fixes-wont-address-adoption-failings (accessed 26 September 2012).

Department for Education (DfE) (2011) *The Children Act 1989 Guidance and Regulations, Volume 4, Fostering Services 2011 Statutory Guidance.* http://media.education.gov.uk/assets/files/pdf/volume%204%20%20%20%fostering%20services%202011%20statutory%20guidance.pdf (accessed 27 September 2012).

Department for Education (DfE) (2012) *Statistical First Release: Children Looked After in England (Including Adoption and Care Leavers) Year Ending 31 March 2012.* www.education.gov.uk/rsgatewayDB/SFR/s001084/sfr20-2012.pdf (accessed 26 September 2012).

Fahlberg, V.I. (1991) *A Child's Journey Through Placement.* London: Jessica Kingsley Publishers.

Farmer, E. and Moyers, S. (2008) *Kinship Care: Fostering Effective Family and Friends Placements.* London: Jessica Kingsley Publishers.

Fostering Network (2012) *Care Figures Highlight Need to Invest in Foster Care.* http://www.fostering.net/news/2012/care-figures-highlight-need-invest-in-foster-care (accessed 2 October 2012).

George, C., Kaplan, N. and Main, M. (1985) The Berkeley Adult Attachment Interview. Unpublished protocol. Department of Psychology, University of California, Berkeley.

Great Britain Parliament (1989) *Children Act 1989.* (Act of Parliament.) London: HMSO. http://www.legislation.gov.uk (accessed 27 September 2012).

Great Britain Parliament (2002) *Adoption and Children Act 2002.* (Act of Parliament.) London: HMSO. http://www.legislation.gov.uk (accessed 27 September 2012).

Great Britain Parliament (2005) *The Children (Private Arrangements for Fostering) Regulations 2005*. (Act of Parliament.) London: HMSO. http://www.legislation.gov.uk (accessed 27 September 2012).

Harris, P. and British Association for Adoption & Fostering (2006) *In Search of Belonging: Reflections by Transracially Adopted People*. London: British Association for Adoption & Fostering.

Hartman, A. (1995) Diagrammatic assessment of family relationships, *Families in Society*, 76:111–122.

Hughes, D.A. (2006) *Building the Bonds of Attachment: Awakening Love in Deeply Troubled Children*, 2nd edn. Baltimore, MD: Jason Aronson.

Hunt, J., Waterhouse, S. and Lutman, E. (2008) *Keeping Them in the Family*. London: British Association for Adoption & Fostering.

Kemp, S.P., Whittaker, J.K. and Tracy, E.M. (1997) *Person-Environment Practice: The Social Ecology of Interpersonal Helping*. New York: Aldine De Gruyter.

Malik, S. (2012) *Adoption Process will be made Fairer and Faster, Says David Cameron*. http://www.guardian.co.uk/society/2012/mar/09/adoption-made-fairer-faster-cameron (accessed 26 September 2012).

Nixon, P. (2007) *Relatively Speaking: Developments in Research and Practice in Kinship Care*. Totnes: Research in Practice.

Ofsted (2011) *Children's Care Monitor 2011*. https://www.education.gov.uk/publications/eOrderingDownload/Children%27s%20care%20monitor%202011.pdf (accessed 2 October 2012).

Pemberton, C. (2012) *Ofsted Inspectors to Look at Adoption Breakdowns*. www.communitycare.co.uk/Articles/06/03/2012/118043/Ofsted-inspectors-to-look-at-adoption-breakdown.htm (accessed 2 October 2012).

Schofield, G. (2000) *Growing Up in Foster Care*. London: British Association for Adoption & Fostering.

Schofield, G. (2003) *Part of the Family: Pathways Through Foster Care*. London: British Association for Adoption & Fostering.

Sinclair, I. (2005) *Fostering Now: Messages from Research*. London: Jessica Kingsley Publishers.

Teater, B. (2010) *An Introduction to Applying Social Work Theories and Methods*. Maidenhead: Open University Press.

Thomas, M., Philpot, T. and Walsh, M. (2009) *Fostering a Child's Recovery: Family Placement for Traumatized Children*. London: Jessica Kingsley Publishers.

4 Youth work

Ainley, P. and Allen, M. (2010) *Lost Generation? New Strategies for Youth and Education*. London: Continuum.

Bradford, S. (2012) *Sociology, Youth and Youth Work Practice*. Basingstoke: Palgrave Macmillan.

Brent, J. (2004) Communicating what youth work achieves: the smile and the arch, *Youth and Policy*, 69: 69–73.

Brew, J.M. (1946) *Informal Education*. London: Faber and Faber.

Brierley, D. (2003) *Joined Up: An Introduction to Youth Work and Ministry*. Milton Keynes: Authentic Lifestyle.

Children's Workforce Development Council (2010) *A Picture Worth Millions: State of the Young People's Workforce*. London: Children's Workforce Development Council.

Coles, B. (1995) *Youth and Social Policy: Youth, Citizenship and Young Careers*. London: UCL Press.

Cook, D. (2008) Some historical perspective on professionalism, in B. Cunningham (ed.) *Exploring Professionalism*. London: Bedford Way Papers.

Darley, G. (2010) *Octavia Hill: Social Reformer and Founder of the National Trust*. London: Francis Boutle Publisher.

Davies, B. and Merton, B. (2009) Squaring the circle? The state of youth work in some children and young people's services, *Youth and Policy*, 103: 5–24.

Davies, B. and Merton, B. (2010) Straws in the wind: the state of youth work practice in a changing policy environment, *Youth and Policy*, 105: 9–36.

Davies, B. and Merton, B. (2012) Managing youth work in integrated services, in J. Ord (ed.) *Critical Issues in Youth Work Management*. Abingdon: Routledge.

Department of Education and Science (DES) (1987) *Education Observed 6: Effective Youth Work*. London: Department of Education and Science.

Department for Education (DfE) (2011) *Myplace Evaluation*. London: Department for Education.

Forrest, D. (2013) Participatory youth work within a 1950s Scottish housing scheme, in R. Gilchrist et al. (eds) *Reappraisals: Essays on the History of Youth and Community Work*. Lyme Regis: Russell House.

HM Government (2004) *Every Child Matters: Change for Children*. London: The Stationery Office.

HM Government (2005) *Youth Matters*. London: HMSO.

Hirsh, B. (2005) *A Place To Call Home: After-School Programs for Urban Youth*. Washington, DC: American Psychological Association.

Hodgson, T. and Jeffs, T. (2012) *Mobex Activity Programmes: A YSDF Funded Initiative*. Newcastle: Mobex North East.

House of Commons (HofC) (2012) *Service Provision: Funding, Commissioning and Payment by Results*. www.publications.parliament.uk/pa/cm201012/cmselect/cmeduc/744/74408.htm (accessed 23 February 2013).

Jozwiak, G. (2013) *Gove: Youth Policy Not a Central Government Priority*. www.cypnow.co.uk/cyp/news/1076071/youth-policy-central-government-priority (accessed 25 January 2013).

Jeffs, A.J. (1979) *Young People and the Youth Service*. London: RKP.

Jeffs, T. (2004) Curriculum debate, *Youth and Policy*, 84: 55–62.

Jeffs, T. and Smith, M. (1994) Youth people, youth work and a new authoritarianism, *Youth and Policy*, 46: 17–32.

Jeffs, T. and Smith, M.K. (2008) Valuing youth work, *Youth and Policy*, 100: 277–302.

Jeffs, T. and Spence, J. (2008) Farewell to all that? The uncertain future of youth and community work education, *Youth and Policy*, 97/98: 135–166.

Lifelong Learning UK (LLUK) (2008) *National Occupational Standards for Youth Work.* http://nya.org.uk/dynamic_files/research/whole%20suite%20of%20Professional%20 and%20National%20Occupational%20Standards%20for%20Youth%20Work.pdf (accessed 18 February 2013).

Mckee, V., Oldfield, C. and Poultney, J. (2010) *The Benefits of Youth Work.* London: LLUK.

Manton, J. (1976) *Mary Carpenter and the Children of the Streets.* London: Heinemann.

National Youth Agency (NYA) (2012) *Annual Monitoring of Youth and Community Programmes Professionally Validated by the National Youth Agency.* Leicester: National Youth Agency.

Oldfield, S. (2008) *Jeanie, an 'Army of One': Mrs Nassau Senior 1828-1877.* Brighton: Sussex Academic Press.

Ord, J. (2011) The Kingston Youth Service: space, place and the Albemarle legacy, in R. Gilchrist, T. Hodgson, T. Jeffs, J. Spence, N. Stanton and J. Walker (eds) *Reflecting on the Past: Essays in the History of Youth and Community Work.* Lyme Regis: Russell House.

Puffett, N. (2012) *Youth Organisation Mergers Vital in Face of Dwindling Budgets.* www. cypnow.co.uk/cyp/news/1075530/youth-organisation-mergers-vital-dwind (accessed 1 December 2012).

Roberts, K. (2009) *Youth in Transition: Eastern Europe and the West.* Basingstoke: Palgrave Macmillan.

Robinson, L.V. (1937) *Children's House: A History of the Hawthorne Club.* Boston, MA: Marshall Jones.

Shildrick, T. and MacDonald, R. (2007) Biographies of exclusion: poor work and poor transitions, *International Journal of Lifelong Education,* 26(5): 589–604.

Smith, M.K. (1988) *Developing Youth Work.* Milton Keynes: Open University Press.

Smith, M.K. (2007) *The Connexions Service in England.* www.infed.org/personaladvisers/ connexions.htm (accessed 1 December 2012).

Titmuss, R. (1971) *The Gift Relationship.* Harmondsworth: Pelican.

Wilding, P. (1982) *Professional Power and Social Welfare.* London: RKP.

Williams, E.I.F. (1937) *Horace Mann.* New York: Macmillan.

Williams, J.E.H. (1906) *Sir George Williams.* New York: Armstrong.

Williamson, H. (2004) *The Milltown Boys Re-visited.* Oxford: Berg.

Wylie, T. (2010) Youth work in a cold climate, *Youth and Policy,* 109: 1–8.

5 Youth offending

All Party Parliamentary Group for Children (2010) *Children and Young People in the Youth Justice System. Report of Seminars Organised by the All Party Parliamentary Group for Children 2009/10.* London: NCB.

Audit Commission (1996) *Misspent Youth: Young People and Crime.* London: Audit Commission.

Bowling, B. and Phillips, C. (2007) Disproportionate and discriminatory: reviewing the evidence on stop and search, *Modern Law Review,* 70(6): 936–961.

Bryan, K., Freer, J. and Furlong, C. (2007) Language and communication difficulties in young offenders, *International Journal of Language and Communication Disorders*, 42: 505–520.

Burnett, R. (2004) One to one ways of promoting desistence: in search of an evidence base, in R. Burnett and C. Roberts (eds) *What Works in Probation and Youth Justice*. Cullompton: Willan.

Crawford, K. and Walker, J. (2010) *Social Work and Human Development*, 3rd edn. Exeter: Learning Matters.

Department for Children, Schools and Families (DCSF) (2010) *Working Together to Safeguard Children*. Nottingham: DCSF Publications.

Department of Health, Department for Children, Schools and Families, Ministry of Justice, Home Office (2009) *Healthy Children, Safer Communities: A Strategy to Promote the Health and Well-being of Children and Young People in Contact with the Youth Justice System*. www.dh.gov.uk/en/Publicationsandstatistics/Publications/PublicationsPolicyAndGuidance/DH_109771 (accessed 1 February 2013).

Earle, R. (2011) Ethnicity, multiculture and racism in a young offenders' institution, *Prison Service*, 197: 32–38.

Egan, G. (2002) *The Skilled Helper: A Problem-Management and Opportunity Approach to Helping*, 7th edn. Pacific Grove, CA: Brooks/Cole.

Hagell, A. (2002) *The Mental Health of Young Offenders – Bright Futures: Working with Vulnerable Young People*. London: Mental Health Foundation.

Harrington, R. and Bailey, S. (2005) *Mental Health Needs and Effectiveness of Provision for Young Offenders in Custody and in the Community*. www.yjb.gov.uk/Publications/Resources (accessed 19 December 2012).

Hill, M. (1999) What's the problem? Who can help? The perspectives of children and young people on their well-being and on helping professionals, *Journal of Social Work Practice*, 13(2): 135–145.

Hurry, J., Brazier, L., Snapes, K. and Wilson, A. (2005) *Improving the Literacy and Numeracy of Disaffected Young People in Custody and in the Community*. London: National Research and Development Centre for Adult Literacy and Numeracy.

James, A. and James, A. (2012) *Key Concepts in Childhood Studies*, 2nd edn. London: Sage.

Jenks, C. (1996) *Childhood*. Abingdon: Routledge.

Junger-Tas, J., Marshall, I.H., Enzmann, D., Killias, M., Steketee, M. and Gruszczynska, B. (2012) *The Many Faces of Youth Crime: Contrasting Theoretical Perspectives on Juvenile Delinquency Across Countries and Cultures*. London: Springer.

McNeill, F. (2006) Community supervision: context and relationships matter, in B. Goldson and J. Muncie (eds), *Youth Crime and Justice*. London: Sage.

Miller, W.R. and Rollnick, S. (2002) *Motivational Interviewing: Preparing People for Change*, 2nd edn. New York: Guilford Press.

Ministry of Justice (2010) *The Youth Justice System in England and Wales: Reducing Offending by Young People*. www.nao.org.uk/publications/1011/reoffending_by_young_people.aspx (accessed 19 December 2012).

Morgan, R. (2006) *About Social Workers: A Children's Views Report*. Newcastle upon Tyne: Commission for Social Care Inspection.

Munro, E. (2011) *The Munro Review of Child Protection: Final Report*. London: Department of Education.

NACRO (2010) *The Use of Custody for Children and Young People*. London: NACRO.

NACRO (2012a) *Reducing Offending by Looked After Children*. London: NACRO.

NACRO (2012b) *NACRO's Response to the Riots, Communities and Victims*. London: NACRO.

Newman, B.M. and Newman, P.R. (2012) *Development through Life: A Psychosocial Approach*. Belmont, CA: Wadsworth.

Parke, S. (2009) *Children and Young People in Custody 2006–2008: An Analysis of the Experiences of 15–18 Year Olds in Prison*. www.justice.gov.uk/inspectorates/hmi-prisons/docs/children_and_youngpeoplerps.pdf (accessed 19 December 2012).

Pickford, J. (ed.) (2000) *Youth Justice: Theory and Practice*. London: Cavendish.

Pickford, J. and Dugmore, P. (2012) *Youth Justice in Social Work*, 2nd edn. London: Sage.

Pitts, J. (2003) *The New Politics of Youth Crime: Discipline or Solidarity?* Lyme Regis: Russell House.

Pitts, J. (2011) Needs and deeds? Youth justice in Finland and England and Wales, *Prison Service Journal*, 197: 15–19.

Prior, D. (2005) Evaluating the new youth justice: what can practitioners learn from research?, *Practice*, 17(2): 103–112.

Prochaska, J.O., DiClemente, C.C. and Norcross, J.C. (1992) In search of how people change: application to addictive behaviours, *American Psychologist*, 47(9): 1102–1114.

Rogers, C. (1976) *Client-Centred Therapy*. London: Constable and Robinson.

Ross, A., Duckworth, K., Smith, D.J., Wyness, G. and Schoon, I. (2011) *Prevention and Reduction: A Review of Strategies for Intervening Early to Prevent or Reduce Youth Crime and Anti-Social Behaviour*. London: Department for Education.

Whyte, B. (2009) *Youth Justice in Practice: Making a Difference*. Bristol: The Policy Press.

Wilkstrom, P.-O. (2012) *Morality Prevents Crime*. www.cam.ac.uk/research/news/morality-prevents-crime/ (accessed 19 December 2012).

Willis, P. (1977) *Learning to Labour*. New York: Columbia University Press.

Youth Justice Board (YJB) (2010) *Developing the Secure Estate for Children and Young People in England and Wales, Young People's Consultation Report*. http://yjbpublications.justice.gov.uk/en-gb/Scripts/prodView.asp?idproduct=501&eP= (accessed 19 December 2012).

Youth Justice Board (YJB) (2012) *Youth Justice Board Statistics 2010/11, England and Wales*. www.justice.gov.uk/downloads/statistics/youth-justice/yjb-statistics-10–11.pdf (accessed on 19 December 2012).

Youth Justice Board (YJB) (2013) *Youth Justice Board Statistics 2011/12, England and Wales*. London: Youth Justice Board/Ministry of Justice.

Youth Offending Team, Inspection (2011) *Inspection of Youth Offending, Core Case Inspection, Case Assessment Guidance*. www.justice.gov.uk/downloads/about/hmiprob/cci-cag.pdf (accessed 19 December 2012).

6 Service user and carer involvement

Adams, R. (2003) *Social Work and Empowerment*, 3rd edn. Basingstoke: Palgrave Macmillan.

Aldridge, J. (2008) All work and no play? Understanding the needs of children with caring responsibilities, *Children & Society*, 22: 253–264.

Aldridge, J. and Becker, S. (2003) *Children Caring for Parents with Mental Illness: Perspectives of Young Carers, Parents and Professionals*. Bristol: The Policy Press.

Arnstein, S.R. (1969) A ladder of citizen participation, *Journal of the American Institute of Planners*, 35: 216–224.

Ballatt, J. and Campling, P. (2011) *Intelligent Kindness: Reforming the Culture of Healthcare*. London: RCPsych Publications.

Barnardo's (2006) *Hidden Lives – Unidentified Young Carers in the UK*. Ilford: Barnardo's.

Beresford, P. (1994) *Changing The Culture: Involving Service Users in Social Work Education*. London: Central Council for Education and Training in Social Work.

Beresford, P. (2000) Service users knowledge and social work theory: conflict or collaboration, *British Journal of Social Work*, 30(4): 489–503.

Beresford, P. and Carr, S. (2012) *Social Care, Service Users and User Involvement*. London: Jessica Kingsley Publishers.

Beresford, P., Adshead, L. and Crofy, S. (2007) *Palliative Care, Social Work and Service Users: Making Life Possible*. London: Jessica Kingsley Publishers.

Braifield, H. and Eckersley, T. (2008) *Service User Involvement: Reaching the Hard to Reach in Supported Housing*. London: Jessica Kingsley Publishers.

Braye, S. (2000) Participation and involvement in social care, in H. Kemshall and R. Littlechild (eds) *User Involvement and Participation in Social Care: Research Informing Practice*. London: Jessica Kingsley Publishers.

Butler, I. and Hickman, C. (2011) *Social Work with Children and Families: Getting into Practice*. London: Jessica Kingsley Publishers.

Carers UK (2012) *Facts About Carers: Policy Briefing*. www.carersuk.org/media/k2/attachments/Facts_about_carers_Dec_2012.pdf (accessed 17 February 2013).

Cooper, J. and Lousada, J. (2005) *Borderline Welfare: Feeling and Fear of Feeling in Modern Welfare*. London: Karnac Books.

Department of Health (DoH) (2002) *Keys to Partnership: Working Together to Make a Difference in People's Lives*. London: Department of Health.

Gosling, J. and Martin, J. (2012) *Making Partnerships with Service Users and Advocacy Groups Work: How to Grow Genuine and Respectful Relationships in Health and Social Care*. London: Jessica Kingsley Publishers.

Green, L. and Wilks, T. (2009) Involving service users in a problem based model of teaching and learning, *Social Work Education*, 26(2): 190–203.

Hart, R. (1997) *Children's Participation: The Theory and Practice of Involving Young Citizens in Community Development and Environmental Care*. London: Earthscan.

Horner, N. (2009) *What is Social Work?: Context and Perspectives*, 3rd edn. Exeter: Learning Matters.

Horvath, A. O. (2001) The alliance, *Psychotherapy*, 38: 365–372.

Hoyes, L., Jeffers, S., Lart, R., Means, R. and Taylor, M. (1993) *User Empowerment and Reform of Community Care: A Study of Early Implementation in Four Localities*. Bristol: University of Bristol.

Hugman, R. (2005) Exploring the paradox of teaching ethics for social work practice, *Social Work Education*, 24(5): 535–545.

Kellet, M. (2006) Children as researchers: exploring the impact on education and empowerment, *Childright*, 226: 11–13.

Levin, E. (2004) *Involving Service Users and Carers in Social Work Education: SCIE Guide 4*. London: SCIE.

Lishman, J. (ed.) (2012) *Social Work Education and Training*. London: Jessica Kingsley Publishers.

McLeod, A. (2007) *Listening to Children: A Practitioners Guide*. London: Jessica Kingsley Publishers.

McLeod, A. (2008) *Listening to Children: A Practitioner's Guide*. London: Jessica Kingsley Publishers.

Molyneux, J. and Irvine, J. (2004) Service user and carer involvement in social work training: a long and winding road?, *Social Work Education*, 23(3): 293–308.

Parton, N. and O'Byrne, P. (2000) *Constructive Social Work: Towards a New Practice*. Basingstoke: Palgrave Macmillan.

Rogers, C.R. (1957) The necessary and sufficient conditions of therapeutic personality change, *Journal of Counseling Psychology*, 21: 95–103.

Roscoe, K.D., Carson, A.M. and Madoc-Jones, L. (2011) Narrative social work: conversations between theory and practice, *Journal of Social Work Practice*, 25(1): 47–61.

Ruch, G., Turney, D. and Ward, A. (2010) *Relationship Based Social Work: Getting to the Heart of Practice*. London: Jessica Kingsley Publishers.

Seden, J. (2005) *Counselling Skills in Social Work Practice*, 2nd edn. Maidenhead: Open University Press.

Teater, B. (2010) *An Introduction to Applying Social Work Theories and Methods*. Maidenhead: Open University Press.

Teater, B. and Baldwin, M. (2012) *Social Work in the Community: Making a Difference*. Bristol: The Policy Press.

Tidsall, K., Davis, J. and Gallagher, M. (2009) *Researching with Children and Young People: Research Design, Methods and Analysis*. London: Sage.

Turner, M. and Beresford, P. (2005) *User Controlled Research, Its Meanings and Potential Final Report* http://shapingourlives.org.uk/downloads/publications/usercontrolledresearch.pdf (accessed 4 March 2013).

Warren, J. (2007) *Service User and Carer Participation in Social Work*. Exeter: Learning Matters.

Warren, L. and Boxall, K. (2009) Service users in and out of the academy: collusion in exclusion?, *Social Work Education*, 28(3): 281–297.

Weinstein, J. (ed.) (2010) *Mental Health, Service User Involvement and Recovery*. London: Jessica Kingsley Publishers.

Weinstein, J., Whittington, C. and Leiba, T. (eds) (2003) *Collaboration in Social Work Practice*. London: Jessica Kingsley Publishers.

White, K. (ed.) (2006) *Unmasking Race, Culture, and Attachment in the Psychoanalytic Space*. London: Karnac Books.

Wilson, K., Ruch, G., Lymbery, M. and Cooper, A. (2011) *Social Work: An Introduction to Contemporary Practice*, 2nd edn. New York: Longman.

Wistow, G. (2005) *Adult Services Position Paper 04, Developing Social Care: The Past, The Present and The Future*. www.scie.org.uk/publications/positionpapers/pp04.pdf (accessed 4 March 2013).

7 Learning difficulties

Association of Directors of Adult Social Services (ADASS) (2005) *Safeguarding Adults: A National Framework of Standards for Good Practice and Outcomes in Adult Protection Work*. London: Association of Directors of Adult Social Services.

Baldwin, M. (2006) Helping people with learning difficulties into paid employment: will UK social workers use the available welfare to work scheme?, *Journal of Policy Practice*, 5(2/3): 91–107.

Baldwin, M. (2011) Resisting the EasyCare model: building a more radical, community-based, anti-authoritarian social work for the future, in M. Lavalette (ed.) *Radical Social Work Today: Social Work at the Crossroads*. Bristol: The Policy Press.

Becker, H. (1963) *Outsiders: Studies in the Sociology of Deviance*. New York: Free Press.

Beresford, P. and Hasler, F. (2009) *Transforming Social Care: Changing the Future Together*. London: Shaping Our Lives.

Beresford, P., Croft, S. and Adshead, K. (2006) *Palliative Care, Social Work and Service Users: Making Life Possible*. London: Jessica Kingsley Publishers.

Brandon, D. and Brandon, T. (2001) *Advocacy in Social Work*. London: British Association of Social Workers.

Brewster, J. and Ramcharan, P. (2005) Enabling and supporting person-centred approaches, in G. Grant, P. Goward, M. Richardson and P. Ramcharam (eds) *Learning Disability: A Life Cycle Approach to Valuing People*. Maidenhead: Open University Press.

Cambridge, P. and Carnaby, S. (2005) *Person Centred Planning and Care Management with People with Learning Disabilities*. London: Jessica Kingsley Publishers.

Carnaby, S. and Lewis, P. (2005) Involving young people with learning disabilities leaving school in planning for the future, in P. Cambridge and S. Carnaby *Person Centred Planning and Care Management with People with Learning Disabilities*. London: Jessica Kingsley Publishers.

Carr, S. (2008) *SCIE Report 20: Personalisation: A Rough Guide*. London: Social Care Institute for Excellence.

Chomsky, N. (2003) *Understanding Power: The Indispensable Chomsky*. London: Random House.

Department of Health (DoH) (2000) *No Secrets: Guidance on Developing and Implementing Multi-agency Policies and Procedures to Protect Vulnerable Adults from Abuse.* London: Department of Health.

Department of Health (DoH) (2001) *Valuing People: A New Strategy for Learning Disability for the 21st Century – A White Paper.* London: Department of Health.

Department of Health (DoH) (2003) *Fair Access to Care Services: Guidance on Eligibility Criteria for Adult Social Care.* London: Department of Health.

Department of Health (DoH) (2006) *Our Health, Our Care, Our Say: A New Direction for Community Services – A White Paper.* London: Department of Health.

Department of Health (DoH) (2007) *Putting People First: A Shared Vision and Commitment to the Transformation of Adult Social Care.* London: Department of Health.

Department of Health (DoH) (2009) *Valuing People Now: A New Three Year Strategy for Learning Disabilities.* London: The Stationery Office.

Department of Health (DoH) (2010a) *Equity and Excellence: Liberating the NHS.* London: Department of Health.

Department of Health (DoH) (2010b) *A Vision for Adult Social Care: Capable Communities and Active Citizens.* London: Department of Health.

Department of Health (DoH) (2012) *Caring for our Future: Reforming Care and Support.* London: Department of Health.

Doyal, L. and Gough, I. (1991) *A Theory of Human Need.* Basingstoke: Macmillan.

Duffy, S. (2003) *Keys to Citizenship: A Guide to Getting Good Support for People with Learning Difficulties.* Birkenhead: Paradigm.

Duffy, S. and Fulton, K. (2010) *Architecture for Personalisation Toolkit: A Toolkit for Exploring Care Management and Community-based Support.* Sheffield: Centre for Welfare Reform.

Ferguson, I. and Woodward, R. (2009) *Radical Social Work in Practice: Making a Difference.* Bristol: The Policy Press.

Flynn, M. (2012) *Winterbourne View Hospital: A Serious Case Review.* http://hosted. southglos.gov.uk/wv/report.pdf (accessed 3 March 2013).

Fook, J. (2002) *Social Work: Critical Theory and Practice.* London: Sage.

Grant, G., Goward, P., Richardson, M. and Ramcharam, P. (eds) (2005) *Learning Disability: A Life Cycle Approach to Valuing People.* Maidenhead: Open University Press.

International Federation of Social Work (IFSW) (2012) *Definition of Social Work.* http://ifsw.org/policies/definition-of-social-work/ (accessed 3 March 2013).

Lavalette, M. (ed.) (2011) *Radical Social Work Today: Social Work at the Crossroads.* Bristol: The Policy Press.

MacConkey, R. (2005) Promoting friendship and developing social networks, in G. Grant, P. Goward, M. Richardson and P. Ramcharam (eds) *Learning Disability: A Life Cycle Approach to Valuing People.* Maidenhead: Open University Press.

Mayer, J. and Timms, N. (1970) *The Client Speaks: Working Class Impressions of Casework.* London. Routledge & Kegan Paul.

NHS (2005) *National Statistics: Adults with Learning Difficulties in England*. London: Health and Social Care Information Centre.

O'Brien, J. and Lyle, C. (1987) *A Framework for Accomplishment*. Decateur, GA: Responsive Systems Associates.

Slasberg, C., Beresford, P. and Schofield, P. (2012) How self-directed support is failing to deliver personal budgets and personalisation, *Research, Policy and Planning*, 29(3): 161–177.

Smale, G., Tuson, G., Biehal, N. and Marsh, P. (1993) *Empowerment, Assessment, Care Management and the Skilled Worker*. London: HMSO.

Small, J. (2009) Assessment and practice in learning disability services, in D. Galpin and N. Bates *Social Work Practice with Adults*. Exeter: Learning Matters.

Teater, B. and Baldwin, M. (2012) *Social Work in the Community: Making a Difference*. Bristol: The Policy Press.

Williams, P. (2009) *Social Work with People with Learning Difficulties*, 2nd edn. Exeter: Learning Matters.

Wolfensberger, W. (1972) *The Principle of Normalization in Human Services*. Toronto: National Institute on Mental Retardation.

8 Physical disabilities

Campbell, J. and Oliver, M. (1996) *Disability Politics: Understanding our Past, Changing our Future*. London: Routledge.

Carers UK (2012) *Policy Briefing. Facts about Carers 2012*. www.carersuk.org/media/k2/attachments/facts_about_carers_Dec_2012.pdf (accessed 18 December 2012).

Contact a Family (2012) *Statistics. Information about Families with Disabled Children*. www.old.cafamily.org.uk/professionals/research/statistics.html (accessed 18 December 2012).

Department of Health (DoH) (1989) *Caring for People – Community Care in the Next Decade and Beyond*. London: Department of Health.

Department of Health (DoH) (2003) *Fair Access to Care Services – Guidance on Eligibility Criteria for Adult Social Care*. London: Department of Health.

Department of Health (DoH) (2007) *Putting People First: A Shared Vision and Commitment to the Transformation of Adult Social Care*. London: Department of Health.

Department of Health (DoH) (2010) *Prioritising Need in the Context of Putting People First: A Whole System Approach to Eligibility for Social Care – Guidance on Eligibility Criteria for Adult Social Care, England 2010*. London: Department of Health.

Department for Work for Pensions (DWP) (2012) *Family Resources Survey, United Kingdom, 2010/11*. London: Department for Work and Pensions.

Evans, C. (2012) Increasing opportunities for coproduction and personalisation through social work student placements in disabled people's organisations, *Social Work Education*, 31: 235–240.

Goodley, D. (2004) Who is disabled? Exploring the scope of the social model of disability, in J. Swain, S. French, C. Barnes and C. Thomas (eds) *Disability Barriers – Enabling Environments*. London: Sage

Great Britain Parliament (2010) *Equality Act 2010*. (Act of Parliament.) London: HMSO. www.legislation.gov.uk (accessed 18 December 2012).

Miller, E. and Gwynne, G. (1972) *A Life Apart*. London: Tavistock.

Oliver, M., Sapey, B. and Thomas, P. (2012) *Social Work with Disabled People*, 4th edn. Basingstoke: Palgrave Macmillan.

Peters, S. (2011) Globalization and disability: disability services sectors for the twenty-first century, in W. Roth and K. Briar-Lawson (eds) *Globalization, Social Justice and the Helping Professions*. Albany, NY: State University of New York Press.

Prime Minister's Strategy Unit (2005) *Improving the Life Chances of Disabled People*. London: HM Government.

Scragg, T. and Mantell, A. (2011) *Safeguarding Adults in Social Work*, 2nd edn. Exeter: Learning Matters.

Southampton Centre for Independent Living CIC (2012) *What Are the 12 Basic Rights?* www.southamptoncil.co.uk/about/12-basic-rights/ (accessed 18 December 2012).

Teater, B. (2010) *An Introduction to Applying Social Work Theories and Methods*. Maidenhead: Open University Press.

Teater, B. and Baldwin, M. (2012) *Social Work in the Community: Making a Difference*. Bristol: The Policy Press.

9 Older adults

Alzheimer's Society (2013a) *Statistics*. www.alzheimers.org.uk/site/scripts/documents_info.php?documentID=341 (accessed 20 January 2013).

Alzheimer's Society (2013b) *Types of Dementia*. www.alzheimers.org.uk/site/scripts/documents.php?categoryID=200362 (accessed 20 January 2013).

Atchley, R.C. (1989) *Making a Reality of Community Care*. London: HMSO.

Batson, P., Thorne, K. and Peak, J. (2002) Life story work sees the person beyond the dementia, *Journal of Dementia Care*, 10: 15–17.

Baxter, K. and Glendinning, C. (2011) Making choices about support services: disabled adults' and older people's use of information, *Health and Social Care in the Community*, 19: 272–279.

Blazer, D.G. (2003) Depression in later life: review and commentary, *Journals of Gerontology, Series A*, 58: 249–265.

Bowling, A. and Dieppe, P. (2005) What is successful ageing and who should define it?, *British Medical Journal*, 331(7531): 1548–1551.

Brooker, D. (2004) What is person-centred care in dementia?, *Reviews in Clinical Gerontology*, 13: 215–222.

Carr, S. (2010) *Personalisation: A Rough Guide. Adults' Services Report 20.* London: Social Care Institute for Excellence.

Chiu, W.C.K., Chan, A.W., Snape, E. and Redman, T. (2001) Age stereotypes and discriminatory attitudes towards older workers: an east–west comparison, *Human Relations,* 54: 629–661.

Cumming, E. and Henry, W. (1961) *Growing Old: The Process of Disengagement.* New York: Basic Books.

Davidson, K. (2011) Sociological perspectives on ageing, in I. Stuart-Hamilton (ed.) *An Introduction to Gerontology.* Cambridge: Cambridge University Press.

Department of Health (DoH) (1989) *Caring for People: Community Care in the Next Decade and Beyond.* London: Department of Health.

Department of Health (DoH) (2000) *No Secrets: Guidance on Developing and Implementing Multi-Agency Policies and Procedures to Protect Vulnerable Adults from Abuse.* London: Department of Health.

Department of Health (DoH) (2003a) *Fair Access to Care Services: Guidance on Eligibility Criteria for Adult Social Care.* London: Department of Health.

Department of Health (DoH) (2003b) *Fairer Charging Policies for Care Home and Other Non-Residential Social Services: Guidance for Councils with Social Services Responsibilities.* London: Department of Health.

Department of Health (DoH) (2006) *Our Health, Our Care, Our Say: A New Direction for Community Services.* London: Department of Health.

Department of Health (DoH) (2009) *Living Well with Dementia: A National Dementia Strategy.* London: Department of Health.

Department of Health (DoH) (2010a) *Improving Care and Saving Money: Learning the Lessons on Prevention and Early Intervention for Older People.* London: Department of Health.

Department of Health (DoH) (2010b) *Prioritising Need in the Context of Putting People First: A Whole System Approach to Eligibility for Social Care, Guidance on Eligibility Criteria for Adult Social Care, England 2010.* London: Department of Health.

Department of Health (DoH) (2010c) *Quality Outcomes for People with Dementia: Building on the Work of the National Dementia Strategy.* London: Department of Health.

Erikson, E. (1950) *Childhood and Society.* New York: Norton.

Fiske, A., Wetherell, J.L. and Gatz, M. (2009) Depression in older adults, *Annual Review of Clinical Psychology,* 5: 363–389.

Gibson, F. (2011) *Reminiscence and Life Story Work: A Practice Guide.* London: Jessica Kingsley Publishers.

Glendinning, C. (2008) The future of adult social care: lessons from previous reforms, *Research, Policy and Planning,* 23: 61–70.

Hall, B. (2012) Reflective social work practice with older people: the professional and the organization, in B. Hall and T. Scragg (eds) *Social Work with Older People: Approaches to Person-Centred Practice.* Maidenhead: Open University Press.

Havighurst, R. (1963) Successful aging, in R. Williams, C. Tibbitts and W. Donahoe (eds) *Process of Aging*. Chicago: University of Chicago Press.

HM Government (2007) *Putting People First: A Shared Vision and Commitment to the Transformation of Adult Social Care*. London: HM Government.

HM Government (2012) *Caring for Our Future: Reforming Care and Support*. London: HM Government.

Holvast, F., Verhaak, P.F.M., Dekker, J.H., de Waal, M.W.M., van Marwijk, H.W.J., Penninx, B.W.J.H., et al. (2012) Determinants of receiving mental health care for depression in older adults, *Journal of Affective Disorders*, 143: 69–74.

Jones, R. (2012) Social work with older people, in M. Davies (ed.) *Social Work with Adults*. Basingstoke: Palgrave Macmillan.

Killick, J. and Craig, C. (2012) *Creativity and Communication in Persons with Dementia: A Practical Guide*. London: Jessica Kingsley Publishers.

Kitwood, T. (1993) Person and process in dementia, *International Journal of Geriatric Psychiatry*, 8: 541–545.

Kitwood, T.M. (1997) *Dementia Reconsidered: The Person Comes First*. Buckingham: Open University Press.

Lymbery, M. (2010) A new version for adult social care? Continuities and change in the care of older people, *Critical Social Policy*, 30: 5–26.

McDermott, O., Crellin, N., Ridder, H.M. and Orrell, M. (2012) Music therapy in dementia: a narrative synthesis systematic review, *International Journal of Geriatric Psychiatry*. Published online, DOI: 10.1002/gps.3895.

NICE/SCIE (2006) *Dementia: Supporting People with Dementia and their Carers in Health and Social Care*. London: National Institute for Health and Clinical Excellence.

Office for National Statistics (ONS) (2012a) *Population Ageing in the United Kingdom, its Constituent Countries and the European Union*. www.ons.gov.uk/ons/dcp171776_258607.pdf (accessed 13 January 2013).

Office for National Statistics (ONS) (2012b) *Community Care Statistics 2010–11: Social Services Activity Report, England*. https://catalogue.ic.nhs.uk/publications/social-care/activity/comm-care-soci-serv-act-eng-10-11-fin/comm-care-soci-serv-act-eng-10-11-fin-rep.pdf (accessed 14 January 2013).

Ostwald, S. and Dyer, C. (2011) Fostering resilience, promoting health and preventing disease in older adults, in I. Stuart-Hamilton (ed.) *An Introduction to Gerontology*. Cambridge: Cambridge University Press.

Rogers, C. R. (1959) A theory of therapy, personality, and interpersonal relationships as developed in the client-centered framework, in S. Koch (ed.) *Psychology: A Study of Science: Formulations of the Person and the Social Context*. New York: McGraw-Hill.

Rowe, J.W. and Kahn, R.L. (1987) Human ageing: usual and successful, *Science*, 237(4811):143–149.

Rowe, J.W. and Kahn, R.L. (1997) Successful ageing, *Gerontologist*, 37(4): 433–440.

Smethurst, C. (2012) Contextualizing the experience of older people, in B. Hall and T. Scragg (eds) *Social Work with Older People*. Maidenhead: Open University Press.

Spector, A., Davies, S., Woods, B. and Orrell, M. (2000) Reality orientation for dementia: a systematic review of the evidence of effectiveness from randomized controlled trials, *Gerontologist*, 40: 206–212.

Van Dalen, H.P., Henkens, K. and Schippers, J. (2008) Dealing with older workers in Europe: a comparative survey of employers' attitudes and actions, *Journal of European Social Policy*, 27: 526-541.

Westerhof, G.J. and Keyes, C.L.M. (2010) Mental illness and mental health: the two continua model across the lifespan, *Journal of Adult Development*, 17: 110–119.

World Health Organisation (WHO) (2002) *Active Aging: A Policy Framework.* Presented at the Second United Nations World Assembly on Aging, Madrid, Spain. WHO.

World Health Organisation (WHO) (2005) *Promoting Mental Health: Concepts, Emerging Evidence, Practice.* Geneva: WHO.

10 Mental health

American Psychiatric Association (2013) *Diagnostic and Statistical Manual of Mental Disorders (DSM-5)*, fifth edn. Washington, DC: American Psychiatric Association.

Anthony, W.A. (1993) Recovery from mental illness: the guiding vision of the mental health system in the 1990s, *Psychosocial Rehabilitation Journal*, 16(4): 11–23.

Bogg, D. (2010) *Values and Ethics in Mental Health Practice.* Exeter: Learning Matters.

Burns, T., Creed, F., Fahy, T., Thompson, S., Tyrer, P. and White, I. (1999) Intensive versus standard case management for severe psychotic illness: a randomized trial, *The Lancet*, 353: 2185-9.

Care Services Improvement Partnership (CSIP) (2006) *Direct Payments for People With Mental Health Problems: A Guide to Action.* London: Department of Health.

Department of Constitutional Affairs (2007) *Mental Capacity Act 2005 Code of Practice.* London: The Stationary Office.

Department of Health (DoH) (1999) *National Service Framework for Mental Health: Modern Standards and Service Models.* London: Department of Health.

Department of Health (DoH) (2000) *The NHS Plan: A Plan for Investment, A Plan for Reform.* London: Department of Health.

Department of Health (DoH) (2008a) *Code of Practice: Mental Health Act 1983.* London: The Stationery Office.

Department of Health (DoH) (2008b) *Refocusing the Care Programme Approach.* London: Department of Health.

Department of Health (DoH) (2009) *New Horizons.* London: Department of Health.

Department of Health (DoH) (2011a) *Improved Mental Health Therapies for Children.* www.dh.gov.uk/health/2011/10/improved-mental-health-therapies-for-children/ (accessed 18 November 2012).

Department of Health (DoH) (2011b) *No Health Without Mental Health: A Cross-Government Mental Health Outcomes Strategy for People of All Ages.* London: Department of Health.

Department of Health (DoH) (2012a) *Mental Health*. www.dh.gov.uk/health/category/policy-areas/social-care/mental-health/ (accessed 18 November 2012).

Department of Health (DoH) (2012b) *Dementia*. www.dh.gov.uk/health/category/policy-areas/social-care/dementia/ (accessed 18 November 2012).

Garety, P. A., Fowler, D. G., Freeman, D., Bebbington, P., Dunn, G. and Knipers, E. (2008) Cognitive-behavioural therapy and family intervention for relapse prevention and symptom reduction in psychosis: randomized control trial, *British Journal of Psychiatry*, 192: 412–423.

Golightley, M. (2009) *Social Work and Mental Health*. Exeter: Learning Matters.

Great Britain Parliament (1998) *Human Rights Act 1989*. (Act of Parliament.) London: HMSO. www.legislation.gov.uk (accessed 20 November 2012).

Great Britain Parliament (2002) *Mental Health Act 1983 (as amended by 2007 Act)*. (Act of Parliament.) London: HMSO. www.legislation.gov.uk (accessed 27 September 2012).

Great Britain Parliament (2005) *Mental Capacity Act 2005*. (Act of Parliament.) London: HMSO. http://www.legislation.gov.uk (accessed 20 November 2012).

Horwitz, A.V. (1982) *The Social Control of Mental Illness: Studies on Law and Social Control*. London: Academic Press.

Huxley, P., Evans, S., Munroe, M. and Cestari, L. (2008) Mental health policy reforms and case complexity in CMHTs in England: replication study, *Psychiatric Bulletin*, 32: 49–52.

Mental Health Act Commission (2009) *Coercion and Consent: Monitoring the Mental Health Act; Thirteenth Biennial Report 2007–2009*. London: The Stationery Office.

Moncrieff, J. (2009) *The Myth of the Chemical Cure: A Critique of Psychiatric Drug Treatment*. Basingstoke: Palgrave Macmillan.

Nathan, J. and Webber, M. (2010) Mental health social work and the bureau-medicalisation of mental health care: identity in a changing world, *Journal of Social Work Practice*, 24: 15–28.

Quirk, A., Lelliott, P., Audini, B. and Buston, K. (2003) Non-clinical and extra-legal influences on decisions about compulsory admission to psychiatric hospital, *Journal of Mental Health*, 12: 119–130.

Tew, J. (2012) Theory in mental health social work, in M. Davies (ed.) *Social Work with Adults*. Basingstoke: Palgrave Macmillan.

11 Domestic violence and abuse

Action on Elder Abuse (2006) *Why Does it Happen?* www.elderabuse.org.uk/About%20Abuse/What_is_abuse_why.htm (accessed 19 October 2011).

ADASS (2005) *A National Framework of Standards for Good Practice and Outcomes in Adult Protection Work*. London: ADASS.

Biderman, A.D. (1957) *Communist Attempts to Elicit False Confessions from Air Force Prisoners of War*. www.gwu.edu/~nsarchiv/torturingdemocracy/documents/19570900.pdf (accessed 26 February 2013).

CAADA (2012) The CAADA-DASH Risk Identification Checklist. www.caada.org.uk/ searchresult.html?sw=DASH (accessed 20 February 2013).

Department of Health (DoH) (2000) *No Secrets: Guidance on Developing and Implementing Multi-agency Policies and Procedures to Protect Vulnerable Adults from Abuse.* London: Department of Health.

Department of Health (DoH) (2005) *Responding to Domestic Abuse.* London: Department of Health.

Department of Health (DoH) (2009) *Safeguarding Adults: Report on the Consultation on the Review of 'No Secrets'.* London: Department of Health.

Department of Health (DoH) (2010) *Written Ministerial Statement. Government Response to the Consultation on Safeguarding Adults: The Review of the No Secrets Guidance.* http://webarchive.nationalarchives.gov.uk/+/www.dh.gov.uk/en/Consultations/ Responsestoconsultations/DH_111286 (accessed 21 February 2013).

Department of Health (DoH) (2011) *Statement of Government Policy on Adult Safeguarding.* London: Department of Health.

Domestic Abuse Intervention Project (DAIP) (2011a) *Power and Control.* www.theduluth-model.org/pdf/PowerandControl.pdf (accessed 23 February 2013).

Domestic Abuse Intervention Project (DAIP) (2011b) *Equality.* www.theduluthmodel. org/pdf/Equality.pdf (accessed 23 February 2013).

Dutton, D.G. and Painter, S.L. (1981) Traumatic bonding: the development of emotional attachments in battered women and other relationships of intermittent abuse, *Victimology: An International Journal,* 6(1–4): 139–155.

Grigsby, N., Hartman, B.R. (1997) The barriers model: an integrated strategy for intervention with battered women, *Psychotherapy,* 34(4): 485–497.

Hacker, F. (1976) *Crusaders, Criminals, Crazies.* Toronto: George J. McLeod.

Hester, M. (2011) The three planet model: towards an understanding of contradictions in approaches to women and children's safety in contexts of domestic violence, *British Journal of Social Work,* 41: 837–853.

Hester, M., Abrahams, H., Harwin, N. and Pearson, C. (2006) *Making an Impact: Children and Domestic Violence: A Reader,* 2nd edn. London: Jessica Kingsley Publishers.

Home Office (1999) *Criminal Statistics.* London: Home Office.

Home Office (2002) *Crime in England and Wales 2001/2002.* London: Home Office.

Home Office (2004) *Developing Domestic Violence Strategies – A Guide for Partnerships.* London: Home Office.

Home Office (2011) *Crime Survey for England and Wales, 2010/11.* www.homeoffice. gov.uk/publications/science-research-statistics/research-statistics/crime-research/ hosb1011/ (accessed 3 March 2013).

Home Office (2012a) *New Definition of Domestic Violence and Abuse to Include 16 and 17 Year Olds.* www.homeoffice.gov.uk/media-centre/press-releases/new-def-of-domestic-violence (accessed 27 December 2012).

Home Office (2012b) *Independent Domestic Violence Advisors.* www.homeoffice.gov.uk/ crime/violence-against-women-girls/domestic-violence/idva/ (accessed 21 November 2012).

Home Office (2012c) *Domestic Violence*. www.homeoffice.gov.uk/crime/violence-against-women-girls/domestic-violence/ (accessed 21 November 2012).

Joint Committee on Human Rights (2008) *A Life Like No Other? Human Rights of Adults with Learning Disabilities*. London: Joint Committee on Human Rights.

Jones, K. and Spreadbury, K. (2008) Best practice in adult protection: safety, choice and inclusion, in K. Jones, B. Cooper and H. Ferguson (eds) *Best Practice in Social Work: Critical Perspectives*. Basingstoke: Palgrave Macmillan.

Kolbo, J.R., Blakeley, E.H. and Engelman, D. (1996) Children who witness domestic violence: a review for the empirical literature, *Journal of Interpersonal Violence*, 11(2): 281.

Lukes, S. (1974) *Power: A Radical View*. London: Macmillan Press.

Morley, R. and Mullender, A. (1994) Domestic violence and children: what we know from research, in A. Mullender and R. Morley *Children Living with Domestic Violence: Putting Men's Abuse of Women on the Childcare Agenda*. London: Whiting and Birch.

O'Keeffe, M., Hills, A., Doyle, M., McCreadie, C., Scholes, S., Constantine, R., Tinker, A., Manthorpe, J., Biggs, S. and Erens, B. (2007) *UK Study of Abuse and Neglect of Older People: Prevalence Study Report*. www.elderabuse.org.uk/Documents/Prevalence%20 Report-Full.pdf (accessed 1 March 2013).

Pritchard, J. (1999) Good practice: victims' perspective, in J. Pritchard (ed.) *Elder Abuse: Work Best Practice in Britain and Canada*. London: Jessica Kingsley Publishers.

Pritchard, J. (2009) *Good Practice in the Law and Safeguarding Adults*. London: Jessica Kingsley Publishers.

Seligman, M. (1975) *Helplessness: On Depression, Development and Death*. San Francisco, CA: Freeman.

Symonds, M. (1982) Victims' response to terror: understanding and treatment, in F. Ochberg and D. Soskis (eds) *Victims of Terrorism*. Boulder, CO: Westview.

Walby, S. and Allen, J. (2004) *Domestic Violence, Sexual Assault and Stalking: Findings from the British Crime Survey – Home Office Research Study 276*. London: Home Office.

Women's Aid (2007) *Cycle of Violence*. www.womensaid.org.uk/domestic-violence-articles.asp?section=00010001002200410001&itemid=1279 (accessed 25 February 2013).

Women's Aid (2008) *Making the Links: Disabled Women and Domestic Violence*. www. womensaid.org.uk/domestic-violence-articles.asp?itemid=1722&itemTitle—aking+ the+links%3A+disabled+women+and+domestic+violence&section=00010001002200 080001&sectionTitle=Articles%3A+disabled+women (accessed 21 November 2012).

World Health Organisation (WHO) (2012) *Violence Against Women*. www.who.int/media-centre/factsheets/fs239/en/ (accessed 25 February 2013).

12 Social work in health care settings

Association of Palliative Care Workers (2006) *Introduction to Palliative Care Social Work*. London: Association of Specialist Palliative Care Social Workers.

Beresford, P., Adshead, L. and Croft, S. (2007) *Palliative Care, Social Work and Service Users – Making Life Possible*. London: Jessica Kingsley Publishers.

Clausen, H., Kendall, M., Murray, S., Worth, A., Boyd, K. and Benton, F. (2005) Would palliative care patients benefit from social workers retaining the traditional 'casework' role rather than working as care managers? A prospective serial qualitative interview study, *British Journal of Social Work*, 35: 277–285.

Croft, S., Beresford, S. and Adshead, L. (2005) What service users want from specialist palliative care social work – findings from a participatory research project, in J. Parker (ed.) *Aspects of Social Work and Palliative Care*. London: Quay Books.

Currer, C. (2001) *Responding to Grief – Dying, Bereavement and Social Care*. Basingstoke: Palgrave Macmillan.

Currer, C. (2007) *Loss and Social Work*. Exeter: Learning Matters.

Department of Health (DoH) (2008) *End-of-Life Care Strategy – Promoting High Quality Care for Adults at the End-of-Life*. London: Department of Health.

Douglas, C. (1992) For all the saints, *British Medical Journal*, 304: 479.

Firth, P., Luff, G. and Oliviere, D. (eds) (2005) *Loss, Change and Bereavement in Palliative Care*. Maidenhead: Open University Press.

Glasby, J. and Littlechild, R. (2004) *The Health and Social Care Divide: The Experiences of Older People*, 2nd edn. Bristol: The Policy Press.

Holloway, M. (2007) *Negotiating Death in Contemporary Health and Social Care*. Bristol: The Policy Press.

Holloway, M. (2009) Dying old in the twenty-first century: a neglected issue for social work, *International Social Work*, 53(5): 1–13.

Holloway, M. and Moss, B. (2010) *Spirituality and Social Work*. Basingstoke: Palgrave Macmillan.

Holloway, M. and Taplin, S. (2013) 'Editorial' to Death and social work – twenty-first century challenges, *British Journal of Social Work*, 43(2): 203–215.

IFSW (2000) *Definition of Social Work*. http://ifsw.org/policies/definition-of-social-work/ (accessed 28 October 2012).

Lymbery, M. (2001) Social work at the crossroads, *British Journal of Social Work*, 31(3): 369–384.

Machin, L. (2009) *Working with Loss and Grief – A New Model for Practitioners*. London: Sage.

McNamara, B. (2001) *Fragile Lives – Death, Dying and Care*. Maidenhead: Open University Press.

Monroe, B., Oliviere, D. and Payne, S. (2011) Introduction: social differences – the challenge for palliative care, in D. Oliviere, B. Monroe, and S. Payne (eds) *Death, Dying and Social Differences*, 2nd edn. Oxford: Oxford University Press.

National End-of-Life Care Programme (NEoLOP) (2010) *Supporting People to Live and Die Well: A Framework for Social Care at the End-of-Life*. www.endoflifecare.nhs.uk/assets/downloads/Social_Care_Framework.pdf (accessed 3 March 2013).

Oliver, M. (1996) *Understanding Disability: From Theory to Practice*. Basingstoke: Macmillan.

Oliviere, D., Hargreaves, R. and Monroe, B. (eds) (1998) *Good Practices in Palliative Care – A Psychosocial Perspective*. Aldershot: Ashgate.

Parker, J. (ed.) (2005) *Aspects of Social Work and Palliative Care*. London: Quay Books.

Paul, S. (2013) Public health approaches to palliative care: the role of the hospice social worker working with children experiencing bereavement, *British Journal of Social Work*, 43(2): 249–63.

Payne, M. (2009) Adult services and health-related social work, in R. Adams, L. Dominelli and M. Payne (eds) *Social Work: Themes, Issues and Critical Debates*, 3rd edn. Basingstoke: Palgrave Macmillan.

Reith, M. and Payne, M. (2009) *Social Work in End-of-Life and Palliative Care*. Bristol: The Policy Press.

Renzenbrink, I. (2008) Social workers within our agencies: the need for 'relentless self-care', in J. Weinstein (ed.) *Working with Loss, Death and Bereavement – A Guide for Social Workers*. London: Sage.

Review Team (2011) *Transforming Your Care: A Review of Health and Social Care in Northern Ireland*. Belfast: Department of Health, Social Services and Public Safety.

Rummery, K. (2003) Social work and multidisciplinary collaboration in primary care, in J. Weinstein, C. Whittinton and T. Leiba (eds) *Collaboration in Social Work Practice*. London: Jessica Kingsley Publishers.

Saunders, C. (ed.) (1990) *Hospice and Palliative Care: An Interdisciplinary Approach* London: Edward Arnold.

Shakespeare, T. and Watson, N. (2002) The social model of disability: an outdated ideology?, *Research in Social Sciences and Disability*, 2: 9–26.

Sheldon, F. (1997) *Psychosocial Palliative Care – Good Practice in the Care of the Dying and Bereaved*. Cheltenham: Stanley Thornes.

Small, N. (2001) Critical commentary: social work and palliative care, *British Journal of Social Work*, 31: 961–971.

Stacey, J. (1997) *Teratologies – A Cultural Study of Cancer*. London: Routledge.

Stevenson, D. and Boyce, S. (2005) *The NHS in Wales: Structures and Services (update)*. Paper number: 05/023. Cardiff: National Assembly for Wales.

Thompson, N. (ed.) (2002) *Loss and Grief: A Guide for Human Services Practitioners*. Basingstoke: Palgrave Macmillan.

Weinstein, J. (2008) *Working with Loss, Death and Bereavement: A Guide for Social Workers*. London: Sage.

13 Alcohol and other drug treatment

Banks, S. (2012) *Ethics and Values in Social Work: Practical Social Work Series*, 4th edn. Basingstoke: Palgrave Macmillan.

Barber, J.G. (2002) *Social Work with Addictions*, 2nd edn. Basingstoke: Palgrave Macmillan.

BASW (2002) *The Code of Ethics for Social Work*. London: BASW.

Best, D., Day, E. and Morgan, B. (2006) *Addiction Careers and the Natural History of Change*. London: National Treatment Agency.

Buchanan, J. (2004) Missing links? Problem drug use and social exclusion, *Probation Journal*, 51: 387–397.

Buchanan, J. (2010) Drug policy under new labour 1997–2010: prolonging the war on drugs, *Probation Journal*, 57: 250–262.

Cabinet Office (2004) *Alcohol Harm Reduction Strategy for England*. London: Crown Publications.

DiClemente, C.C. (2006) *Addiction and Change*. New York: Guilford Press.

Heather, N. and Robertson, I. (1997) *Problem Drinking*, 3rd edn. Oxford: Oxford University Press.

HM Government (2008) *Drugs: Protecting Families and Communities: The 2008 Drug Strategy*. London: Crown Publications.

HM Government (2010) *Drug Strategy 2010: Reducing Demand, Restricting Supply, Building Recovery: Supporting People To Live A Drug Free Life*. London: Crown Publications.

Hunt, N. and Derricott, J. (2001) Smackheads, crackheads, and other junkies: dimensions of the stigma of drug use, in T. Mason, C. Carlisle, C. Walker and E. Whitehead (eds) *Stigma and Social Exclusion in Health Care*. London: Routledge.

Lloyd, C. (2010) *Sinning and Sinned Against: The Stigmatisation of Problem Drug Users*. London: UKDPC.

Miller, W.R. and Rollnick, S. (2002) *Motivational Interviewing: Preparing People for Change*. New York: Guilford Press.

National Treatment Agency (NTA) (2002) *Models of Care for the Treatment of Drug Misusers: Promoting Quality, Efficiency and Effectiveness in Drug Misuse Treatment Services in England. Part 2: Full Reference Report*. London: National Treatment Agency.

National Treatment Agency (NTA) (2003) *Confidentiality and Information Sharing*. London: National Treatment Agency.

NHS Information Centre (2012) *Statistics on Alcohol: England, 2012*. https://catalogue.ic.nhs.uk/publications/public-health/alcohol/alco-eng-2012/alco-eng-2012-rep.pdf (accessed 10 January 2013).

Reuter, P. and Stevens, A. (2007) *An Analysis of UK Drug Policy: A Report by Professor Peter Reuter and Alex Stevens*. London: UKDPC.

Roberts, M. (2011) *By their Fruits . . . Applying Payment by Results to Drugs Recovery*. London: UKDPC.

Rogers, C. (1961) *On Becoming a Person: A Therapist's View of Psychotherapy*. London: Constable.

Smith, K. and Flatley, J. (2011) *Drug Misuse Declared: Findings from the 2010/11 British Crime Survey England and Wales*. London: Home Office.

Watson, J. (2012) The good, the bad and the vague: assessing emerging conservative drug policy, *Critical Social Policy*. Published online before print 6 September 2012, doi:10.1177/026018312457861.

14 Housing and homelessness

Belcher, J.R. and DeForge, B.R. (2012) Social stigma and homelessness: the limits of social change, *Journal of Human Behavior in the Social Environment*, 22: 929–946.

Benbow, S., Forchuk, C. and Ray, S.L. (2011) Mothers with mental illness experiencing homelessness: a critical analysis, *Journal of Psychiatric and Mental Health Nursing*, 18: 687–695.

Brammer, A. (2010) *Social Work Law*, 3rd edn. Harlow: Pearson Education.

Cebulla, A. (1999) *Housing Benefit and Supported Accommodation. Research Report No. 93.* Leeds: Department of Social Security.

Department for Communities and Local Government (DCLG) (2006) *Homelessness Code of Guidance for Local Authorities*. London: Department for Communities and Local Government.

Department for Communities and Local Government (DCLG) (2010) *Technical Note – Rough Sleeping Statistics in England – Autumn 2010.* www.gov.uk/government/uploads/system/uploads/attachment_data/file/7379/1846366.pdf (accessed 24 February 2013).

Department for Communities and Local Government (DCLG) (2011) *Vision to End Rough Sleeping: No Second Night Out Nationwide*. London: Department for Communities and Local Government.

Department for Communities and Local Government (DCLG) (2012a) *Statutory Homelessness: July to September Quarter 2012 England*. London: Department for Communities and Local Government.

Department for Communities and Local Government (DCLG) (2012b) *Making Every Contact Count: A Joint Approach to Preventing Homelessness*. London: Department for Communities and Local Government.

Department for Communities and Local Government (DCLG) (2013a) *Rough Sleeping Statistics England – Autumn 2012 Experimental Statistics*. London: Department for Communities and Local Government.

Department for Communities and Local Government (DCLG) (2013b) *Homelessness Data: Notes and Definitions*. www.gov.uk/homelessness-data-notes-and-definitions (accessed 24 February 2013).

Department for Work & Pensions (DWP) (2012a) *Housing and Heating Costs*. London: Department for Work & Pensions.

Department for Work and Pensions (DWP) (2012b) *Housing Benefit and Council Tax Benefit. General Information Bulletin*. London: Department for Work and Pensions.

Homeless Link (2012) *Homeless Watch: Survey of Needs & Provision 2012. Homelessness Services for Single People and Couples without Dependents in England*. London: Homeless Link.

Homeless Link (2013) *Facts and Figures*. http://homeless.org.uk/facts#.USoNkqVjBSU (accessed 24 February 2013).

Maslow, A. (1954) *Motivation and Personality*. New York: Harper.

Office of the Deputy Prime Minister (ODPM) (2005) *Causes of Homelessness Among Ethnic Minority Populations*. London: Office of the Deputy Prime Minister.

Reeve, K. (2011) *The Hidden Truth about Homelessness: Experiences of Single Homelessness in England*. London: Crisis.

Rogers, C.R. (1957) The necessary and sufficient conditions of therapeutic personality change, *Journal of Counseling Psychology*, 21: 95–103.

Saleebey, D. (2012) *The Strengths Perspective in Social Work Practice*, 6th edn. Boston, MA: Pearson.

Sundin, E.C. (2012) P-1171 – what are the risk factors for becoming and staying homeless? A mixed-methods study of the experience of homelessness among adult people, *European Psychiatry*, 27(Supplement 1): 1.

Teater, B. (2010) *An Introduction to Applying Social Work Theories and Methods*. Maidenhead: Open University Press.

Williams, S. and Stickley, T. (2011) Stories from the streets: people's experiences of homelessness, *Journal of Psychiatric and Mental Health Nursing*, 18: 432–439.

Zlotnick, C., Robertson, M.J. and Lahiff, M. (1999) Getting off the streets: economic resources and residential exits from homelessness, *Journal of Community Psychology*, 27: 209–224.

15 Asylum seekers and refugees

Border and Immigration Agency (BIA) (2007) *Planning Better Outcomes and Support for Unaccompanied Asylum Seeking Children*. London: Home Office.

Centre for Social Justice (CSJ) (2008) *Asylum Matters: Restoring Trust in the UK Asylum System*. www.centreforsocialjustice.org.uk (accessed 17 October 2012).

Cohen, S. and Wills, T.W. (1985) Stress, social support and the buffering hypothesis, *Psychological Bulletin*, 98(2): 310–357.

Crawley, H. (2007) *When is a Child not a Child? Asylum, Age Disputes and the Process of Age Assessment*. www.ilpa.org.uk/data/resources/13267/Executive-Summary-Age-Dispute.pdf (accessed 21 January 2013).

Crawley, H. (2010) *Chance or Choice? Understanding Why Asylum Seekers Come to the UK*. www.refugeecouncil.org.uk/Resources/Refugee%20Council/downloads/rcchance.pdf (accessed 21 January 2013).

Dennis, J. (2007) The legal and policy frameworks that govern social work with unaccompanied asylum seeking children in England, in R.K.S. Kohli and F. Mitchell (eds) *Working With Unaccompanied Asylum Seeking Children: Issues For Policy and Practice*. Basingstoke: Palgrave Macmillan.

Department for Children, Schools and Families (DCSF) (2006) *Working Together to Safeguard Children: A Guide to Inter-Agency Working to Safeguard and Promote the Welfare of Children*. London: The Stationery Office.

Department for Children, Schools and Families (DCSF) (2007) *Safeguarding Children Who May Have Been Trafficked*. Nottingham: DCSF Publications.

Doyle, J. (2012) *Fears Over Asylum Claims as Six More Olympic Athletes Go Missing When They Are Meant to Return Home.* www.dailymail.co.uk/news/article-2188496/Fears-asylum-claims-Olympic-athletes-missing-meant-home.html (accessed 21 January 2013).

Fell, B. (2013) Social work practice, asylum seekers and refugees, in M. Davies (ed.) *The Blackwell Companion to Social Work*, 4th edn. Chichester: Wiley-Blackwell.

Fell, B. and Fell, P. (2013) Welfare across borders: a social work process with adult asylum seekers, *British Journal of Social Work*, advance access published 29 January 2013, doi: 10.1093/bjsw/bct003.

Fell, P. and Hayes, D. (2007) *What Are They Doing Here? A Critical Guide to Asylum and Immigration*. Birmingham: Venture Press.

Friedman, M.J. (2003) *Post Traumatic Stress Disorder: The Latest Assessments and Treatment Strategies*. Kansas City, MO: Compact Clinicals.

Furness, H. (2012) *Three Sudanese Athletes Attempt to Claim Asylum After Going Missing in Britain*. www.telegraph.co.uk (accessed 17 August 2012).

Greenslade, R. (2005) *Seeking Scapegoats: The Coverage of Asylum in the UK Press*. London: IPPR.

Hayes, D. (2009) Social work with asylum seekers and others subject to immigration control, in R. Adams, L. Dominelli and M. Payne (eds) *Practising Social Work in a Complex World*. Basingstoke: Palgrave Macmillan.

House of Commons (2007) *The Treatment of Asylum Seekers*. London: House of Commons.

Humphries, B. (2004) An unacceptable role for social work: implementing immigration policy, *British Journal of Social Work*, 34: 93–107.

International Organization for Migration (2012) *Assisted Voluntary Return for Families and Children*. London: International Organization for Migration.

Kasiram, M. and Khosa, V. (2008) Trauma counselling: beyond the individual, *International Social Work*, 51(2): 220–232.

Kidane, S. (2001) *Food, Shelter and Half a Chance: Assessing the Needs of Unaccompanied Asylum Seeking and Refugee Children*. London: BAAF.

Kohli, R.K.S. (2007) *Social Work with Unaccompanied Asylum Seeking Children*. Basingstoke: Palgrave Macmillan.

Kohli, R.K.S. and Mather, R. (2003) Promoting psychosocial well-being in unaccompanied asylum seeking young people in the United Kingdom, *Child and Family Social Work*, 8: 201–212.

Kohli, R.K.S. and Mitchell, F. (2007) *Working with Unaccompanied Asylum Seeking Children*. Basingstoke: Palgrave Macmillan.

Leggett, S. I. (2008) *Enhancing Social Work Practice with Refugee Children in Exile*. Norwich: Social Work Monographs, University of East Anglia.

Mitchell, F. (2007) Assessment practice with unaccompanied children: exploring exceptions to the problem, in R.K.S. Kohli and F. Mitchell (eds) *Working with Unaccompanied Asylum Seeking Children*. Basingstoke: Palgrave Macmillan.

NRPF Network (2011) *Social Services Support for People with No Recourse to Public Funds – A National Picture*. London: NRPF Network.

Parker, J. (2000) Social work with asylum seekers and refugees: a rationale for developing practice, *Practice*, 12(3): 61–76.

Parker, J. and Penhale, B. (2008) *Working with Vulnerable Adults*. Abingdon: Routledge.

Raval, H. (2007) Therapeutic encounters between young people, bilingual co-workers and practitioners, in R.K.S. Kohli and F. Mitchell (eds) *Working with Unaccompanied Asylum Seeking Children: Issues for Policy and Practice*. Basingstoke: Palgrave Macmillan.

Refugee Action (2006) *The Destitution Trap: Research into Destitution Among Refused Asylum Seekers in the UK*. London: Refugee Action.

Refugee Council (2012) *Asylum Statistics*. www.refugeecouncil.org.uk/Resources/ Refugee%20Council/downloads/briefings/Asylum%20Statistics%20%20Aug%202012. pdf (accessed 20 December 2012).

UK Border Agency (UKBA) (2012a) *Current Support Amounts*. www.ukba.homeoffice. gov.uk/asylum/support/cashsupport/currentsupportamounts/ (accessed 16 August 2012).

UK Border Agency (UKBA) (2012b) *Employment*. www.ukba.homeoffice.gov.uk/asylum/ support/employment/ (accessed 16 August 2012).

UK Border Agency (UKBA) (2012c) *Section 4 Support*. www.ukba.homeoffice.gov.uk/ asylum/support/apply/section4/ (accessed 16 August 2012).

Vernon, G., Ridley, D. and Lesetedi, D. (2008) Home office syndrome, *British Journal of General Practice*, 58(552): 510.

Watters, C. (2001) Emerging paradigms in the mental health care of refugees, *Social Science and Medicine*, 52: 1709–1718.

Weaver, H.N. and Burns, B.J. (2001) 'I shout with fear at night': understanding the traumatic experiences of refugees and asylum seekers, *Journal of Social Work*, 1(2): 147–164.

Wright, F. (2012) Social work practice with unaccompanied asylum-seeking young people facing removal, *British Journal of Social Work*, advance access published 23 November 2012, doi: 10.1093/bjsw/bcs175.

16 Rehabilitation and corrections

Boswell, G. (2002) Imprisoned fathers: the children's view, *The Howard Journal*, 41(1): 14–26.

Brannen, J. (1988) The story of sensitive subjects, *Sociological Review*, 36: 552–563.

Bretherton, I. (2010) Parental incarceration: the challenges for attachment researchers, *Attachment and Human Behaviour*, 12(4): 417–428.

Burnett, R. and Roberts, C. (eds) (2004) *What Works in Probation and Youth Justice*. Cullumpton: Willan Publishing.

Cann, J., Falshaw, L., Nugent, F. and Friendship, C. (2003) *Understanding What Works: Accredited Cognitive Skills Programmes for Adult Men and Young Offenders*. London: Home Office.

Carter, P. (2003) *Managing Offenders, Reducing Crime: A New Approach*. London: Home Office Strategy Unit.

Clifford, J. (2010) Managing a murderous identity: how men who murder experience life imprisonment and the concept of release. University of Bath, unpublished PhD thesis.

Corston, J. (2007a) *A Review of Women with Particular Vulnerabilities in the Criminal Justice System.* London: Home Office.

Corston, J. (2007b) *The Corston Report.* www.justice.gov.uk/publications/docs/corston-report-march-2007.pdf (accessed 13 January 2013).

Crawley, E. (2004) *Doing Prison Work: The Public and Private Lives of Prison Officers.* Cullompton: Willan Publishing.

Crawley, E. and Sparks, R. (2005) Older men in prison: survival, coping and identity, in A. Liebling and S. Maruna (eds) *The Effects of Imprisonment.* Cullompton: Willan Publishing.

Crow, I. (2006) *Resettling Prisoners: A Review.* Sheffield: University of Sheffield and NOMS.

Cullen, F. and Gilbert, K. (1982) *Reaffirming Rehabilitation.* Cincinnati, OH: Anderson.

Edgar, K., Aresti, A. and Cornish, N. (2012) *Out for Good.* London: Prison Reform Trust.

Egan, G. (2010) *The Skilled Helper: A Problem-Management and Opportunity-Development Approach to Helping*, 9th edn. Belmont, CA: Brooks/Cole.

Farrow, K. (2004) Still committed after all these years? Morale in the modern day probation service, *Probation Journal,* 51(3): 206–220.

Feeley, M. and Simon, J. (1992) The new penology: notes on the emerging strategy of corrections and its implications, *Criminology,* 30(4): 449–474.

Foucault, M. (1977) *Discipline and Punish: The Birth of the Prison.* London: Penguin.

Garland, D. (2001) *The Culture of Control: Crime and Social Order in Contemporary Society.* Oxford: Oxford University Press.

Goffman, E. (1961) *Asylums: Essays on the Social Situation of Mental Patients and Other Inmates.* Chigaco: Aldine.

Goffman, E. (1963) *Stigma Notes on the Management of Spoiled Identity.* London: Penguin.

Gojkovic, D., Mills, A. and Meek, R. (2012) *Accommodation for Ex-Offenders: Third Sector Housing Advice and Provision.* Working Paper 77. Birmingham: Third Sector Research Centre, University of Birmingham.

Harper, G. and Chitty, C. (2005) *The Impact of Corrections on Reoffending: A Review of What Works.* http://rds.homeoffice.gov.uk/rds/pdfs04/hors291.pdf (accessed 3 January 2013).

Hedderman, C. (2007) Rediscovering resettlement: narrowing the gap between policy rhetoric and practice reality, in A. Hucklesby and L. Hagley-Dickinson (eds) *Prisoner Resettlement: Policy and Practice.* Cullompton: Willan Publishing.

Her Majesty's Inspectorate of Prison and Probation (2001) *Through the Prison Gate: A Joint Thematic Review.* London: Home Office.

Home Office (1991) *Custody, Care and Justice: The Way Ahead for the Prison Service in England and Wales.* Command Paper 1647. London: HMSO.

Home Office (1999) *What Works, Reducing Re-Offending: Evidence Based Practice.* London: Home Office.

Home Office (2004) *Reducing Re-Offending: National Action Plan*. London: Home Office.

Home Office (2009) *Integrated Offender Management Government Policy Statement*. London: Home Office/Ministry of Justice.

Howard, P., Clark, D. and Garnham, N. (2003) *An Evaluation and Validation of the Offender Assessment System (OASys)*. London: OASys Central Research Unit.

Kemshall, H. (1998) *Risk in Probation Practice*. Aldershot: Ashgate.

Kendall, K. (2004) Dangerous thinking: a critical history of correctional cognitive behaviouralsim, in G. Mair (ed.) *What Matters in Probation*. Cullompton: Willan Publishing.

Lewis, C.S. (1971) The humanitarian theory of punishment, in L. Radzinowicz and M. Wolfgang (eds) *Crime and Punishment*, Vol. 2. New York: Basic Books.

Losel, F. (2012) Offender treatment and rehabilitation. What works?, in M. Maguire, R. Morgan and R. Reiner (eds) *Oxford Handbook of Criminology*, 5th edn. Oxford University Press.

McGuire, J. (ed.) (1995) *What Works: Reducing Re-offending*. Chichester: Wiley.

McGuire, J. (2006) General offending behaviour programmes: concept, theory and practice, in C.R. Hollin and E.J. Palmer (eds) *Offending Behaviour Programmes: Development, Application, and Controversies*. Chichester: Wiley.

Maguire, M., Hutson, S. and Nolan, J. (2007) *Accommodation for Ex-Prisoners in the South West Region: Final Report*. www.unlock.org.uk/userfiles/file/IAG/housing/maguire_accommodation_report.pdf (accessed 3 January 2013).

Martinson, R. (1974) What works? Questions and answers about prison reform, *The Public Interest*, 35: 22–54.

Maruna, S. (2010) *Understanding Desistance from Crime*. London: NOMS.

Miller, W.R. and Rollnick, S. (2002) *Motivational Interviewing: Preparing People for Change*. New York: Guilford Press.

Ministry of Justice (MOJ) (2011) *Resettlement of Released Prisoners*. www.justice.gov.uk/offenders/before-after-release/resettlement (accessed 16 January 2013).

Moore, R. (2012) Beyond the prison walls: some thoughts on prisoner 'resettlement' in England and Wales, *Criminology and Criminal Justice*, 12(2): 129–147.

Phillips, C. and Bowling, B. (2012) Ethnicities, racism, crime and criminal justice, in M. Maguire, R. Morgan and R. Reiner (eds) *Oxford Handbook of Criminology*, 5th edn. Oxford: Oxford University Press.

Pincus, A. and Minahan, A. (1973) *Social Work Practice: Model and Method*. Itasca, IL: F.E. Peacock.

Prison Reform Trust (PRT) (2012) *Bromley Briefings: Prison Factfile*. London: Prison Reform Trust.

Prochaska, J. and DiClemente, C. (1984) *The Transtheoretical Approach: Crossing radational Boundaries of Therapy*. Homewood, IL: Dow Jones Irwin.

Raynor, P. (2007) Theoretical perspectives on resettlement: what is it and how it might work, in A. Hucklesby and L. Hagley-Dickinson (eds) *Prisoner Resettlement: Policy and Practice*. Cullompton: Willan Publishing.

Reid, W.J. and Epstein, L. (1972) *Task-Centred Casework*. New York: Columbia University Press.

Roberts, A.R. (ed.) (2005) *Crisis Intervention Handbook: Assessment, Treatment, and Research*, 3rd edn. New York: Oxford University Press.

Rogers, C.R. (1951) *Client-Centered Counselling*. Boston, MA: Houghton-Mifflin.

Rollnick, S. and Miller, W.R. (1995) What is motivational interviewing?, *Behavioural and Cognitive Psychotherapy*, 23: 325–334.

Senior, P., Wong, K., Culshaw, A., Ellingworth, D., O'Keeffe, C. and Meadows, L. (2011) *Process Evaluation of Five Integrated Offender Management Pioneer Areas*. www.justice.gov.uk/downloads/publications/research-and-analysis/moj-research/evaluation-integrated-offender-mgt-pioneer-areas.pdf (accessed 6 January 2012).

Social Exclusion Unit (2002) *Reducing Re-Offending by Ex-Prisoners*. London: Social Exclusion Task Force.

Williams, B. (1992) *Probation Values*. Birmingham: Venture.

Worrall, A. (1992) Equal opportunity or equal disillusion? The probation service and anti-discriminatory practice, in B. Williams (ed.) *Probation Values*. Birmingham: Venture.

17 Self-harming

Bell, J. (2011) Disentangling self-harm and suicide, *Youngminds*, 112: 26–27.

Bell, J. (2013) Self harm and suicide: positive pastoral strategies for schools, in N. Purdy (ed.) *Pastoral Care in Post-Primary Schools – A Critical Introduction*. London: Bloomsbury.

Best, R. (2006) Deliberate self-harm in adolescence: a challenge for schools, *British Journal of Guidance and Counselling*, 34(2): 161–175.

Department of Health (2004) *National Service Framework for Children, Young People, and Maternity Services*. London: HMSO.

Harbour, A. (2008) *Children with Mental Disorder and the Law: A Guide to Law and Practice*. London: Jessica Kingsley Publishers.

Hassan, T.B., MacNamara, A.F., Davy, A., Bing, A. and Bodiwala, G.G. (1999a) Lesson of the week: managing patients with deliberate self harm who refuse treatment in the accident and emergency department, *British Medical Journal*, 319(7202): 107–109.

Hassan, T., MacNamara, A. and Bodiwala, G. (1999b) Authors' reply, *British Medical Journal*, 319(7214): 917.

Hawton, K., Saunders, K.E.A. and O'Connor, R. (2012) Self-harm and suicide in adolescents, *The Lancet*, 379: 2373–2382.

Horrocks, J., Price, S., House, A., et al. (2003) Self-injury attendances in the accident and emergency department: clinical database study, *British Journal of Psychiatry*, 183: 34–39.

Joiner, T. (2005) *Why People Die by Suicide*. London: Harvard University Press.

McDougall, T., Armstrong, M. and Trainor, G. (2010) *Helping Children and Young People Who Self-Harm: An Introduction to Self-Harming and Suicidal Behaviours for Health Professionals*. Abingdon: Routledge.

Mental Health Foundation and Camelot Foundation. (2006) *Truth Hurts: Report of the National Inquiry into Self Harm Among Young People*. London: Mental Health Foundation.

Miller, D.N. (2011) *Child and Adolescent Suicidal Behaviour: School-Based Prevention, Assessment, and Intervention*. New York: Guilford Press.

National Institute for Clinical Excellence (NICE) (2004) *Self-Harm: The Short-Term Physical and Psychological Management and Secondary Prevention of Self-Harm in Primary and Secondary Care*. www.nice.org.uk/cg16 (accessed 31 December 2012).

NSPCC (2008) *Gillick Competency or Fraser Guidelines: An Overview*. London: NSPCC.

Rudd, M.D., Joiner, T. and Rajab, M. (2000) *Treating Suicidal Behavior*. New York: Guilford Press.

Schneidman, E. S. (1996) *The Suicidal Mind*. Oxford: Oxford University Press.

Scottish Executive (2002) *Choose Life. The National Suicide Prevention Strategy and Action Plan*. www.scotland.gov.uk/Publications/2002/12/15873/14466 (accessed 31 December 2012).

Scottish Executive (2007) *A Report on Implementation of the UN Convention on the Rights of the Child in Scotland 1999–2007*. www.scotland.gov.uk/Publications/2007/07/30114126/0 (accessed 8 January 2013).

Social Care Institute for Excellence (2005) *Deliberate Self-Harm (DSH) Among Children and Adolescents: Who is at Risk and How is it Recognized?* www.scie.org.uk/publications/briefings/briefing16/ (accessed 7 January 2013).

Trainor, G. (2010) Adolescent self harm, *APSA Practitioner Briefings*, 3 March

Walker, S. (2012) *Responding to Self-Harm in Children and Adolescents: A Professional's Guide to Identification, Intervention and Support*. London: Jessica Kingsley Publishers.

Walsh, B. W. (2006) *Treating Self-Injury: A Practical Guide*. New York: Guilford Press.

Williams, M. (2001) *Suicide and Attempted Suicide*. London: Penguin.

Index

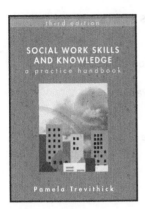

SOCIAL WORK SKILLS AND KNOWLEDGE
A Practice Handbook
Third Edition

Pamela Trevithick

9780335238071 (Paperback)
February 2012

eBook also available

Since its first publication in 2000, this best-selling text has been an
invaluable resource for thousands of social workers preparing for life in
practice. Written by an influential academic-practitioner, it is widely regarded
as the leading book in its field.

Key features:

- 4 new chapters that integrate theory and practice in a Knowledge and
  Skills Framework
- 80 social work skills and interventions
- 12 appendices describing a range of different social work approaches

www.openup.co.uk

 OPEN UNIVERSITY PRESS
McGraw - Hill Education

CRITICAL ANALYSIS SKILLS FOR SOCIAL WORKERS

David Wilkins and Godfred Boahen

9780335246496 (Paperback)
2013

eBook also available

Analysis is a critical skill for social workers, yet it is a skill that many practitioners find very difficult. This book will help social workers to improve their analysis skills by offering a very basic, step-by-step model to develop an analytical mindset. It shows how analysis can be woven into the whole process of social work engagement, resulting in better decision making, more efficient ways of working and, ultimately, better outcomes for social work service users.

Key features:

- What analysis is, and why it is such an important skill in practice
- The skills that underpin critical analysis, e.g. time management, planning, critical understanding, logical thinking, research-mindedness, creativity, communication, reflection and hypothesising
- The role of emotion and intuition in critical analysis

www.openup.co.uk